BEFORE I DIE AGAIN

Also by Chad Varah

The Samaritans: befriending the suicidal
Telephone Masturbators
Notny Sbornick Russkogo Pravoslavnogo Tserkovnogo Peniya

BEFORE
I DIE AGAIN

Chad Varah

CONSTABLE · LONDON

First published in Great Britain 1992 by
Constable and Company Limited
3 The Lanchesters, 162 Fulham Palace Road
London W6 9ER
Copyright © 1992 by Chad Varah
The right of Chad Varah to be
identified as the author of this work
has been asserted by him in accordance
with the Copyright, Designs and Patents Act 1988
ISBN 0 09 470580 1
Set in Linotron 11pt Sabon by
Servis Filmsetting Limited, Manchester
Printed in Great Britain by
St Edmundsbury Press Limited
Bury St Edmunds, Suffolk

A CIP catalogue record for this book
is available from the British Library

My thanks to Isabel Vincent, who typed it all
C.V.

For friends all over the world, especially
PETER and HAYAT
(Lord and Lady Palumbo of Walbrook)

Contents

Illustrations   8

Chapter 1   11
Chapter 2   41
Chapter 3   75
Chapter 4   102
Chapter 5   129
Chapter 6   149
Chapter 7   190
Chapter 8   228
Chapter 9   241
Chapter 10   263
Chapter 11   287
Chapter 12   319
Chapter 13   349

Index   371

Illustrations

The illustrations in this book come in two eight page sections, between pages 128 and 129 and pages 224 and 225 respectively.

All the photographs come from the author's own personal collection with the exception of the photograph of H.R.H. The Duchess of Kent which is reproduced by permission of the Yorkshire Evening Press.

Le livre de la vie est le livre suprême,
Qu'on ne peut ni fermer ni rouvrir à son choix.
Le passage attachant ne s'y lit pas deux fois,
Mais le feuillet fatal se tourne de lui-même.
On voudrait revenir à la page où l'on aime –
Et la page où l'on meurt est déjà sous nos doigts.

A. de Lamartine

1

I am in a condemned cell, awaiting death. (Not for the first time.) All around me are other cells. You are in one of them. That makes a bond between us. We are in the same boat – I mean, situation.

You will have guessed that the condemned cell I am in is my body, which I must be taken from on a date unknown to me but certainly within the next twenty-five years. Then my corpse, useless to me but useful to the teachers of anatomy to medical students, will be whisked away for dissection. I hate waste. If you wish to treat the mortal remains of your dear ones with reverence, or have your own so treated, that is up to you. If I am taking the funeral or cremation I will be considerate of your feelings, but I cannot regard a dead body as he or she. Only an 'it' can be burned or buried without a qualm. When I say in the Creed that I believe in the resurrection of the body, I do not mean the revival of disintegrated corpses – gruesome idea. I mean I believe that we shall live again in a body which comes to earth in the only known way, through the birth-canal of a mother. Whenever I say the Creed, I assert my belief in reincarnation.

In my condemned cell, I cannot hear you, but you can hear me. I may possibly hear *from* you, if we both live long enough. I greet you, you who are reading this book or having it read to you, in English or in translation. I don't know, or care, whether you will pay attention to everything I say or even understand most of it, so long as you take from it what you find useful.

The words I use sometimes have meanings or shades of meaning that are personal to me, and the same words have different meanings for you. But after making allowance for that difficulty, you will soon, if you stay with me, know a great deal about me, whilst I shall

11

still know no more about you than I know now, which is nothing; except that you are a fellow human being who wanted to know what it was that I wished to say before I die. Before you die.

I do not know your age, sex, appearance, occupation, beliefs, prejudices, skills, intelligence, nationality, disabilities, or the colour of your hair, eyes, skin, or shoes – if you wear shoes. For me it is enough to know that you are human. *Homo sum – nihil humanum a me alienum puto* (I am a man, I count nothing human alien to me). It is as if all the many faces of people I have known or seen are merged together into one, to form someone of any race of either sex who is old enough to understand some of my thoughts. It is this someone, you, whom I have in mind as I write, and although a true dialogue is not possible in the circumstances, I am not talking to God or to myself, but to you, whose imagined presence will influence what I say, and how I say it.

Why would you, why would anyone, be interested in my auto-biography? It is a fact that in our day biography appears to be the favourite form of reading of many of those who read books at all. I can only suppose that curiosity about those who are alleged to have done interesting things and met interesting people is not the only motive: there must surely be some desire to gain insight into the reader's own experiences, and to gain courage in coping with the human predicament which the reader shares with the writer. A good biography will surely not only amuse, excite or perhaps shock, but lead the reader to have more understanding and to be less harsh in judging the human nature we all share.

This can of course happen only if the writer is sincere and honest. It would be too much to ask for 'the truth, the whole truth, and nothing but the truth' because the whole truth would be far too long and mostly boring, and it would be unkind to reveal everything that one knows about other people. Two precepts not observed by every-one these days are '*De mortuis, nil nisi bonum*' and 'Don't kiss and tell'. If you, reader, are scandalized by some of the things I shall write it will not be because I have been careless of the reputation of those who cannot now defend themselves. I shall not be as careful of myself as I aim to be of others.

When you live to be eighty, the majority of the people you used to know have either died or grown away from you. The other day I was rearranging books in the library – my eight-roomed semi-detached house has one room lined with shelves which I call the library, even though only about 3,000 of my books are in it – and I found the record of my 1961 appearance on Eamonn Andrews' *This is Your Life* programme. Looking at the photographs of the people who were so important to me at that time, I realize that only my wife and the four children I then had are still part of my life, and Eamonn Andrews himself is dead. If I were to be done again, the people around me in the group photograph would be different; and if I had been done twenty years before, they would have been different again.

It isn't only the people who come into one's life and, after a shorter or a longer time, leave it who change. One changes oneself. I can try to remember exactly how I felt and what I did all those years ago, but how can I judge what other people did? Surely to judge them by criteria which probably didn't then exist, by standards which I didn't myself then have, in the light of knowledge and inventions which were not yet available to mankind, would do them an injustice? This same injustice is wreaked against historical characters, who may well have been neither much better nor much worse than their contemporaries, but are judged to be good or bad by people who did not have to live in their circumstances or under their handicaps. We may suspect that those who so glibly judge them would have cut a pretty poor figure themselves in their situation; and, indeed, perhaps did, because I am convinced that we were our ancestors, and will be our posterity. It is possible that when we judge harshly some character from the past we may be passing judgement on a previous incarnation of our own, though this is statistically very unlikely. The number of people in the world today is about 4,000,000,000,000 and the number of people whose names and deeds have come down to us in history is so tiny by comparison that the odds are overwhelmingly in favour of our having come and gone many times without leaving any trace that could now be identified.

I was born on 12 November 1911 at the vicarage, Barton upon Humber. The house still stands, though reduced by the knocking down of various bedrooms my father had built on as the number of his children gradually increased to nine; it is now used as offices, and the vicarage is a red-brick building opposite, in what used to be known as the Big Garden to distinguish it from the Little Garden around the house. The churchyard path separated the two. The room where I was born was the first-floor front, on the right.

13

In the day time, any sunlight would have been muted by that great beech tree just the other side of the churchyard wall which was not much smaller then than it is now. When night came, though there were still some oil-lamps in use in my earliest years, the room would have been lit by gaslight, which gives out a welcome warmth and a comforting bubbling sound. The window does not look on to St Peter's church itself, a pre-Norman building with extensive Gothic additions, founded by St Chad in 669. Father named his firstborn after the saint who converted Mercia in the seventh century – one of twelve heathen Mercian boys who had been captured in war against the Kingdom of Northumbria, and had been saved from a sticky end by the intercession of good St Aidan of Holy Island (Lindisfarne), who said to the Christian king, 'Give them to me, my Lord, and I will bring them up as my own sons and send them to convert their countrymen.' Several did well, but the one who became Apostle of Mercia was Chad (originally Ceoddha or Ceaddha – the 'a' being masculine termination). The combination of what has become an unusual Christian name with the surname Varah led many people to think it isn't English, but it is in fact pure Anglian. There are more churches in England dedicated to St Chad than to any other saint who is not in the New Testament.

Old St Peter's was built all in one piece some time in the first half of the tenth century, and only the part east of the tower was demolished and replaced by later buildings.

My father was the Reverend William Edward Varah, Vicar of Barton upon Humber from 1910 until ten days before his death in 1945. Much of the time he was Rural Dean of Yarborough North and an honorary Canon of Lincoln Minster. He always topped the poll for the elections to the Barton Urban District Council, which he pressurized on many subjects including the need for a Humber Bridge. He never lived to see it, but there it is now, the world's longest single-span suspension bridge, and very beautiful. When it was opened, I was glad to be televised in front of it to say that all those years ago my father had persuaded the town council to vote £10,000 towards the cost of a bridge, which was an immense sum in those days for a town of 6,000 inhabitants. He was a well-known authority on pre-Norman architecture and history, and scholars came from all over the world to consult him and also to see the Saxon part of the church in which I was baptized.

It is easy to see why he was chosen to be Vicar of Barton; but why was he chosen to be my father? Did I choose him, or did God or my

14

guardian angel choose him for me? Do we choose our parents when we come, not in utter nakedness nor in entire forgetfulness but trailing clouds of glory from God who is our home?

My father was a very strong character, a man of principle with firm beliefs and convictions, and furthermore a man with the moral courage to speak what he believed whether it would make him popular or unpopular. It used to embarrass me often in my youth that he so frequently said things which other people only thought but were too shy to voice. As I have grown older, I have admired this more and more and am inclined to do the same thing myself. I doubt if I embarrass my children as much as my father used to embarrass me by this means, but maybe I am as unaware as he apparently was. Maybe they blush or cringe inwardly more than I realize; or did when they were younger.

My father was a Tractarian. He belonged with great figures in Anglican history such as Keble, Pusey, Liddon – he was delighted when I got rooms in Pusey Quad in Keble College – and the son of his elder brother was christened Liddon. He had a great feeling for the English Church and for English, as against Roman and Papist, Catholicism. He loved the Book of Common Prayer and knew how to speak Cranmer's prose in such a way that his flock could understand it. Although I argued with him frequently and passionately and came to reject many of his religious, philosophical and political ideas, I was powerfully influenced by him. As a child I naturally hated him as well as loved him, and did not feel guilty about hating him because I felt justified. I now remember him with gratitude.

Before saying more about him, I must refer to the most important of the circumstances surrounding my birth, namely the mother who bore me. Why did I choose her to provide me with the body with which I was born into the world? Or why was she chosen for me?

My mother, née Atkinson, was christened Marie. Father didn't like this name, and on her marriage on 25 January 1910 she changed it to Mary.

During my childhood Mother appeared to me rather as an appendage to my father, even though he was normally shut up in his study and she was around the house in places one frequented such as the warm kitchen. One took it for granted that Father was the one who knew things and to whom one listened, and to whom Mother listened. One took it for granted that Mother was good at everything to do with running a house: cooking, baking, sewing, mending, knitting, dressmaking, tailoring, cleaning, laundering, ironing and everything else necessary to make a large house run smoothly when, as the number of children increased and the purchasing power of Father's income diminished, the amount done by my mother with the aid of the older children increased proportionately.

I gather that when I was born, before the First World War, my parents had four indoor servants and two outdoor in addition to my nanny and some casual help.

Even during the war my mother's task increased as the number of servants diminished, but after the war there was only a daily to 'do the rough', by which was meant scrub the kitchen, scullery, and passages and any cupboards with tiled floors on hands and knees, and also clear out the grates, polish with black lead, separate the cinders from the ash, throw the ash into the ashpit behind the outside privy and re-use the cinders when laying the fire again with newspaper and sticks. In addition, there were the women who came on Monday to wash, and a different pair of women who came on Tuesday to iron. Later on these were reduced to one woman for both tasks, but the cleaning woman still came daily.

My father was born at Braithwell in 1862, where his father was the Master of the old endowed school, built in 1673, which still stands. He was the dominant son, though Uncle George was older. My mother was born in 1888 at Boston Spa. After their marriage in 1910 they had a honeymoon in London for several weeks before going to the vicarage at Eastville in the Fens. So my father must have been forty-nine and my mother twenty-three when I was born, as their birthdays were both in August.

Our surname appears on tombstones at Wickersly and Maltby, the oldest, now indecipherable, being dated 1480, and the oldest legible until recently being of 1597 (the same date as the silver-gilt chalice I use every Thursday). It seems that the reason why Varah is an uncommon name is that for centuries those of us who survived have mostly been girls.

My mother had a baby every year for eight years, then a stillbirth which we didn't know about until much later, and a ninth child six years after the eighth. Father gave us good old pre-Norman saints' names: Edward Chad, Audrey Mary, Dorothy Margaret, Rosalind (she added Mary at her confirmation), Winfrid Edmund, George Hugh, Mary Elgiva, Albery Veronica and William Oswald.

The sexes were segregated. By the time there were eight of us, the bedroom next to the nursery had been turned into a proper bathroom and the hip baths previously used were abandoned, so Father had to have a little room built above the pantry for Winfrid (later known as Edmund) and Hugh. In the very middle of the bedroom floor was a little room lit only by a skylight, where the nurserymaid used to sleep until after the departure of the last one, Shucksmith (the youngest of twenty children of a man who was unemployed, at least during the day). Later I slept in this room myself for a while. The three eldest girls slept in the north bedroom, and the two younger girls in the four-poster bedroom. I myself slept in what had been Father's dressing-room, immediately above the front door and hall, on one side of which was the 'best bedroom', for visitors, and the other side my parents' bedroom – except for a period when, having been in a children's hospital in Hull with a mysterious stomach ailment, I convalesced for a year or more in a balcony room made by an ingenious transformation of the window in Mother's dressing-room.

There was a water-closet upstairs, but during the day we hardy males went to an outside privy between the ashpit and the coal sheds, whose roofs were covered for some reason with fleshy *Sempiternum vivens*. Under the privy seat was a large oblong wooden box covered with pitch inside, which Daddy used to drag each week through the yard and the Little Garden and across the churchyard path and up into the Big Garden to tip the contents into a hole dug in the orchard, which produced splendid apples. If you think 'Daddy' means my father, you are not thinking about the closing year of the First World War, when I was still calling my father Sir and the girls called him Father. Daddy was the surname of the gardener. I think the war hadn't quite finished when the box wore out and had to be replaced and I saw the new one when the joiner brought it. I asked him why it was daubed with pitch and he said it was to make it watertight. I reasoned that if pitch kept urine in it would keep pond water out, so what we had was a boat. A hundred yards away, across Beck Hill and down a grassy slope, was the Beck. I know the word 'beck' should mean a small stream, and in fact a small stream did run into it, but the Beck was a pond, about sixty yards in diameter, whose level was controlled by a sluice. From our house you could see the great church of St Mary reflected in this pond which acted as a huge looking-glass. Equally, from St Mary's churchyard you could see the reflection of the great church of St Peter plus old St Peter's plus the vicarage.

With much puffing and panting, I managed to drag this box down to the Beck and launch it, leaping aboard with a bit of wood to act as a paddle. It wasn't the right shape for a boat. Only a few yards from shore, it overturned and deposited me in the water, from which I emerged spitting newts, with green weed in my hair. I ran back home, and in at the back door, where fortunately there was water on the tiles anyway, as it was washing day, and Mrs Wrack was helping my mother to do the weekly wash. It was decided that I should strip off all my wet clothing and have a warm bath in a hip bath in front of the kitchen fire, lest I 'catch my death'. My mother was evidently anxious to get me into dry clothes before my father returned from wherever he was. I expect she thought I had been sufficiently punished for my naughtiness by the fright I had had, and she was pleased that I had not drowned, because in the middle the Beck was about eight feet deep at that time. Relieved though I was by a purely practical and remedial approach to the situation, I remember being aghast at the thought of taking off my clothes in front of Mrs Wrack. She obviously had the intention of bathing me, but I snubbed her with the statement that I had been bathing myself for more years than she had been working for us.

When my father eventually appeared, I was clothed and in my right mind, and he decided to treat the matter lightly and indeed to dine out on the story. I often had to listen to him telling people about my adventures boating on the Beck.

The first act of mine which perhaps qualifies to be called Samaritan occurred early in 1917. I was, as usual in the winter, getting in my mother's way in the kitchen, where a huge coal-fired range kept the room warm. I could enjoy the smell of baking bread (my mother baked every day except Sunday) and often have my presence rewarded by a hot 'new cake' liberally spread with butter, or better still with bacon dripping from the frying pan. I was poring unenthusiastically over a tattered copy of Dr W. Smith's *First Latin Primer*, my father having one day removed my book of natural philosophy and substituted this dreary tome, saying curtly, 'Learn Latin from this – I'll correct your exercises,' when the doorbell rang. I ran to answer it with alacrity.

The visitor was a tall, pasty-faced young man in a black suit and clerical collar, who was sweating and trembling with fear and saying he had an appointment to see my father. I took a dislike to him even before he patted me on the head and called me his little man, but I nevertheless felt sorry for him, for he was clearly dreading his coming encounter with my father, a strong character who was not afraid to say what he thought. It was many years before I discovered what it was the young man was frightened about. He had (I was told) been recommended by my father for some free training for the ministry on condition that he served for some years in the Mission Field, and after ordination had conveniently discovered that his health would not allow him to be boiled and eaten by cannibals, so had worked safely in this country and had not repaid the cost of his training.

My father was using the dining-room instead of the study to save fuel, and I led the young man into the Awful Presence, astonished that the visitor hadn't turned to stone under the glowering he got. In an attempt to soften my father, I stayed, chattering, telling jokes and being consciously 'cute', and the visitor played up to this, praising my wit and enquiring how old I was.

'He's five,' said my father, dismissing the subject and me.

'Five and a quarter!' I cried; and that is how I know when the incident happened. I went reluctantly back to my Latin Primer, having failed to save the young man from the wrath he assuredly deserved.

As the number of my brothers and sisters grew, so did my responsi-bilities as the eldest: 'Why did you let him (or her) do so-and-so?' I occasionally escaped to have a few days' holiday with Uncle George at Old Brumby near Scunthorpe, whose daughters I addressed as Auntie Elsie and Auntie Ida, because they were adult. I met my cousin Uncle Liddon only once, a strapping soldier in thick khaki with puttees and huge boots, who lifted me effortlessly with one hand and pressed me against the ceiling. He wasted away in a German prisoner-of-war camp, and his name wasn't on the war memorial because he hadn't died in action. When Uncle George wasn't playing the piano to me or taking me for long walks, I would haunt Frodingham Iron and Steel Works and watch the men tipping molten slag.

Once when I was staying there – I think it was in 1921 or 1922 – Alan Cobham's Air Circus was in town, utilizing a large meadow. I wish I had taken more notice of the aeroplanes: I could doubtless find out from the records of the period, but that would be cheating. I don't, in fact, remember anything except that they were biplanes and that one was (for those days) large and the others were small. The large one was taking people for rides. It cost ten shillings to go for a ten-minute spin, and when I was there there were no queues, I think because ten shillings was a very great deal of money in those days, rather than that people were nervous. I don't know how I managed to raise the ten shillings: it may have been half-price for children, and I may have had to raise only five, but during the whole of my childhood I can't remember ever having more than a few pennies at any given time, except once. The big plane that people went for rides in had no seats in the cabin, which was about six or seven feet wide and maybe fifteen feet in length, if I remember rightly, with looped rope around the walls to hold on to as you stood, and a sliding door which an attendant obligingly opened in flight so that we could see out. It gives me the horrors now to think of myself standing at the very edge while flying over Scunthorpe peering over with fascination at the familiar steelworks and slag heaps, blissfully unaware that a slight lurch could precipitate me without a parachute to the ground.

After our ten-minute ride, there was a draw: tickets of admission, which I think were a shilling for adults and sixpence for children, were all numbered, and several were drawn out of a hat and those drawn were entitled to a free flight in a little aeroplane with room for only one passenger behind the pilot, or two if they were small enough to sit side by side. I was one of the lucky ones, and was slightly nervous as we came down because of the wind whistling past – there was no canopy or other protection though the pilot himself had a windscreen. Just before landing we clipped some trees, which took a little of the fabric off one wing.

At home I was expected to be usefully employed at all times, and it was fortunate that when I was happily wasting time I could always hear Father coming, because either shortly before or shortly after his marriage he had had a bad accident with a pony and trap, which had broken his leg, and it was badly set so that when eventually it healed it was a couple of inches shorter. Whenever my father referred to 'my accident', he always added, with an expression that made it clear he was reliving it, that he hadn't known there was so much pain in the world. As a result of it, he had to wear a built-up surgical boot, and had to clump along with a dot-and-carry sound which made his approach very recognizable to those who were doing what they ought not to be doing. He was able, nevertheless, to ride a bicycle, which he mounted by standing on the step that protruded from the axle of the back wheel. One could also ride behind him standing on this step, and one's foot became very tired indeed. He had been, Mother said, a fine figure of a man before his accident; even after it he had immense stamina and could, for instance, ride long distances on his bicycle, whether with a child on the back or not.

Shortly before the church clock in the great tenth-century tower struck ten in the morning or five in the afternoon, Father would set out to say Mattins or Evensong in Old St Peter's, which he boasted was the oldest church in England in daily use for worship.

If I was playing in the Little Garden when the clock was shortly to strike ten or five, Father would come stumping along the path and would say to me, in the tone of one conferring a favour, 'You can come with me to Mattins [or Evensong, as the case might be] if you like.' The possibility that one would prefer to go on playing never crossed his mind, and the possibility of being truthful about the matter never crossed mine. I often felt resentful at these interruptions, as I trotted along behind him up the churchyard path and up the few steps and past the broken tombstones near the great beech tree under which I would hide when playing hide-and-seek, quite undeterred by the human skull and other bones I found in there – parsons' children whose playground is a graveyard are not to be scared by a few old bones – and then past the cross which marks the site where St Chad planted a wooden one in the year 669 and said, 'Here we will build a church.'

Once inside these ancient yard-thick walls, scarred by the attempts of the Danes to burn them down and by the marks of arrows being sharpened by the defenders, I felt as much at home as in the vicarage next door. There would sometimes be other worshippers besides myself and my father, and of course the younger children got roped in later. I may have picked up the unvarying responses by hearing them, but I can't have been quite three at the time when I was reading the even verses of the psalms, which of course changed every time, antiphonally with my father. By the time I was nine, I knew the whole psalter off by heart, and retained it until a few years ago.

I started at my dame school, Mrs Cooper's, at the age of four. The building is still there, behind a double-fronted house alongside the left-hand side of St Mary's churchyard.

I didn't learn as much as I learned from reading in my father's library. This contained a few books of 'natural philosophy', which was what science was then called and which I read with avidity, and one very precious shelf full of volumes of Dent's Everyman's Library. These were possibly taken over by my father from his predecessor, one of whose sons, David Hogarth, was translator for Dent's from Russian and Spanish; I read Tolstoy's *Anna Karenina*, Dostoevsky's *Letters from the Underworld* and the plays of Ibsen. In the drawing-room, in a case with glass doors, were more frivolous works, such as the collected novels of Dickens, Scott, Thackeray and Lord Lytton, as well as Tennyson, Keats, Byron and of course Shakespeare. It was when I went into hospital in Hull that I came across books specifically written for boys, such as the stories of R. M. Ballantyne, Captain Marryat and Fenimore Cooper, author of *The Last of the Mohicans*. I became, naturally, a Mohican – I even remember that I was called Fleetfoot, and was as skilled with bow and arrow as any Robin Hood.

I shall always be grateful to the dame school for the multiplication table and for the Two Duties, which of course went out of fashion with its 'Order myself lowly and reverently to all my betters' when it was decided that nobody was better than anyone else. I got a real appreciation of English from my father, the Book of Common Prayer and my dame school.

We had, of course, copybooks, and we learnt to write copperplate by copying pothooks and maxims, thus improving one's handwriting and one's character at a stroke. My character must have needed a lot of improvement, not to mention strokes, because at her eightieth birthday party Julia, with whom I had shared the 'big table', reminded me that I had been caned every day by Mrs Cooper. The girls were punished only by having to spend half an hour or so holding a 'back board', a thick piece of wood about a yard long, four inches wide and three-quarters of an inch thick with handles at the ends, which the girl had to hold in her two hands with palms facing forward and elbows by her side, and force down behind her shoulders so as to encourage an erect posture. One day I was sentenced to an hour of the back board because I had already been caned once or twice that day, and came to the conclusion that girls had the best of it.

When I observed that, as soon as they were old enough to help, my sisters were rarely allowed to read quietly in a corner but had to engage in household chores which it was alleged would be good training for them, I changed my opinion about girls having it easy. In fact, I soon discovered, and still believe, that with certain exceptions it is boys who have it easy: presumably most of them will have to make up for it by being born girls in their next incarnation, especially the ones who can justly be described as male chauvinists. The really vicious ones should be reborn as Asian or African Muslim women. It will, of course, be their own higher self which chooses this destiny – karma is not a punishment, but a consequence and an education.

A great many of the standards and values that were taken for granted in the world I was born into were being changed, apparently for ever, by the Great War. It is amazing to me now how little impact that war made on me, as a child who did not read newspapers nor have much conversation with adults, in the days before radio jabbering everything as it happened was a child's constant companion. Barton was by no means exempt from the carnage of the trenches: the war memorial recorded the names of 165 Barton men who gave their lives in the First World War. In a town of about 6,000 inhabitants, that meant there was hardly a family that was not bereaved. We had appropriate prayers at the services of course and my father had to minister to those whose husbands and sons and brothers were listed as dead or missing, and we met some wounded in our streets. Nevertheless, the war seemed far away, for wars were still fought by the armed forces, and did not to any great extent involve civilians directly. Indeed, the only thing that stands out clearly in my memory as a sign that we were at war is being plucked from bed by my nanny and carried to a window and held there, blinking sleepily, to see a Zeppelin, silver, beautiful and unreal, caught in the searchlights. Years later I was crossing the Humber from New Holland to Hull on the paddle-steamer now tethered near Westminster Bridge when the R34 exploded and pieces of the envelope, silver on one side, pink on the other, but no bodies, fell on to the deck.

When I was in hospital at the age of about eight, I read from morning till night; and back at home, convalescing on my 'balcony', I read from morning till night. I was never lonely, and preferred books to company.

When I was well enough to go to school, Father sent me on principle to his own church school in Queen Street, where I was so far ahead of Standard VII that they had to create a special Ex-VII. I was in a room with about twenty working-class boys who were surprisingly nice to me, especially when they discovered that far from my being teacher's pet, the headmaster seized every pretext for caning me savagely, possibly resenting the fact that my father, as Chairman of the Managers, was his boss or perhaps having discovered that I had (once) kissed his daughter Kathleen on the lips. I was very short-sighted and could not see the blackboard, so when he said what he was writing as he wrote it, I could remember, but if he didn't, I hadn't a clue and was caned for inattention. It was in fact the other boys who were inattentive, as most of them spent much of the time masturbating under the protection of their desks, competing to see who could carry on till the last moment as the teacher approached, without being caught. You may think it snobbish by today's standards, but at that period the other boys and I instinctively understood that it wouldn't have been suitable for the vicar's son to join in.

My father knew nothing whatever about the technicalities of sex, and the subject was never discussed at home. After mother had borne him a child every year for nine years, the ninth one stillborn, my godfather, who was also our family doctor, Dr Percy Birtwhistle (known until his death at a ripe old age as the *young* doctor, because he had succeeded his father in the practice) tried to explain menstruation to my father, presumably with a view to attempting some rhythm method of contraception, but my father was so painfully embarrassed by the whole discussion that Dr Percy couldn't bring himself to continue the attempted explanation. Five years later, number ten (ninth surviving), William Oswald, was born.

I might well have grown up in fearful ignorance but for the fact that I was one of three parsons' sons in the diocese of Lincoln who were 'adopted' by a returned missionary Bishop, Dr John Edward Hine (same name, same family as the cognac). I call him 'doctor' not only because he had five doctorates, but because he had started off as a doctor of medicine and had gone to Central Africa for UMCA as a medical missionary.

Bishop Hine was a tall, solemn, impressive figure with a shock of white hair and a great white beard, too ascetic to look like Father Christmas, who lived with two spinster sisters.

He confirmed me when I was twelve. One day when I was on holiday with him at the Subdeanery in Lincoln he called me into his study and said, 'You are twelve, are you not?'

I said that I was.

'I don't suppose', said the Bishop, 'that your parents have told you anything about sex?'

'Certainly not,' I said. 'They always give the impression that it is

24

something one does not talk about. There hasn't been much about it, either, in any of the books I've read, except the Bible. I have, of course, seen dogs and horses copulating, and once when I was staying on Uncle Charlie's farm at Brampton-en-le-Morthen I got up early one morning and was fortunate in seeing a litter of piglets being born, and was a bit shocked to realize àt that moment how we really came into the world.'

'Not a bad beginning,' said the Bishop, 'but it's time you knew the facts. I shall sit here at my desk, and you may sit behind me in that easy chair, and you may take the cat upon your lap.' When we were thus settled, the Bishop gave a most lucid and systematic explanation of human sexuality. Now that I am a recognized authority on the subject myself, I doubt if I could much have improved on the account the Bishop gave in 1923 or 1924. As he spoke, an enormous number of things fell into place, and a great many old wives' tales which my scientific mind had in any case doubted were happily relegated to limbo.

When the lecture came to an end, I sat there, feeling elated, with a sense of 'knowledge is power'. I also felt slightly relieved to know that masturbation, of which I was a devoted practitioner and had been since before puberty, is a normal manifestation of adolescence. I had not, in fact, been particularly worried, unlike many boys of my generation, because as a scientist I never believed the horror stories that were circulated by adults anxious to frighten one off the practice. For instance, 'Everyone who looks at you will know,' was to me totally unconvincing, because when I looked at people, I didn't know, so why should anyone else? Especially in view of the fact that other people were less observant, less intelligent and generally less likely to be recognized as geniuses than I was?

We attended church two or three times on a Sunday according to age, and strictly followed the Christian Year. We celebrated Advent not quite as rigorously as Lent, but with solemnity and much thought of the Four Last Things, and not a hint of a carol until Christmas Eve. There was immense excitement as Christmas approached, and much hiding away in corners to make things or wrap them up in mysterious parcels, for each of us had to contrive some sort of present for each of the others and for our parents. We'd gather holly and ivy from the garden to decorate the house – a sprig of holly must go behind each of the pictures hanging on the

25

walls – and from the churchyard would cut a suitable evergreen, usually yew, as a Christmas tree. It would stand seven feet tall in its bucket of close-packed earth in the bay window of the drawing-room. It would mysteriously get decorated after the Midnight Eucharist when we children were in bed, with decorations kept from year to year and little coloured candles in holders that clipped on like a bulldog clip. Smaller presents would actually be hung on the tree and larger ones piled round the base of it. But on Christmas Eve, all would be bustle and preparation and expectation. For us, Christmas was a Christian festival and all the feasting and exchanging of presents was something arising out of the commemoration of an historic and mystic event.

Whether we had been to the Midnight or not, we all went to Mattins, in a church decorated in much the same fashion as our own home, and heard the Christmas story and sang the Christmas hymns. Sometimes we would encounter other children who would speak of the presents they had *had*: their families had adopted some new-fangled habit of hanging up stockings, in or near which all their presents were put, and as soon as they woke in the early dawn they would open all their presents in their beds, and that was the end of that. We felt sorry for them: our giving and receiving of presents hadn't yet begun, and would continue for the twelve days of Christmas.

After an unhurried mid-day Christmas dinner of goose (later turkey) and Mother's vintage plum pudding, we trooped into the drawing-room with gasps of wonder and pleasure as we saw the Christmas tree lit up and the log fire blazing. The blinds, which had been lowered to prevent us from peering in, were raised to reveal the snow outside, deep and crisp and even. We all made ourselves comfortable and sang a carol, and then, at a nod from Father, Mother would go towards the tree with a pair of scissors. Each of us in turn would receive one present, which we would open carefully, untying the knots in any string, winding up the string, folding up the paper neatly, and then thanking the person who had given the present (or writing a letter of thanks if the giver was not with us) before playing with it or reading it or whatever. Each of us, whilst opening our own present, was the centre of attention, because no one else was opening one at the same time, and everybody was keen to see what we had got and what pleasure it was giving us. Much of the delight came from this leisurely sharing: and nothing got broken. The youngest were given their presents first, so that their

26

patience should not be too much strained, but they knew better than to clamour for another one even after everybody had received a parcel.

Each of us in turn would sing a carol or do a recitation of some kind or play a piece on the piano, and the party would continue until tea-time, when there was Christmas cake and other cakes and in later years crackers with paper hats. Then all of us would go off to church for Evensong. We would go to the tree every day for another round of presents until Twelfth Night, when all the remaining presents would be given out and the tree and decorations taken down and the tree burnt on a ceremonial bonfire. Having one present a day meant that it really had our attention and we extracted the maximum possible benefit from it, both that day and later. We learned some very important lessons from Christmas, as it was celebrated at the vicarage in those days: self-control, care and consideration, tidiness, thrift, making the best – truly, the best – of everything we had, and giving no mere perfunctory thanks to those who benefited us.

Perhaps because we had an academic and somewhat authoritarian father, we four boys all found a friend in the town who did not belong to the class with which we could mix socially, such as Mr and Mrs Nowell, whose garden abutted on to ours, and my godmother Mrs Uppleby of Barrow Hall, who lived in considerable state. Mine was Harold 'Pop' Eastoe, a spry man, not very tall, but perky and agreeable in his manner, with slightly bulging eyes. His hands were reddened by filleting fish and skinning rabbits in all sorts of weather as well as by weighing out potatoes and having to wash his hands a lot. He sometimes washed them with invisible soap while poised behind the counter listening respectfully to a customer's requirement. He must have looked a very ordinary little man to everyone except his wife, though he was well respected and a keen churchman who was both a bell-ringer and a sidesman. Later, when you no longer had to be gentry, he was a churchwarden. I spent hours lounging about the shop and listening to his pithy remarks, and soon was welcome to go up to his living-room – he lived above the shop. I had hardly seen inside any houses in Barton other than those I called at socially. I don't suppose it crossed my mind at the time how truly I loved this man with whom I would seem to have had so little in common.

Pop wasn't the captain of the bell-ringers – that honour belonged to Arthur Hoodless, a joiner who lived a few hundred yards away at the bottom of Holydyke, opposite the grey Wesleyan Chapel. His apple-cheeked wife had more gaps than teeth in her ready smile, and one of their children was a retarded boy with whom they were both wonderfully patient. He was a conscientious workman: if Arthur made you a coffin, it was so well made it seemed a pity to bury it.

You always knew when Arthur or one of the other joiners was going to be making a coffin, because you would hear the Passing Bell. When anyone died, somebody would be sent to tell the verger to ring the Passing Bell, and pay sixpence for half an hour or a shilling for an hour. After a few warning strokes at the rate of one a minute, there would come three quick strokes together. 'Ah,' you would say, 'three for a child – I wonder if Mrs So and So's baby died soon after birth?' Then another three: 'Hm, six for a woman – maybe it was the mother who died in childbed?' Another three: 'Nine tailors [equals tellers] makes a man – now will that be young Whosit who had the accident and is in Hull Infirmary, or will it be old Whatsit who's been bedridden for weeks?' One wouldn't have to wait long for the answer, because after a pause would come a steady sequence of strokes in number equalling the person's age. The rest of the half hour or the hour would be taken up with one 'knoll' (knell) per minute.

Our friend Miss Molbs, headmistress of the church school, produced Shakespeare plays in the Assembly Rooms. I remember what a fine Orsino Arthur Hoodless made in *Twelfth Night*, every inch a Count, though of course speaking broad Lincolnshire. Pop played the part of Sir Toby Belch, and I played the part of Feste, the fool. When Miss Molbs moved away to Nottingham, she twice invited me to stay with her in order to hear music: the Carl Rosa opera company's performances of *Tosca* and other operas; and a piano recital by the great Russian composer Serge Rachmaninov, a tall, austere, aristocratic figure who when applauded hysterically managed to look aloof without being ungracious.

At the end of the concert, when the time came for him to play an encore, everyone in the audience began shouting out the one word: 'Prelude'. His resigned expression showed that he knew which prelude they meant – the Prelude in C sharp minor which was not only a fascinating piece but also had the macabre story attached to it (with what justification I don't know) that it depicted somebody buried alive hammering more and more frantically on the lid of his coffin. It was just the kind of story to appeal to me at that age, and I did in fact play the Prelude myself, which is not as fiendishly difficult as it looks at first glance with all those accidentals. But I had also struggled with another of the preludes which I thought far superior, so in the instant between the tumult and the shouting and Rachmaninov turning back to the piano, I shrieked, 'In G minor!' For a second Rachmaninov looked straight into my eyes, slightly raised one eyebrow, sketched the merest trace of a shrug as he turned down the corners of his mouth, and then sat at the piano and banged out his Prelude in C sharp minor. I still treasure the message he signalled to me in that second: 'My dear chap, you know and I know that the G minor is superior, but the C sharp minor isn't bad and we must give the public what they want, must we not?'

When I was thirteen, Father decided it was time for me to go to public school, and he chose Worksop, where my cousin 'Uncle' Liddon had been prefect of chapel and captain of football. It was a Woodard school with a High Church tradition in a most beautiful situation in that part of Sherwood Forest called The Dukeries. The school was built on Clumber Estate which belonged to the Duke of Newcastle, and just opposite the main gates were the main gates of Welbeck, the estate of the Duke of Portland. The schoolboys at Worksop in those days had the run of both estates except, of course, the immediate vicinity of Clumber House and Welbeck Abbey. I started off in Form 3A and my house was Fleur de Lys, now renamed Pelham.

My first week in 3A I was bottom of the form, because I hadn't got the hang of doing things the way they did at this school and at prep schools, like the other boys. By the second week I was top, and remained monotonously there until the end of the term, when I was moved up to the Fourth Form.

I was not allowed to take part in games on medical grounds, so when not cheering on the school XV or XI would go for long walks in Sherwood Forest – deep into Clumber, or across the road and up the drive to Welbeck, sometimes even exploring the tunnels, though this was forbidden. A mad Duke of Portland had not been able to bear seeing carts go across his land, so as carts *had* to pass if the ducal revenues were to be maintained, he built these fantastic cuttings and tunnels so that carts could be unobserved by him as they passed on their lawful occasions. Now that Welbeck House is an army college, *their* boys will have the run of those tunnels, no doubt.

I enjoyed the chapel services. Viscount Mountgarret had built a magnificent chapel for it, and the choir was excellent. An advantage of a chapel-centred school was that Sunday was made the most enjoyable day of the week: after church, twice, in the morning, there was better food than usual and a long free afternoon and best of all, some kind of entertainment in the evening. It might be a film, such as Cecil B. de Mille's *The Ten Commandments*, or it might be a singer or other musician, or an entertainer reading from Dickens and other dramatic works.

In the Fourth Form I spent a lot of time in the laboratory and neglected the subject I had hated ever since my father had forced me to learn it by myself at an early age, namely Latin. My punishment for this I brought upon my own head: at the end of the year, I failed an exam called the Lower Certificate by two marks in the Latin paper, which was essential. This was the only exam I have ever failed in my life, and my *amour propre* took a heavy blow. My father rang all the changes on the possible stresses in the sentence 'You failed an examination?' Only the word 'an' didn't get under-lined in tones of outrage and disbelief.

This led to my being put into VB, not VA, as one likely to pass the School Certificate but unlikely to get exemption from Matriculation. The maximum number of credits one *could* get in those days was nine, and I decided to get these and did. I was allowed to go straight up into the Upper Sixth, to take the Higher Certificate in one year instead of two.

I was always greatly helped by a retentive memory. I remembered everything I read with attention, often after reading it only once. For example, for English we had two set books, Chaucer's *Prologue* and Shakespeare's *Macbeth*. Both of these I knew off by heart, and I won't bore you with the huge stretches of them I can still remember. When out for walks with friends of mine such as (at that time) Brittain and 'Ginger' Dixon and Eacott, we used to practise 'gob-bets' on one another: the one who had the book would fling two or three words at the rest of us, and we should have to identify where these words came from and what were the words before and after. To even things up a bit, they used to throw only one word at me: 'brown' one of them would yell, and I'd have to say, 'a not-heed hadde he, with a broun visage.' Then we would all giggle, because there was a master who was exactly like that, with a very brown face and a crew cut – what we would nowadays call a skinhead. He was disappointingly normal in other ways; we really liked masters with eccentricities, such as the one called Dr Barton who went into class with a little suitcase from which he took all kinds of paraphernalia to make himself green tea, or maté, to which he was quite literally addicted.

The previous year, the Oxford and Cambridge Joint Board had appointed *Twelfth Night* as the Shakespeare play for the School Certificate, and the headmaster always saw to it that the school play was the one set for the examination, to give us all an extra chance of getting to know it. Although I wasn't doing the School Certificate that year, I learned *Twelfth Night* off by heart, and when this came to the knowledge of the prefects, one of them had me appointed prompter, so that I could prompt the players when they dried up without the disadvantages of my predecessor, who had tended to lose his place in the book and drop the torch with a clatter at the crucial moment.

The first play I took part in as well as prompting was *Macbeth*, in which I played the third witch. There was one occasion when I failed to prompt someone because my mind was far away, and the dreaded headmaster, instead of telling me to come to his study afterwards to be caned, simply sang out sarcastically, 'Dreaming about Cutie, I suppose!'

I knew then the meaning of the expression 'his blood ran cold'. I tried to look like an absent-minded professor but managed to look only like the village idiot as I enquired, 'Cutie, sir?'

'Well, carry on then, and stop staring at Boyd!' snapped the headmaster and I knew with relief that he didn't after all know anything except that nearly all the boys dreamed of Cutie. I wasn't likely to stare at Boyd, dressed as Lady Macbeth with falsies, when Cutie didn't need falsies.

Ah, Cutie! How, on her first appearance in Hall, did she flutter the hearts and penes of all except the smallest boys and the most dedicated homosexuals!

The policy of the school was to have all females on the staff, matrons and maids (this is not a classification into married and virginal), as old and unlikely to distract the pupils as could possibly be found. Until the arrival of Cutie, not a single female about the place attracted even a passing glance or speculation.

In Hall, we were waited on by surly grandmothers. One day, however, their ranks were decimated – whether by 'flu or by senility

31

we never enquired – and one of them was allowed to bring her granddaughter to help out. This girl, dark and rather pretty, had been crammed into one of the shiny black uniforms with lace-edged white pinnies and cap, and on her appearance in Hall that night, there was a collective gasp. One boy was heard to remark in the sudden silence which followed that her 'chest' was going to burst the buttons of her blouse any minute.

The little boys continued wolfing their food, and the bigger boys who were deeply involved in what we called 'romantic friendships' continued their conversations, but the majority of the boys from the Fourth Form upwards were twisting necks and swivelling eyes in an attempt to get a glimpse of her as she passed about her maidenly occasions, whilst appearing to be getting on with their dinner. Eventually, we stood for the Latin grace known to non-classics as Retford Brewery because it began *Retribruere Domine Deus*. The masters strolled out from the high table at the far end and the rest made a mad rush towards the exit for the lavatories and for prep. I followed at leisure, and waited outside the double doors, watching through a crack until the other maids had retreated to their cups and only Cutie still busied herself clearing the tables. I nipped back smartly in and went up to her, and said, 'When you came up from Worksop today, do you remember passing a new building called the Sanatorium?' She replied that her grandmother had pointed it out to her. 'Good,' I said. 'On the opposite side of the path is a large clump of gorse, with a way at the back into the middle of it. Meet me there on your way home this evening.'

'I'll be with my grandmother,' she objected.

'Tell her you have to go back for something and will catch her up,' I said, adding firmly, 'You *be* there!' That was how I 'bagged' Cutie. The prefects and other bloods who tried to nobble her during the next few days never knew why she was so unresponsive. She and I were not able to meet very often, nor for very long, and I'm not going to tell you what we did or didn't do, because she might just conceivably be identifiable. Except that I didn't 'ruin' her, as it was then described.

Macbeth, *Julius Caesar* and Shaw's *St Joan* were not well furnished with damsels. Opportunities for transvestitism were few and far between in our school plays. In *St Joan* there were many boys who would have fancied J. W. B. Wilkinson but for the fact that the character would insist on wearing armour, which must have been a considerable anaphrodisiac all through history.

32

Talking of armour, another thing I got off on medical grounds was the OTC. It must have been very tedious for most of the boys to have to change into rough, scratchy khaki with puttees in order to drill and otherwise play at soldiers. On top of everything else, they had to go to camp, and while some of them enjoyed it, others came back with horrifying tales of bullying. One we didn't know whether to believe or not was of a boy being 'shot up the arse with a blank cartridge' and thereby 'ruined for life' (for what? one wondered).

It is not surprising that I was listed as a swot, seeing I had no involvement in rugger, hockey, cricket, gym, the OTC, or any other form of muscular Christianity unless you count being drafted with two other boys into the Rover Scouts in 1928, without ever having been a Wolf Cub or an ordinary Scout, in order to go to the Jamboree in Arrowe Park, Birkenhead. We were in the Rover Service Camp, which meant toiling from morning till night at an allotted task and having practically no time to cook the rations that were supplied. My task was directing traffic all day at one of the main crossroads, and answering silly questions from Scouts from all over the world, which hardly counts as athleticism although it was very tiring.

I was quite content with the sort of life I had made for myself in that unhappy school, though I should have liked to be a prefect in order to be able to stay in bed longer and have certain other privileges. Then came the day when a new housemaster was appointed for Fleur de Lys, and excitement in the school was intense when it was learned that the headmaster had succeeded in persuading H. P. Jacob ('the fastest three-q. England ever had') to join the staff as our housemaster. We were much envied by the other houses, but I myself gave a resigned shrug and said to myself, 'Bang goes all chance of being made a prefect by a man who is openly described as Rugger Master, though he would also teach some harmless subject to the smallest boys.'

The first night H. P. Jacob was with us, there appeared on the house notice board a notice saying, 'To be house prefect, Varah, E.C. Signed H. P. Jacob, Housemaster.' I was flabbergasted. I asked the Head of House, Sandy Christison, about it. He was a hero on the rugger and cricket fields and was prefect of chapel which meant that among the school prefects he was second to the head of the school. He had once seized upon a pretext to beat me ferociously with a slipper, which, if it has a substantial heel, can be very painful

33

when one is wearing only pyjamas. This was a couple of years before, and as Christison had seemed to go out of his way to be decent to me after that episode, I decided that this was as near as he could be expected to get to admitting that he shouldn't have beaten me, so I bore him no ill will.

Christison told me of his conversation with our new housemaster. 'There's a boy here', Jacob had said, 'who is in the Upper Sixth and who is the only boy in the school, perhaps in the country, to get nine credits in the School Cert, so what has he done to make him unfit to be a prefect?'

'He's a dirty swot, sir,' replied Christison, disposing of the matter, as he thought.

'That', stated H. P. Jacob, 'is what a public school is for, Christison, and don't you forget it. You and I and other comparative dimwits who happen to be Good at Games must not suppose that the *only* purpose of this place is proficiency with varying sizes and shapes of *balls*.' Christison did very well to remember such a long sentence verbatim nearly ten minutes after it was spoken to him.

I said to myself, 'That man has been *fair* to me! I must *do* something to show my appreciation – but what? What on earth can a chap who is "off games" do to please the fastest three-q. England ever had?' Then I got it. The long list of things I wasn't allowed to do didn't include an activity which was organized only once a year, namely cross-country running. It was obvious, of course, that had any medical man thought of it he would have forbidden cross-country running before anything else; but it hadn't been thought of because it wasn't listed as a school activity. There was a recognized five-mile cross-country course, through a very attractive part of Clumber Woods (how nice for the Duke of Newcastle to have such extensive grounds that he can have a school and its playing-fields and a five-mile cross-country course in them and not notice) and once a year practically the whole school took off on this course on what was called 'the Dorm Run', because the competition was between dormitories who entered all their members except the halt and the lame. The first 300 or so boys were numbered from 1 to 300 in the order in which they panted home, and the house with the lowest number of points won. In addition, the first eight received their school running colours and the first twenty their house running colours – this in addition to colours given for athletics events on sports day.

I decided that someone who was too weedy to play rugby and too likely to break his specs at cricket and whose swimming style was shaped by being thrown in at the deep end and left to find a way of not drowning, was unlikely to be good at anything requiring the physique and co-ordination of an Apollo, but that staggering around a cross-country course might be just the ticket. He would only need practice and perseverance. That meant that if it hurt, you ran harder.

So from that day forward, every day of term and twice on Sundays, a lanky figure in singlet and shorts would set off laboriously on the cross-country course, accompanied by the jeers of small boys who knew that this particular prefect would beat them only for some genuine and serious breach of the rules and not for rude remarks he was forced to agree with.

It was agony for the first few weeks, but gradually it became easier and I forced myself to go faster. Hutcha hutcha higher higher hutcha hutcha higher higher, said my breath, interspersed with the occasional groan.

At last the great day came, at the end of the second term after I began this torture. An account of the race would be boring so I will only tell you that to practically everyone's astonishment, I came in ninth. This meant that I just missed my school colours, but I had my house colours, and H. P. Jacob said, 'Well done, Varah.'

One day when I was in the laboratories by myself, having done the five-mile course in twenty-seven minutes, I found myself fascinated by white phosphorus. Like most of the solid elements, this one is rarely encountered in its pure form. It was first isolated by distillation from urine. White phosphorus had a bad record in the last century because of the illnesses it caused among the match-girls who used it to make matches. It was because of the dangers to health that red phosphorus was substituted.

Just as water bears no resemblance to the hydrogen and oxygen which compose it, and the harmless fluorides used to prevent dental caries have no resemblance to the corrosive gas fluorine, so the phosphates which are used as fertilizers show no trace of the interesting characteristics of the element phosphorus. White phosphorus looks like yellowish church candles as it lies there innocently in its jar under water, without which it would ignite spontaneously in the atmosphere.

I didn't know then that of all the elements essential to human life, the one we are in gravest danger of running out of is phosphorus. We keep letting it be carried by rivers to the bottom of the sea, from whence it is for all practical purposes irrecoverable.

I can't remember now what experiment I was going to do with the phosphorus, but I took a stick of it from the jar with tongs, and holding it carefully on a plate of glass was cutting a small piece off ready to plunge the large piece back into the jar and the smaller piece into a beaker of water, when my knife slipped, the stick of phosphorus skidded, and landed on the tiled floor. There it broke, which is strange, because usually you had to chip bits off – there must have been fractures across it already. The speed with which all three or four pieces – one small one being on the bench – started producing P_2O_5 (phosphorus pentoxide) was impressive. Clouds of this dense white 'smoke' filled the laboratory, and I didn't notice that while putting the small piece in the beaker, I had put my foot on one of the pieces on the floor. This meant that wherever I walked in the laboratory, I left bits of white phosphorus on the floor, all of which began to give off phosphorus pentoxide.

Eventually I managed to scrape all the phosphorus off my shoe but by now the laboratory was full of smoke which was pouring out of the windows. The next thing I knew, the fire brigade had come up from Worksop and people were breaking down the door to rescue me. I had locked the door to keep out curious small boys and other potential trespassers. They found me lying on the floor at the far end of the laboratory, tying a wet cloth round my mouth in preparation for making a dash for the door. They thought I was unconscious, but of course I was simply finding breathable air, which is usually near the floor because of draughts. A fireman carried me out, trampling through the phosphorus on the floor. When I could struggle free, I told the fireman that it was phosphorus, but they didn't want to listen until I pointed out that they were causing little explosions and leaving puffs of smoke wherever they trod. Eventually the chemistry master came and supervised the scraping up of the remaining phosphorus, now safe under the sheet of water. Later I was summoned to the headmaster's study, and found him holding a bunch of birch twigs neatly bound together like a besom without a handle.

I was told the enormity of the offence of burning down the laboratory (which you will realize I hadn't done) demanded birching rather than caning. I was somewhat relieved at this news, but didn't show it. The headmaster had often boasted of his prowess with a cane, saying that he could lay two weals across a boy's bottom within a quarter of an inch of one another, and then use the remaining strokes all on that tender ridge between the two. I decided that birching, though spoken of with bated breath, was probably more spectacular but less painful – I guessed it would lacerate the skin but leave no deep bruises. I was told to lower my trousers and bend over, which I did. The headmaster did not appear to be angry: when it was all over, he told me kindly to go to the Matron to have disinfectant put on the wounds.

Boys who had suffered crippling caning from him at one time or another were looking at me with awe as I limped along the cloisters towards the stairs that led to the Matron's surgery – a place of dread, where boys would go with boils on their necks (or sometimes on their behinds) to have these treated with red-hot antiphlogistine, or, if very unlucky, to have them squeezed. I later made a nice profit by charging sixpence for people to have a good look at my backside on bath night. There were many takers, in spite of the rival attractions of a prefect who suffered the embarrassment of an immense erection whilst lying in his bath and failing to subdue it – streams of boys passed the end of his bath, squinting sideways, and reappeared going in the opposite direction, like a stage army. I was relieved when he leapt out and wrapped a towel round himself, so that my customers would not be distracted.

It was strange how inadvertent erections on bath night were so feared that many little boys got them through concentrating too hard on trying to avoid them. Yet some, at least, of the same ones who would have been mortified to 'get big' *coram populo* would compare penis sizes in the lavatories and even, in some cases, engage in competitions to see who could ejaculate furthest. There was one boy who had quite an obsession about size and would often stand alongside me in the 'pee stalls' wishing to engage in comparisons, using my appendage as a yardstick (if yardstick is the word I am looking for). 'Is mine bigger than last time you saw it?' he would hiss. I would untruthfully reassure him on this point, enthusing over the circumference since the length was rather a sore point with him. Though several boys boasted of the feat, he was the only one I actually saw standing in the doorway of one of the 'bogs', and ejaculating upwards with such force as to hit the lintel of the admittedly not very high doorway. I declined to engage in this contest. I'd have tried it for Cutie, in the unlikely event of her wishing me to do so, but not for another boy.

37

Masturbation, which at that period was called 'tossing off', was a favourite occupation, particularly useful in getting warm in a cold bed, and also a favourite topic of conversation. The exaggerated boasts of some boys reached the ears of the headmaster, who decided to conduct his own survey of the prevalence of this habit. We got the impression that he wanted to know all about it rather than stamp it out, though of course he did not wish Worksop's prowess on the rugger field to be imperilled by frantic masturbation to the point of exhaustion the night before a big match. For his survey, he assembled the older boys together, one form at a time, and gave a talk which was so elliptic that some of the dimmer brethren didn't know what he was on about. At the end, we were all given a blank piece of paper, and told to write on it nothing whatever except a number, this number being the answer to the question, how many times a week did we 'do it'? 'Do what?' whispered the dimmer brethren, who had already written their name and form on their piece of paper. Once everybody was clear what the number was to represent, and had written his reply, shielding it with his other hand from his neighbour's gaze, the papers were collected up for study and analysis.

As far as the Fifth Form was concerned, it could be called 'Varah's Revenge', because I had persuaded my cronies to put down between forty and fifty (I myself had put fifty) for the number of times a week. It nearly drove the headmaster crazy. The two possibilities were equally unacceptable: one, that half a dozen boys were masturbating more than half a dozen times a day, and the other, that half a dozen boys were mocking him on what was practically a sacred subject (well, the survey took place in a class called Religious Knowledge). He did the only thing he could, which was to repeat the survey for my form. His qualifications included that of barrister at law, but all his skill availed him nothing when facing a class of innocently receptive boys to whom he did not wish to admit that he was worried about their previous answers. Of course, as you will have guessed, my little prank had become known to several boys in the class, though not to all – we daren't risk there being a sneak amongst us – so the number of boys putting figures between forty and fifty increased somewhat. The headmaster was as much in the dark as ever: was the increase caused by more boys mocking him than before, or by more boys deciding to tell the truth at last? As far as I am aware, he went to his grave without knowing.

*

38

The term after the School Certificate, four of us who were regarded as being 'good at sums' and were to sit for scholarships at about the same time that we took the Higher Certificate, were allocated to the Second Master, whose name was O'Meara but who was known to everyone as Buz, for extra maths. This was a tremendous experience, because Buz had been Second Wrangler, which means that he was second of the top twenty-five in the first class in the Mathematical Tripos at Cambridge. He usually wore ginger or mustard-coloured plus fours, had a red face and only one eye, and was thought to be called Buz because of his habit of saying tut tut, which in *Hamlet* is buz, buz, though he pronounced it tmut tmut. This was only one of several peculiarities of speech, another of which was his inability to say the letter L for which he substituted R; but he couldn't otherwise say R very easily and tended to substitute M. For instance, Lund became Rund, and Milner, whose father was a professor at Sheffield where he himself hoped to get a scholarship, became Miwner. He could manage the third of us, 'Ginger' Dixon, but I naturally became Vahma. We assembled in his room for the first time to hear the marks we had obtained in Elementary Mathematics in the School Certificate. He explained that there were three papers at 100 marks each, but the examiners always deducted one mark on principle, so that the possible total for the three papers was 297. He then read: 'Rund, 294 – must tmy harder. Dixon, 295 – could do better. Miwner, 296 – mop bad. Vahma, 297 – h'm, we'oo, er, open your exercise books and we'll do a rittle cow-curas (calculus).'

The other three boys always scrambled for the seat on Buz's left, so that they could grimace and generally misbehave in the safety of his blind side. I never joined in this scramble, because I was convinced that I, on his right, was on his blind side – that his glass eye looked more real than his real one, and that I detected a faint sardonic quirk of his lips whenever the boy on what was *assumed* to be his blind side did something particularly outrageous.

We really did get through an enormous amount of work, though. When the time for the examinations approached, however, we began to get a little anxious about the fact that we hadn't done anything except calculus. One day we said to him, 'Sir,' we said, 'what about solid geometry, sir? What about conic sections, sir? What about higher algebra, sir? And did we do enough trig (trigonometry) in the Fifth, sir?'

'Boys,' replied Buz, 'tmust me. I have been thwough the examination papers for the rast ten years, at all the praces where you are sitting for scommer-ships, and in none of them have there ever been fewer than fwee questions out of ten on cow-curas, and sometimes there have been four or even five. Any boy who gets two and a half questions wight is sure of a scommer-ship. It would be a work of' – I can't begin to spell the word 'supererogation' as he pronounced it – 'to do anything but cow-curas, but if it would ease your consciences, we can spend a few ressons on the hommors of statics and dynamics.'

'But, sir,' we chorused, 'are we even up to scholarship standard in calculus?'

Buz cackled wickedly. 'Scommer-ship standard? Scommer-ship standard?' he chortled. 'I have taken you boys up to finals standard, degmee standard. You can teach bright boys anything, if you don't ret them suspect it's hard!'

Buz was right. We hated statics and dynamics, and we did all get our scholarships. I was the luckiest: in the examination for my group of colleges at Oxford I was not altogether pleased with the way I had done in the physics paper, although I had found an ingenious method of doing one of the practical questions which occurred to no one else and gained marks for ingenuity even though it gave a totally incorrect result. I could hardly believe my eyes when I opened the mathematics paper, and saw that out of the ten questions nine were calculus and one was elementary trigonometry. In thirty-five minutes I had finished the entire paper and gone out into the quad for a smoke, having been warned by the invigilator that under no circumstances would I be allowed to come back. I told him I had completed all ten questions, and he looked at me in a manner appropriate to an idle boaster who didn't even know when he was out of his depth and was in any case a slave to nicotine. So, thanks to Buz and his obsession with cow-curas, I got my scholarship, or rather exhibition, and the school celebrated with a half-holiday.

At the end of the summer term 1930 I left Worksop. In spite of looking forward enormously to Oxford in the autumn, I felt really distressed as a taxi took me down the drive for the last time, to catch the train to Barton.

2

I fell in love very easily – except in one instance, I managed not to
fall in love with two girls in the same village at the same time –
and thoroughly enjoyed writing poems to girls and whispering to
them in the dusk or the moonlight the sort of romantic nonsense I
was later to encounter with a shock of bashful recognition in James
Branch Cabell's *Jurgen* – the only book I've reread every year since I
discovered it. It seemed to me jolly sensible to be able to experience
transports of ecstasy from looks, letters, kisses, and touching of
hands (I'm not going to say we never touched anything else) rather
than to engage in that miserable contest, which I so often heard an
account of from both sides, in bewilderment or exasperation. Not
having it with girls one liked very much was a more satisfactory
policy than having it with girls one didn't even like. On top of
everything else, knowing how to please a girl – and being confident
of being able to please *any* girl – is, no matter what the Purity
League may say, a better preparation for the *grand amour*, or for
that matter for marriage, than waiting until the wedding night to
treat a girl in the same inept way as the easy fornicators who had
disappointed half the parish.

It was at this period of my life that my father began to make
serious use of my services, not simply as a server and a choir man,
but as reader of the lessons at the parish church and as a lay reader
down at St Chad's, by the waterside. I don't know whether it did
any good to the faithful at that mission church, but it did a lot of
good to *me*, because I made up my mind from the very beginning
that I would not write out sermons and would keep any headings I
had jotted down on a piece of paper in my cassock pocket, to be
produced only if I got absolutely stuck. Forcing myself to work out
in my mind what I was going to say beforehand, and then saying it,

41

looking at the people to whom I was speaking, was wonderful practice and although my sermons must have been pretty tedious in those days, I started a habit which I have continued throughout my life of speaking without notes. I fear I was often a long way above the heads of the congregation, though I hope not quite so far as that parson in the *Punch* cartoon addressing bemused yokels (which St Chad's congregation were not) with the words, 'Aha! I know what you are going to say to me – you are going to say, "Apollinarian-ism"!' Decades later I did without notes when preaching at Westminster Abbey whilst the late Eric Abbott was Dean. Afterwards he, who had been Warden of my theological college at the end of my time there, said, 'I'm immensely proud of you, Chad.' As usual, I'd thought out the sermon more carefully than if I'd written notes.

I went up to Oxford in October 1930 to read chemistry at Keble College. I had fallen in love with the place when I went there for my 'scommer-ship' examination and later for my College Entrance exam (I had been excused Responsions because of getting at least five credits in the School Certificate), and the longer I was there, the more I loved it. I still love it. I was allocated rooms at what was then P.3.11 – that is, rooms No. 11 on the third staircase of Pusey Quad, where my scout was Joe Boodell. I didn't know anyone else on my staircase, though I had a nodding acquaintance with Felix Arnott who had the room above mine, as he reminded me fifty years later when we met in Brisbane, where he was Archbishop. I made hardly any friends in College because I decided to become cosmopolitan and collect interesting foreigners. The ones I came to know were Michael (Misha) Matejić, who was Serbian; George She, who was Hong Kong Chinese; and a Russian postgraduate student, Nikolai Zernov. Misha was the only one I saw regularly.

All undergraduates had a Tutor, and a Moral Tutor, the latter being *in loco parentis*. My Moral Tutor, Dr George Parkes, was also my Tutor at that time, being a chemist himself.

Did I waste, or largely waste, my three years at Oxford? I did not think so at the time, in spite of the people who tried to make me feel guilty about seldom attending lectures and spending most of my time collecting interesting foreigners; and I certainly do not think so now. It would be useless to ask me whether I would do the same again, because I am not the same – no longer feeling my way uncertainly towards a purpose in life – and Oxford is not the same – no longer a place where you learned how to think, unlike Redbrick universities where you accumulated knowledge, but a place where you now have to have a good mind and also work hard. It would be an oversimplification to say that at Oxford in those days you didn't need to memorize facts if you knew where they were to be found and what use to make of them, so that instead of storing up masses of grist you worked on the efficiency and accuracy of the mill into which the grist would be fed; because you didn't need to be a scholar at all to get in, if you had the money and if possible a family connection or came from a renowned school or were proficient at some form of sport. Only in law were feats of memorization vital, which was why so many Indians did well at it, it was said.

As I look back at my life I identify a complex of different and sometimes conflicting traits. For instance, I can easily become absorbed in a task and work at it industriously, even obsessionally, forgetting to eat or rest; but I can also procrastinate, give in to my disinclination to tackle an unappealing duty, be lazy about boring routine. There are times when, like Oscar Wilde, I 'can resist anything except temptation', and I don't want to excuse my dilettantism at Oxford by saying I was searching for the influences which were going to be important to me and therefore did not need to be too firmly committed to incarceration in the Bodleian Library. I have to face the truth that I did well at school because my lucid mind and exceptional memory were disciplined by schoolmasters who not only taught me but made me work, whether (as was usually the case) I felt like it, or whether I didn't. At Oxford this discipline was almost entirely removed, and I found myself with a freedom I had never had before – not at home, not at school – and which I often used unwisely.

Can you imagine what it was like to come from a strict home and a strict school to that sweet city with her dreaming spires, with little control exercised over the way one's time was spent? There was, of course, the need to get up at a certain time if one wanted breakfast, and to be in Hall on time for other meals, and to be in college by 11 p.m., and to write the essays enjoined by one's Tutor. Oh, and to attend chapel five times a week whilst living in college. Attendance was reduced when living in digs (in my case, only in my third year) to four or three times, or even twice, according to distance – so by taking digs in St Clements, over Magdalen Bridge and intended for Magdalen men, chapel attendances could be skipped altogether or cut to once a week. Remember that one of the new freedoms was the freedom not to practise the religion of one's childhood or of one's schooldays, but to proclaim oneself an agnostic: not as a pose, but because (as St Paul put it) 'when I became a man, I put away childish things.' At eighteen one wasn't a man in those days, and one now blushes to remember how often one behaved like a foolish child, but the rejection of a faith, however admirable, inherited from someone else was (and I believe still is) an essential step towards finding one's own faith. Never missing Holy Communion on a Sunday was not a sign that the process had been completed, but a testimony to the power of what had been inculcated during impressionable years.

I had gone up with an exhibition (a less pecuniarily advantageous scholarship) in natural science, having won it in physics and mathematics which I had studied at school along with chemistry. The colleges were in groups for the scholarship exams and more than one might offer an award. I chose the one from Keble because it was the most generous and because the college, though full at that time of theologians and historians, was conveniently opposite the Clarendon laboratories. Much as I admired (and still admire) the buildings of Magdalen, I did not agree with those who despised the architecture of Keble: I found the proportions noble, and the nearness of a bathroom to all the rooms desirable, if less romantic than crossing a couple of quads in one's dressing-gown in deep snow, like one of my acquaintances in a medieval foundation.

Nowadays, it seems the reason why Keble is the most popular college is that it has retained a formality some others have lost: you still wear gowns and dine in Hall after a Latin grace and are waited on by 'scouts' instead of queuing in a cafeteria. Scholars and exhibitioners wore long gowns rather similar to those of graduates, whilst commoners wore scrappy little things barely covering their jackets. We also sat at the Scholars' Table, presumably so that we might engage in erudite conversation above the heads of commoners. I can't remember this ever happening, but I do remember religion and politics were barred, and you could be 'sconced' for mentioning a lady's name. A 'sconce' was a huge vessel containing anything from two to seven pints of beer for which the person sconced had to pay. He must 'down' it, either at once or after it had been round the table one or more times. I was sconced on my first night for downing another chap's sconce, having misunderstood. I then downed my own, and ate no dinner, bloated with about four pints. I'd never drunk beer before.

The first two terms were for preliminary exams of those not reading classics or mathematics, which needed two years each for

Honour Moderations and Finals. For most subjects you took Pass Mods, that is, no class was awarded until you took your Finals; but for natural science you took 'Nat. Sci. Prelim' which for me was in chemistry because I was intending to take chemistry for my Finals. Although I enjoyed the laboratory work, I hated reading up endless experiments done by other people in volume after volume of a *Zeitschrift* in German, and was easily tempted away from this tedious exercise by friends proposing morning coffee at the 'Super' Cinema, dispensed by a slight, dreamy, languishing girl called Lily about whom I was briefly silly. I didn't realize at the time that it was Finals work I was being set at the Clarendon, because, working for the Higher Certificate, as A levels were then called, and which I passed a year too soon and again at the proper age, to boost the school's results, I had learnt enough chemistry at school to pass Nat. Sci. Prelim with one hand tied behind my back.

I had one very good tip from my Tutor, Dr George Parkes, for which I shall ever be grateful. It was to attend lectures, not required for Nat. Sci. Prelim, on atomic chemistry, given by Frederick Soddy. I didn't know at the time that being taught by Soddy would make me a historical character; I only knew the lectures were fascinating. The subject would now be called atomic physics, about which Soddy knew more than anyone else except perhaps Rutherford. It was Soddy who had discovered isotopes, a word from the Greek which means 'in the same place' items. In the same place as what, *in* what, you will ask. In the same place in Mendeleev's Periodic Table as another form of the same chemical element of a different atomic weight. Atomic theory demanded that atomic weights of elements should be pretty well exact integers, yet some had figures after the decimal point, however carefully you did and re-did the estimation. Since an element is a form of matter which remains the same however much you divide and subdivide it, all parts of it must have the same atomic weight, and an element with a different atomic weight must be a different element. Soddy did what is now called 'lateral thinking' to discover that the explanation of the non-integral atomic weights was that the elements concerned were a mixture of forms of *the same element* of different atomic weights all of which *were* integers.

You will realize the importance of this when I tell you that the heaviest element found in nature (that is, not made, as are plutonium and the other trans-uranic elements, in the laboratory) is uranium, and that it is a mixture of three isotopes of atomic weights 235, 237 and 238, the last being by far the greatest part; and that it is of U235 that bombs working by nuclear fission can be made. So without Soddy's discovery (made independently some months later by Aston at Cambridge) there would be no atomic bombs and no possibility of electrical power from nuclear power stations.

By 1931 Soddy knew that *if* (and it was such a big IF I want to put it in capitals) U235 could be separated from U238, in quantities which were not achievable, a mass of U235 of what is called critical mass (brought about, for example, by two smaller masses being rapidly forced together), its atoms would spontaneously split explosively, releasing an amount of energy calculated theoretically by that genius Albert Einstein (the famous formula $e = mc^2$). When you realize that 'c' is the velocity of light (in metres per second, if you are measuring mass in grams: $299,792,456.2 = 186,282.397$ m.p.s.) you will see that the square of it gives an enormous multiplicator. To release this almost inconceivable amount of energy instantaneously is to cause an explosion of a magnitude previously undreamed of.

The first and second uses of the 'atom bomb' on Hiroshima and Nagasaki raised warfare to a new dimension and stunned Japan into surrender – thereby saving millions of Japanese as well as Allied lives which 'conventional' victory would have cost. The horror people feel at it is not, of course, misplaced: those who died slowly and those who still suffer paid and pay a terrible price for Japanese militarism and atrocities. (Those whose bodies were converted in an instant into black shadows on the pavement had as merciful a death as it is possible to have.) The terror of nuclear war has kept the peace for all the years that have elapsed since, and 'mutually assured destruction' is the best deterrent sinful men have found. The advocates of unilateral nuclear disarmament seem to me to have a fear of suffering and death such that it has taken away their senses – except, of course, those who were peaceniks until the events of Eastern Europe of 1989, and knew exactly what they were up to. Of course, in 1930 we atomic chemistry students were not planning to make atom bombs because, *inter alia*, in the unlikely event that we were aware U235 was fissionable, we also 'knew' that it was not possible to separate significant quantities of U235 from the mixture of uraniums found in nature. It needed the exigencies of war, a dozen years later, to provide the scientists and the money to transform the impossible into the merely difficult and expensive. I might have been one of those scientists if I hadn't decided, after Nat. Sci. Prelim, to enter some other Final Honours School, instead of chemistry.

It is my belief that God didn't give us the possibility of energy from nuclear fission simply in order to overthrow the Axis and Japanese tyrannies and to provide a future world government with unassailable authority, but so that we might have an inexhaustible source of energy when we had either frittered away the fossil fuels he had laid down for us long before we appeared on earth, or found the use of them contributing too much to the 'greenhouse effect'. Non-scientists are having frightening success in stampeding the general public into the belief that it is entirely beyond the wit of man to generate nuclear power safely or to dispose safely of its radio-active products. If the French can do it (and they've proved they can), so can we. To say this is not to minimize the dangers that must be guarded against: human carelessness at Three Mile Island, human foolhardiness at Chernobyl, of the same kind that produced the non-nuclear tragedy of Bhopal. What sort of scale of values puts avoidable Chernobyl above the ruin of our whole planet by the destruction of the rain forests and the burning of coal, gas and oil?

Naturally, I am in favour of harnessing the wind and the tides, and pursuing the research that will eventually bring us fusion power (nuclear energy by the fusing of light atoms instead of by the split-ting of heavy ones). We should emulate the French *now*. From the first success in November 1991 to commercial production will take years, possibly decades. As John Drinkwater wrote:

Knowledge we lack not, knowledge thou hast lent,
But, Lord, the will: there lies our bitter need.
Help us to build, above the deep intent,
The deed, the deed.

Study for chemistry Finals seemed to consist largely of learning and repeating other chaps' work instead of doing original research. But an even greater objection was that it kept one involved with things rather than people. I was beginning to emerge from the aloneness and self-sufficiency of my childhood, modified by the friendships I had made at school, and was now finding great satisfaction in meeting the most interesting people I could find in Oxford. Most of these were foreigners, because on the whole I avoided the politicians and the gilded youth, though I did occasionally speak at the Union (Bishop Hine had paid for me to become a Life Member) during the time John Boyd-Carpenter was President. He was wonderfully kind to me, gauche as I think I was – and I'm quite proud to remember that in the (in)famous 'King and Country' debate I was one who didn't get called to speak but did vote that this House *was* willing to fight for its king and country.

As a boy, I had read a lot of Russian novels and in my last year at school had taught myself some Russian. I included verse translations from Russian as well as from French in the anthology of schoolboy verse *After School Hours* which I edited and persuaded Basil Blackwell to publish. (I even got a £10 advance.) It was natural for me to join the Oxford University Russian Club, and I found there was no competition to become Secretary of it. I did not at that time like either of my Christian names, so I adopted the name Vladimir (accent firmly on the second syllable, Vlad-EE-meer, please) because St Vladimir, Prince of Kiev in the ninth century, was a Varyagh. My English friends started to call me Vlad, which is *not* the abbreviation of Vladimir (Volodya is, if you can call it an abbreviation), and I reluctantly accepted what seemed to me a sissy practice of using first names, which we had never done at school. People there didn't even *know* the first names of Varah, E.C.

One of the few Russians in the Russian Club was Prince Leonid Lieven, who kindly taught me how to pronounce the language. All the other members of the Committee, except the beautiful, intelligent, disdainful (or shy?) Countess Tania Vorontsov, were Serbs – Prince Mihailo (Misha) Dragishe Matejić (ić is pronounced itch), the Princes Stojan and Vojislav (Voki) Veljković, Princess Stanka Losanić – except for John Plamenac (c, no accent, pronounced ts), later a Don, who was Montenegrin. All these titles reflected the fact that people from the Balkans could afford to study at Oxford only if they were rich and upper class.

Misha was almost my only friend at Keble, and when I became very friendly with Voki it created a difficulty, because the Veljkovići were the female line of the Obrenovići, the royal family displaced by the Karadjordjovići with the help of politicians led by Misha's father. I was never close to Stojan, who languidly claimed the throne but was unlikely to do anything about it, but as I was walking down The High one day with Misha on one side and Voki on the other, the tension between them caused me to insist that they end a feud which was now meaningless. When we got back to my room we decided to become blood brothers (eighteen-year-olds were much younger in those days) and as we didn't know the proper method of effecting this, we gingerly scratched the balls of our thumbs to draw a few drops of blood, and each shook hands with the other in such a way that the tiny wounds approximated. Whether we exchanged any blood at all is doubtful, and of course this was long before Aids made us wary of body fluids, but it was the thought that counted, and it made me happy when they went off to ride together on Port Meadow.

I was less happy when they agreed that Misha should teach *me* to ride. Apart from being put as a small child on the back of a carthorse so wide that I did the splits, painfully, and occasionally driving a pony called Toby who pulled a little vehicle called The Tub when I visited my Uncle Charlie, a farmer at Brampton-en-le-Morthen, I had no experience of horses nor desired any. Misha assured me that riding was easy: he could do it before he could walk. So we hired a couple of hacks and took them to Port Meadow, where Misha insisted on attaching Serbian cavalry spurs to both our boots. He dug his into his beast which charged off with an indignant squeal. My nag started bouncing and, as I tried to hold on, *my* spurs dug in, and he (or she) tore after the other one. The more I tried to hold on by my heels, the more I spurred the creature on, and I began to slide towards the front until I was straddling its neck. This was uncomfortable for both of us, and my four-legged friend had the solution: he lowered his head, depositing me on the ground, tried not to step on me but with so many legs caught my shin with the toe of one and my back with the knee of another, took a tumble and then got up and began to eat grass. I lay there in agony feeling as if my back was broken, and Misha rode back, a resentful and disappointed teacher of an inept pupil.

'You'll have to mount again immediately, or you'll lose your nerve!' he commanded.

'I don't care if I do,' I groaned, 'as I'm going to keep clear of horses from now on.'

'Nonsense,' he said, helping me up and heaving me on to the back of my horse. I briefly passed out with the pain and this seemed to convince him that he must walk and lead both horses to the Radcliffe Infirmary. Every step was agony and it was weeks before the pain subsided – apparently some muscles had tried to tear away from the bone, or something equally dire. I had an injection against tetanus because of the wound on my left shin. (I still have the scar.)

49

We decided to change the name of the Russian Club to the O.U. Slavonic Club (Slovyanski Klub) and to try and enlist all Slavs by getting other nationalities to speak at meetings. One of the most interesting I obtained was Paul Selver, a Czech who had published an anthology of Czechoslovak poetry translated into English by himself. Thanks to him I became familiar with the poems of Vrhlicky, Březina, Machar, Sova and Bezruč, another step in the process of becoming cosmopolitan, a citizen of the world. An interesting glimpse of how manners change in the space of a lifetime: I was shocked when Paul Selver, walking with me along The Corn, lit a cigarette. I was keen smoker myself, but in 1931 well-bred people didn't smoke in the street.

It was about this time that I decided not to register for chemistry Finals. I went to see my Tutor, George Parkes, and told him my decision. He was a Yorkshireman who had never lost his broad accent, and later became Senior Proctor (in charge of the university's policing of undergraduates). 'We shall miss ye at Queen's lab,' he said, referring to the small stone building in Queen's Lane known irreverently as 'the lab of one beaker', though its equipment had been adequate for his needs and mine. 'There'll be a terrible paucity of drama, unless soom oother oondergrad makes a 'abit of putting 'is 'ead in the poison cupboard instead of 'is 'ands.'

'I only did it once,' I protested.

'Ye only die once,' he remarked drily. Experiments with arsenic and cyanides had to be done in a glass-fronted cupboard from which he had had to rescue me when I flopped unconscious.

I hastily changed the subject and asked him in what Final Honours School I could get an Honours Degree without doing any work, because lighting my cigarettes at Bunsen burners in the labs was ruining my social life, even though I stayed up to all hours arguing with my friends about the meaning of meaning and the shortage of beautiful women undergraduates. 'Varah,' he said, 'that is a most immoral question. 'Owever, since ye've asked it, Ah'll answer it: PPE. A bright lad like you should get some sort of honours without doing no work whatsoever. *If*, o' course, you can fix Set Books. Let's see what they are.' He consulted a book on his desk and chortled. 'Ah reckon these'll stoomp ye,' he said. 'Kant, *Kritik der reinen Vernunft*. Also, Kant, *Grundlegung zur Metaphysik der Sitten*. You'll be longing for *Zeitschrift für Chemische Studien* afore ye've finished wi' yon.'

Critique of Pure Reason and *Groundwork of the Metaphysics of*

Morals didn't sound exactly un-put-downable, but I was sure I'd think of something when the time came. I was free of the labs of which I had once dreamed, starry-eyed. Philosophy, Politics and Economics, with a paper on Psychology, was called 'Modern Greats' because Greats (Classics) was what you studied if you were a philosopher, but you didn't get as far as Descartes. From Descartes onwards it was therefore *Modern* Greats, but it didn't command the same respect.

The shortage of desirable damsels which I'd mentioned to Dr Parkes but on which he made no comment was somewhat alleviated by girls who were neither Town nor Gown. These were the Scandinavian girls of good family who had come to live in Oxford in order to learn to speak English with an Oxford accent. They were scattered around in many lodgings but a number of them were conveniently near me at 2 Keble Road, mothered by Mrs Beake. I never, of course, dreamed that half a century later that would be the address of the Oxford University Night Line — an offshoot, like all other Night Lines, of The Samaritans.

I didn't hold it against Mrs Beake, who was as thin as a rail and smoked incessantly, that she regularly told me of someone of good family she had known who declared of her, 'Mrs Beake is a perfect lady.' I concentrated on being a perfect gentleman, and was allowed readier access to her precious charges than anyone else. Not all were blondes: the tall, slender Astri Aubert (later Fru Scott-Hansen) was, but my other favourite, Kari Staubo, was brunette. These two I was later to visit in Norway. The reason I didn't propose to Kari, lovable as well as beautiful, was that I had no job or income and her father was a rich shipowner. Jolly Ingeborg, from Sweden, whom I visited in Stockholm, was blonde, but Vips (Vibeke) from Denmark was a cute little brunette. All these, and others at 2 Keble Road, encouraged me in my plan to form an O.U. Scandinavian Club so that Frökens from all over Oxford could be assembled where undergraduates could get to know them and — well, make sure they *did* speak English with an Oxford accent.

I had to go to the Clarendon Building in The Broad to get permission from the Proctors, hoping they wouldn't remember how often I'd been 'progged' for being in a pub (which wasn't then allowed) or out without a gown after 9 p.m., or both. The Proctor, accompanied by stocky, muscular chaps in blue suits called 'bulldogs' or 'bullers', would raise his mortar board to you three times, and you would reciprocate with your own square, in the unlikely event that you had it with you (otherwise you would bow), and he would say, 'Good evening. Are you a junior member of this University?' When you admitted it, he would demand to know your name and college and next day a missive would summon you to attend and be fined, usually ten shillings, which really hurt all but gilded youth. It was no use running away, as the bulldogs would catch you unless you were in The Giler and your college was St John's, which has a walled-off rectangle in front which counted as being in college. John's men could leap over this wall and jeer at the glowering bullers who might not follow. I once escaped in this way, but don't know what I'd have done if they'd watched me bang on the door and the Porter had repudiated me.

I still remember with pleasure an attempted progging later when I must have looked younger than my age and I was able to reply, 'No, sir, I am a *senior* member of this University;' and another on a visit to Cambridge when I was able to enquire with polite innocence, 'Is there a University here?'

Behold me, then, facing sceptical Proctors and seeking leave to found the O.U. Scandinavian Club, 'for the study of Ibsen, Strindberg, Björnstierne Björnson *et al.*,' and 'to listen to the music of Grieg, Sibelius, Palmgren . . .' The Proctor looked at me long and intently as I added, 'And, of course, to promote Anglo-Scandinavian relations.' I guess what saved me was his assumption that with a name like Varah I must be some sort of Scandinavian myself, moved by patriotism. I did, in fact, spell my first name on our club posters as Edvard.

The club was wildly successful, and I as President was able to afford to hire a hall and a grand piano and engage the Organ Scholar of Keble, Joseph Cooper (later well known on TV) to play the Grieg Piano Concerto. While still a schoolboy at Clifton he'd played the Rachmaninov 2nd, so this presented no difficulty. It reassured the Proctors, though our biggest attendances were when we held dances (strictly forbidden in those days) in Woodstock Road, with chaps keeping *cave* at every corner so that if a Proctor approached the band would disappear and the girls and their partners would be doing anything except dancing: listening to a lecture by me, or teaching us a song. I can still remember an unsuitable one for a learned society, in waltz time, beginning '*Varje litet ord av kärlek, Vil jeg viska nu til dig* . . . (every little word of love,

52

will I whisper now to you).' It was a false alarm that time, but when the Proctors *did* look in, everyone was racing toy motor-cars which I had bought at Woolworths across the dance floor, and they found nothing in *Excerpta e Statutis* to prohibit a serious club from wearing evening dress and playing with toys and shrieking.

The members were a loyal lot, and *did* attend in force at Rhodes House when summoned to hear a distinguished visitor, such as H.E. Baron Palmstierna, the Swedish Ambassador, who spoke on Erik Gustav Geijer and gave me a fine English translation of this great writer's *Letters from England*. (When, in the '70s, my dear friend Roger Pilkington married into the Geijer family, it was a joy to give him this by now rare book.)

Dr Parkes remained my Moral Tutor, of course, but my Tutors for PPE were the late Billy Reade, Sub-Warden; Harry Carpenter ('The Carp'), then a layman but later Bishop of Oxford and a good friend, his wife Urith (née Trevellyan) becoming a friend of my wife; and Maurice Hugh-Jones, whom I often see when, as an Honorary Fellow, I dine at High Table, and who has never once recalled, dear man, that he must have thought me in 1932 unlikely ever to do anything useful let alone to be so honoured by our College. My tutorials must have driven them mad: I would read them my ill-prepared essays scribbled the night before they were due, and then discuss with them some point that interested me in a way that must have made them wonder why, if I could think and reason clearly, I inflicted such muddled nonsense upon them in my papers.

Not quite all my friends were foreigners or from other colleges, and at first I kept up with a few chaps who had been at school with me, particularly Wearing King who was at Worcester and whom I hadn't previously known well as he was in a different house, and a classic, and a scrum half. We used to meet for coffee fairly regularly. In 1938, he and I were to drive round Scandinavia for a holiday during which I paid some visits to old friends from the Scandinavian Club.

Another English friend was David Sherwood, who lived in Cadogan Square and later went into hotel management. He and I were both courting a blonde girl called Joyce who lived in North Oxford. (Yes, of course I remember her surname and address.) She chose him to canoodle with (he was very good-looking) and relegated me to the role of confidant. We men were very helpful to one another in those days, and when they had the idea that they'd like to listen to Beethoven's Ninth while they embraced and kissed, I let them do this on my carpet while I changed the records – you'll realize gramophone records were 78s in those days and each side lasted only about three minutes, when you had to turn the disc over, change the needle, and rewind the clockwork. It was obvious to me that for David to do this would have risked diminishing the girl's appreciation of classical music. As it was, they both said it was an unforgettable experience; and as for myself, I have always preferred to do one thing at a time.

A very different kind of friend was Langford James, whose ambition it was to be an actor and who managed to get walking-on parts at the Playhouse in Woodstock Road. I often went there, not to see him carrying a spear but to feast my eyes on Thea Holme. She and Stanford Holme (brother? husband?) were the leading lights of the Playhouse, and I envied Langford James his closeness to her. He had a passion for climbing and no talent for it, as he was big and clumsy and always drank too much before setting out. I let him persuade me to accompany him in the enterprise of setting a jerry (chamber-pot) on the highest pinnacle of Keble College chapel. After we got safely down, *I* drank too much, and woke with a hangover to see a crowd in Liddon Quad looking up at something gleaming white on the skyline. I felt sick when I remembered that I'd risked my life at the bidding of Langford James: I wasn't excessively mature, but I knew better than to do what I didn't want to do for a 'dare'. My partner in crime materialized by my side and bleared up at the jerry.

'Did we do it, then?' he whispered.

'*We* did it as far as the difficult bit, and then *I* did it,' I growled. 'Never again!'

The Dean was instructing Baker, the college porter, to get it down, and Baker, a large sergeant-major type, was indicating tersely that if the Dean wanted it down . . . The scouts were hurriedly sent to search all rooms to see whose jerry was missing; it was, of course, Dr Parkes's; ours had no handles, nor pink roses round them. If ever you do such a foolish thing, pick a jerry with a handle – floral decoration optional – so you can hook a couple of fingers round it and still have the use of both hands on the way up. A don – I think it was Jolliffe – came out with a gun and shot at it: it replied 'ping'. In the end they had to get scaffolding put up at a cost, I was told, of £50. I felt bad about that, and did not join the Alpine Club, and was not one of those who climbed the pediment of the Ashmolean and tied an umbrella to the hand of the figure seated there, though I felt a bit wistful when I saw it in position the next day – by God's good providence it was pouring with rain.

I never joined OUDS but did support their performances at the New Theatre in George Street. The presentation I shall never forget was of James Elroy Flecker's *Hassan*, with professionals playing the chief parts. Thea Holme was a ravishing Yasmin, and Peggy Ashcroft was marvellous as Pervaneh. George Devine played the Caliph. I bought the play and knew it by heart after reading it twice. I can still remember chunks of it. To add to the magic of Flecker, the music was by none other than Delius. Early on, there was a slight disturbance as a man four rows ahead of me scrambled out, leaving his companion embarrassed. A Magdalen man next to me muttered that the one left was C. S. Lewis. This was the first time I saw him, but it was years before I met him.

I have mentioned a good many friends, English and foreign, but I was still very much an alone person. I loved to wander round Oxford, by day or by night, and would stare at the twin towers of All Souls in the moonlight, or gaze at night through the crumbling gateway on South Parks Road across the lawns of Trinity, where on bright days they played bowls or croquet – this gateway is no longer crumbling and the romance is gone. I still enjoy taking people round Oxford and can manage twenty colleges in an afternoon if they can keep up with me.

I'm not sure who introduced me to the Anthroposophical Society – it was probably Arthur Wrigley, but how did I meet *him*? A little group met every week to study the works of Dr Rudolf Steiner, and for some reason I was chosen by the others to recapitulate what had been said the previous week. I could never remember much of this, so simply gave my own thoughts. Some of Steiner's ideas I thought outlandish (for example, planting at a certain phase of the moon) but his book *Die Philosophie der Freiheit* appealed to me very much. Eventually a few of us went on a trip to Birmingham to visit the Sunfield Children's Home in Weoley Park Road, Selly Oak, and what was being done for epileptic and other handicapped children there interested me more than the discussions we'd been having. Whilst I was still an undergraduate the work was moved to a country house in Worcestershire – Clent Grove, near Kidderminster – with a farm used for organic fertilization, Broome Farm, attached. Tasting organically grown fruit and vegetables for the first time, no matter when planted, I was converted, but when war came Broome had to change to artificial fertilizers to achieve greater bulk.

I was one of those who went over at weekends to help in decorating the mansion in a style I mentally labelled 'anthroposophical', feeling myself a part of the community (largely German) presided over by Herr Geuter and his wife Maria ('Mutter'): about a hundred adults looking after perhaps eighty children. There was a wonderful fellowship there, and those of us who worked in the kitchens, preparing vegetarian meals and (if unskilled, as I was) washing up, were constantly singing, in English or German, mostly songs composed by one of the leaders, Michael Wilson, a first-rate violinist. Thirty years later Eamonn Andrews did him on *This is Your Life*, shortly after he'd done me, and it was good to see him again and to appear with him, even though our paths had been so long separated.

I can still remember some of those songs, or at least the words and the baritone parts of them:

In the quest of the Holy Grail
Do we wander from land to land;
In our duty we shall not fail
If in God's light we stand.
But if falsehood and doubting
In the heart hold sway
There is vanished from the soul
The light of day . . .

The member of staff who had come to Oxford each week to take charge of our meetings was David Clement, a young man with whom I felt at ease because it seemed to me 'he had no guile'. I wish I could remember when it was that he and I had a conversation which was to me crucial. It may well have been in my last term: Trinity Term 1933, when I imprudently hired a punt on the Cherwell for the whole term instead of by the hour, day or week. Remember this was my Finals term and I ought to have been swotting day and night instead of taking a succession of girls in summer dresses punting on the Cher, and showing off my amazing skill with a quant and my encyclopaedic knowledge of the varying consistencies of the river bottom. (Ah, those narrow stretches where the girl had to part the trailing willow caressing her face as we glided towards one of the hidden places where the punt could be secured by paddles stuck in the mud and used for amorous dalliance.)

Oh, yes, David Clement, you will remind me. Whatever we had

been discussing, his answer implied a belief in reincarnation. 'You don't believe in reincarnation, do you?' I asked.

'Yes, I do,' he replied firmly. 'Don't you?'

I heard myself saying, 'Yes, of course!' because suddenly I did. It was like a revelation of beauty and order and *fairness* in the universe: it was the missing piece which made sense.

I didn't normally mix with the rich, though some of them joined the Scandinavian Club. I had very little money, and most of what I had went, wastefully, on cigarettes – and not your ordinary Players Navy Cut at 11½d for 20, but fancy hand-made brands from S. P. Ora, Sobranie, and 'Russian' (nothing of the sort, just foul, with smart black paper and gold tip). This must have been to impress people, and maybe it did if they were easily impressed. One day I was lighting one of these when an elegant fellow sauntered by, and drawled a request to try one, as he'd run out. We chatted for a while and then to my surprise he invited me to dine with him at The George. I hesitated, because if he forgot who was paying, I hadn't enough on me to cover one, let alone two. The rich aren't always aware (how could they be?) that some people have to be careful. My father had always impressed on us children that there was no shame in being poor – Christ had been poor – and that it was apostasy to behave as if it were the worst sin, but I wasn't always able to display the same moral courage as he did. However, on this occasion I forced myself to say, firmly, 'Look, I enjoy talking with you, but we don't move in the same circles. I'm up on a scholarship and can't afford to eat at The George.'

'I promise you it's on me,' he replied quietly, and off we went. He was obviously well known there, and they recommended the lobster. A disadvantage of being well-known and pleased to be so is that you can easily be taken advantage of. There was very little meat in the shell and it was almost impossible to extricate. Cauffield-Stoker – I'd gathered his surname and that he was at The House (Christ Church) – was busy being witty about his vacation experiences, but I'd somehow missed the location and therefore had no idea in what exotic language he was amazingly proficient when he spoke of joking with the natives in the vernacular. It couldn't have been Choctaw, because it was an island.

'Will you have anything else, old chap?' he enquired hospitably, pushing his almost untouched plate aside. 'I'm not very hungry.'

Well, *I* was. I scanned the bill of fare and saw that mutton (not all of which was called 'lamb' in those days) was not an extravagant choice. He was well-bred in concealing his surprise, and when it came, I think it was genuine hunger that led him to order the same.

'Did you', I asked, 'find your fluency in the vernacular made you an object of great interest to the local damsels?' The answer engaged us happily for the rest of the meal. We made no arrangement to meet again so I still don't know what 'the vernacular' was – Cypriot? Malagasy? Taiwanese? He paid by cheque but I couldn't read his initial.

The Warden of Keble at that time was Beresford James Kidd, a formidable character whom I met only at Monday Club, the name we gave to the straggle of chapel defaulters who presented themselves at his Lodgings on a Monday morning. It would never have occurred to me even to contemplate the possibility that all his successors would become friends of mine.

My last term wasn't all punting, writing for *Isis* and *Cherwell*, and lecturing to other undergrads on subjects unrelated to my faculty. I spent a good deal of time in Blackwell's, not actually *buying* books, but handling and skimming through volumes I ought to have mastered. In particular, having learnt from Schwegler's (I hope I've remembered the splendid fellow's name correctly) *History of Philosophy* what Kant was on about – and my admiration for this Schwegler for having managed to grasp it was unbounded – I could then turn to Kant's own works and find quotations which illustrated the various points, and memorize them. His German was not too difficult to parody, but his habit of using ninety-three commas and one full stop per five pages made him a bit difficult to quote verbatim. Mind you, we weren't examined on the German text, but on an English translation, but I thought it would impress the examiners if I quoted extensively from the original by the simple expedient of putting down what I thought Schwegler said he said, and translating this into Kantian German. It might have worked better if I'd been able to resist the temptation to reveal that I considered the *Grundlegung* a load of codswallop.

It wasn't only Kant that I dipped into in Blackwell; the good Schwegler gave me other useful leads, and guided by him I bought a couple of volumes of Spinoza which I still have. This was because about twice a term it was necessary actually to *buy* a book to avoid embarrassment. I noted the most prolific writers on various subjects, too: for example, no one wrote more on aesthetics than E. F. Carritt.

When the dread day of Schools arrived (the finals exam) I presented myself in sub-fusc suit and white tie and gown at the Examination Schools in The High and struggled to conceal the inadequacy of my studies and to demonstrate what a clever fellow I was, sometimes by answering a question slightly different from the one asked, or by putting any dubious statements or opinions in inverted commas and attributing them to someone who would command more respect than I. If only it had all depended on 'I for ingenuity'.

I guess there were many undergraduates in the same boat and perhaps not all were as enterprising or audacious as I, but of course there were also those who had worked solidly and deserved their success, as I myself had deserved it when I sat my Scholarship Exam.

When one had written the papers, there was still another hurdle: the 'viva' (short for *viva voce*, by the living voice – that is, oral). You went into a room to be faced by about five gowned examiners, any of whom might fire questions at you about what you'd written or even about what you'd failed to write (because you didn't know). At that time, Oxford philosophers were all Kantian to a man, and one of them barked at me almost before I'd shut the door behind me. 'How', he asked, 'do you justify your outrageous description of the *Grundlegung* as a work of fiction?' His companions snorted in sympathy. If I'd had any sense I'd have humoured the fellow and let him overcome me in argument and feel immense satisfaction at having plucked a brand from the burning. Instead I proceeded to justify my *lèse-majesté*. 'Immanuel Kant', I told him, with an insufferable air of being his instructor, 'always distinguished between the *Ding an Sich*, "the thing as it is in itself", which must be to us for ever unknowable, and the *appearance* of the thing, which is all we can ever know. He defines metaphysics as the study of the *Ding an Sich* and then proceeds to write a large book about this which he has declared unknowable. That is why I described the *Grundlegung* as a work of fiction.'

Nobody laughed. Nobody applauded. The assembled Kantians could have been used to refrigerate a hot room. Then one of them enquired of his colleagues: 'Does anyone have any further questions for this – er – ahem – candidate?'

A smallish man shuffled some papers and hitched up his gown. 'Mr Varah,' he said, 'I see that in your answer to a question about aesthetics you have used a sentence which you say is a quotation from *The Theory of Beauty* by E. F. Carritt. I cannot find the words, or indeed that sentiment, in that work.' Oh dear!

'I – I may have confused the book with another,' I said. 'It may have been from his *Introduction to Aesthetics*.'

'I cannot find it in that book, either,' stated the tiresome fellow.

'Or – or *A History of Aesthetics*,' I offered desperately.

He shook his head solemnly. 'Not that either,' he murmured.

'Or *Aesthetics for Beginners* . . .' But he was continuing to shake his head. 'Carritt wrote a great many books on the subject,' I pleaded. 'Isn't it possible that you haven't read every word of every one of them?'

He rose to his feet. 'Young man,' he said, not unkindly, 'I think the beautiful moment has at last arrived to acquaint you with the fact that I am Carritt.'

I guess my jaw dropped. The Kantians were simmering with suppressed enjoyment at my discomfiture. Doubtless after I'd gone they would bellow with laughter at the rout of the undergraduate who had poked fun at Kant.

Without another word, I slunk out. If you want to know the definitive meaning of the word 'slunk', just observe my exit from this room.

I went to see my Moral Tutor and told him how E. F. Carritt had set a trap for me and I had fallen right into it. Dr Parkes laughed so much I thought he might do himself a mischief. 'Varah,' he said, 'you don't deserve sooch luck. If Ah know Carritt – and coom to think of it, Ah do know Carritt – 'e'll dine out on yon story the 'ole of next term. 'E'll give ye a good mark, lad – you see if 'e doesn't. Ye should scrape a Second, which isn't bad for someone 'oo's coot as many lectures as you 'ave.'

But then I told him about the Kantians, and his merriment subsided. 'Ye daft 'a'porth [halfpenny-worth],' he said sombrely. 'Whatever got into you? You'll be lucky to get a Third.'

Many years later, I was staying at the Deanery in Durham when John Wilde was Dean, and at dinner the conversation took a turn which prompted me to tell the story of my being caught out by E. F. Carritt. A fellow guest whose name I hadn't caught slapped his thigh. 'So it was true!' he exclaimed. 'We were never sure the old man hadn't made it up. Oh, how good to have it verified – 1933, wasn't it?' My fellow guest was David Carritt. E.F.'s version had improved the story, making me say, 'I can only suppose you aren't as familiar with the works of Carritt as I am!'

During one vacation, being short of money, I got a temporary at an institution in north Oxford calling itself Beaumont College, which foreign students – not connected with the university – cou improve their English and study English literature. I was never an *illiterate* scientist, but I prepared my lectures on Shakespeare and Shaw – the prescribed authors for that part of the course – very carefully. I had read most of the plays of both writers, and my students were impressed to be told that I had actually met Shaw, twice. I declined to tell them what we had talked about, because leaving them wondering was more impressive than admitting that all we had said to one another was 'Howjerdo' on both occasions. One of these was when he bumped into me in the London Underground as I absent-mindedly made to go down an up escalator from which he was stepping, and the other was when he came to Oxford to lecture to the October Club, a small band of Red revolutionaries who succeeded in enticing the great man when the rest of us (myself included) had failed. Surely the author of *The Quintessence of Ibsenism* ought to have addressed the Scandinavian Club?

The October Club enormously increased its membership by refusing admittance to non-members, so my membership card decorated my chimney-shelf for a term, though naturally I never attended any other meetings. My name on the list did not, however, pass unnoticed by our security services, and it gave me a comforting feeling that our chaps didn't miss many tricks every time I was vetted in subsequent years to see whether I might be a secret Bolshie. The fact that I would have cheerfully joined the Mormons to hear Shaw speak, and that the same applied to others who had paid to attend one solitary meeting of the October Club, didn't make me feel at all annoyed that Special Branch was wasting its time on unlikely subversives.

Shaw gave the Oxford Reds short shrift. 'You are, I take it,' he began in his Dublin accent – that is, beautiful English in no way resembling a stage Irishman with a brogue you could cut with a knife (at arl at arl) – 'prepared, indeed eager, to shed blood in the cause of Red revolution? To hang the wicked capitalists from the nearest lamp-post with your own hands? Because if not, you're a lot of imposters, fakes, charlatans, posers.' I can't remember the whole lecture but when I read his *An Intelligent Woman's Guide to Socialism and Capitalism* it seemed familiar. After the lecture the chastened comrades hustled him away before I could say, 'Mr Shaw, I'm an imposter: I paid the sub simply to hear you speak.' Would he have replied 'More fool you!' or 'Better than spending the money on cigarettes and booze'? We shall never know, now. Why didn't I, like E. F. Carritt, improve the story?

One of my pupils at Beaumont College was Armand Cornelissens, a Flemish poet who was to have a considerable influence on my life, because he invited me to spend a long vacation with him in Holland, to give him practice in spoken English.

My time at Oxford ended abruptly at the end of my last term when I had a motoring mishap ('30s jargon for 'car crash'). You remember Arthur Wrigley, through whom I encountered the Anthroposophical Society? He had had a 1928 Morris Cowley with a Hotchkiss engine offered to him, and had the bright idea of sharing the modest purchase price with 'seven other devils more wicked than himself', of whom I was one. The reason for having eight co-owners was that there were then, as now, seven days in the week, so by taking it in turns each of us would have the use of the car for five useless days and for one Saturday and one Sunday, per term. He was foolish to include me, because although I purchased a driver's licence, which I still have somewhere, I didn't know how to drive properly. Pop Eastoe had once or twice taken me up Toft's Road, Barton, in his own vehicle, so I knew how to start, stop, go faster, go slower – I could even, if I took my eyes off the road to look at my feet, change down by double-declutching, a mystery unknown, I believe, to modern drivers. What I couldn't do was steer. Pop kept telling me to look well ahead so we didn't jerk from side to side all the time – he himself rested one hand negligently on the wheel and made only tiny adjustments except when turning corners, whereas I hung on with both hands and looked a yard ahead of the bonnet.

But it was as well I did that and never got up any speed because the awful truth dawned on him one day that I was turning the wheel the opposite way to the way I wanted the car to go. 'Stop!' he yelled suddenly, startling me so that I stamped on the accelerator instead of the brake. He kicked my foot away and grabbed the handbrake. Ashen, he was, apart from his five o'clock shadow. He forced himself to speak calmly. 'If you want to turn left', he asked, 'which way do you turn the wheel?'

'Why, clockwise,' I said.

'This isn't a bloody boat!' he screamed. It was the only time he ever screamed at me. 'It doesn't have a ruddy rudder!'

I reminded myself of this every time I drove, and turned the wheel anti-clockwise to go left. I had to admit it worked, but Pop lost interest in instructing me. 'You'll never make a natural driver, Chad,' he opined. 'Not what I'd call a natural, born driver.' It wasn't until 1938 that I took this verdict seriously, and, as you shall hear, gave up driving for good.

None of this was, of course, known to Arthur Wrigley, and I became an owner-driver (well, one-eighth of an owner-driver) at the age of twenty. My Saturday turn came after everyone else's, but Arthur was still in residence. As I took over the car, he said, 'I suspect someone's had a bit of a mishap and didn't tell me, because the hood won't go up.'

'Never mind,' I said, anxious to be away. 'I don't suppose it'll rain.' I planned to drive to Clent and back, so was quite pleased when he said, 'For some reason, it only seems happy at 55. It won't do *much* more, but doesn't seem to like doing less.' There was, of course, much less traffic in those days, so it wasn't quite as dangerous an enterprise as it now seems, even to me. But the 'mishap' for which the last driver was responsible damaged more than the hood: it damaged the steering. Having confessed to you my heretical belief about the way to steer when being 'taught' by Pop, you may suck your teeth disbelievingly and suspect that what was faulty was not *the*, but *my* steering. I can only tell you what happened and leave you to judge for yourself. I was bowling along at 55 m.p.h. with the engine purring happily, and when it began to rain I used only mild expletives about the inoperative hood. The road curved gently to the right, and I turned the steering-wheel (I promise you) gently clockwise. But the car continued in a straight line, so I turned less gently and the wheel spun, unattached, while the vehicle obeyed Newton's First Law of Motion. Surprisingly, I remembered to stamp on both pedals (no, *not* the accelerator: the clutch and the brake) and all would have been well but for a substantial tree which was eccentric enough to interrupt the otherwise harmless stretch of hedgerow. Still obeying Newton (a Lincolnshire man like myself) I catapulted over the windscreen, luckily unimpeded by the unserviceable hood, but catching my left shin on something sharp before landing in a heap on the grass verge, the road having now curved somewhat to the left. The V-shaped scar still keeps company with the horse-kick scar, and the damage to my back was very similar to that caused by my violent encounter with Port Meadow.

63

I recovered consciousness to find myself in bed in Shipston-on-Stour Cottage Hospital having an anti-tetanus injection. The next day Arthur Wrigley turned up and was very nice about the car being a write-off – he let me think the insurance would give him a tidy profit and I didn't know whether this was true or just to make me feel less guilty. I besought him to get me transferred to Clent for my treatment and convalescence, which the insurance would also cover, and after an interminable day's wait this was arranged. I was driven, not painlessly, to Clent Grove to be looked after by a German lady, Dr Walter. She used Rudolf Steiner's methods, which appeared to be similar to homeopathic remedies, and included an archaic medicament, arnica, which had a wonderful effect on my bruises.

As soon as I was able to be up and about, I did what I could to help the community. Translating texts and even poems from German to English may not have contributed much, but I was an assiduous washer-up and an enthusiastic unskilled worker with the children who were our *raison d'être* and principal means of support: those parents who could afford to pay did so, and even my own two weeks' convalescence was charged to the insurance company, who must have been amazed to get a receipt like a medieval scroll.

On previous day visits I'd taken a special interest in a skinny little girl called Vera, who wasn't one of the many epileptics but was there because she just couldn't hear at all, even though examination proved that there was nothing wrong with her hearing apparatus. Apparently, they decided, she simply didn't want to hear: I was never told whether this was in her karma. Among the exercises designed for her was one where three helpers took it in turns to hold her ankles and her hands and play loud octaves on a piano, so that one could plant her foot firmly on a step of a 7-step pair of steps while another kept her from falling, matching each step to the appropriate note on the scale, up and down, for an hour at a time. If we could sing in tune, we also sang the tonic sol-fa, or intoned, 'Well done, Vera!' on the appropriate note.

Some months later, on my first day up, I went into a big room and saw Vera at the far end, with her back to me. Forgetting that she couldn't hear, I called 'Vera! Come here, darling!' and she turned and ran to me and precipitated herself into my arms.

The person with whom I shared my joy at Vera's improvement was an attractive Austrian girl called Ilse Gmeiner. I had noticed her on one of my first visits and always looked out for her. It wasn't possible to sit with her at every meal because there were two shifts

and duties came first, and she or I might be waiting on table –
though I was more likely to than she as she was more experienced
and useful. It was an Utopian community where we were all equally
regarded and valued but very much unequal in skills and functions.
We would no more have queried Friedrich Geuter's leadership than
we would have thought we could replace Michael Wilson at his
fiddle when he was playing a Bach violin sonata. I can tell you, it is a
wonderful experience to be part of a community where 'From each
according to his ability, to each according to his need' is not taught
or discussed but practised as if it were the only possible way. Doing
it on a larger scale or with people who hadn't freely elected to join
wouldn't work. Even at Clent if the question, 'Why should I do
this?' came to mind, it was answered every time we clapped eyes on
a handicapped child. It was a way of life, not an ideology imposed
on an unwilling nation by power-hungry politicians: it seemed to me
to be close to the life of the early Christians who 'had all things in
common', and whose own description of their religion was 'The
Way'.

My stay at Clent to convalesce from 'a slight accident' seemed less
and less convincing the longer I remained, and my father wrote
ordering me to come home. When I made excuses to delay, he sent
Mr Gilbert Nowell to fetch me in his car, but I was too happy in the
place to be persuaded to leave for a life in Barton which at that time
could have no object or purpose. But my father was a very determined man, and a week or so later he himself arrived, driven by a
parishioner, and insisted that I return with him. There was no
possibility of refusal, and while he and Herr Geuter sparred with icy
politeness, I went and packed, and said goodbye to the few friends I
could find. Ilse was not one of them.

We didn't talk much on the way back, but my father had some
blunt ways of describing the sort of organization he had had to
rescue me from. Imagine in our own day a respected clergyman
whose eldest son had been conned by the Moonies or had joined
Rajneesh, and you will understand his anxiety, and the relief he and
my mother felt when he had me safely home. Of course, the comparison is inappropriate: the work at Clent was worthwhile work;
Anthroposophy was too deep and intellectual to appeal to silly
young things behaving irrationally out of rebellion against parents,
society or whatever; and I still have respect for those who follow it;
but from my father's point of view it was worse than heretical, it
was 'a cult'. This was long before even ecumenism and interdenomi-

national activities became fashionable – not that my father, bless him, would have considered being fashionable an argument in favour of anything. Everyone in Barton knew that the Established Church was what God willed them to belong to, and the Vicar would have no truck with 'dissenters', whether chapel folk or papists.

So there I was in limbo, missing Oxford, missing Clent, at a loss to know what to do, living at home (at that time it wasn't thought of disapprovingly as 'living off one's parents' except in the wage-earning classes) and unable to contribute anything except by taking services at St Chad's mission church by the waterside (a stone's throw from where the Humber Bridge now reaches the south bank). I did a little freelance writing – my first acceptance was from *Punch*, but I built up a great collection of rejection slips through thinking that I knew better than the *Writers' and Artists' Yearbook* and writing what I wanted to write rather than what was likely to sell. I had hardly any money for stamps, let alone cigarettes, and my father was rightly furious that I had omitted to pay my last term's battels (bill for items from the college buttery) and wouldn't be allowed to take my degree until this sum was paid. My poor father had by this time all eight of his other children at fee-paying schools and had to persuade Barclays Bank to increase his overdraft.

Pop Eastoe was, of course, an immense comfort at this time, though he insisted wisely that I see my father's point of view and be decently contrite and subdued.

It was Alec Oldridge who came temporarily to the rescue. He was manager of a brickyard and tile factory at Goxhill, a few miles further east than New Holland, on the bank of the Humber. He and I sat together in the choir stalls, and my moderate baritone followed his rich and accurate one as we sang the harmonies of hymns, psalms, and settings for the Eucharist. Although we seldom met outside church or at the Assembly Rooms, I thought of him as a friend. One day he asked me if I'd like to come and do some special work requiring chemical knowledge at Goxhill (or 'Gowshall', as it was commonly pronounced). Without hesitation, I said yes. 'Don't be in too much of a hurry,' he warned. 'This is a project of my own, not authorized by the bosses, so I won't be able to pay you what an Oxford BA should get. The most I can take out of petty cash would be 16s a week, but of course I'd take you to work with me in the car, as long as you don't ask to drive.' (One's prowess soon becomes widely known.)

My mother didn't know why I had to wear my oldest clothes for chemical experiments in a nice clean laboratory, but she approved of Alec, as did everyone who knew him, and prepared a lunch box for me each day. There was, in fact, no laboratory, and the bit of analysis of clay I had to do I did at home, with materials bought from a local pharmacist. I could well afford these out of my sixteen shillings, or four-fifths of £1, because that was in no way to be compared with the technical equivalent of 80p today. It would, for instance, have bought me three slap-up lunches at the Strand Palace, if I'd been in London, and extravagant, and entertaining two girls at once.

Alec's investigation was brilliantly conceived, and designed to make millions for the owners of the yard. 'D'ye know owt abaht clay?' he asked as we drove off the first morning. On his way to the yard, he spoke in Lincolnshire dialect, just as my father did when visiting parishioners who found 'educated Northern' almost as difficult as 'Oxford'. He, of course, being a Yorkshireman, had had to learn it: I had grown up with it and switched to it as easily as I now do to French or Dutch. Alec might have used the second person, 'Doos thou knaw,' as he would to his workmen. To Southerners, all northern dialects sounded the same, warm and uncouth, with broad vowels. They would have been astonished to learn that a Yorkshireman might have said 'on th'roo-ad to th'yaard', abbreviating 'the' to 'th'', and a Lancashire man would shorten it further to 't': 'ont' rood tut' yaard', whereas we Woldsmen (not Yellowbellies, please: the Fens are well south of Lincoln, half-way to London) – we Woldsmen just left out 'the' altogether.

So, we wor on way to yard, me and Alec, when he asked if I knew owt about clay, and he was relieved when I said, 'Only its approximate chemical composition,' because it seemed the Humberside clay was different from any other clay in the world except some in a remote part of Hungary.

It turned out that there were basically two kinds of bricks, common and facing. Common bricks were used for inside walls as they would never be seen, or for building factories, where it didn't matter. Facing bricks were for the fronts of houses, and were either very red, as at Barton (as were the roofing tiles), or 'rustic', as made at Crowle, with roughened surfaces and all sorts of purple and russet shades. Now, said Alec, the top one-and-threequarter feet of the clay at Goxhill would make excellent facing bricks if it was skimmed off the other seven or so feet, but that wasn't the practice: the whole lot went wastefully into common bricks. But it didn't need a bright lad like me or Alec himself to work *that* out: below the Humberside clay, of which there was still a large but not inexhaustible supply, was an unusable clay similar to that in Northamptonshire: enough of it to last for a century. It was unusable because it contained large numbers of chalk pebbles each about the size of a pea, with a few slightly larger. Any brick in which one or more of these was embedded would 'blow' in the kiln (pronounced, please, 'kill').

'Of course,' I said, showing an intelligent interest. 'Calcium carbonate plus heat equals calcium oxide or quicklime plus carbon dioxide gas, which would ruin the shape of the brick, and when the brick got wet the quicklime in it would turn to calcium hydroxide.'

Alec agreed he couldn't have put it better himself and said that there did exist a type of pug mill different from that used at Goxhill to turn spits of clay into brick-shaped lumps of clay with three holes in them to lift them by. This other mill had rollers to crush any stones in the clay to powder before extruding it.

'Wouldn't help,' I interjected. 'The chalk would do the same damage whether it was in lumps or powder.'

Alec said he knew that without any Oxford geniuses telling him, and quickly re-lit his pipe without taking his eyes from the road. 'We'll look over the yard ('ovver yard') and then discuss it further,' he ruled.

Looking ovver yard involved a great deal of walking, mostly through slippery clay. We saw it being dug, and transported to the pug mills, and extruded, cut with wires into threes, lifted off by men with three-pronged wooden forks and taken away to be dried in immensely long wooden sheds with tiled roofs but no sides. When dry they would be carefully stacked in the kiln which, when full, would be fired. When the process of burning the clay into bricks was complete, the kiln would be unloaded and the bricks stacked for taking away. What impressed me most was the skill of the men who controlled the operation of the kilns. Alec and I wandered about on the tops of kilns with the man responsible for each, who would uncover in turn the holes through which coal dust would be introduced in small quantities to keep the fire going. The man could tell at a glance how much coal dust to put in. It varied from one feeding hole to the next, and had to be exactly right. If it was too hot, the bricks might be distorted or discoloured, if not hot enough, the bricks would not be burnt right through. Alec himself was capable of doing this skilled job, but contented himself with a few esoteric exchanges with the man whose job it was.

It was a matter of weeks between putting clay forms into the kiln and taking them out again, burnt and cool enough to handle, so there was no time to be lost in preparing our specimens. We spent a lot of time in the diggings, selecting half-spits of clay which I carefully labelled and put into the wheelbarrow trundled by a scornful peasant engaged to do the heavy work attached to this namby-pamby exercise. What would he have said if he had known that the next day Alec was going to bring his mother's sausage machine, and ruin it by using it to chew up gobbets of clay and extrude them in a convenient cylindrical shape?

I won't weary you with the details. Under Alec's supervision I made sausages, carefully marked for identification, of every type of clay and many mixtures of one type with another in varying proportions. I also made by hand some miniature bricks in case the behaviour of a cylindrical shape in the kiln was different from that of the shape of a standard brick, $9'' \times 4\frac{1}{2}'' \times 3''$. Naturally, any samples containing clay with chalk pebbles in it used such clay both with the pebbles as they were and with the pebbles crushed as in a mill with rollers. In both cases they were mixed with different proportions of normal clay.

Whenever a kiln was nearly full, Alec and I would put the results at the very top of the pile, where the heat was greatest, under the sceptical eye of the workmen responsible for loading, one of whom referred to 'them toy bricks' and the other, more daringly, to 'them pricks o' thine', mumbling so that you couldn't be sure whether he'd said bricks or pricks. The workmen were deeply suspicious of 'young feller from Oxford college', believing that any resulting change would mean fewer jobs or more work for those that still had jobs. Even Lincolnshire workmen, splendid fellows, were not entirely immune to the gloomy prognostications of trouble-makers.

The day on which the first kiln we loaded was cool enough to empty was a very exciting one. The samples we extricated were interesting and in some cases confirmed our theories and in other cases not. I noted the information gained from them and devised a new series of experiments based on what we had learned. When our investigations were complete, Alec was cock-a-hoop at the discovery that it *was* possible to utilize a good deal of the hitherto unexploited clay. A certain proportion of the lower-quality Humberside clay, from lower than one-and-threequarter spits down, could be mixed in with the first one-and-threequarter spits, and still give good facing bricks; and it was possible to use a number of spits (which I shall naturally not reveal to you) of the pebbly clay underneath along with the remaining common-brick Humberside clay to make common bricks which would not 'blow' in the kiln if the mixture was put through the kind of mill which crushed any pebbles. With my help, Alec prepared a report for his bosses, and looked forward to the congratulations and increase of salary he could expect when he revealed that they owned vastly more usable clay than they had ever supposed. In addition, there would be a properly paid job for me.

I could hardly believe my ears when, over a pint for Alec and a drowned whisky for me, Alec told me the result of his meeting with the bosses. 'Very inter-*est*-ing,' one of them had said. 'But it'd mean a lot of new equipment. We 'ave our market for common bricks, and we've never sold facing bricks, and although we 'ave the capital for new mills, it'd mean a lot of oopset. So we don't think we'll bother, like.' Thus they flatly turned down profits of millions. Alec was as if pole-axed, and as for me, my job had come to an end.

Alec went on to be a tremendously successful man in his own field, and I lived to bless the day when I had *not* become scientific adviser to a brickyard.

So there was I again, living at home still, making little progress with my freelance writing, and happy to accept an invitation from Armand Cornelissens to spend a couple of months with him in Deventer, giving him practice in English. He taught English, French and German at the Middelbare Koloniale Landbouwschool (College for Colonial Agriculture) in Deventer, in the province of Overijssel. He lived in a small modern house in Raalteweg on the outskirts of the town with his wife Heliane, who was French, his son Tristan, and his daughter Eva – a tiny, pestilential girl who is now the charming Mrs Krebbers of New York. I had to speak English to Armand and French to his wife, and in my free time bicycled into town and learnt Dutch by chatting up the more personable of the girls in the cigarette kiosks. It wasn't until nearly the end of my 'holiday' that I ventured to speak Dutch in front of Armand and his friends, which caused them to laugh until they choked because I was speaking Dutch with a broad Overijssel accent. I was subsequently able to correct this, and speak in the same much admired '*deftig*' manner as the inhabitants of The Hague – a sort of Oxford Dutch.

I spent four long holidays with Armand, and it will be convenient to run them into one and deal with them now. I visited every part of the Netherlands, from Leeuwarden and Groningen in the north to Maastricht in the south, and from the North Sea coast to the German border. I travelled by bicycle, or train, or bicycle taken *on* a train, or by a method which was practically unknown at that time, hitch-hiking ('*meerijden*'). I think I was one of the pioneers of hitch-hiking in Holland because of people being intrigued by an Englishman speaking Dutch, and giving them the unaccustomed pleasure of hearing their own language spoken with a foreign accent.

The only excursions on which Armand accompanied me were to his birthplace, Gent, the heart of the Flemish Movement (Vlaamsche Beweging), which was for most Flemings a political movement but for Armand and his friends was purely cultural. The poets, painters, sculptors and engravers of Gent formed a close-knit coterie of which Armand was a member-in-exile, and I was accepted as his friend. The ones I knew and liked best were Josef Cantré, a sculptor in the summer and engraver of woodcuts in the winter; Maria De Keijzer, painter, and her sister Sidi, poet; René De Clercq, story-writer and poet. The artists were more fortunate than the poets: tourists of many nationalities could admire Josef Cantré's great statue of Eduard Anseele and most of my visitors admire the painting Maria De Keijzer gave me and which hangs now in my drawing-room. But who could read the poems and other writings? So Armand asked me to translate *Levensverlokkingen* and Sidi De Keijzer her *Deining*, and René De Clercq the story that was appearing in weekly parts in a newspaper. The difficulty was not in the translation but in finding a publisher. The nearest we got to success was with my translation of the classic Karel van de Woestijne's *De Boer die Sterft* (A Peasant Dies) for which Josef Cantré made woodcut illustrations. Karel van de Woestijne had, as is usual with aristocrats, a great understanding of and affinity with the peasants, and his prose-poem resembles the Authorized Version of the Bible in making poetry of simple, colloquial words.

My other failure to get a translation published was after the war, during which Piet Bakker's *Ciske de Rat* was read by every Dutchman. At the end of the war he asked me to translate his exciting book about the conflict in the Netherlands East Indies, entitled *De*

Slag (The Battle). I read it and was fascinated by it and translated the first chapter and gave a summary of the rest of the book, but didn't find a publisher because at that period people wanted to forget about the war – even their own war, let alone that of our Dutch allies.

At the time of my holiday with Armand in 1934, the seeds of war were already being sown. Against the advice of Armand and all his friends, I decided to take a trip across the German border, whence came frightening tales of Hitler's Brownshirts. I decided to take one of the buses which crossed the frontier with peasants transporting their produce. One such went from Zutphen (where the dying Sir Philip Sidney said, 'Thy need is greater than mine') and Doetinchem to Emmerich, on the north bank of the Rhine. I had studied Baedeker carefully and knew that on the other side of the Rhine was Kleve (Cleves, where Anne of Cleves came from), with a castle called the Schwanenberg. It is typical of my mentality that I familiarized myself with the diagram of this castle, filling my mind as usual with useless information.

I reasoned that at the frontier, the only formality would be a uniformed officer poking his head into the bus without entering, enquiring 'All locals? All regulars?' and receiving an affirmative growl, not only because I had enlisted the other passengers in my support (they advised me to talk German with a Dutch accent rather than Dutch with a German accent) but because the Dutch hated the Germans and wouldn't have given them the correct time, let alone the fact that there was an English spy among them. (The late Greville Wynne once told me I would never make a spy because I would never stand up under torture. I could only agree.)

Arrived in Emmerich, my Dutch comrades urged me not to be late for the bus back. My exploration of the town went smoothly until, when turning a sharp corner, I almost banged noses on a young Brownshirt. His right arm shot up and he yelled, 'Heil Hitler!'

'That is not my name, my mister,' I replied politely. 'I am a stranger here.'

'You Dutch', he said, misled by my almost hawking gutturals, 'think you can be funny with us, but you are a little people and we are a Great Nation!'

I tried to walk on, but he barred my way.

'My country, Great Britain,' I said, 'is also a Great Nation.' I pulled out my passport and thrust it under his nose, jabbing my finger at the words as I read them aloud in English: '. . . request and

72

require, in the name of His Majesty . . .' Whilst he was still flabbergasted, I nipped back around the corner again and slipped into a shop, closing the door quietly behind me. The old lady behind the counter summed up the situation incredibly quickly and gestured towards her back room. I hid there, and when the Brownshirt looked in the old lady, busy with her ledger, and apparently deaf as a post, muttered something in Hebrew, and he went. She then let me out the back way, but not before I had bought as much as I could, for hers was one of the shops guarded by huge posters saying that it was Jewish and loyal Germans wouldn't buy there. Many were also guarded by Brownshirts.

I decided to cross the Rhine on the little ferry, and boarded it, but before it left the jetty my Brownshirt adversary boarded it and began searching for me. As the little steamer pulled away, I jumped back on to the jetty, and hid. When it returned, there was no sign of him, so I crossed with it, only to find him waiting by the tram stop. I had the feeling that hours must have passed as I went backwards and forwards across the Rhine until at long last I was on the Kleve side when the tram was there and he wasn't.

I took the tram into Kleve but it wasn't long before I was in trouble again. A Brownshirt youth of about fourteen was tormenting a little group of boys – I don't know whether they were Jewish or not – and he would neither leave them alone nor let them go. I told him to stop it, and he replied insolently, so I smote him. Well, I was bigger than he was. As he fell, he hit his head on a wall, and the other boys skedaddled. I departed the scene more leisurely, but looking round I saw that he was standing up, not much the worse for wear but screaming German oaths before turning to go in the opposite direction, doubtless to fetch his father and other larger Brownshirts. I decided it was time to visit the Schwanenberg.

Of course, several of them came looking for me, but the ignorant oafs had no idea about the layout of a medieval castle even though it was their own chief tourist attraction. I was able at times to perch on a ledge watching them scurrying around just below and never thinking of looking up.

While waiting for them to give up, I worked out the way to the Dutch frontier, and as soon as it was safe to do so, I set off in the right direction. Just outside the town, a couple of middle-aged Brownshirts stepped from concealment and seized me, and began marching me off in the direction, I supposed, of the nearest concentration camp. At a suitable moment I hit one of them below the belt

73

– well, he was bigger than I was – and outran the other to a stile leading to a little wood, in which he lost me. Then I made my way across interminable fields until I came to an unmanned frontier post. At least, I thought it was unmanned until a man in uniform ran out of the hut and grabbed me. My strength was as the strength of ten as I struggled with him, believing my life and liberty to be at stake, but when he shouted to his fellow officer to help him he shouted in Dutch; and I stopped struggling. I said to them in Dutch, 'I am an Englishman, escaping from the Brownshirts.' They picked me up, dusted me down, gave me very good coffee, and arranged for me to have a lift on a lorry going to Nijmegen. Now, Nijmegen is an interesting city, but all I wanted to do was to get back to Deventer and tell Armand and his friends that they had been quite right – sneaking into Germany had been a daft idea.

But that was a year after the events I must now describe. My job at the brickyard ended, I had nothing to do but follow my favourite occupation, reading. My father was less exasperated by my 'hanging about the house' if I was reading an improving book. It was about this time that he came into the kitchen one day – I hastily put my feet to the floor and threw my cigarette into the range – and found me reading *La Vie de Disraeli* by André Maurois. He didn't know whether to be gratified that I was reading French for pleasure, or outraged that I was giving my attention to one who had opposed his beloved Mr Gladstone. 'A mountebank!' he pronounced. 'Never could stand the feller.'

'Did you know Disraeli, then, Father?' I asked.

'I knew him,' he replied darkly. 'I knew him, but never liked him. I had many an argument with him.'

'Did you have any correspondence with him, Father?' I asked eagerly. 'Have you any letters of his?'

'Look in the second drawer down in my bureau,' he said. 'That's where they'll be if I haven't thrown them away. You can have them if they interest you!' Alas, he had thrown them away. And they only interested me as things to sell, in order to get money to buy cigarettes.

3

I T was about this time, 1934, that I was invited to stay again for a week with Bishop Hine. He was no longer Bishop of Grantham, having reluctantly relinquished that suffragan see in order that Archdeacon Blackie might be consecrated to it – he could become Assistant Bishop of Lincoln but the Archdeacon couldn't be consecrated as such. However, Bishop Hine still lived in the Subdeanery though he was shortly to move a hundred yards or so to Canteloupe Chantry South. The first time we sat down in his study – the same one where he'd transformed my entire future by telling me the truth about sex at the age of twelve – he said without preamble, 'Chad, you are wasting your life. Why don't you go to the theological college here? You like academic life, and you're at a loose end, and one can never know too much, and it would please your father, to whom you must be something of a disappointment.'

'But Bishop,' I protested, 'I don't want to be ordained. I don't have a vocation.' He then gently instructed me in the meaning of 'vocation', he having gone to Central Africa as a doctor, a medical missionary. Before the afternoon was over, I had agreed to go to the Bishop's Hostel (as it was usually called, though its official name was Scholae Cancellarii) on the understanding that at the end of the course I didn't need to be ordained if I didn't then wish to be.

My father didn't go overboard at the news, but my mother told me that he was very relieved and happy about it.

Life at the Bishop's Hostel was monastic. But Bishop Hine was right: the ordered life of the college appealed to me very much, and we had the finest staff any theological college had had before or since. Three of them became bishops (not that that's anything to go by) and one of these was my own tutor, the Subwarden, Michael Ramsey, the scholar-saint who was to become Archbishop of Can-

75

terbury. Although he was only a few years older than I, he already had the gravitas of a future prelate – except when I was teasing him in the common room. He had several mimickable habits, such as folding his arms very high up his chest and waggling his bushy eyebrows up and down, especially when seated; or when standing, holding his right arm firmly pressed to his hip while wagging an admonitory finger. When amused, his rhythmic laugh would some-times get out of control, and become almost hysterical. This particu-larly happened if I sat opposite him with my arms folded high, waggling my eyebrows, and beginning to giggle. It always ended by his having to retreat from the room, but it didn't upset him, because he knew that we all loved him.

There were only about three dozen of us at that time, and almost everybody got on well with everybody else. Apart from Stephan Hopkinson and Richard Hill, with whom I am still in regular touch, I remember 'Farmer' Bloom, the late Stephen Chase, Jim Eckersley, Edward Grimston, Francis Noble, John Park, Everard Sampson, Ronny Sibthorp, Frank Wright, and of course Arthur Partridge whom I nicknamed Art. Part. Bart. when he was voted the student least likely to become a bishop (he was the only one who did, as far as I know). I went through a stage of being childishly amused at the English way of spelling Chumley Cholmondeley and Fanshaw Featherstonehaugh, so I named Hill 'Huddlebill', Chase 'Chuddle-house', Noble 'Nodbubble', and so on.

Huddlebill was my most constant companion. He had been a farmer and found it easy to get up, so it was his job to call me in the morning, just in time for me to slip a cassock with a zip over my pyjamas for chapel, after which, in the gap before breakfast, I could dress and shave, with Huddlebill talking to me whilst I shaved. The local tailor, when I took one of my father's discarded cassocks to be reduced in girth and seamed up apart from a zip at the top, informed me, 'They don't put zips in cassocks.' They still don't, but I have my original one which of course I can't get into any more.

One day there was delivered to the common room by mistake (it should have gone to the Warden's house) a renewal form for the college's entry in *Minerva Jahrbuch*, a German publication some-thing like a *Who's Who* plus an educational directory. The Nazis were increasing their grip on Germany, and I wanted to show my contempt for them, so I filled in this form in a manner which must have aroused their suspicions if they had had the faintest trace of a sense of humour. I changed us to the University of Scholae Cancellarii, made it co-educational, affiliated it to Clark's College (a correspondence school) and gave us a most eccentric curriculum. I changed the names of the staff: not, as I remember, our revered Eric Mascall, author of *He Who Is*, the best book about the Almighty, in my opinion; but the late Eric Ashdown, who tried to teach me church history and went on to become Bishop of Newcastle, became the Reverend Aloysius Ashpit; and there were other changes I no longer remember. Of course, retribution was bound to come when the form came again a year later to be revised, if, as I'd calculated, Minerva had unsuspectingly printed my spoof. By the time this happened, the late Eric Abbott had replaced Leslie Owen as Warden (the former went on to be Warden of Keble and later Dean of Westminster, the latter became Bishop of Lincoln) and I myself, after a term or two with 'the Abbot', had become curate of St Giles, Lincoln, and was beyond the range of any disciplinary action at the Bishop's Hostel. The Revd Aloysius Ashpit was understandably the most outraged, and contended that, even in Nazi Germany, *Minerva Jahrbuch* should be furnished with accurate information. I was, and am, impenitent.

You may find it hard to believe, but I had become rather devout – in fact, probably more so than at any other stage of my life, until a year ago. This was alongside a more assiduous practice than I have been able to achieve in the world outside the theological college. But I still didn't want to be ordained. To show you the extreme lengths to which I would go to avoid this unwished consummation, I confided in Leslie Owen that I was not a suitable person to be ordained, having had unspecified sexual relations with an unspecified number of unnamed girls. It shows how different the mid-'30s were from the '90s that he insisted that my father, the last person in the world to be able to take a balanced view of this, should be informed. This led to enormous embarrassment, but they both decided (without my having said any such thing) that I was properly penitent, and need not hesitate to go forward to ordination.

As the dreaded time approached, I made a last attempt to escape. I went to see dear old Bishop Hine to remind him that he had said that if at the end of the course I did not wish to be ordained, I needn't be. His old sister received me and told me that he was very ill but she was sure he would like to see me. I tiptoed into the sickroom, and told him why I did not intend to be ordained. He made no reply, but was obviously listening, so I told him again, giving my reasons at greater length. The third time, they began to sound unconvincing even to me, and I dried up. He then opened one eye and gave his verdict: 'Scruples,' he said, and closed his eye. Now, it's unlikely that you know the meaning of this word in theological circles. It means rationalizations whereby one tries to excuse oneself from not doing one's plain duty by making out that it would be against one's conscience. I could see no way of being able to plead 'not guilty' to this. I just did not want to be on the other side of the great gulf between human beings on the one side and parsons and maiden aunts on the other. (No disrespect to maiden aunts intended: dear Miss Violet Hine was typical of the admirable creatures I had in mind, though an aunt only, I think, to a succession of Sealyhams.) 'You are right, as always,' I said. 'I will be ordained.' I then went over and kissed him on the forehead (a thing I had never done before) and said goodbye. He didn't answer. Outside the room, Miss Violet said, 'Wait a moment – I'll just go in and switch on Evensong for him on the wireless, he likes to listen to that.' She went in, and switched it on. He murmured, 'Switch it off,' and died. She came and told me; and I had immediate practice in one of the things that separates parsons even from maiden aunts.

So what chance did I have, being press-ganged by a saint on his deathbed? I felt that I had just received a life sentence, and that, of course, is what it was.

The ordination service in Lincoln Minster was an occasion of very mixed emotions. Bishop Nugent Hicks, nicknamed for some reason I never discovered 'Bumbo', conducted the Making of Deacons and the Ordination of Priests in the presence of a large congregation which included my father, sitting in his stall of Stow-in-Lindsey as an Honorary Canon. I was conscious of the emptiness of Bishop Hine's stall, Langford Ecclesia, in which I had normally sat when his guest. It was a particular pride for my father that after attending the same theological college he had attended, I was reading the Gospel in the same place where he had read it all those years before – the Deacon who has done best in the general ordination examination is rewarded by being chosen to read the Gospel at the ordination service.

But lest we should think of it too solemnly, I must mention that I was in charge of a student called Woollaston who was stone deaf, and was preparing for a ministry among the deaf and dumb. He wasn't himself dumb, having gone deaf later in life, but needed to be nudged when the time came to give the answer to the Bishop's questions. If you look at the Prayer Book of 1662 you will find that there are several questions addressed to the candidates, and that the answer in each case is, 'I will so do, the Lord being my helper.' However carefully I timed my nudges, Woollaston always came in with a huge voice, varying from rasping to squeaky, with these words out of time with the others. It was difficult to concentrate on one's own dedication in these circumstances. I sometimes used to meet him in Lincoln afterwards and would talk to him in finger-spelling, and he would reply in speech, with the result that it was I who received pitying glances from the passers-by.

My introduction to the work of an assistant curate was sudden and traumatic. I had been given my 'Title', as it is called – you have to be ordained *to* a job – by the Revd R. N. Daniels, who was vicar of the new housing estate of St Giles, most of which was situated between the Wragby and Nettleham roads on the east side of Lincoln. He had been a printer, and had served a curacy at St Botolph Boston; as indeed had Michael Ramsey. He had married into one of the res-pected old families of Boston; Miss Oldfield was a proficient organ-ist, and often played at the Minster for Dr Gordon Slater (who called his best-known hymn tune 'St Botolph'). It was this lady I encountered when I reported for duty at 10 Lee Road. She opened the door and greeted me with great relief. 'Oh, Mr Varah, I'm so glad you've come: Mr Daniels [not, in those days, 'Nicholas', you'll notice] is down with the 'flu, and he was due to take a funeral at St Peter in Eastgate, and I haven't been able to find a replacement. You will just be in time if you hurry – I see you have your bicycle.'

I didn't have to go back to my lodgings at 11 Austen Walk (all the streets on the estate were literary – the church that was being built at the time was in Lamb Gardens) because I had dumped my robes where I would be using them, namely at the wooden hut which served as a church on the Wragby Road. I gathered it was third-hand, having started its career as a venereal hospital during the First World War. It's not easy to ride a bike in cassock, surplice and scarf, especially with an ankle-length funeral cloak rolled up and balanced on the handlebars, but I managed to arrive at the cemetery chapel in time to lead the coffin into the building. I noticed that it was a very small coffin, so I did the order for the burial of a child. As we came out to go to the grave for the committal, it began to rain, so I put on my cloak and a black skull-cap from my cassock pocket, and walked with the undertaker in front of the coffin, the mourners following behind in the car.

'Your first time, sir?' enquired the chirpy little undertaker. I admitted that it was. 'Then I'd better show you the ropes,' he said. 'The most important thing is, don't turn your 'ead to me when we talks, like you were doing now, as the mourners mustn't get the impression we're 'aving a cosy chat.' I accepted his advice and kept my head facing the way we were going. From then on, we talked out of the sides of our mouths, like stage villains. 'And when you laughs,' he pursued, 'try not to let your shoulders shake.'

'I'm not likely to laugh,' I replied shortly. He was unabashed.

'We usually exchange jokes with the clergyman, sir,' he said. 'No point in getting morbid.'

'My good man,' I said, remembering to keep my head from turning towards him – in those days we often addressed the lower classes thus – 'do you know what the word "morbid" means? It means "of or pertaining to death". If a funeral isn't morbid, I'd like to know what is.'

'Well, sir,' he conceded, 'be that as it may, when you've done as many as I 'ave . . .'

We paced on in silence, getting soaked. At length we'd passed all the gravestones and were proceeding towards what looked like a ploughed field. 'Where on earth are we going to?' I asked.

'Unconsecrated ground, sir,' he informed me soothingly. 'Just up to the top there.'

'But she wasn't a Roman Catholic,' I protested. (Roman Catholics preferred unconsecrated ground because they didn't trust our bishops' consecrations but wanted to consecrate each grave themselves.)

'It doesn't matter what religion a person is, if it's a suicide,' stated the undertaker.

I could hardly believe my ears. '*Suicide?*' I hissed disbelievingly. 'At *that* age? Why?'

'Well, sir, we don't usually know, do we? But it so 'appens that she was at the same school as my girl, and she told 'er one day as 'ow something 'orrible 'ad 'appened to 'er, said she'd started bleeding between 'er legs, like. Didn't know what it was. Didn't 'ave nobody she could ask. O' course, my girl didn't know what it was, neither.'

I was stunned. I splashed on as if in a dream. It never occurred to me then, or later, to ask *how* she had killed herself, and I still don't know. I could only think that when her period started it was to her something horrible and mysterious and, worst of all, 'she didn't 'ave no one she could ask.'

At last we came to the grave. The gravediggers, poor fellows, had each an old potato sack over his head, to try to keep off the worst of the rain. The bearers took the coffin from the hearse and stumbled across the uneven ground, followed by the few mourners from the car, all in black. The coffin was speedily lowered and the soggy clay kept falling on it. I made the committal as quick as possible so the mourners could get back under cover. I continued standing at the head of the grave looking down on that small coffin. I said, half aloud, 'Little girl, I never knew you, but you have changed my life. I promise you that I, who was taught about sex by a saintly old man when I was younger than you, will teach children your age what they need to know, and be someone they can ask, even if I get called a dirty old man at the age of twenty-four.'

Then I realized the gravediggers wouldn't start filling in the grave until the mourners were out of sight, so I squelched back to the hearse, in which they had kept me a seat by the driver.

I still have that cloak, a bit moth-eaten round the collar. I still wear it for funerals, one of the latest being of someone whom I would probably never have met but for that little girl: Jean 219, one of the earliest Samaritans.

I had the opportunity to begin to keep my vow to that little girl that very night. The old hut was in constant use, and could be adjusted to be a church or a church hall by people so practised that they could do it in a few minutes. Secularization was always announced by people lighting cigarettes and pipes. Except the youth club: the young weren't allowed to smoke in those days.

The youth club members were a boisterous lot, but of course much more polite and biddable by the clergy, their teachers and their parents, than youngsters tend to be nowadays. They naturally wanted to see how far they could go with the new young curate, because of course some parsons are weaker than others and some tend to be indecisive and soft. I was never one of these. It was no great trouble to keep order amongst the players of table-tennis and billiards and make sure everybody got a turn and to see there was no horse-play near the gramophone, to which some youngsters would dance. Some would be playing chess or draughts or dominoes or cards, and one would have to ensure that those chasing around the hall didn't upset these sedentary pursuits.

The way the new young curate was to be tested was to utter four-letter words in his neighbourhood, *sotto voce*, so that he could hear but not be entirely sure what he had heard. When I made no response, they became bolder and bolder. I suspected, and later discovered it to be true, that most of them didn't know the meaning of the words they used. My opportunity came when a girl snatched the ping-pong ball and ran off with it, pursued by a girl with a bat who had been playing. 'I'll sod you!' she shrieked.

'Stop!' I yelled as if on a parade ground. 'Everybody gather round! Come on, now!' I retrieved the ping-pong ball, took the needle off the gramophone record and said, 'Now listen, all of you! You boys have been saying words you think are rude in the hope of embarrassing me and getting the girls to admire you, and you girls were beginning to join in. Well, I don't think you know the meaning of those words, but anything you want to know, you can at all times ask me. But first, I've something to ask *you*!', and I pointed at the girl who had been threatening the other girl. 'You said you would "sod" her.' There was a lot of nervous giggling and shuffling of feet. 'Do you know what the word "sod" means?' I demanded. Silence. 'Does anybody know?'

A few of the boys muttered, 'Nossir.'

'Then I'll tell you,' I announced. 'In the Old Testament you can read about two cities whose inhabitants were so wicked that God destroyed their cities with a volcano. They were called Sodom and Gomorrah.' A boy laughed, and I rounded on him. 'Don't tell me you always thought they were husband and wife!' I said; and everybody laughed. This released a little tension, as I'd intended. 'Now,' I continued, 'it is believed that the Sodomites were in the habit of having sexual intercourse (and if you don't know what that is, ask me another time – don't ask some adult who might lie to you or punish you for asking) using the back passage instead of the proper one.' You could have heard a pin drop. I had deliberately avoided four-letter words, but it was probably the first time an adult had mentioned sexual intercourse in their hearing. 'So we now use the verb "sod" to mean that action, and the noun "sod" to mean a person who performs that action. Now, does anybody think it could be done by a girl? Well? . . . Well?'

General agreement: 'Nossir.'

'Right,' I said. 'Then in future you girls are not to say you'll do it; and of course you boys are forbidden to start any volcanoes around here! Now we'll break for refreshments.'

Remember this was 1935. I didn't know then that anal intercourse between consenting adults wasn't a sin, though I did know God wouldn't strike you dead for it.

That's as nearly as I can remember how it went on that first evening, and I wondered afterwards whether I'd been wise, and whether there would be deputations of parents accusing me of corrupting the youth I was supposed to keep on the straight and narrow. I needn't have worried. It seemed that not a single youngster mentioned anything about it to any grown-up, but the attendance at the church youth club increased the next time we met.

As the time for refreshments approached on that second occasion, a certain restlessness was manifested, and the members tended to form themselves into a group around me. 'I told you the other evening', I announced, 'that you can always come to me with your questions and get a straight answer. I have the feeling somebody wants to ask me something.' Silence. Some of the boys were nudging one another, to no effect. 'Most of the questions to which adults won't give you a straight answer are about sex,' I encouraged them.

Eventually one boy, pushed forward by his mates, asked: 'Sir! Is it true that if you . . . you know . . . in bed, like . . . you go mad?' Emboldened, one of his mates added helpfully, 'Or have hair grow on the palms of your hands?' And a third, fourth and fifth chorused: 'Or go blind, sir?'

'*If* it were true,' I answered firmly, 'we'd all be blind, wouldn't we?' (I'd been tempted to say 'you', but decided that 'we' was more honest.) This was a marvellous opportunity to deal with an important subject which worried most youngsters. I rationed myself to three minutes on the subject of the harmlessness of masturbation before calling for refreshments to be served.

The pattern was established. Before refreshments, we would have quite a brief but strictly accurate explanation of something that youngsters wanted to know. At first it was always about sex, but later other subjects came up, mostly concerned with the rights and wrongs of various kinds of human behaviour. The club membership grew and grew, and that of the rival secular club on Outer Circle Drive began to diminish, until I persuaded the young blonde social worker who ran it, Miss McAlister Brew, to change to a different night so that the young people of the parish could go to both.

A much respected middle-aged member of the congregation, Mr Stringer, volunteered to help with the youth club. He and his wife had no children, which was a pity, because they would have made excellent parents. His wife always referred to him as 'Clem', but I insisted on addressing him formally and the youngsters followed my example. If ever things got a bit out of hand, he would take his pipe from his mouth and say not very loudly, 'Now, lads!', and order would be restored.

We had services on most days, and three on Sundays. I would have to preach at least once a week and of course teach in Sunday School and take Sunday School teachers' preparation classes. I had regular consultations with my vicar, who was an amiable man and very humble: he would constantly be doing something he described as 'picking your brains'. His sermons were better than mine at that time, because he was content to teach. The only fault I ever found in him was that his house tended to be cold because of his theory that all doors should be left open so that the entire house would be heated by one or two fires, instead of heating one room and encountering cold when you left it.

I lodged at 11 Austen Walk with Mr and Mrs Sidney Orme, their son Sidney and their daughter Joyce, who was about ten, I suppose, and who behaved to me like a niece or a much younger sister. She often pestered me when I was reading or studying, so I christened her Pest, but spelt it with a long-tailed 's' that looks like an 'f', so that it was pronounced Peft. Mrs Orme was a good cook and a kind-hearted woman. Her husband Sid was a quiet man, leaving most of the talking to his wife. I always addressed them as Mr and Mrs Orme.

About half-way through my year as a deacon, the new church was finished and the old hut became permanently a church hall. Human nature being what it is, the congregation grieved for the old hut for some months. A redundant church called St Peter-at-Arches (this meant it was near the Stonebow) was to have been transported lock, stock and barrel to the new housing estate of St Giles, but when they came to pull it down the stone crumbled, apart from the superior stone of the windows and mullions. So the new church had had to be built of brick apart from its facings, windows, and pinnacles on the tower. It did have the pews and other furniture, and what had been the high altar became the altar in the side chapel. The consecration of this church was of course a great event in the life of the parish.

It occurred to me about this time that teaching my youth club about sex was all very well, but babies were being born all the time who would be wrongly taught from the word go, and the ill effects would be difficult to reverse. One ought, I thought, to begin sex education with young couples coming to be married, so that their transformed attitudes would be communicated to any children they might have.

We always start our ministry with a year as a deacon, and during my first year I didn't take any weddings because a deacon can't, for the simple reason that it requires a priest to give a blessing just as it does to give an absolution. Male and female deacons are allowed to take weddings nowadays, but they ought not to. Although I didn't take weddings, I did prepare young couples for marriage. As soon as we knew abut their intention to marry, which at latest would be when they came to put up the banns, I would with the vicar's permission get them to come round to my lodgings for a talk in preparation for marriage. This is now fairly standard procedure, but was practically unheard of in those days. Most of the clergy didn't even go through the order of service with them, to make them familiar with the wording and purpose of it, let alone explain the three reasons for Holy Matrimony with particular reference to the second ('in order that the natural instincts and affections, implanted by God, should be hallowed and directed aright'). I made sure that they knew all that they needed to know in order to have a successful sexual relationship in their marriage.

The people of St Giles were an agreeable lot, and there were many near-saints in the congregation, but I don't suppose there is any parish without one or two sourpusses, so one day a delegation appeared at 10 Lee Road to complain to the vicar that 'that new young curate of thine is gathering young couples in Mrs Orme's front room and talking dirty to them, and Mrs Orme says she isn't going to stand for it, and he'll have to go elsewhere.' Mr Daniels, dear man, lit another cigarette (he was practically a chain-smoker) and said mildly, 'I think you have it slightly wrong. What Mrs Orme actually said was that if the young couples preparing for marriage were going to come not only from St Giles but from all the nine parishes of Lincoln, the front room wouldn't be big enough to hold them, and Mr Varah would have to transfer his classes to the school.' We were loyal to one another, my vicar and I. He told me he couldn't have given these talks himself, but was very glad that I gave them.

At the end of my year as a deacon, I easily passed the examination to go on to the priesthood, but a day or two before the ordination in the Minster I went down with 'flu. Dear old Bumbo was very kind about it. He knew that if I wasn't ordained before the end of the year, it would look in my records in *Crockford's Clerical Directory* as though I had been a deacon for two years, even though it might only have been for thirteen months. This would be a sign that I had in some way disgraced myself and had my ordination postponed. He therefore arranged with my vicar to come and ordain me in St Giles on St John's-Day-in-Christmas, 27 December 1936. I am still the only person to have been ordained in that church.

In those days we parsons got a full month's holiday every year, and in 1936, my first year as a priest, I paid what was to be my last visit to my friend Armand in Deventer. I visited Utrecht, where the Old Catholic Cathedral was, and met the Archbishop's Suffragan, Bishop Lagerwij, titular Bishop of Deventer (where there was no Old Catholic Church) to ask him whether I might be the first Anglican priest to take advantage of the Bonn Concordat of 1934, establishing full intercommunion between the Church of England and the Old Catholic churches of the Netherlands, Germany, Switzerland and Poland, by celebrating the Sacred Liturgy in Dutch. He was very keen that this should happen, and chose Sint Jacobus (St James's) Church, whose priest at that time was Pastoor Bakker. I was to do a Stille Mis (a Said Mass) at 8 a.m. and a Gezongene Mis (Sung Mass) at 10.

The said celebration went quite well and the people seemed pleased, but I made a fearful mess of the Sung Mass, having rashly assumed the parts I would have to sing would be the same as in the Church of England and the Roman Church. They weren't, not by a long chalk. I got scolded afterwards by two old men, who said I'd quite spoilt it for them, though one of them added that my Dutch sermon had been rather good. I don't know whether any other Anglican priest has since celebrated the Old Catholic liturgy in Dutch, but several Dutch priests have celebrated the Anglican liturgy in English. I think the first was my friend Andries Zwart, who served as a curate of All Saints, Hertford. Naturally, I joined St Willibrord's Society, named after the Apostle of the Netherlands, which exists to promote fellowship between the Anglican and Old Catholic churches. What we have in common is that we are both *reformed* Catholic Churches who have liberated themselves from Rome, we in the sixteenth century, the Dutch in the eighteenth century, and the German disciples of Dollinger in the nineteenth century. An odd item of interest is that the Polish Old Catholics in the United States sent missionaries to Poland and established a small Old Catholic church there. The Swiss Old Catholic church is called 'Christkatoliche', so in German Switzerland if you say you're Catholic they may ask, 'Oh, Roman or Christian?'

In 1937, the year of the Paris Exposition, I heard of a flat in the rue d l'Assomption available for a month at a very reasonable rent. I decided to get to know Paris, improve my French (which was theoretically sound but of little practical use) and see the Exhibition. It proved to be a very commodious flat on the first floor, within easy reach of Métro Ranelagh. On my first evening I went to Montparnasse, leaving Montmartre (the other artistic and literary quarter) for another day. I was going to spend the evening over a Pernod or even, dangerously, an absinthe, listening to the wit and criticisms of the literati in Le Dôme or La Coupole. A glance into each of these crowded places convinced me that I would be wasting my time: the hubbub was tremendous, and nobody looked like a distinguished writer or critic, or rather, like my ideas of these. I had to admit that the most scintillating conversation in colloquial French would probably have passed right over my head, and I made for a quieter place called La Palette.

I sat at the bar and ordered a Pernod. Before long a young Frenchwoman a few years older than I came and sat next to me, and called for poker dice and a board on which to throw. She was dressed in a smart blue suit over an immaculate white blouse. As I watched her throw with interest, she invited me to play with her, 'for drinks'. I could not possibly have allowed her to pay even if I had won, but the poker dice served merely as an excuse for striking up a conversation. She was patient with my halting, schoolboy French, and remembered to speak to me slowly and distinctly. We got on well, and my French kept on improving, as I had a pretty large vocabulary in my head and a good knowledge of the grammar – I only lacked practice in speaking. By the time we parted, we had agreed to meet again the next morning.

87

I didn't feel at all certain that the young lady *would* meet me the following morning, but she did, and when I said how fortunate it was that she had the day off from work, she said that she had been ill and her doctor had insisted that she take a holiday from work until the end of the month. She had been with her family in the depths of the country and had got bored and had come back to Paris, and now was at a loose end. I didn't hesitate. I asked her whether she'd like to be my guide and companion during my stay in Paris: I couldn't afford to pay her much, but could and would pay for all meals, transportation, and entry to museums. She accepted with alacrity. I then asked her name: it was Yanine Maincent; I told her mine, using the French version of my first name, Edouard, and not mentioning my occupation.

Yanine proved to be an excellent guide. There was no part of Paris she didn't know, and in a surprisingly large number of places she herself was known. Her conversation was witty and amusing, and I fairly soon improved at keeping up with it.

She had a healthy appetite and after a couple of days of two good meals a day plus innumerable coffees and snacks, she was beginning to get some colour in her cheeks and some spring in her step. We walked almost everywhere because she said that was the only way to see Paris, and of course she was right. Thanks to her, I had an intimate knowledge of the whole of metropolitan Paris by the end of the month; much later, as Secretary of the Orthodox Churches Aid Fund, I was to acquire an intimate knowledge of non-tourist Paris, namely the slums of Montrouge, Malakoff and Clichy, where the Russian *émigrés* were served by their impoverished *émigré* priests.

The only thing she asked me to buy her, apart from the agreed meals and so on, was a pair of gloves: she said she felt naked without them. But by about the fifth day she was in a state of some distress, and confided that she had been thrown out of her room. I had never asked where her room was, but as she wasn't working she probably hadn't been able to pay the rent. I felt very mean about having a big flat all to myself while she was homeless. After five days I felt I knew her sufficiently well to invite her to move into my apartment until she could get another room, on the strict under-standing that this was a brother-and-sister arrangement – I had in fact no designs upon her, and she had shown no signs of coquetry towards me. She brought her few possessions – you could hardly call it luggage – and the first thing she wanted to do was some ironing. I didn't then know the word *repasser*, so she demonstrated.

While she was ironing, I couldn't help noticing what a dreadful condition her underclothes were in – such a contrast to her smart exterior – and I made up my mind that our next stop would be Printemps, a department store which even a mere man would know about. It was delightful to see her pleasure at being fitted out with all that she would need and I admired the thrifty way in which she shopped, not wanting to be extravagant with my money – a real Frenchwoman, who would make an excellent housewife one of these days, I thought. I had no means of knowing at that time that she was unlikely to be allowed to follow her vocation.

She soon established a pattern for our days. When we returned from exploring Paris in the late afternoon, hot and dusty and somewhat footsore, she would throw off her clothes, make a dive for the shower, and without bothering to dry herself, would wash the underclothes she had worn that day. By the time I emerged from the shower, drying myself, she would be ironing the previous day's laundry, including mine, still naked but now dry. It was astonishing to me that she showed no self-consciousness whatever: she wandered about, getting on with her little tasks, not flaunting herself in the least, as though it was the most natural thing in the world. After the first couple of days I began to think it was, though I didn't do it myself. Then we would both dress to go out to dinner and, very occasionally, because for the French dinner takes up a whole evening, a theatre or film. When we got back, we would go to our separate rooms, and I would read for a while before going to sleep, as I always do. I would wake up in the morning to hear the slight noises she made as she cleaned the flat, and if I tottered along to the bathroom while she was thus engaged, I would see that she was in her working clothes – that is, her birthday suit. She seemed to think she could only keep her clothes immaculate if she didn't wear them while engaged in household duties.

It never occurred to me at the time to wonder what she thought of my lack of evident arousal by the proximity of her unclothed body. She had no means of knowing that I was going through a period of voluntary celibacy. I think the most likely explanation is that she desperately needed the kind of undemanding relationship we had, and wasn't inclined to look this gift horse in the mouth.

Yanine was my teacher, and from her I learned *argot* as well as colloquial French (it must all have changed now – slang does), but sometimes she learned from me. For instance, I taught her to appreciate the pictures in the Louvre, and the Russian music in the

Orthodox Church in rue Daru. Until she met me she had never been to the Bibliothèque Nationale, where I spent an hour researching the poems of Francis Jammes, knocking off only when she was evidently bored.

I was due to return to England the day after Yanine was due to return to work, with the permission of her doctor. On her last day, I carried the little valise I had bought for her to the top of the steps of Métro Ranelagh (she wouldn't let me come further), thanked her for all she had done for me, and gave her a parting present of 200 francs, which in those days was a sum worth having. 'Shall we ever meet again, I wonder?' I said.

'No, Edouard,' she replied firmly. 'We shall never see one another again, but I shall never forget you, my Englishman.' She started down the steps, saying, 'It will be strange going back to work . . .'

I called after her, 'Yanine, you told me you were having a holiday, but you didn't say from what, and I never asked.'

She turned and came back up the steps and looked at me wide-eyed, her jaw dropping slightly. 'That's right!' she exclaimed. 'I never got round to telling you, but it was never meant to be a secret. I am a prostitute.' Then she flitted down the stairs, and I never saw her again.

On my way back to the empty flat, I commended her fervently to God, praying that she might be safeguarded in her arduous and sometimes dangerous occupation, and might prosper enough to be able to retire in middle age to the country from which she came.

Back in Lincoln, I felt the need for a piano, as well as one or more guest-rooms. I didn't go searching for a house of my own, but when I heard of a suitable one for rent in Ruskin Avenue I couldn't resist it. It belonged to the mother of a Mr Stan Hollowday, who lived opposite with his Russian wife, Yana. Stan was a Continental travel-ler for Ruston Bucyrus Excavators and was in Central Europe three weeks out of four, leaving his wife with their son Mark and his Greek-Cypriot nanny. He had been manager of an asbestos mine at Amiandos, Cyprus, which was where he met his wife, whose mother had taken refuge there after the Russian revolution, leaving their immense fortune behind in Kharkov.

My interest in things Russian, and my penchant for collecting interesting foreigners, led me to spend many hours of my free time in fascinating conversation with Yana across the road. Our tastes in music were the same, and we would listen to favourite compositions such as Rachmaninov's Second Piano Concerto (played on old 78 r.p.m. records by Rachmaninov himself) again and again. Various Sunday School teachers would come from time to time to do a bit of cleaning or cook me a meal, though I wasn't very interested in food in those days and managed pretty well on my bachelor cooking plus a proper meal most lunchtimes at the Nightingale pub on Nettleham Road.

During my time at Lincoln I visited Barton occasionally, and on a couple of occasions preached for my father in one of the two great parish churches there, St Peter's or St Mary's. (The verger no longer trundles hymn books and cassocks back and forth between them in a huge wheelbarrow, because St Peter's has now been taken over by the National Trust, and St Mary's is the only parish church.) I am afraid my sermons were a great disappointment to my father, though he didn't say so. They were a disappointment to me, too, since I knew they were far below my usual standard because I was trying too hard in the presence of a congregation many of whose members had known me since childhood, and of my father and mother. I guess I am always at my worst in front of people I know, because I do best when I am carried away by my subject and care nothing about what impression I am making; this is difficult in front of your nearest and/or dearest.

After three years in Lincoln, I was tempted away by someone who had been at theological college with me and who had gone to serve *his* Title in Putney, London – Stephan Hopkinson. His vicar had given Stephan the job of finding a fellow assistant curate to work with him at the parish church of St Mary the Virgin, at the south end of Putney Bridge. The vicar himself worked with another curate at St John's, near the vicarage in Ravenna Road, which served the most affluent area of the parish. There were two other clergy at All Saints', on Putney Lower Common near the hospital.

I was rather excited by the thought of living and working in London even though it meant I must give up being a householder and go into digs once again. My lodgings were found for me by Stephan and his wife Anne – he had, unusually in those days, become engaged while still a theological student, to a rising young opera singer, and was now married to her and the first of his children had been born. The road where he lived and I was to live was Deodar Road, alongside the river to the east of Putney Bridge, and passing underneath the railway bridge which carried the 'underground' railway across the Thames from Putney Bridge to East Putney and thence to Wimbledon. The houses whose gardens ran down to the river were very desirable, and it was in one of these, No. 93, that I went to lodge with Mr and Mrs Robert Fletcher-O'Borne.

Mrs O'Borne, whom I did not then know as Mrs Ob, let alone Nelly, came from 'England beyond Wales', namely Tenby in Pembrokeshire. She was older than her husband, and until she married (and perhaps even after) had spent her life in 'good service', by which she meant in the households of titled people, as a cook. I have never had such meals put before me before or since as were served up by Mrs O'Borne, picked at by me in my unregenerate days, and finished off with gusto by her husband. I had the large front room facing on the street, a bedroom upstairs, and what little I ate of these fantastic meals, all for a ridiculously small sum: the next best thing to being in 'good service' was to have what Mrs Beake would have called 'a perfect gentleman' to wait on hand and foot.

I don't think I ever saw her sitting down at that period. She would stand respectfully, little over four feet high and tell me at great length what her 'mam' had told her when she was a little girl or what Sir Thomas (with whom she had been in service and whose firm 'made the banknotes') had one day said about her cooking. In time I was to know all these stories, with their digressions and parentheses, off by heart, learned to close my ears to them and concentrate on the book I always read at table until marriage deprived me of this pleasure. I felt sorry for Mr O'Borne, fed like a duke though he was, because he had had this for years and could not, like me, ignore it, though sometimes he would whistle under his breath, like royalty trying not to be driven mad by the National Anthem.

Church life in London at that time appeared to me to be more superficial than I had been used to in Lincolnshire, though there were many devout and regular members of the congregation, and there were various parish societies and clubs, some of which met in the old church hall on Putney Bridge Road, a stone's throw from my lodgings. People were very formal when one visited their homes, and one missed the warmth of the northerner. Although I am by nature an unsociable person, requiring a large ration of aloneness in my day and hardly ever knowing the painful experience of conscious

92

loneliness, I was missing my Lincoln friends, especially Yana Hollowday, and had no friends at all in Putney, as you could hardly count Stephan, tied up as he was with his wife and child and his parochial duties. He was very left-wing at that time, and much involved with his cousin Sir Richard Acland, whom he helped later to form a party called Common Wealth, which never really came to much.

Of the subjects I'd had to study for PPE, politics was the most boring. I had reacted against my father's conservatism with socialist arguments which exasperated him, but as a scientist I couldn't find any evidence for the belief that human nature would be so transformed by socialism that people would work harder for the common good than they would for themselves and their families. Then he had cut the ground from under my feet by abandoning the land-owning classes on a matter of religious principle, in 1928 or 1929. My father had been very committed to the revision of the Book of Common Prayer of 1662, and was wholeheartedly in favour of the document eventually produced in 1927. This was somewhat changed in the hope of making it more acceptable to Parliament in 1928, and my father campaigned everywhere for 'The Book of Common Prayer with additions and deviations proposed in 1928'. He urged the sitting Tory MP to vote for it, but he voted against. My father told the MP that he would lose his seat at the next election because he himself would grit his teeth and vote Labour and urge others to do the same. I was astonished, but received a salutary lesson in what conviction can do when, at the next election, our constituency of Glanford Brigg (the same Brigg celebrated by Delius in 'Brigg Fair') rejected Sir Berkeley Sheffield and elected the Labour candidate, whose name was Quibell. I have used the technically illegal 1928 Prayer Book throughout my ministry, and I still use it.

In 1938 I preached a controversial sermon in Putney parish church at the time of Munich. Chamberlain had returned from a visit to Hitler with his bit of paper (whatever your age, you must have seen him waving it on TV) and saying it represented 'peace in our time'. I poured scorn on this. 'Peace?' I sneered. 'Sacrificing Czechoslovakia won't win peace; it simply means that when war comes, the Škoda armament factories will be making arms for the enemy instead of for us! The most advanced democracy in Europe has been thrown to the wolves, and we are told this is a distant country of which we know little. Know little,' I yelled, 'and care less!' There were complaints to the vicar, but I stood my ground. I wasn't consciously or unconsciously trying to please Stephan, I was speaking indignantly, out of heartfelt conviction.

I wasn't to know that within a few months of preaching against appeasement and for Czechoslovakia I should find myself sitting every Monday lunchtime next to the exiled president of Czechoslovakia, Eduard Beneš. I had not been surprised to find that the category 'minister of religion' in the Putney Rotary Club was occupied by Stephan, and as he and I worked for the same 'firm' I was allowed to become what was called 'an Additional Active Member'. (I remained a Rotarian from 1938 to 1953, when I resigned because I could no longer keep up my near 100 per cent attendance record.) Beneš, having taken refuge in England, was living in a house in Gwendolen Avenue, Putney, and was happy to join the local Rotary Club, where I was given the honour of sitting next to him at our luncheons because my knowledge of Russian (not Czech) was about the same as his knowledge of English, and we managed to converse.

In sharp contrast to my association with the respectable burghers of Putney in the Rotary Club was my attempt to make useful contact with the street-corner boys of the neighbourhood. They tended to hang about in groups when it got dark on winter evenings, with apparently no clear purpose, but doing a lot of running around, shouting, and wrestling one another. They played a peculiar game where one of them would stand bent as if for leapfrog, with his head down and his hands against a wall, with two others behind him in a similar position, all bracing themselves because the others would leapfrog on to the 'bridge' thus created, until there might be as many as seven on top of the first three, whereupon the whole thing would collapse amid insane shrieks of laughter. The various gangs didn't have much to do with one another and certainly didn't fight, but kept to their own territory.

Everybody thought it was ridiculous of me to have joined the gang which scampered about nearest to Deodar Road, because they were in their early or mid teens, and I was twice the age of the youngest of them. It was pretty exhausting running around with them, and I didn't at all enjoy their piling on top of one another game, which did no good at all to one's subfusc suits, but I persevered and at last was able to move them indoors, into the old church hall. There were, of course, complaints from other users of the building that that dratted youth club broke things and left the place untidy, but I fended off these criticisms and collected the members of another couple of gangs, who really appreciated having somewhere to meet that was out of the cold and rain. In answer to questions at our weekly staff-meeting about why none of them had begun to attend church, I replied that our services were simply not designed to appeal to working-class boys of that age group. As nobody suggested that we should change the form of service to suit the presumed tastes of 'Varah's ruffians', the discussion usually petered out. I did myself feel, however, that the amount of time and energy I put into it was hardly justified by any noticeable results – I didn't even get many of the sort of questions about sexual morality which I had had constantly in my youth club in Lincoln, though, come to think of it, I must have prevented a few unwanted pregnancies.

The rest of the social life of the parish was much more civilized. The part of the parish belonging to St Mary's, and to some extent All Saints' at the other end of the Lower Richmond Road, had two very successful clubs, the Rambling and Social Club for those in their late teens and early twenties, and the Social Guild for the twenties and thirties. The members of both were regular members of the congregation. The secretary of the Social Guild was a girl called Doris Susan Whanslaw, whose family lived in Rotherwood Road, on the edge of my visiting area. Her father was a bell-ringer, her mother active in the women's work and her sister Marjorie active in the Rambling Club. She herself was a member of the Parochial Church Council and a Sunday School teacher.

There were several attractive young women in these clubs and in the Sunday School, and some had of course noticed the arrival in their midst of an eligible unmarried young man. You may be a little surprised, having read about my way of life before ordination, to know that I was not anxious to acquire any sort of girlfriend. I was not ready to be married, if indeed an unsociable person like myself was ever going to be ready, and I had resolved not to break any hearts nor cause any scandal. Three or four young women found occasion to call upon me to discuss various parish matters, but they were always coolly received by Mrs O'Borne who was exasperatingly vague about the likely hour of my return. With one exception: Miss Whanslaw. She was always invited in, plied with tea, and entertained while she waited for my arrival with accounts of what Mrs O'Borne's mam had said to her on various topics, or what Lady Waterlow had said in praise of her cooking, and (it goes without saying) what a perfect gentleman I was and what a wonderful husband I would one day make for some fortunate lady. (This was, I tell you sincerely and with no false modesty, an exaggeration.)

It began to seem as though whenever I came in in the late afternoon, this charming young lady was being entertained by Mrs O'-Borne. I had to admit that she was very agreeable company, but I did not want her to get a false impression. I mentioned the matter to Stephan and Anne, but there were no allies there: they both thought what an excellent parson's wife Miss Whanslaw would make, though they didn't put it quite so crudely; and of course they were right. But I did not want it to be *this* parson. On my day off I often used to go and drop in on Wearing King, who had been at school and Oxford with me and had gone into educational administration. He had a flat in Shaftesbury Avenue, which he regarded as the centre of the world, and affected to believe that if you went too much beyond Piccadilly Circus you would find yourself out in the country. Most of his neighbours, apart from one dentist, were expensive prostitutes, with whom he loved having a purely neighbourly, chatty relationship. Wearing took a glum view of my situation. We arranged for him to come on a Rambling Club outing so that he might meet the subject of our discussion. I felt sure that Susan (her family called her Doris but I preferred her second name) would come on the outing if I mentioned that I was going on it, and sure enough she did.

The three of us strolled along together, chatting easily. At one point in our rambling we came upon a tree which had been cut down and trimmed so that a log about twenty feet long lay on the ground. Susan sat on one end of it to rest, and a foolish young man picked up the other end of it, lifted it as high as he could, and then dropped it. Her jarring must have hurt Susan dreadfully, but she wouldn't admit it. I was very angry with the young man, and Wearing said, 'You know I think you're more fond of her than you admit!' Then he added: 'She's very attractive, you know!'

'Oh, do you think so?' I enthused. 'Well, now . . .'

'Oh, no, you don't!' he snapped. 'I'm not the marrying kind.' In fact, he later married twice, but that's another story.

'Neither am I!' I told him. 'I have no right to make some girl unhappy, even if she thinks she wants this, because she doesn't know me and doesn't know how unready for it I still am. Besides, what if I got married to someone I'm certainly very fond of, and fell madly in love with someone else?' He couldn't answer that.

That was the year, 1938, that Wearing and I took our summer holiday together for the first and only time, driving round Scandinavia. In Malmö we were able to hire a large black Ford V8 motorcar. We decided there was no point in having the freedom a car gave if we went the direct way to Stockholm which was followed by the railway, so we agreed to drive up the then unfrequented Baltic Coast road.

It was an amazing experience to drive for three days further and further north through miles of forest and lake, and then breast a rise at dusk and look down on Stockholm, all lit up on either side of the great gulf called Mälaren, and on the island between. There was a liner lit up in the harbour, and the whole place looked quite magical. We stayed at the Ritz Hotel, which no longer exists, and made contact with Ingeborg, a jolly blonde whom I'd known in the Scandinavian Club and whose father was an engineer. We felt very much at home in this distant·northern city once we were in the company of somebody who actually lived there. We drove her to the coast at Saltsjöbaden (salt sea-baths) and kept her and other Swedish bathing beauties under close observation.

We continued north to Uppsala, a combination of Oxford and Canterbury. (Lund, near Malmö is a combination of Cambridge and York; each city is one of their two great universities and their two archbishoprics). It was, oddly enough, the Archbishop of Uppsala, Dr Erling Eidem, whom we were going to Uppsala to see – he'd been a friend of my father when the former was a professor at Lund, and he remembered him well and gave me a signed photograph to give to him. He was impressed by my knowledge of the Swedish Lutheran Church, which of course I had gained from my father, who had told me with great emphasis that whereas the other Lutheran churches, including those of Denmark and Norway, had lost the Apostolic Succession, Sweden had in fact retained it, though, he added glumly, they didn't seem to take much account of this.

From Uppsala we aimed the car at Oslo via Orebro and the frontier at Hån. Here we were able to make contact with Astri, who told us where to stay, showed us round, and talked nostalgically of her time at 2 Keble Road. When we didn't find Kari Staubo at her Oslo address, Astri managed to discover where was their place in the country, on the coast on the way to Gothenberg. We found Kari on the beach having just emerged from a swim, and looking as beautiful as ever. As we walked towards her she couldn't at first believe her eyes, and then she rushed forward and flung her arms round me, dripping wet, and covered my face with salt-tasting kisses. Why had I ever left this girl, I asked myself – but of course the answer was still the same as it had been at the time. It was hard to tear myself away, but we had calculated rather narrowly the time it would take us to get the car back to Malmö by the agreed date.

Somewhere between the Norwegian frontier and Gothenberg, I think on the way to a place called Uddevalla, I was for once driving in the depths of the country, probably with my mind still on Kari, when I failed to notice a Swedish peasant driving a cart from a field on one side of the road to another field on the opposite side of the road; or rather, not driving, because he was fast asleep, but sitting there, doubtless aware that the horse knew the way. Why, I asked myself, did he not pull up at the edge of the road and wait for our important vehicle to pass? I hadn't noticed that he was asleep. The horse was not impressed by a Ford V8, so by bouncing along the grass verge on the left (the Swedes drove on the left at that time, just as we still do) I managed to miss the back of the cart by about four inches. The peasant never knew how near to disaster he had come, but I did; I pulled the car up as soon as I could, got out and walked around and got in at the other side saying to Wearing, 'Move over and drive – I'm never going to drive again.'

'Not drive again?!' shrieked Wearing, to whom this sounded like heresy, if not paradise lost. 'Why ever not?'

'Because', I said firmly, 'I am a bad driver. Unco-ordinated, absent-minded, impatient, and generally unfit to be in control of a lethal implement called a motor-car. I promise you, I shall never drive again.' And I never have. And I've never regretted it. I know it makes me an eccentric, because the roads are full of bad drivers who continued to drive like crazy, and I mean crazy.

I remember the outbreak of war very vividly. That Sunday I had been given the duty of celebrating and preaching at All Saints' on Putney Lower Common, just opposite the hospital, and was in the middle of my sermon when one of the churchwardens came hurrying up the nave and waved a piece of paper at me. I leaned over and took it from him, read it, and then announced to the congregation as follows: 'I have just received an important communication, but before I tell you about it I should like you to know that I intend to continue with the service and I hope all of you will stay until it is ended. But if any of you feel you must get home, please leave quietly. The notice I have just received is that we are now at war with Germany. God save the King.' I had barely finished when everybody rushed out of the church, and I had to complete the service by myself.

As I pedalled past the slit trenches that had been dug on Putney Lower Common, the siren sounded – that banshee wail to which we were to become so well accustomed. Like many people, I felt a mixture of apprehension and exaltation: at last we were going to stand up to the ogre Hitler.

The All Clear sounded: the unidentified aircraft that had set off the alarm had proved to be one of ours. Thus began what was soon to be known as the 'phoney' war, during which we were able to make up for some of the past neglect of our armed forces, partly owing to the success of pacifist propaganda.

Stephan had been offered his first benefice, St John's, Barrow Island, Barrow-in-Furness in the Diocese of Carlisle, in which his father was Archdeacon of Westmorland. Stephan invited me to go with him as his curate, and I agreed on condition that we were equal partners.

When I told Susan that I was going north with Stephan, she was distressed. It shows how unperceptive I was at that time that I was surprised by this. We had been accustomed to meeting several times a week, and although I had a number of friendly acquaintances, she was the only one who could be described as a friend. When I thought about it I could see that she had every reason to suppose that our friendship would lead to courtship and marriage, and it was 'just like a man' (well, I am a man) not to have considered this seriously before. I had become genuinely fond of Susan and could not bear to see her looking brave and unhappy, but what if marriage to the person I was at that time made her even more unhappy? Wouldn't it be kinder to an attractive and affectionate girl with so many admirable qualities to let her get free of me and be courted by someone more worthy of her? Don't forget that in those days respectable people had to be sure to get it right first time, as divorce was scandalous, and for the clergy unthinkable.

After some weeks of agonizing over it, without the advantage of an unprejudiced person to discuss it with (for The Samaritans didn't exist in those days or I would certainly have got in touch with them), I proposed to Susan in the church hall kitchen at some event at which she was helping. She refused me. 'Go on, just this once,' I said; and she agreed. She insisted that I go home with her to tell her mother, who I guess wasn't quite sure whether to be disappointed that her warnings that no good would come of it had been proved wrong, or relieved that her daughter's friendship with that unpredictable young man was going to have a happy – or at least not unconventional – ending after all.

My own parents were equally concerned with propriety. I had to take Susan to be vetted. She was an immediate hit with my mother, but found it rather an ordeal to be called into my father's study, doubtless to be questioned about her churchmanship and Christian beliefs. Whatever it was, she passed, and it was the general consensus among my family and friends that I didn't deserve such a paragon. I could only agree.

I was now priest in charge of Putney parish church. Stephan came up from Barrow, where he had arranged digs for us, to solemnize the marriage, bringing with him his daughter Jennifer who was to be a bridesmaid along with my sister Audrey. Mrs O'Borne was proud to substitute for my mother, who was unable to travel, and Wearing was my best man. As the bride appeared, looking elegant and happy, he muttered out of the corner of his mouth, 'We've been in some tight corners together, old boy, but this is one you won't get out of.' Well, I knew *that*.

We were married on 27 January 1940, a Saturday, and my duties at St Mary's didn't end until midday on the Sunday, so we booked at the Rembrandt Hotel for the first night of our honeymoon in order that I shouldn't be too far away for the 8 a.m. Holy Communion at Putney. Ignoring the gibes of those who thought it excessive to take two girls on one's honeymoon, we arranged for Susan's friend Alice Wren to stay at the hotel in order to spend with her the hours that I should be absent on my ecclesiastical duties. I left instructions to be called at 6.30 a.m., which they thought so odd that I explained I had to take a service at Putney at 8. A good thing I revealed this: it enabled the night porter to call me at 5 a.m. with the news that eighteen inches of snow had fallen during the night, so that I should have to walk to Putney and had better start as soon as I was dressed. Have you ever tried walking several miles in eighteen inches of snow? I can assure you there are few things more exhausting. I arrived, sodden, at a few minutes to 8, and took the service for no fewer than two parishioners who lived only a stone's throw away – or should I say a snowball's throw? A hot bath and a huge breakfast at Mrs O'Borne's got me fit for the 11 a.m. Mattins and sermon, and by the time I was free to resume my honeymoon, some trains were running. We were able to get to Oxford, where we were booked into the Golden Cross for two nights. I was due to start my new duties at Barrow-in-Furness on 1 February, so we had planned to break our journey also at Chester.

There didn't seem to be any other guests at that charming old coaching inn except Anthony Asquith, a film producer. I managed to show Susan many of the sights of Oxford, in spite of the snow and ice, but we didn't see much of Chester as the whole of our time seemed to be taken up in waiting for trains. I had always taken such difficulties in my stride when alone, but it's a different matter when you have someone with you that you have to look after and protect from hunger, boredom, and cold. I also discovered, like all young husbands at that time, that 'a penny bun costs fourpence', because the young lady has to have a tuppenny one, and you have to have the same as she does or she would be embarrassed. This doesn't, of course, apply only to buns.

4

WE arrived in Barrow-in-Furness late, but on the correct day, and the first impression was of a Siberian prison camp. As we slithered on the thick ice, Susan must have been thinking perhaps she would have been wiser to stick to her original 'no'.

We were to have two rooms and a share of kitchen and bathroom with a Miss Baxter, at 26 James Watt Terrace. This was only a few yards from Stephan and Anne's vicarage. Later, we were able to splash out and take the commodious house next door to theirs. The prosperity of the town depended upon Vickers Armstrong's shipyard which was on Barrow Island, separated by a short bridge from the mainland and therefore within the bounds of our parish of St John. The church was a large, bare, concrete structure with a flat roof, which soon came in useful for fire-watching. It was typical of the town that it elected a Labour town council and a Conservative Member of Parliament, the reasoning being that socialist builders of submarines and aircraft carriers dare not risk electing a government which might be pacifist and reduce orders to the shipyard.

Barrow was the windiest place I've ever lived in; in fact, the local paper published a cartoon of two chaps in a desert with not a breath of air moving, both holding on to their hats, the caption reading, 'Ah see tha cums from Barrer, too.' Many of the parishioners lived in The Buildings, which were misery to visit though they kept one in training for mountain-climbing. Clothes-lines high across the street were steel cables which could be wound in from either end to bring in laundry which was doubtless clean but didn't look it because of the grime that settled on it.

It must have been difficult for Susan adjusting to life in the north, which she had never previously experienced, as well as to married life. Fortunately, she got on well with Anne, as she had done before we were married, and sometimes on our day off the four of us would go to the Lake District, where the women would picnic and knit (Susan was a most accomplished knitter) while the men would scramble up the nearest peak. During our time in Barrow I climbed all the Lake mountains except Skiddaw, which I thought boring.

The most memorable *real* climb (as distinct from scrambling) was with Stephan up the north face of Scafell. We were not equipped for rock-climbing, because we didn't want our spouses to know what we were up to, so we set off together wearing casual clothes and walking-shoes and mackintoshes, taking our bicycles on the train. I discovered on the journey that Stephan had the ambition to repeat a climb named after his grandfather, Sir Alfred Hopkinson, which as far as he knew hadn't been repeated. We got to the base of the sheer cliff which was the north face of Scafell, managed to identify Hopkinson Climb and started up it. I had never before clung to a sheer face with toes and fingertips, and after what seemed an interminable and exhausting climb, I found myself stuck. I was sitting astride a cornice, and could see no way of going either forwards or backwards, though I didn't care to look too closely at the quarter-mile drop beneath us. Stephan edged down again, identified a point at which an essential foothold was missing, and managed to jam his fingers into a crevice so that I could tread on the back of his hand. 'Just put your right foot on my hand,' he urged. 'Don't give up now – we're nearly at the top, and then there's an easy way down.' I was thinking of an even easier way down if I missed a hold, because of course we had no ropes, but we made it to the top and the way down was indeed easy on the other side. It's an exhilarating feeling, having been close to death and having survived. When we got back, we did not tell our wives what we had been up to.

War-time shortages meant that there were few toys for the children at Christmas, so Susan and others formed the Santa Claus Guild, which was to meet regularly over tea and homemade cakes for various kinds of needlework and knitting, including the making and stuffing of soft toys. Husbands who worked in the shipyard were enlisted to make wooden and metal toys, some of which were most ingenious, and almost all of which were 'foreigners'. I had never previously heard the word used to describe things made with the employer's machinery and the employer's materials in the employer's time for one's home or for the church Christmas bazaar. It was more practical to make wooden than metal toys, and I fear it may have done no good to certain metalworking machines to be used on timber.

Even before the phoney war became a real one, anti-aircraft sites were set up all around Barrow to protect the docks and the shipyard. It was very lonely and boring for the men stationed miles from anywhere, and I was one of those who volunteered to visit the sites and give educational lectures. These were much appreciated, and led to lively discussions. Sometimes I took Anne Hopkinson with me to sing for the audience, and needless to say this was much more popular than my lectures. Her biggest hit was Stephen Adams's 'The Holy City'. I learned that the most enviable job in the army below the rank of Major was WO1: he was waited on hand and foot, and received far more respect than the junior officers.

After Germany invaded the Netherlands, I became even more involved with Dutch sailors than with British soldiers. Fishermen from Egmond and Ijmuiden simply sailed their trawlers across to England and were eventually stationed at Barrow-in-Furness as minesweepers. Because of my knowledge of Dutch I was appointed chaplain to the Dutch minesweepers, and because of my familiarity with the Old Catholic Church I was very acceptable to them, Egmond and Ijmuiden being the only two places in the Netherlands with a large Old Catholic population. I was able to celebrate the Old Catholic liturgy for them either on shore or on board ship. A less pleasant duty was to take memorial services on all the other ships after one of the trawlers struck a mine and went down – the first to be lost was the *Carolina*. I had been specially friendly with the mate, Cornelis Ploeg, who was very clever at metalwork and made me a tiny pair of clogs from brass from a mine.

After the war I made a point of visiting Egmond and Ijmuiden to renew acquaintance with some of the minesweepers who returned safely, and to visit the widows of those who did not return, including Mevrouw Ploeg. It was a great comfort to her to spend an hour with someone who had often seen her husband during the years when they were parted by war and unable even to communicate with one another, and to hear my account of the last conversation I had had with her husband before he set out on his final journey.

I was able to organize Christmas parties for the minesweepers during my two years as their chaplain. It seemed to me that what these men, far from home in a strange land, would appreciate more than anything else would be to celebrate Christmas on the day on which they were accustomed to exchange presents at home, namely

6 December, St Nicholas's day, known in Dutch as 'Sinter Klaas', at a party arranged specially for them with a slap-up home-cooked meal and feminine companionship without competition from the men of our congregation (not necessarily in that order). Susan, who was herself a good cook, organized the ladies of the parish to provide a spread which hardly looked like war-time scarcity.

The men of the congregation found it a little difficult to understand why, once they had put up trestle tables and a Christmas tree and done the necessary electrical work, they should be required to make themselves scarce. However, I was adamant. The result was that once the sailors were full of good food and 'good cheer', they were invited to dance to a radiogram with ladies hand-picked by me for their warmth and friendliness and their lack, as far as I could ascertain, of excessively jealous husbands or boyfriends. The minesweepers were still talking about the wonderful Christmas party six months later. I hadn't, of course, been able to organize serious girlfriends for them, nor was I acquainted with any local ladies whose favours were for sale. It's possible that the sailors were better acquainted with the availability of such services than I was. I only know that their friendly dancing partners at the Christmas party didn't continue to meet them, and no marriages resulted.

Barrow was on the whole a rather selfish place, which couldn't really compare with Lincoln, or even Putney, but something was soon to happen which would change all that. The 'something' was, paradoxically, the blitz on Barrow. It lasted for eight successive nights, then one night was missed, and then there was a ninth night of very heavy bombing directed at the shipyard and the docks. We, of course, were between the two, and received a lot of the near misses. During those ten days and nights Barrow became a warm, loving, neighbourly place to live in. The tenderness with which people greeted one another, finding themselves still alive after a devastating night, was something that would have been unimaginable before.

We had, of course, never experienced anything like it before but after the first night we organized ourselves as if we all knew exactly what to do: fire-watching on the flat roof of St John's, visiting people in the shelters to cheer them up and say prayers with them, co-operating with the air-raid wardens and, in the case of us clergy, meeting every morning at 10 to say Mattins together, report on everyone's well-being or otherwise, and allocate rosters of duty.

By the fifth night of the bombing we were veterans, experiencing a heady mixture of trepidation and exaltation. It seemed to us that we had never before lived to the full. Certainly every minute was precious. And we were *needed* – needed not only by the fraction of the population which formed our congregations, but by everyone. By the eighth night, we had adjusted to the ominous droning of the enemy planes, the crash of their bombs and the even louder racket made by our own anti-aircraft guns, rather as explorers acclimatize themselves to the Arctic or the scorching desert. When there was no bombing on the ninth night, we were uneasy and restless and couldn't catch up on missed sleep. The bombing on the tenth night came as a relief, but, as I have already told you, it didn't last. That was the end of our blitz.

The war, of course, continued to have an impact, the most noticeable aspect of which was the presence of large numbers of soldiers in the church from time to time. Units stationed in the neighbourhood came at times arranged with Stephan for a service which I normally took, and on these occasions they almost completely filled the church. The first time they came I detected a good deal of resentment in the ranks at having to come to church. I decided to take the bull by the horns, and deal with it straightforwardly. At the beginning of the service, I said to them, 'My spies tell me that a good many of you would rather not be here. If that is so, I could say the same. Naturally, as a priest, I like being in the house of God and I am quite content with my job of taking services, but I am accustomed to a congregation which has come of its own free will, wishing to join with me in worshipping God and to listen to any instruction I am able to give from the pulpit. The only way of dealing with this situation that I can think of is to have the sermon at the beginning of the service and to use it to deal with the question: Ought there to be compulsory church parades for the armed forces of the Crown in a supposedly Christian country, fighting an enemy, Hitler, who has absolute power in his country and is not influenced by any Christian in its population? But first, let's see if we can choose some hymns you would enjoy singing.'

The atmosphere began to improve, and some of the men began to suggest their favourite hymns on which we took a vote. After the first one, the ice was broken, and I did my best to present the arguments in favour of an army in war-time being instructed in the principles of its country's established religion.

We were two years in Barrow-in-Furness. One terrible day in September I had a brief letter from my mother, saying that my sister Dorothy had been killed in her ambulance in London and that Hugh Nowell had gone down with his submarine. (Mrs O'Borne lost her only son, Percy, a pilot officer, at about the same time.) My sister Audrey was living and working in London, and Dorothy was staying with her at her flat in Russell Square, and driving an ambulance for the borough of Holborn from a base in Moon's Garage. This was the beginning of the Blitz, and people weren't used to it: even the bravest were terrified. Lincoln House in Holborn had been hit, and Dorothy had collected injured people on a couple of journeys with her ambulance when it was time for her to return to base and have a rest. The girl who was to replace her on duty was literally paralysed with fear, squatting on the floor, frozen, unable to move or speak. I was told later that Dorothy tilted her tin hat at a jaunty angle and said she would do this girl's duty for her. She paused only to light a cigarette, and drove off to her death. The first one-ton bomb that fell on London fell on her ambulance and on a fire engine with seventeen firemen. There was, mercifully, no funeral: all that was found was part of a foot recognized by a blue sock. This was buried at Putney Vale Cemetery, where I had so often officiated, in a mass grave for Holborn civilian war dead.

Apart from my first experience of death as a small boy, this was the first death that had hit me where it hurt most. Of all my five sisters, Dorothy had been closest to me and my grief at her death was such that I knew nothing could ever hurt so much again. It was at least twenty years before I could speak about her without wanting to burst into tears. That Christmas, as Susan and I were doing our Christmas shopping on Dalton Road, I saw something in a shop window which caused me to say, 'I think Dorothy would like that...' and suddenly realized that the little girl who had shared my childhood Christmases was no longer with us. I burst into tears, and to Susan's great embarrassment could not stop sobbing for a long time.

Yana Hollowday, from whom I hardly ever received letters once I was married, wrote: 'Like a fairy into thin air, in the dawn and a flash.' Dorothy had been nicknamed 'Fairy' by her fellow students at teacher-training college, and I never learnt why. At their school, my five sisters pronounced their surname 'Vah-ruh' to rhyme with Lara, which is the way I myself pronounce it, but my father always made it rhyme with Sarah, and I suppose this version may have been corrupted to 'Fairy', as she was of average height and build and not at all elfin. She had been married for about six months when her husband went to sea and she moved to London. I think it was another six months before he returned to this country and collected her few belongings from Barton, where I guess he had a cool reception, because my father had put him beyond the pale when he married Dorothy without his prior knowledge and without having met him.

Whilst at Barrow I was offered my first benefice by Provost William Kay, of Blackburn Cathedral, who as Vicar of Blackburn had the patronage of most of the churches there. He offered me Holy Trinity, a huge cruciform example of Victorian Gothic, black with industrial smoke, standing impressively on a hill called, heaven knows why, Mount Pleasant. All the housing round it was poor, and most of it has now been demolished. When we went to look at it, Susan and I got on well with the Provost, who was to become a dear friend until his death many years later, but her heart sank when she saw the vicarage. It was built in the same blackened stone as the church, and had nineteen rooms and five cellars. It had been enlarged in the time of a predecessor, Dr Moffatt, who had had ten children but was succeeded by a Mr Thornton who had neither wife nor children, and he by Canon Perry, my immediate predecessor, who had been there for thirty-four years and had changed nothing during that time. A whole block was taken up by the vicarage, the church, the school, and the church hall. Only the church now remains, and it has been taken over by the National Trust. My successor built a red-brick vicarage in place of the huge stone one; it has recently been used as a worship centre.

Susan was now pregnant, and was happy to think that she would be more 'settled' in a vicarage, even such an enormous one, than as a curate's wife in a rented house. We moved early in 1942, and our daughter Felicity was born on 2 June with the invaluable assistance of 'Humpy', Nurse Humphreys, introduced to us by Anne Hopkinson. Humpy had always been resident midwife in Anne's family and had in fact brought Anne into the world. She was an immensely impressive and reassuring figure, and was responsible for the choice of name for what I think she said was her 200th baby. Susan and I had been disputing about the name in Humpy's presence. I had come out very strongly in favour of Xenia Yseult, which Susan thought outlandish. She herself wanted Rachel. She had the Londoner's tendency to turn an 'l' into a 'w', so I was able to sneer that I did not want my daughter to sound like a sneeze, pronounced to rhyme with 'atishoo'. 'I always think', murmured Humpy comfortably, bent over her sewing, 'that Felicity is a nice name.' At this, hostilities ceased. I still regretted not having a daughter whose initials were XYV, but when Susan said, 'We could add Mary, after your mother,' I said, 'And of course Dorothy' – and hastily left the room to hide in my study my still inescapable tears at the mention of her name.

Holy Trinity was very much a CMS (Church Missionary Society) parish, which in that part of the world meant that it was moderate evangelical, with a Cross but no candlesticks on the altar, coloured stoles but not eucharistic vestments for the 8 o'clock Holy Communion, Choral Mattins and sermon at 10.30, Sunday School at 2 and Evensong and sermon at 6.30. Whilst at Barrow I had preached for Alan Eccleston at Frizington in Cumberland and fallen in love with his Parish Communion/Parish meeting setup, so I was keen to institute the Parish Communion at 9.15 as the only Sunday morning service. But I knew I couldn't do this until I had won over the congregation, which was large and faithful.

Fortunately for me, my predecessor had become perfunctory over the years, which gave me an unexpected ally in the shape of Miss Dugdale. Miss Dugdale was a highly respected and devout little old lady who had taught in Sunday School so long that most of the present teachers had been taught by her when they were children or young adults. I didn't realize until afterwards that the whole fate of my ministry rested on her verdict on the new vicar. Since it was wartime, there was a blackout, and the unshaded electric bulb placed on the altar to allow the priest to read the service not only cast grotesque shadows all over the building but also infringed the regulations. So I was able to substitute two candles to enable me to read the Epistle and the Gospel. Several people sucked their teeth disapprovingly as they reported this to Miss Dugdale, who didn't always attend at 8 but never missed Mattins. My critics were silent as she raised a ladylike hand. (It came as a shock to me when I discovered that she was by profession a grocer, who was driven nearly mad by the task of weighing out a full two ounces of butter eight times from a pound when the government made no allowance for the fraction lost in the dividing and turning of the scale. Her own ration tended to disappear in giving full weight to her customers.) She had attended Mattins, which I was accustomed to take slowly and distinctly, bringing out the meaning of the text so that the Elizabethan language would not defeat those who hadn't been brought up with it, as I had, and it seems Miss Dugdale was enthralled to hear the familiar words lovingly pronounced, and everything done with great care and reverence. 'As long as 'e conducts the service in the way God meant it to be conducted, 'e can 'ave *ten* candles for all I care ... or stand on 'is 'ead!'

That settled that, except for the few diehards, one of whom was a churchwarden. I had pointed out to the Easter Vestry that the vicar and parishioners should agree, if possible, on two churchwardens of the parish, and only if they could not agree would the vicar choose one and the people the other. They preferred to do it the way they had been accustomed to, so I gave in, as I usually do when disagreements are academic and not on points of principle. I then proceeded to appoint as 'my' churchwarden Mr Reg Rozee, who was prepared to work loyally with me and who became a good friend right up to his death. In due course I was able to introduce the Parish Communion, parish meeting and parish breakfast. The 1928 Prayer Book allowed one to combine *shortened* Mattins with Holy Communion, thus making a service which had ingredients familiar both to those who liked Holy Communion every Sunday and to those who were brought up on Mattins. It was very scriptural, of course, having four readings in addition to the psalm and canticles. But it was a bit on the long side.

I enjoyed teaching regularly in the day school. I sought every opportunity to be with, and to encourage, the youngsters of the parish and those who had charge of them, without neglecting the influential groups of older people, such as the Young Men's Club, most of whose members were young when my predecessor was first appointed, and the Girls' Friendly Society, who had been girls many years before and who used to meet once a week in the large vicarage kitchen. They were a great help to Susan in understanding the Lancashire way of life and thought, and she became very fond of them and they of her. As a southerner, who until she met me had never been further north than Regent's Park Zoo, she found it more difficult to fit in than I did, because though I had worked in the south, I came from the north – not, heaven forfend, from Yorkshire, like my forbears, or there might have been a War of the Roses, but from North Lincolnshire, neutral in that war. Even I could not help when Miss Maud Smalley complained to Susan about people 'camping' at the back of the church after a service: her vision of people setting up tents and lighting camp fires was dispelled only by Mrs May Hindle, who explained that 'camping' meant chatting or gossiping. 'I'll go and camp her a bit,' meant 'I'll go and have a chat with her.' But I think she never understood that 'oo' meant 'she', and that therefore 'oo says' wasn't a question. It was at this time that, being now a mother herself, she became an active member of the Mothers' Union.

Naturally, of course, a great deal of time had to be devoted to our daughter. Though there was never any lack of pram-pushers or baby-minders, it was a hard task running a very large house and being an amiable and accessible vicar's wife and looking after a small baby with very little help from its father, besotted with the child though he was. This was war-time still, with its shortages and deprivations, blackouts and anxieties, but not, in Blackburn, much fear of being bombed. Having been through the heavy bombardment of Barrow-in-Furness, I didn't know whether to be amused or outraged when someone pointed out to me a corner where two small houses were missing, they having been destroyed in 'our blitz'.

Apart from playing the piano and the gramophone, and of course reading, I had not had a hobby. I don't remember how I came into possession of an old Zeiss-Ikon camera which took photographs on glass plates, not film, but it was certainly in the winter, because my first photographs were of the church when there was snow on the ground, which gave sufficient light for the photograph to be correctly exposed. I made a dark-room in one of the cellars, and with my training in chemistry found it very easy to master the techniques of developing and printing black and white photographs. With my knowledge of physics, I managed to make a workable enlarger from an old magic lantern by extending the distance between the plate and the lens with a long cardboard tube, and using bromide paper instead of contact paper, fixed to an easel at a distance. Although I had a safelight, by being systematic about where everything was placed, I could work entirely in the dark, until the moment came to

111

switch on my makeshift enlarger. It always gave me great pleasure to take a photograph of the bride and groom after a wedding, and nip down to the cellars while the official photographer was posing group after group, develop the plate, wash it a little, put it in the enlarger, put the plate back in water and the print in the developer, rush back before the official photographer had finished, and present to the bride an 8″×6″ photograph of herself and the groom, damp and not properly fixed, with the promise to supply a properly finished one in due course. Nobody at this period ever got a photograph of the wedding before leaving the church grounds except from me.

The young couples who came to be married had, of course, attended preparation classes at the vicarage, in the course of which I explained to them all they needed to know to make their sex life happy and successful. Nearly all of them found this helpful and welcomed it, but unlike Lincoln, few of them mentioned it to other people so I didn't get so many young couples from other parishes in Blackburn coming for sex instruction as I had had in Lincoln. However, the total number was sufficient for me to amass some interesting statistics over a period of six years. The most important of these concerned accurate knowledge of the whereabouts and function of the clitoris. Let's not waste our time on two places of decimals, but simply note that, very roughly, out of each five couples only one of the men and two of the women knew sufficient to be fairly sure of the woman having an orgasm. This was in spite of the fact that *three* out of five of the women (and of course five out of five of the men) knew how to masturbate. This meant that one out of five women, in thinking of her own sexual satisfaction, made no connection between that produced by her own masturbation and that likely to be produced on the honeymoon. They remained convinced that the movement of the penis in the vagina would automatically produce an orgasm without the clitoris being directly stimulated, which is not of course true except for a tiny minority of women who have such a sensitive clitoris that they respond to the 'drag' which, during coitus, pulls the hood of the clitoris rhythmically across the glans clitoris.

The only explanation I could think of for this anomalous behaviour was that women have been so terrorized by the church, directly or indirectly through their mothers, about 'not touching yourself down there', that they have not dared to reveal to their husbands what they knew about the manipulation of the clitoris, and thought

112

that if they didn't achieve orgasm the 'proper way' – that is, in intercourse – there must be something wrong with them. No wonder it came as a tremendous relief to the young ladies whom I instructed along with their fiancés to know that their clitoris was a gift of God to enable them to enjoy sexual satisfaction, with or without a partner, and any husband who was dubious about the effort involved could simply be labelled as one who didn't know as much about sex as the vicar.

One of my churchwardens, Cyril Brierley, was responsible for my engaging in a very rash escapade, which even in war-time briefly hit the headlines. His wife Betty's brother, James Isherwood, had married a nurse from Queen's Park Hospital, where I frequently visited patients, and had a son by her, whom I baptized. Moira Isherwood was a Roman Catholic but made no difficulty about Kevin being baptized in the Church of England and was apparently very happy in her marriage. It was therefore a shattering blow to the whole family when one day, with the child in her arms, she kissed her husband as usual before he went off to work as an ambulance driver at Queen's Park Hospital, but when he returned after work she and the child had vanished and there was a note to say that she had left him for good and he should not try to find her. He was distraught, and so was Cyril, and the two of them came to see me to ask if I would help them.

We felt pretty sure Moira would have gone back to her father in Mullingar, County West Meath. It would be difficult to get her, or more importantly the child, back from the Republic of Ireland, unless they, or he, could be smuggled across the border into Northern Ireland. They were asking me in effect to go to Mullingar secretly, without any Roman Catholic whatever in the Blackburn area knowing that I had gone, to persuade her to come back, or to let me bring the child back; and if she refused . . . They didn't specify, but I knew quite well what they had in mind.

Before departing, the missing wife had been careful to gather up every scrap of correspondence that she had had since her marriage, except one letter which she overlooked because it had been used as a bookmark. This letter was obviously one of a series from a nun, telling the girl that she had committed a grave sin in marrying a Protestant, and worse, allowing her child to be baptized a Protestant: unless she left her husband and brought the child to where they could both live as good Catholics she would undoubtedly go to hell. I think it was this relentless harassing of a girl I remembered as sweet and gentle in private life – she had been a very competent nurse – and plainly in love with her husband, as you had to be to make a mixed marriage in those days, which decided me to accept the challenge.

I needn't weary you with the elaborate arrangements I made to be absent without anybody knowing except my wife and those in the plot. Naturally, it came as a terrible shock to my parishioners when the news of my quixotic expedition broke at a time when any of them would have sworn that I was in my vicarage.

Arrived in Dublin, I stayed at a bleak hostel run by the Irish Church Mission, a very Protestant organization dedicated to luring Roman Catholics, and particularly priests, away from their allegiance to the Scarlet Woman. Though I felt even more ill at ease there than I would have done in a papal seminary, I knew they would not betray me, and they were able to put me in touch with a reliable Protestant taxi-driver and a trustworthy English children's nurse. I had to meet the taxi-driver in what turned out to be a genuine smugglers' den – a meeting place for drivers who specialized in unauthorized crossings of the frontier by unpatrolled routes. (This was, of course, long before the IRA.) I arranged that I myself would go to Mullingar by train, and my driver would pick up the English nurse and drive there and meet me at an agreed rendezvous at any time within an hour or two of my arrival there. In the light of subsequent events, I wondered whether my smuggler was as 'reliable' as the ICM assured me. It might have been difficult for him to avoid giving any clue to his cronies about the nature and purpose of the English toff he had been conspiring with.

On my way back, I had to pass along Upper Liffey Street, where I was accosted by a young woman offering to 'gam' me for ten shillings. Thanks to Yanine, I knew that the French verb 'gamahucher' meant 'to afford oral-genital satisfaction to a male', but was surprised to find that abbreviation of it in the mouth . . . on the lips . . . used by a Dublin prostitute. I declined politely and she followed me, reducing her price first to five shillings, and then to half a crown. (If you don't know pre-decimal currency, the prices were one half, one quarter and one eighth of £1 in the days when £1 would buy 400 cigarettes.) Just as we approached a corner, she hung on to my jacket, which I wrenched free just as her ponce sprang at me from round the corner shouting, 'Let go of my tart!' Before I knew what was happening, he punched me two or three times in the face, breaking my spectacles and knocking me down. I resisted the temptation to fight back, not wishing to imperil my mission, and picked up my specs and ran. I got away the more easily because the girl was angrily shaking her ponce, shrieking at him that he should have waited until she was gamming me before hitting me, because then she could 'have held on'. As I made my way back to the Mission, I reflected that a good argument in favour of not consorting with such women offering greatly reduced prices was that you would *not* find yourself having your face smashed in while your penis was firmly held by a strapping wench's teeth. Back at the ICM, I tended my wounds, cobbled up my spectacles, and had a very unrestful night in preparation for the next day's great adventure.

I felt very much alone as I got myself to the station with a single ticket to Mullingar. It was dark when I arrived there, and I had avoided getting into conversation with anyone *en route*. This was all, of course, strictly Secret Service stuff: I had to find my way around an unknown town without asking anybody, and be as unobtrusive as possible without arousing suspicion thereby. I had been given the name and address of a Protestant elderly lady who would be willing to put me up for one night provided I could get in and out of her place without being seen. She was unhappy about the whole arrangement, and I sympathized with her, because she had to live there and I would soon be leaving forever. I paid her well, and after 'tea' she opened up and entered into the spirit of the thing, giving me invaluable local information: yes, the girl was back with a little boy; the address was so-and-so, and I would find it thus-and-thus in relation to the station; the father was still a powerful drinker and unlikely to be home except at night; the road to the border was past such-and-such a garage, not far from the little bridge near which I had instructed the taxi-driver to wait with the English nurse in the back.

The following morning whilst I was going up the rather steep street towards the house, I saw Kevin playing on the pavement a few doors down from his home. He recognized me, and I was tempted to lead him to my taxi and get him over the border before his mother even knew an emissary of his father was in Mullingar. But however hard I tried to convince myself that Moira had done it to her husband so couldn't complain if it was done to her, I felt that I must talk to her and try to persuade her to come with me or, if not, to allow me to take the child. I still think I would have got clean away

115

with Kevin if I had hardened my heart, and it would have saved me a lot of grief, but I don't regret having taken him by the hand and gone into the house to be greeted with astonishment by his mother.

We men aren't nearly as aware as women of the standard of furnishing in a place we are seeing for the first time, but even I could not help contrasting the room I was visiting with the neat suburban house Moira had left.

I tried to persuade her to come back to Jimmy with me, but, although she spoke of him as though she missed him and indeed was still in love with him, she was adamant, and I was angry at the brainwashing to which she had been subjected.

She offered me a cup of tea, which I accepted, and as she stood up to get a cup from the wall cupboard, she was silhouetted against the window. Whilst we sipped our tea, I said casually, 'Fair's fair – let Jimmy have Kevin, and you keep the one in your belly.' She shrugged her shoulders and said, 'The Church wants them both.' That decided me to carry out the original plan.

She agreed to come for a walk with me before my train back to Dublin, and she pushed Kevin in a kind of pram. I managed to get us moving in the direction of the little bridge, and when we reached it I unstrapped Kevin and carried him on the pretext of showing him ducks on the water. While she too was looking at them, I suddenly sprinted across the bridge, both car doors opened simultaneously, I thrust Kevin into the arms of the nurse in the back and got into the front myself, and we were all set to drive over the border to Omagh when Murphy's Law foiled us. The car didn't start. When the driver finally got it going, Moira had caught up, and was hanging on to the door handle. The driver wanted to stop, I wanted to go on as I felt sure she would let go before we picked up speed and would not be hurt; however, the driver insisted on stopping, so I leapt out, dragged her away and half-carried her about twenty yards back, sat her down gently on a grass verge with apologies for manhandling her, then sprinted back to the car and this time off we went. I had calculated that by the time she got back to the Gardai (police) or to the presbytery, we should be too near the border to be stopped on a route that was carefully planned. What I hadn't counted on was that she wouldn't go back, but on to the garage from which she could, and did, telephone. The result was that shortly before the border two Gardai stepped from a parked car ahead of us and signalled to us to stop. My driver refused to try to get past them. One of the men drove me and Miss Fisher and the child (who was quite happy with her) back to Mullingar, and the other accompanied my driver.

This adventure would take up a disproportionate amount of my story if I were to go into more detail. The driver and the nurse were released as my innocent dupes, and I was charged with child-stealing. I was released on bail, and allowed to go back to England until the time of the trial. Needless to say, I was intensively questioned by reporters, who had quite a field day. One of them asked me why my face was bruised and my spectacles broken, so I told him that I had been mugged in Dublin before setting out on my mission. The result was that I was interviewed by a senior police-man, who gained my admiration by telling me that his men had already identified the couple who had attacked me, and that they would have a hefty period of imprisonment if I cared to press charges, but he would advise me not to do so in view of my profession and the fact that the accused would claim that I had 'sought bad company', which I thought a rather odd expression, worth memorizing. He strongly advised me to say that as a Christian I felt bound to forgive those who had injured me and therefore would not be pressing charges. In no condition to argue, having lost my voice (at that time my weak spot in times of severe hardship), I told him, though not for publication, that I did not as a Christian believe that we had any duty to forgive those who were not at all repentant. I never knew whether I had been betrayed, deliberately or carelessly, by my taxi-driver, but how did the Gardai get their car to a point only a few miles short of the border without passing us?

I arrived back to enormous gratitude from Cyril and Jimmy and their family, and the delighted attentions of the local press and photographers, the *Northern Daily Telegraph* (daily) and the *Blackburn Times* (weekly). To my surprise, I received a hero's welcome from my congregation, and even my few opponents, who had thought my two candles and my coloured stoles were leading them, vainly resisting, in the direction of submission to the Pope, now regarded me as an intrepid Protestant David challenging the papal might. I imagine Susan found the whole thing pretty distasteful, but could hardly say so when all her friends were praising me to the skies.

I eventually had to go back to stand trial, and of course Cyril and Jimmy came with me. A defence fund had been established in Blackburn and there were many generous contributions to it, so that in the end I was not completely ruined financially.

The Irish – Roman Catholic almost to a man, except for my

solicitors – were surprisingly nice to me, and the reason became clear when my counsel, Mr Nugent, in conducting my case made it clear that under Irish law it is the father who must say what happens to the child, and the mother must not take the child away from the father's care and custody, even if she is Roman Catholic and he is Protestant. Moira had had no right to do what she did, and however ill-advised his client was to take the matter into his own hands instead of allowing the inevitably slow process of the law to take its course, he was only trying to put right what had been put wrong, and should not be severely punished. 'Which of you,' he thundered, 'if, God forbid, such a thing should happen to you, would not go to your priest, as Mr Isherwood did to his, to seek his help? And which of you would not be amazed and delighted if the response of your priest was the same as the response of my client, risking his reputation, his freedom, perhaps even his life, in order to redress a wrong? Would you not be proud to have a priest like that?'

I was embarrassed by all this, but it seemed to do the trick, or something did, because I was found not guilty of child-stealing, since I had had in my pocket the father's written authority to repossess his child who had been illegally taken away from him. I was, however, found guilty of common assault, in that when my car was pursued by the child's mother, I had physically removed her from its vicinity. For this offence, I would be sentenced to six months' imprisonment, unless I would consent to be bound over to keep the peace for one year, which of course I did. I had to keep the peace only in the Republic of Ireland, which would not be difficult as I had no intention of visiting it again for many years. But the great triumph was that the court awarded the custody both of Kevin and of the unborn to Jimmy, who thanked the court, accepted the custody of Kevin, and stated with some dignity that he did not wish to deprive his wife who had deserted him of a child he had never known, and could not be certain was his.

I think I owe it to Anna Isherwood and to her mother to say that when I met Anna about twenty years later her resemblance to Jimmy was most marked.

You'd think there was enough drama in real life for me to be satisfied with it, but I had always enjoyed amateur dramatics. The parish hall at Holy Trinity had an excellent stage, and was much used for concerts and sing-songs to cheer people up in war-time, so it was easy to start an amateur dramatic group, whose performances were very well received by crowded audiences.

The most successful play I produced was called *Glorious Morning* (I forget the name of the author), about a totalitarian state in which a young girl had a spiritual vision and began to preach about it. She was encouraged and protected by her father, a stubborn old peasant (the part had been played in the professional theatre by that splendid old actor, Herbert Lomax). I myself, exceptionally, played a part in it: the scientist reluctantly drawn by the girl's prophecies away from his pro-State atheism. I haven't read it for forty-five years, but I remember it as a well constructed and moving play. Sometimes we did two one-act plays in an evening: amongst these were *Campbell of Kilmhor*, J. M. Synge's *Riders to the Sea*, Arnold Bax's *The Cloak*, and John Drinkwater's *X=0, a Night of the Trojan war* – a play it wasn't quite as dangerous to put on during the Second World War as it had been when it was first performed during the First.

The hall was also used for whist drives, dances, and such romps as those of Scouts and Guides, Brownies and Cubs as well as, of course, the Sunday School's overflow from the day school.

Susan now became pregnant again, and as the months went by, my scientific mind was rendered suspicious by the *rate* of growth of her circumference. If it's going to be a multiple birth, it isn't the actual size ('once round my wife, twice round a gasometer') that counts, but the fact that if twins double their size, the two of them together quadruple the volume. As the time of delivery approached, I felt convinced we were going to have twins, although there was no record of any twins in our family. An X-ray at the hospital a week before the birth was due revealed that Susan was carrying triplets. Naturally, the doctor hadn't wished to do an X-ray at an earlier stage for fear of damaging the foetuses, but when at last they felt it was reasonably safe, it was fascinating for me to see how you could tell how many offspring you were going to have by counting the backbones – the other bones simply made an indecipherable jumble, but the backbones curved clearly downwards towards three faintly discernible heads.

We already knew that dear old Humpy wouldn't be available, and it was just as well, because our doctor at that time, Dr Pendlebury, arranged with the authorities that we should be supplied with three Queen's Nurses by day and one by night for a month. We had nineteen altogether, and they were splendid girls.

119

We turned the north wing of the vicarage into a hospital, and sterilized sheets were hung at the entrances to it which few people were allowed to pass. One of the few was Susan's mother, who had come to keep house and look after Felicity.

At last the day came when the nurse on duty summoned Dr Pendlebury, and there began a period of hard labour for Susan and anxiety for her mother and me. Not knowing how long labour would last, I had to keep on with my duties. I came back to the vicarage at one point to find Susan's mother in the large kitchen, her ear glued to the wall. No, the delivery room was not on the other side of that wall: it was an old house, and there was a speaking-tube connecting the kitchen with the room above, where Susan and her entourage were. Emmy-Nell ('M-in-L'), as I always called her, invited me to listen, which I did briefly, feeling uneasy about this eavesdropping. I had heard one yell, and as I couldn't believe Dr Pendlebury was beating up the nurses I assumed this was Susan. It wasn't the fashion in those days, as it is now, for the husband to be present at the birth, and doctors and nurses in those days were happy that there should be no useless bystanders whose sterility was doubtful to say the least of it (if you see what I mean).

I was making myself a coffee when Emmy-Nell came and called me from my study and when I followed her to the kitchen her ear was once again at the speaking-tube. She let me take her place for a moment, and I heard the unmistakable sound of a baby's cry. It was five hours before I was called from my work again, which must have been a terrible time for Susan, but then the third one was born five minutes later, with the assistance of forceps. I was allowed to see Susan, briefly, and found her bearing up amazingly well after her long ordeal, but was shooed away after inspecting the three red-faced, yelling boys. It appeared that the first two were uniovular twins and the third one, with ginger rather than mousy hair, was a fraternal twin to the other two. They weighed $4\frac{1}{2}$ lb, $4\frac{1}{4}$ lb and $4\frac{1}{2}$ lb, so no wonder their mother was so huge, and got so tired carrying this great weight around.

It seems that uniovular twins are caused by the father, and fraternal twins by the mother producing two ova at once, so Susan and I were both 'to blame' for this particular variety of triplets. They were not Blackburn's only triplets: seventeen months earlier, three girls had been born at Samlesbury, and these I gathered were all identical. I never saw them and they never got together with my triplets.

Twins occur once in 80 births and triplets once in 17,000, but of course not all survive. I was told that to have triplet boys all surviving was one chance in about 2,000,000. As soon as the doctor permitted, they were constantly photographed, both for local and national papers, and photographed again when they were christened at Holy Trinity by the then Bishop, Wilfred Askwith. This time Susan didn't argue about the names: I selected three sets of three names and allocated one from each set to each triplet. The sets were the patron saints of England, Scotland and Wales; the three favourite disciples, Peter, James and John; and the three archangels, Michael, Gabriel, and Raphael. This meant that each boy had at least one name that wasn't at all outlandish and could choose a name which suited his avocation in due course. George Peter Michael was always called by his third name, and Andrew James Gabriel and David John Raphael were always called by their first names.

From the very beginning, Felicity Mary Dorothy was very much involved. At two and a half years old she was talking well, and told us that she was 'a chambermaid', because she was always running up and down stairs with a chamber-pot. She was very interested in her little brothers and liked helping to look after them.

Naturally, however, she didn't want to be forgotten. I remember one occasion when I was pushing the special pram we had had built which had two of the boys at one end and one at the other, and Felicity was walking along with me holding on to the handle. Every few yards somebody would stop and peer at the triplets with exclamations of admiration and delight – it was nearly impossible to get anywhere because of the constant interruptions. On one of these occasions, in a brief pause, Felicity was heard to say, 'Daddy has a little girl, too.' It tore at my heart, and I put the brake on and picked her up and walked away and made a great fuss of her while the triplets were admired by parishioners. Thereafter, I always ignored the triplets and concentrated on Felicity when the boys were being admired and praised. I saw quite a lot of her during the first month, when we had the three Queen's Nurses. But when they were withdrawn I had to do my share of taking care of the triplets. Susan would go to bed early and I would do the midnight feed, which as you may possibly know from experience involved feeding and changing and burping and potting; with three of them to do I would be lucky to get to bed by 2 a.m. Susan would get up to do the 6 o'clock feed whilst I caught up on sleep. We did, of course, meet at lunch-time. Even with all the help that was given by the Girls' Friendly Society and other parishioners, it was a difficult time, but the little boys were an immense joy to us both and to Felicity.

The triplets were born on 19 October 1944, so it was still war-time. Two things will illustrate this very well: I had to go to five different shops in order to obtain nine Chilprufe vests (each baby had to have one on, one to wash, and one spare), even though I had the necessary coupons; and when the GFS came to meetings at the vicarage, many of them would come bringing a huge 'cob' of coal wrapped in newspaper under their arms, and toss it on arrival into the coal-shed, saying, 'Yon's to keep triplets warm' (pronounced to rhyme with harm). I couldn't have imagined the people of Putney, kind though they were, being seen dead walking down the street with a lump of coal under their arm. No wonder we both loved the warm and unaffected people of Lancashire.

Our enormous house had the same coal ration as a two-roomed cottage – not that there were many of these; mostly the houses were two up and two down. It got very cold on the south side of the house, looking on to Cleaver Street, where I slept for a while to avoid disturbing Susan by returning from the night-nursery to her bedroom at 2 a.m. This was nearly the death of me, not from pneumonia, but because subsidence had caused the south wall of the house to lean very slowly and steadily outwards, until one morning it reached the point where the timbers supporting the ceiling finally had no ledge to rest on and came crashing down with such force that the two single iron bedsteads which were all we could afford for that room were bent into a V touching the floor by the immense weight suddenly falling upon them. Anyone sleeping there would have been cut in half.

I missed this fate by a few minutes, having gone downstairs to make a telephone call, in the midst of which came this enormous, terrifying crash. I told the person on the line that I would have to ring later because I thought a bomb had fallen on the vicarage. When I went upstairs and opened the door of the room in which I had been sleeping, it was all in darkness because the fallen ceiling and the timbers above it were propped at an angle from a few feet into the room up to a point where the ceiling had met the south wall, thus completing blocking the windows. The clouds of dust were so great that I quickly shut the door again to prevent the house from being smothered. It was a very expensive business putting a new ceiling in that room, fixed in such a way that the same accident couldn't happen again.

*

When I took over Holy Trinity, its fine Victorian neo-Gothic proportions were marred by a plethora of timber. Not only the west end but also the transepts were covered with galleries, giving the church seating for about 1200 people. Although congregations were very good they didn't even fill the floor level, and the only people who went into the gallery as a rule were teenagers getting up to whatever teenagers do want to get up to when not easily observed by the parson. I didn't want to deprive these youngsters of this hebdomadal joy, but wanted to reveal the proportions of the building which in any case was ripe for restoration. We decided to do the work of demolition ourselves, and then sell the timber, and I discovered once again that you can get the young men of the parish doing anything provided that you work alongside them. It was pretty exhausting, but at last it was done, the timber cleared away, and the church filled with scaffolding to allow the interior to be made good, where necessary, and repainted.

The opening up of the church prepared the way for me to put into effect a new idea I had had, namely a Harvest of Industry, or Industrial Harvest Thanksgiving. The rural Harvest Thanksgiving was, as in pretty well every church in an industrial area, still celebrated at that time with the fruits of the earth *not* grown by the parishioners nor by anyone within twenty miles or more. I pointed out to them that by buying cauliflowers and enormous vegetable marrows at the local greengrocer the industrial workers of the parish were not offering to God the fruits of their labours, and if the service was to be meaningful to them, they must offer that upon which they themselves had worked. I wasn't so foolish as to abolish the apotheosis of the pumpkin, but relied upon it being eventually overshadowed by whatever the fairy godmother turned it into, which in this case happened to be a whacking great boiler along with more portable items. I had for weeks impressed it upon the congregation that the only *things* that would be acceptable as offerings would be things on which the people presenting them had personally worked. Any items not easily saleable could be redeemed by the person or firm presenting them by an agreed monetary contribution, so that what was offered at the altar was without doubt *given*, and was for the time being in the possession of the church.

My parishioners worked in many different industries, the majority of them (at that time) in textiles. The nearest industrial enterprise to the church was very industrial indeed; Foster, Yates and Thom,

123

Boilermakers. I went to see Mr D. P. Welman, the managing director, and explained to him my idea for a Harvest of Industry. He mentioned that he was an agnostic, so I explained to him the Christian philosophy of work, illustrating it by quotations from the book Ecclesiasticus. 'Why,' cried Mr Welman, 'that's exactly my philosophy. The only difficulty is, that my men wouldn't be able to carry the smallest of our products, even if it would go through your door.'

He then took me and showed me the smallest boiler, which towered above us both. 'I'd love to have that one!' I enthused. 'And would you be willing to read the first lesson, from the chapter of Ecclesiasticus which I've quoted?'

'I'd be honoured,' he replied, and I quickly took my leave, leaving him to grapple with the problem of how to get the boiler into the church and out again. (They took down the doorway of the north transept, brought the boiler in, rebuilt the doorway, and reversed the process to get the boiler out again.)

Naturally, the boiler got us magnificent publicity, as did the other items that were too big to be carried and offered at the offertory along with the home-made bread, the home-made grape wine, and the alms.

I don't think anyone who was there will ever forget the opening of the service (shortened Mattins and Holy Communion) at our first Industrial Harvest Thanksgiving. I know I never shall. The sanctuary had been completely cleared, and during the first hymn two coopers from the brewery rolled two enormous barrels which they had themselves made all the way up the nave and into the sanctuary, where they up-ended them in such a way as to make the base of a makeshift table. They were closely followed by two carpenters with a door they had themselves made, which they laid on the two barrels to form a table. They in turn were followed by women weavers with calico or some other tough cloth they had themselves woven, with which they covered the table. Then came weavers with fine lawn or some similar material to serve as the fair linen cloth. Then there were ladies who had embroidered an altar frontal, and then a turner with candlesticks he had himself turned. And so on: I think you'll be able to imagine the rest.

A man who had opposed the offertory procession when I first introduced it said to me after the service, 'Now I understand what you were on about, Vicar, when you were so dead set on 'avin' that there offertory procession.'

Why do I have to explain the Harvest of Industry after more than forty years? Is it not something widespread, taken for granted in the industrial parishes of our country? You know that it isn't. Why isn't it? Is it not as valid as the Parish Communion, which, in however distorted a form, did transform the worship of the whole C. of E.?

I think the clergy are more to blame than their people. Some just could not get out of a rut and give a strong lead. Some didn't want the Holy Communion to be important. Some couldn't grasp the difference between industry and commerce, so that instead of having parishioners offering themselves and their work, they had them badgering long-suffering shopkeepers to give goods manufactured half a world away. There may have been a few Harvests of Industry around the country, but the only one I heard of, apart from that introduced by me at Blackburn and in my next parish, was at All Saints', Handsworth, Birmingham, where they doubtless had a wonderful display of hollow ware.

Every summer a team of clergy chosen from all parts of the diocese was assembled to go to Blackpool to take part in the Blackpool Sands Mission. We were put up in a small hotel and each day went in pairs to preach on different parts of Blackpool beach, supported by little groups of worshippers from the nearest churches. I remember that at the time of Hiroshima I was on this mission with, among others, a very powerful preacher whose name I forget. Everybody was talking in terms of a new era having begun that day, and I was particularly keen to get any details of the atomic explosion because of my interest in the matter when I had been studying under Soddy all those years before. I can still hear my preaching partner booming out to the very shaken crowd, 'Flee from the wrath to come!' He made it sound like the beginning of Armageddon, but I felt relieved by the Japanese surrender, and was convinced that millions of Japanese as well as Allied lives must have been saved by this *coup de grâce*. We weren't, of course, to know that the nuclear age would be one of peace between rival superpowers because of their possession of the A bomb, and later the H bomb, with the inescapably associated threat of mutually assured destruction if either side launched an attack.

Once the war was over (and I will not weary you with accounts of how we celebrated VE Day and VJ Day), it became possible to go abroad again. We decided to take a party of parishioners to the

125

Continent. This was before anyone had heard of Benidorm – there were few package holidays, and none of my flock would have made use of one – so those who enrolled for a holiday with me in the Netherlands regarded themselves, and were regarded by envious friends, as exceptionally adventurous. No matter that Albert Hindle and others had returned from more exotic places such as the Gold Coast (now Ghana) full of glowing accounts of the devoutness and kindness of the 'CMS Christians' there whom our Sunday Schools had for so long supported – this didn't count, because he had been taken there willy-nilly by the army and enjoyed its protection. Besides, the denizens of the Gold Coast spoke English, not double Dutch.

I've already mentioned to you my interest in the Old Catholics of Holland and elsewhere, so you will not be surprised to learn that I had arranged for the greater part of our holiday to be spent as guests of Old Catholic families in Rotterdam and Amsterdam. Thanks to Pastoor Raymaekers in Rotterdam and Pastoor Zwart in Amsterdam, our holiday would be as different from the average beach-centred package tour as it is possible to be. We were a group of Anglicans being entertained by Dutch fellow-Christians with whom we enjoyed full intercommunion. None of our lot, except myself, spoke any Dutch, but most of our hosts spoke at least some English. Even so, I was in fairly constant demand as an interpreter.

Molly Fletcher, a Sunday School teacher, had been deliberately placed by Pastoor Zwart with a family who had one son of about her age, Ap (short for Albert) Milet de Sant Aubyn, who had always been too shy to say boo to any girl. He managed to say more than that to Molly, with the result that later there was a wedding joining Anglicans to Old Catholics.

I had arranged that the party should make a day excursion to Liège, so that its members might boast of having visited two Continental countries. Almost everyone was happy to pay the additional cost, and I arranged for a responsible person to be in charge of the party in Liège during my absence elsewhere in Belgium.

I had at that time an obsession with railways and railway time-tables, and had worked out that almost immediately on arrival at the central station in Liège, Molly Fletcher and Susan and I could catch a little train to a place in the Ardennes called Hotton, and could spend several hours there before catching a train back to rejoin the party in Liège. The reason for the expedition to Hotton was that Molly was still grieving over her first boyfriend, killed in the Ardennes and buried at Hotton. She had never seen his grave, nor had she ever hoped to be able to do so. She hadn't the slightest idea of where Hotton was, and certainly not how to get to it from Amsterdam. I had borne this in mind when planning the trip, but had naturally said nothing to Molly in case it wasn't possible. When Ap began to show an interest in her, I realized it had to be *made* possible, as I felt sure she wouldn't be able to accept that her first love was dead unless she had prayed by his grave. She was fairly tearful on the journey to Hotton, but Susan was splendid with her, allowing me to 'be unsociable' and study the landscape through the carriage window.

Arrived at Hotton, I secured a decrepit taxi to take us to the war-grave cemetery and leave us there. We had already purchased provisions for a picnic, including a local cheese of the kind called '*carré*'.

There was no one in charge of the cemetery – I think it may have been some kind of holiday – but we divided it into three and took one section each, inspecting every white-painted metal cross, looking for the name of the soldier to whom Molly had been engaged. We checked and double-checked, and then Molly collapsed on the ground in tears, with Susan comforting her. I meanwhile, having noticed that not all the grave spaces had a cross, and that a few had been fairly recently cleaned up or even repainted, went off and found a hut in which this activity might have taken place. Sure enough, I could see crosses stacked in there through a crack in the boarding. I broke into this hut without a qualm, and eventually found the missing cross. I carried it to the part of the cemetery where there were most missing crosses, and set myself the task of working out exactly which was the correct grave for it. On every cross were tiny figures relating to plots, row, and position in row, and I was happy to be able to plant the cross on the correct grave. Susan cleaned up the grave space while Molly gathered wild flowers, and I found an abandoned pot to put them in and got my camera ready. Then Molly put the flowers by the cross and knelt there, and I took several photographs which showed both her and the wording on the cross clearly, and which doubtless she still treasures.

We then went into an adjacent field to have our picnic, but wherever we moved, we couldn't get away from the smell of pig dung, or whatever it was. Eventually we realized we were carrying the smell with us: it came from the *carré*. Upon realizing this, Molly collapsed in helpless laughter, which soon turned into convulsive sobs. I held her tight until they died down. At last she blew her nose, and announced calmly, 'Now I can say yes to Ap.'

The glowing reports brought back to Blackburn by those who had accompanied me to the Netherlands whetted the appetite of my parishioners for foreign travel, and when I announced the following year, 1948, that I would be leading a party to France, the trip was quickly oversubscribed. All travel was, of course, by train, ferry, and train again: we went first to Paris, where we stayed in a cheap and scruffy hotel in Montmartre, and after a night at a delightful hotel at Jougne near the Swiss border (to recover from the long train journey) we continued on through Switzerland to Martigny. Here we changed to the funny little train that corkscrews up the inside of the mountain, giving spectacular views, and then goes along to Chamonix, back in France. There we stayed, not for the ski-ing but for the mountain scenery and some gentle scrambling up the lower slopes of Mont Blanc.

Left: My paternal grandfather. Right: My father as a student

Left: My father at 75. Right: My adopted uncle J.E. Hine, Bishop of Zanzibar 1907

Left: The author with his Nanny 'Winnow'. Right: Aged two

Aged four with sisters Audrey, Dorothy and Rosalind

Corner of the vicarage drawing-room

Left: My maternal grandmother. Right: My mother

My sister Dorothy

With two brothers and five sisters (youngest boy not yet born)

Left: My sister Dorothy just before she was killed. Right: My mother and my sister Veronica

Wedding of sister Rosalind to Jack Nurcombe, showing my brothers Bill, Edmund and Hugh and sisters Veronica and Elgiva

Left: My portrait of daughter Felicity done with home-made enlarger. Right: With my wife and Vivien and Eamonn Andrews on set of *This is Your Life*

My son Michael with teammates Boulter, Grant, Carter and coach after breaking World Records for 4 × 800 yards and 4 × 800 metres at Crystal Palace

With my wife and our triplet sons

My wife, my daughter and myself with the triplets at christening of Charles
at St Stephen Walbrook

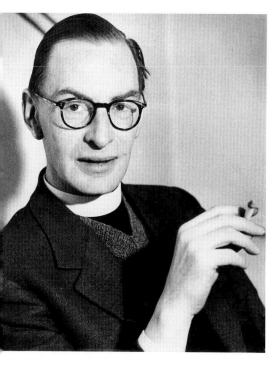

Left: Attack on apartheid in *Picture Post* had to show author was white, so Bert Hardy took this.
Right: My wife as Mothers' Union Diocesan President for Southwark

Visiting the Patriarch in Moscow 1955
with Roland Clark, Christopher Bourne *et al*

wife as Mothers' Union Overseas Chairman

HRH The Duchess of Kent, Royal Patron and Samaritan 1500/1/1 addressing annual conference

World's longest serving male Samaritan George 75/1/1 with the tools of his trade (map of the parish in background)

I took this photograph of my secretary Suzan Cameron for *Spotlight* Directory of leading actresses

5

MY chief extra-parochial activity was editing the diocesan magazine, *The Crosier*, and if it hadn't been for this chore it is unlikely that I would ever have met Marcus Morris. In 1947 I had the idea of calling together a conference of diocesan editors at Whalley Abbey to explore the possibility of improving our publications by syndicating amongst us articles by well-known writers whose services individually we would not have been able to afford, and I invited one person whose magazine was not diocesan but parochial, and to some extent nationwide – the Revd Marcus Morris, vicar of St James Birkdale, Southport. His magazine, *The Anvil*, resembled in format and in other ways, though with far fewer pages, the popular little magazine *Lilliput*. He and I took to one another straight away, and dominated the little conference, the other diocesan editors welcoming my lead and Marcus's flair. At an intermediate stage towards a full-blown society for Christian publicity we founded *Interim* as a vehicle for syndication of first-class articles. The first author I wrote to was C. S. Lewis, Fellow of Magdalen College, Oxford. I told him about our scheme and asked if he had in some drawer a manuscript he hadn't yet placed. He kindly sent me a brilliant little piece called 'Where the Shoe Pinches', and with his permission I changed the title to 'The Trouble with X', under which title it appeared in all our diocesan magazines. We each paid 7s 6d and C. S. Lewis got £10, which wasn't bad in those days.

Marcus and I continued our friendship, and I began to write for *Anvil*. No one who knew him would be surprised to learn that he had swept off her feet and married the beautiful and charming leading actress of the Southport Repertory Company, Jessica Dunning.

Marcus was disturbed by the fact that children were reading 'horror comics' produced for the kind of GI in this country who had been described as OK *except* that they were 'overpaid, overdressed, oversexed and over here'. Our American comrades-in-arms were very attractive to our young women whose boyfriends, if any, were overseas or at any rate stationed elsewhere, because they were a source of nylons, chocolate, chewing-gum and other delights unobtainable in war-time. Naturally, strip-cartoon stories designed to appeal to these characters sought to provide crude thrills by horror and violent sex, which was not precisely what English parents wished their sons, let alone daughters, to peruse. Marcus was convinced that what attracted the children to these horror comics was not their content so much as their telling stories by the method of strip cartoon. He was perhaps the first person to recognize this, especially the strip cartoon's importance to those who did not derive much pleasure from stories told in words only, because of their lack of imagination. He was convinced that there would be an immense demand for a strip-cartoon magazine telling the kinds of stories designed to appeal to boys rather than to adult but immature GIs. It was obvious that the boys would want adventure, such as cowboys and Indians, cops and robbers, as well as humour, and science, but it required Marcus's exceptional perception to realize that adventure must include adventures in space, and also the adventures of Christian heroes.

None of his dreams would have become possible but for his discovery of a brilliant artist in the same town, Southport, namely Frank Hampson. (I have written the story of Frank Hampson in the *Dictionary of National Biography*.) Frank was not only a most talented artist but also one who could tell a story compellingly in a series of pictures, and for a story about the future could devise space-ships and other equipment which had not been invented. Marcus engaged his services under the auspices of the 'Society for Christian Publicity' and set him to work on producing a dummy of the proposed magazine. The original provisional title was *Junior Post* and the hero of the space fiction was the chaplain to the Space Fleet, Lex Christian; but Christian heroes were transferred to the back page of the magazine and Hampson came up with Dan Dare, Space Pilot of the Future.

Although St James Birkdale was a rich parish, Marcus could not ask it to support this new venture as well as his expensive parish magazine *Anvil*, so I began writing many of the articles in *Anvil* free

130

of charge under different names, so as to save money for the new project, which I completely believed in. Though I could never have conceived what eventually the first issue of *Eagle* would look like, I felt sure that we were on to a winner, and only regretted that I didn't have the means to provide financial support except by writing free of charge. I did not know that I should shortly be removed from Lancashire to London, and that this move would turn out not to be a desertion of Marcus and his exciting project but in the truest sense of the word providential. I cannot now doubt that the creation of *Eagle* was part of the divine plan for Marcus, for me and for his other associates, at that time and later.

You will remember that Stephan Hopkinson had been responsible for my move from London to the north-west. Whilst I was still working hard to make Holy Trinity Blackburn a lively parish in the best traditions of the Church of England, Stephan had moved back to London again, as vicar of Battersea. This gave him the patronage of all the many churches in what had originally been the parish of Battersea, and he kept offering them to me as they fell vacant. One that attracted me was Christ Church, but I was too wrapped up in what I was trying to do at Holy Trinity to consider it very seriously, and not long after I inspected it it was destroyed by bombs and the vicar's mother killed. The war was over by the time Stephan offered me the one I eventually accepted in 1949, St John with St Paul on St John's Hill, Clapham Junction.

Here again I would be following somebody who had been there a very long time: Canon Kennedy-Bell had been vicar of Clapham Junction for twenty-eight years. St John's Church in Usk Road had been destroyed in the bombing but the school was left, so once again I would have a church school. Attached to the parish was the chaplaincy of St John's Hospital, Battersea, a hospital of 500 beds consisting largely of geriatric wards. It was the income from this chaplaincy which would make me very much better off than I had been at Blackburn, and this was important with four growing children. It was a wrench to leave Blackburn, but I felt I owed it to Susan to take the opportunity of being back in South London, within easy reach of her mother and the rest of her family and friends.

We were to have what by our standards was now a rather small house, with only thirteen rooms, at 68 North Side, Wandsworth

Common, just outside the actual parish. Susan and I were sitting on packing-cases in this empty house waiting for the furniture to arrive when we were visited by one of the churchwardens, Mr Peters. He broke the news to us that the income would be less than we had been told: £150 p.a. for the hospital chaplaincy instead of £450 p.a. This meant that I would be receiving less, instead of more, than at Blackburn. When asked why we had not been informed of this before leaving Blackburn, Mr Peters said disingenuously that the PCC didn't think we would come if we knew these depressing facts in advance, and they had wanted us to come.

This was rather rich, in view of the fact that at the PCC meeting to make the final decision the other churchwarden had said that the members of the congregation wished for my assurance that I wouldn't change anything. Since I didn't really want the job, I had been in a good position to say firmly that in the unlikely event of my agreeing to come, I should change *everything*. The congregation had dwindled until the numbers matched the times of the services (eight at 8 a.m., eleven at 11, and six or seven at 6.30 p.m.), so not changing anything would have condemned the parish to extinction, which I was not interested in doing. Unless, I said, I received a *unanimous* request to accept the benefice, and a *unanimous* undertaking to support me loyally in any changes I might think fit to make, I should turn it down. I had then retired to let them debate the matter, feeling fairly sure that I should be able to return to the parish I had come to love and my faithful flock; but on returning to the meeting I was told that they had agreed and begged me to accept the benefice.

I had often observed the truth of the words of the hymn,

> God moves in a mysterious way
> His wonders to perform,

and so it was in the matter of my reduced income. I was Marcus's London representative, and had a copy of the dummy which he had sent to a great many publishers without effect; in desperation he had authorized me to try to sell the project to the *Church Times*. They were totally uninterested in *Eagle* but very interested in *Anvil* and eventually bought it (the paper still owns the title). What they paid saved the *Eagle* project from going under. Whenever Marcus came to town I met him at a café in Piccadilly which no longer exists (how could they pay the rent and rates on that situation when a couple of clergymen not wearing dog-collars sat there for hours over a cup of

132

coffee?) and we constantly improved the proposed content of the magazine.

Eventually the beautiful day arrived when Marcus, still in Birkdale, received a telegram (yes, reader, there were still inland telegrams in those days) from Hulton Press, saying: 'DEFINITELY INTERESTED STOP DO NOT CONTACT ANY OTHER PUBLISHER STOP COME AT ONCE.' When Hulton decided to go ahead with *Eagle*, it was ironic that they spent more on promotion before a single issue hit the streets than the total capital of the *Church Times*.

Marcus and his family moved to the London area, and he was given an office in Hulton's then premises in Shoe Lane. I am telling you about the early history of *Eagle* in order to keep it all together, though of course at this time I was trying to revitalize my parish of Clapham Junction and giving only my spare time to *Eagle*. Marcus had assembled a staff, and he had other friends besides me working with him. My task, when *Eagle* first moved to London and started preparing for publication, was threefold: first to be Marcus's trusted adviser, secondly to write a text serial story, and thirdly to read about a quarter of a million words a week of unsolicited manuscripts submitted. I found the last a tedious task. I suppose I was too conscientious in reading on when it was already plain that the piece wouldn't do, remembering my own feelings on receiving rejection slips in my early days as a freelance writer. Only occasionally was anything usable.

Since there had to be *some* text in the magazine, in order that our readers might take longer to get through it and therefore feel they were having their money's worth (because strip cartoon takes less time per page to peruse than solid text takes to read) I was commanded to write a serial story. This I entitled *Plot against the World*, with a boy hero called Jim, his girl companion in adventure (no romance, of course) called Pru, and a heinous villain called Baron Figtree. I had what I still think was a good beginning, giving the readers the feeling that however humdrum their life, they might suddenly drop in (literally) on a fiendish plot: I had Jim walking along the street and suddenly falling down a manhole which someone had carelessly left open, and sliding down into a coal cellar, such as many people had in those days. Unable to get back up the chute again, Jim explores and finds other cellars including an empty wine cellar with what I described as 'bins' all along one wall.

133

These were like enormous stone bookshelves a yard high and with upright slabs a yard apart, so that there were cubic spaces in which to put bottles or cases; and Jim discovered that at the back of one of these, not properly shut, was a slab that pivoted vertically. He turned it, and crawled through into a room beyond (where, of course, plotting was taking place). Unfortunately, the artist who illustrated the story had never been in the wine cellars of Barrow Hall or been told by the cellarman that those shelves were called 'bins', so he drew barrels, which made nonsense of Jim's secret way into the underworld.

I was too busy to plan out the entire story, so I made it up as I went along, and didn't know at the end of each instalment how the obligatory 'cliff-hanger' was going to be resolved. It's not a method of writing I would now recommend.

It was a wonderful relief the day I came across two typescripts sent by the agents Pearn Pollinger & Higham which enthralled me, and which I felt sure would appeal strongly to the top 50 per cent of our readership, intellectually. I wrote immediately to the agents offering them double the usual payment, and asking to see any other stories by the same writer. He was then comparatively unknown, but is now famous. His name was, and is, Arthur C. Clarke. Years later, visiting him at his home in Colombo, Sri Lanka, and being shown all his amazing gadgetry, including a huge dish which brought him television pictures, I reminded him of his first story to appear in *Eagle*, 'The Fires Within'. He immediately went to a bookshelf and took out a paperback collection of his stories containing 'The Fires Within', and wrote a most generous appreciation of me on the flyleaf as his 'discoverer'. You won't be surprised when I tell you it was stolen. I have now stopped lending books from my library, except to my grandchildren (after noting the title and date), but I used to love to share books that had given me pleasure, and whether from carelessness or sheer dishonesty the damnable tribe of book bandits has deprived me of some of my greatest treasures.

My chief job on *Eagle* was as scientific and astronautical consultant to Dan Dare. With an Anglican priest brilliantly occupying the editor's chair, his staff weren't going to be surprised at another Anglican priest having such an appointment – they'd probably have been more surprised if they knew that I spent slightly more time doing sex therapy than scrutinizing the artwork for the Dan Dare stories to make sure that nothing he did, however far-out and astounding, was actually impossible (such as travelling at more than the speed of light), and that nothing concerning the *known* features of any planet was in any way inaccurate.

I remember on one occasion one of Frank Hampson's beautifully drawn pages showed Dan Dare stopping for a while on Mars, on the way to Venus, and visiting archaeological remains which indicated that Mars had been inhabited but was so no longer. This was itself a terrible mistake: there are so few planets in the solar system where *any* form of intelligent life might flourish, that to throw one of them away in this manner was improvident, to say the least. We were going to *need* Mars one of these days. (I didn't know then, of course, that I would one day be given the job of scripting a Dan Dare story on a much more difficult planet, namely Mercury.) However, it wasn't about the waste of a perfectly usable planet that I urgently rang Marcus Morris, but about the fact that the archaeological remains on Mars included a short flight of stone steps, and you could see as Dan Dare walked down them that they were identical to similar remains on earth.

'What's wrong with that?' enquired Marcus. 'I don't see what all the fuss is about.'

'You can't be expected to,' I said. 'That's what you keep me for. The gravity on Mars is so much less than on Earth that the relative sizes of treads and risers have to be totally different. With that low gravity, staircases would be much much steeper.'

Marcus said he would take my word for it and I assume took the necessary steps (joke). He was never one to gush, but I could tell he was secretly pleased, because he was a stickler for accuracy. Everything in his beloved strip-cartoon magazine (he wouldn't allow it to be called a comic) had to be of the best: superior paper, superior printing, superior scripting, superior art work, even a high standard of English except where it was necessary to show that a character was speaking dialect or was uneducated or foreign.

Nobody knew more than Marcus himself about how to make a first-class magazine which would appeal to its readership, and he had an amazing mastery of all the technicalities. He did, of course, surround himself with people he could trust to keep watch on certain aspects of the job: in addition to myself as scientific adviser, he had Ruari McLean for typography (in those days there were Dolcis shoe shops everywhere and Ruari's design for the name Dolcis was known to a million people for each one who knew *his*

135

name), James Hemming to keep watch on matters of child psycho-logy, and other less obvious behind-the-scenes people. Someone, for instance, had to answer letters from readers: *Eagle* was selling three-quarters of a million copies a week and each one was read by several people besides the purchaser – his brothers *and* sisters, and (often before him) his father. If any proof of Marcus's genius were needed, it was provided by the fact that he created a magazine which suited the boys for whom it was intended in every possible way, and also gained the approval of their parents and schoolmasters. I remember Marcus was delighted with a letter from one of two English Royal brothers saying that at their school a notice on the board had prohibited 'comics', but these junior Royals had gone to the head-master to say 'Oh, but sir! . . .' Whereupon an addition had been made to the notice: ' . . . except *Eagle*'.

Of course, all this time I was working hard to wake up my parish and to make a go of it. My work for *Eagle* had to be done late at night, and I went up to the offices in Shoe Lane only once or twice a week unless specially summoned. But as long as you remember that *Eagle* was not my main work, then or ever, as it was Marcus's, it will be convenient for me to tell you now something about *Eagle* in those early, exciting days and how it came about that I discovered, or rather Marcus discovered, the unusual talent which was to trans-form completely my activities as a writer for the rest of the twelve years that *Eagle* continued under its creator's editorship.

You can find elsewhere the story of Marcus and his other associates in proper chronological order, but this is *my* story, not the story of *Eagle*. Indeed, at the same time that I'm writing this, Marcus's daughters are writing his biography and you may be sure that anything I am telling you I will already have told them.

For me, the great turning-point came when one day Marcus took me to lunch at the Ivy, a restaurant then favoured by many in what used to be Fleet Street who had fairly lavish expense accounts. This was intended purely for us to have the pleasure of being together, but it wasn't long before we got to talking shop. After a while he was suddenly plunged deep in thought, and as everybody eats faster than I do, I didn't interrupt him but went on enjoying victuals of a standard to which poor parsons are not accustomed, accompanied by some very decent claret. (By the way, do you share my disgust at the habit some journalists have, when describing a banquet, of writing: 'Boeuf en Croute Wellington *washed down* with Vosne Romanée'? They have picked up the cliché – just as, when cub reporters, they learnt to conclude the report of the wedding by saying, 'Mrs Thistlethwaite *presided* at the organ' – without stopping to visualize the horrid picture of eminent persons filling their mouths with meat and two veg and, whilst it is half chewed, washing it down their gullets with huge swigs of a wine that should be sipped rather than gulped.)

I was savouring every delicious mouthful, and sipping appreciatively at my St Emilion, when Marcus suddenly barked, 'Have you ever read the Acts of the Apostles?' That's the way the more flippant clergymen address one another, and I replied straight-faced, 'Of course, I did it for Divinity Subsid.' This, though meant as a piece of persiflage, was in fact true: for Higher Certificate (which preceded what are now called A levels) I did physics, chemistry and mathematics with divinity as a subsidiary subject. He then explained to me that Frank Hampson was on the verge of a nervous breakdown through overwork. He had been scripting, and with his assistants drawing, two pages of Dan Dare plus the back-page story of St Paul entitled 'The Great Adventurer', and had said to Marcus that it would be a great relief if he could get someone else to script the rest of the current back-page story and the whole of the next one. I said I'd have a bash, and he assured me there was no hurry – the following morning would do.

I began by studying the proofs of the back pages which hadn't already appeared in the paper, reread the Acts of the Apostles, and decided that another four or five instalments would finish off the story neatly. I made a tentative decision about how much of the story I intended to cover in the next instalment, and sat down at my typewriter at about 11 p.m.

I didn't sit long. Having typed 'The Great Adventurer' at the top of the page with the episode number and my name, the word CARTOON at the top of the left-hand half of the page and CAPTION at the top of the right-hand half, and then 'Frame 1', I got up and began pacing backwards and forwards with my eyes shut, occasionally banging my forehead with my fist. I was seeing the story in my mind's eye in 3D and in colour and mentally walking around this visualization to get the best angle on it. Nobody had told me to do this: it just seemed to me obvious that a strip-cartoon story was not a written story which someone then illustrated, but a story which was thought in pictures, with the minimum amount of text in speech

137

balloons or thought-clouds or captions. It seemed to me that unless you could vividly imagine the story, you couldn't script it.

When I, or any other of the rare breed of visualizer-scriptwriters, are telling a story in pictures, we see the pictures very clearly in our mind's eye, and take a series of snapshots. Of course, if I were scripting a film, I would be specifying moving pictures.

So when I've finished pacing around bashing my forehead and seeing the story unfold behind my closed eyes, I sit down at my type-writer and I begin typing on the left-hand column headed 'cartoon'. For each 'frame' I type the angle of the shot, the distance of the shot, the relative position of the characters, their gestures, facial expressions, clothing, weapons, implements, details of any architecture or landscape or foliage, and if relevant the nature of the source of light and the direction of any shadows. When I move on to the next frame, I have not forgotten exactly how the previous frame looked in my mind's eye, because I have filed away somewhere in my mind an outline of the entire page of 9, 10 or 11 frames. The whole page is more exciting if there is a variation in distance and viewpoint and angle. These variations are not put in arbitrarily, but in accordance with the dictates of the story. You don't move arbitrarily and un-thinkingly from a medium shot with two or three characters, to a distant shot showing them in the middle of a crowd, to a close-up show-ing the face of one of them speaking, scowling, laughing, sneering — everything is calculated to draw the reader's attention to what it is important for him to grasp. If, for instance, two men are talking, and one of them is going to pick up a coin surreptitiously behind his back so that the first one doesn't see this, you would show the two characters half length with the hand of one of them approaching a coin on a table or shelf behind, and then in the next frame you would zoom in on the hand and the coin in a close close-up.

You may be wondering where this ability to visualize in 3D in colour came from. All the time I was working for *Eagle* my mother was still alive, and one day she was talking to me about my work in a mildly disapproving way. She evidently thought it was *infra dig* for a clergyman, not to mention an Oxford graduate, to be writing for what she persisted in calling 'comic cuts', which was the name of a blotchy children's strip-cartoon publication which had existed, if I remember rightly, since my childhood, though naturally I hadn't read it, being too busy with Dostoevsky's *Letters from the Under-world* and similar juvenile reading. I explained to her about visuali-zation, just as I have explained it to you, and said it could only be done by people who had this gift of seeing things very clearly in their mind's eye. 'Doesn't everybody?' enquired my mother innocently. I then realized that this was one more thing which I had inherited not from my academically brilliant father but from my dark horse of a mother.

I felt it a great honour to be scripting for Frank Hampson, the most brilliant strip-cartoonist there has ever been. But it wasn't only an honour: it was also extremely well paid. As I told you, I had suffered a drop in income on moving from Blackburn to Clapham Junction, but now I was able to live well on my *Eagle* earnings and provide for my family, using my benefice income to pay a secretary. Naturally, my brethren in the other parishes in the Deanery of Battersea thought it was most eccentric for a clergyman to employ a secretary instead of a curate, but I explained to them that if I had a curate I would be chained to my desk while the curate did the pastoral work among the people committed to *my* charge, whereas I could do my own pastoral work by chaining my secretary to my desk and letting her deal with all the boring admin and correspondence. The question was solved to my brethren's satisfaction when one of them called at the house when my wife and I were both out and had his enquiry dealt with very competently by Dionne Gale; he reported back that the sight of her left him groggy and stammering. She was a stunningly beautiful girl, very restful on the eye when one was dictating, but not as brilliant at shorthand as her successor, an elderly lady who lodged near the church and turned the vestry into an office. She would have been ideal if her typing had been able to keep pace with her shorthand. It was an old Olivetti typewriter which you probably can't visualize, but I could type on it with two fingers, and thumbs on the space bar, faster than she could. Unfortunately, after only a few months she died suddenly in her bath. She was Scottish and very well educated, with apparently no family or friends, and I wish I had been kinder to her. *Her* successor was Vivien Prosser, who worked in the vicarage as Dionne had done.

None of my secretaries had anything to do with my scriptwriting. This could only be done late at night when I was uninterrupted and could concentrate on the very exhausting process of visualization.

Marcus's choice of St Patrick for the next back-page story really put me on my mettle. It was difficult for Susan to understand, when I sat with a glazed look, that I was working hard; she considered that if I 'wasn't doing anything' it was little enough to ask that I should 'be sociable'. Alas, I am not a sociable person. If we had people in, she would have to find an opportunity to hiss at me, 'You were miles away – come back! – be sociable.' Needless to say, she was very popular in the parish, making steady progress upwards in the Mothers' Union and becoming, not long after, Diocesan President for the Diocese of Southwark, which was the biggest step towards her becoming eventually, years later, Central President, which means President for the whole world.

A very exciting thing happened in the course of my scripting St Patrick. I found that he had been born at Ailclyde, which we now call Dumbarton, of a Roman patrician family, and that he and his younger sister Lupait had been captured by bandits and taken to the coast of Antrim, where they were sold into slavery. After six years, Lupait died of ill treatment and privation, and Patrick escaped from Antrim. After many adventures which don't concern us now, he eventually returned to his birthplace and in all his subsequent adventures he is accompanied by 'his sister Lupait'. How come, when she had died many, many years before? No certain solution to this problem could be found by scholars poring over musty tomes. They mostly engaged in intricate manoeuvres with the chronology. It needed a visualizer to solve the problem.

When I came back to Ailclyde after an absence of many many years (naturally, when I say 'I', I mean Patrick, with me looking through his eyes), the first person I saw walking down the street towards me was Lupait, the same age that she had been when she was with me in Antrim. I am not looking up the final artwork as I tell you this, but simply remembering my creative process. 'Lupait, my little sister!' I shouted, and she flung herself into my arms. When we got to our family house, our mother greeted her by the name 'Tigris' and, forcing myself to think with my head instead of my heart, I realized that this girl, the image of my beloved martyred sister Lupait, had been born long after we were enslaved. I planned to go back to Ireland and convert the people there to Christianity, and Tigris said that she would go with me, would share my work for the rest of her life, and would take the name 'Lupait' because she would be doing what dear Lupait would have done if she had not died when she did.

All this simply means that to tell a story about an historical character well, you have to get inside the skin of the character and feel his or her experiences as if they had really happened to yourself.

As staff scriptwriter/visualizer it was my duty to visualize any script the editor wanted drawn for the magazine, and I often found

140

myself doing scrappy bits or short series which didn't give me the satisfaction I got from the back page. One such, which I remember, was entitled 'It Couldn't Happen, But It Did', rather along the lines of Ripley's 'Believe It Or Not'. It was an immense labour *finding* incidents which could be scripted under this heading, as they had to be veridical. I remember my favourite one was of someone who had jumped out of a blazing aircraft at 20,000 feet and landed unharmed in a deep snowdrift. Believe it or not!

I didn't always do the back-page stories for *Eagle*, though I think I did every one that was drawn by Frank. The existence of *Eagle* inspired artists and scriptwriters to do serious work. Although Marcus's instinct for what the boys would like was infallible, Hulton Press did arrange for a market-research survey of readers' preferences to be done every fortnight. The researchers listed every single item in the paper, including the advertisements, and then they would ask the selected 2,000 children to say of each item whether they were very interested in it, quite interested in it, not very interested in it or not interested at all. The first, minus the fourth, had added to it half the second minus the third. The back-page Christian adventure stories were almost invariably fifth in popularity out of thirty-two or so items, beaten only by Dan Dare, cowboys and Indians, cops and robbers, and Ashwell Wood's exploded drawings. I can't resist telling you at this point that when *Eagle*'s first sister paper *Girl* appeared, the back page was always by me, with different artists, and was always top in popularity – apart from the week that 'Belle of the Ballet' started, when all the little balletomanes managed to push that strip a decimal point ahead for just that one issue. But I mustn't tell you now about the sister papers or the annuals or the carol services, because we have already gone sufficiently out of chronological order.

For the first three years of *Eagle*, I was still vicar of St Paul Clapham Junction, and trying to make my inner-city parish useful to at least some of its inhabitants. I made a deliberate decision to concentrate on the young people, because the old people had, as I toughly put it, 'had their chance – if they hadn't been converted by now they never would be'. And they were unlikely to give up attending, the few who did, because their attendance had become a habit – a good habit, in my opinion, but there was obviously no need to stand on one's head to attract them.

Next door to the church was the Hughes Memorial Hall, used for the meetings of every kind of church society and for dances and jumble sales and nativity plays, as well as for the youth club. There was a tendency at that time for gangs of young fellows, sometimes accompanied by a few girls, to go round both church and secular youth clubs and entertain themselves by disruptive behaviour or even terrorizing the members. My youth club was beginning to flourish when I heard on the grapevine that the most dangerous, or at least most feared, of the gangs was going to wreck it. I told my members I didn't want any heroics from the boys nor cold-shouldering of the intruders from the girls. If it comes to a fight, I said, we haven't a chance. Let us see if we can make being in the club more entertaining than smashing it up. They agreed it was worth a try.

So when the dreaded evening arrived, suddenly the girls were very noticeable and the boys not, and the invaders found themselves being invited to dance, whilst their leader, a pasty-faced young fellow with a shock of carroty hair, was greeted by me. I welcomed him and his companions and tried to discover what he was interested in. It turned out that he had an unexpected love of opera. I had in fact an operatic record with me, as well as some other classics, which I occasionally inflicted on the members instead of the eternal dance music they never seemed to tire of, and I told Carrottop I'd like to play him something. When the dance record ended I put on 'O Mimi tu piu non torni', sung by Koloman von Pataki. There was considerable grumbling among the dancers, both 'ours' and 'theirs', which seemed to unite them a bit, but nobody was going to start smashing the place up without word from their leader – and lo, he had been deep in conversation with the bloody parson, and now was listening rapt to a dreary, boring record the said parson had inflicted on the company.

In those days, of course, records lasted only three minutes, but even so, I took it off half-way through and said to him, looking him squarely in the eye, 'I guess we'd better let them dance again – we don't want a riot, do we?'

'I can't understand them not liking that,' he complained. 'I've come to the conclusion they just don't *listen*.'

'But you're different,' I said, 'and that's doubtless why you are, I gather, the leader of the gang. I'd like to invite you to bring them all again next week.' This was a new experience: all the other clubs had been trying to think of ways of keeping them out or fighting them off. Most of them became regulars, and no, they did not start attending church, or at least not immediately.

You will not be surprised to hear that I not only introduced the Harvest of Industry into my new parish, where it was more difficult because there was less industry and more population, but also the Parish Communion followed by parish breakfast and parish meeting. Curiosity about the new vicar and the new service brought a number of lapsed churchgoers to join the eight parishioners displaced from the 8 a.m. service and the eleven parishioners displaced from the 11 a.m. service to make a sizeable congregation at 9.30. It was then up to me to make them want to come again.

The people who could always be counted upon to be there were those who were responsible for something: singing in the choir, reading a lesson, taking the collection, doing the offertory procession, ringing the bell, cooking the breakfast. I decided to increase enormously the number of jobs, and to request members of the youth club to volunteer for these, initially once a month. You may find it hard to believe that in the end I created forty-four jobs to be done at the Sung Eucharist, and I decreed that any job allocated to a person who did not turn up, or who did not turn up in time, just would not be done. (I guess I was a fairly bossy person then. Perhaps I still am.) For instance, if the bell didn't summon you to worship, the bell-ringer hadn't come and no one else was allowed to touch it. If the two persons welcoming the congregation as they arrived didn't turn up, the congregation didn't get welcomed. If the people handing out books didn't turn up, the congregation had to find their own. If the candle-lighter didn't light the candles, the candles remained unlit. If the person collecting the intercessions didn't come, there were no intercessions of a special nature that day. This meant that everyone given a job felt a sense of responsibility and knew he or she would be missed – not in the easy, insincere way that people say, 'Oh, we did miss you', but *genuinely* missed, with some disappointment or even exasperation. (Of course, I had a supply of wafers and wine so that in the unlikely event that the person baking the bread or offering the wine didn't turn up in time, the congregation and myself would not be deprived of the Sacrament.) Before long the Sunday morning congregation averaged a hundred and four, the majority of them young, and the majority of *those* previously unconnected with the church. I know this is not a very impressive number, but it was an improvement on eight at 8, eleven at 11, and six or seven at 6.30 p.m.

*

143

Mention of the Harvest of Industry reminds me of two other things I want to tell you, one of which is that we had the ordinary (rural) harvest thanksgiving as well, and balanced it and made it meaningful by observing Rogation Sunday in the old way – that is, by going around the fields singing a litany in procession and praying for God's blessing upon the growing crops. Naturally, we didn't do this in Battersea, but in Surrey, by making a connection with the church at Limpsfield Chart. Our congregation went there in what I was brought up to call a fleet of charabancs, and we felt sure that our rural brethren would 'doubtless come again with joy, bringing their sheaves with them'. Indeed, they did: their arrival *en masse* for our harvest thanksgiving later in the year made it real for us and allowed us to return their hospitality.

The other thing the Harvest of Industry put me in mind of was that we were sufficiently industrial to have some chance of raising funds for the church by levying a Church Rate on business premises in the parish (and on any private householders who were willing to contribute in this way, though of course a Stewardship Campaign was more appropriate for private individuals and we used that too). It was the church treasurer, Douglas Drakeley (whose wife Dorothy was a great help to Susan with the Mothers' Union) who first drew my attention to the Act of Parliament of 1919 and the provision in it for the churchwardens of any parish to levy and demand and collect a Church Rate. This Act of 1919 is commonly called the Enabling Act; it set up the National Assembly of the Church of England, known for short as the Church Assembly, now replaced by the General Synod. The whole democratic structure of the Church of England dates from 1919, and the Church Assembly was empowered to enact legislation which would be made law by Parliament unless Parliament felt there was good reason to refuse in a particular instance. Before 1919 the Church was not democratic at all: the business of the Church was carried on in each parish by the incumbent and his two churchwardens, and Parochial Church Councils did not then exist.

There had in the old days been a compulsory Church Rate which the incumbent and churchwardens could levy, demand and collect on rateable properties within the bounds of the parish. You may imagine how much this was resented by ratepayers who did not belong to the Church of England, and even more by those who weren't Christians at all, such as Jews. (We didn't at that time have any appreciable number of Muslims.) The idea of committing

144

people to prison for not paying a rate which they conscientiously felt obliged to refuse to pay troubled most people in the Church, and there was a very strong and widespread feeling that there ought not to be any penalties whatsoever for non-payers. The Enabling Act of 1919 took account of this feeling by substituting a Voluntary Church Rate for the compulsory one, but it remained a Statutory Rate which was not requested or begged for but levied, demanded and collected. The choice of the word 'voluntary' was perhaps unfortunate in that some people took it to mean that it didn't matter whether you paid it or not; that without any conscientious objection you could freely decide that you'd rather keep the money, since there was no penalty for non-payment. But of course the Church would have been very ill-advised to accept this interpretation because one enormous advantage of a Statutory Rate which you did not go cap in hand for but demanded, as you were authorized by Parliament to do, was that the Rate could be paid out of your gross income before tax, and not out of your taxed income as would be the case if you were making a charitable donation. It was chiefly business firms which benefited from being able to pay the Church Rate in the same way as their general rate or water rate, as part of the expenses of running their business. Private householders didn't have the same incentive to welcome it, but the Church Rate worked well enough in my parish at Clapham Junction to give me the necessary experience for its full-scale application in my next parish, which I shall tell you about later.

Life was so busy in 1950 that I am afraid I neglected my friends and my brothers and sisters, to whom I always felt very close even if I didn't see them for a while. You will remember how shocked I was by the death of the sister closest to me, Dorothy, killed driving her ambulance in London in 1940. The next closest to me was my youngest sister, Veronica, who had married a rising young actor called Frederick Gibson. He had played the lead in *Young Woodley* on the West End stage, but his theatrical career was interrupted by his being called up into the RAF. After the war, they went to live in Frognal Lane, Hampstead, and had two children, Simon and Susan. Veronica and I were, of course, at opposite ends of London, but I deeply regret not having made time to visit her more often.

The hardships of her life seem to have been responsible for her

145

going down with tuberculosis, and she was transferred from a London hospital to Harefield, where she had a pneumonectomy. I regularly visited her there, where she was wonderfully brave and patient, but had obviously barely survived the massive surgery involved in a pneumonectomy at that time. She told me that in the course of the operation her oesophagus had been damaged, and that this did not readily heal, the only possibility being development of 'proud flesh' around the wound, which apparently didn't happen.

Regular visitors learn their way around a hospital, and we parsons are particularly unhampered by visiting hours because we must be free to visit our parishioners at any time (except when they are actually being operated on or having a bed-pan administered). So I arrived one day at the door of her little ward without having encountered anyone. Two nurses were doing something difficult to interpret with an awkward thing covered with twisted blankets which they propped up, turned, laid prone, up-ended, breathing hard with the effort. I backed away out of sight on tiptoe, feeling instinctively that I was intruding on nursing intimacies in which I could have no part. Only when I was round a corner did I realize that the thing they were engaged with was the corpse of my sister. A message had been telephoned to my home about her death, but had not arrived till I was already on the bus for Harefield.

When the nurses called me in, the body was composed and prepared for display: for some hours it would bear an adventitious resemblance to the person who had inhabited it, and it would be a mercy if it were hidden from sight before decomposition had set in to a degree which could not ignored. The sweet, brave, eager spirit of Veronica was no longer there, and could not be sought in those mortal remains, in that ward, even in her home or anywhere upon earth. One could be close to her only in memories, and in prayer to the Father of all of us in Whom, living or dead, we all live.

'Doesn't she look lovely?' whispered one of the nurses, and I did not correct her. Hospital staff, like funeral undertakers, are accustomed to dealing with bereaved persons whose theology is even shakier than their own, and find it convenient to use the personal pronoun instead of the impersonal 'it', for the same sort of reason presumably that sedatives are sometimes given to the bereaved to postpone their realization that someone they have cared about has actually *died*. I said the commendatory prayers by the body, and then went back to my duties, one of which was of course to speak with Veronica's husband. It was 4 July 1951, and a few days later I

146

conducted the burial service in Hampstead Cemetery, which I have of course never visited since. As far as I know, Veronica had never been there.

I didn't cry as bitterly or as long as I had for Dorothy, not because I loved Veronica less, but because the heart's scar tissue is less sensitive than the not-yet-wounded heart.

Derick (his own abbreviation of Frederick) arranged for Simon to be cared for by one of his family, and Susan and I took little Susan to grow up for about a year with our triplets.

You may be wondering what was happening to my family whilst I was busy all day and part of the night with my various activities, some of which, like daily visits to the wards in St John's Hospital, weekly visits to teach in my church school, St John's in Usk Road, and weekly attendance at the Battersea Rotary Club, I haven't even mentioned. There was a happy day early on in my time in Battersea when many press photographers recorded my leaving my vicarage hand-in-hand with my five-year-old triplet sons, taking them to their first day at my church school. My father had insisted on sending me to one of his two church boys' schools for a couple of terms in order to show the parishioners that he thought the schools were good enough for his own children, and I felt it right to do the same. Unfortunately, times had changed, and the school wasn't even like the one at Holy Trinity Blackburn, having classes of forty or more and a fair proportion of pupils who didn't want to listen. At one stage I engaged my youngest brother Bill (later to become famous as headmaster of the then happily old-fashioned school of St Mary Bryanston Square) and his wife Phyl, also a teacher, but even they couldn't make up the gaps in my poor sons' education in the conditions they found there, and eventually we sent two of them away to a prep school where we hoped they would be as happy as Felicity was at Norland Place, Holland Park (they weren't).

This is my story, not my children's, so I shall say no more about them at this stage except that they loved to come with me to church and Sunday School, but best of all to visit the hospital. At that time, children were strictly prohibited at St John's Hospital, Battersea. The geriatric cases who filled most of the wards could see their grown-up children and grandchildren, but not little ones, so they never saw a child from one year to the next until I began to take my children, particularly the boys, on visits to the geriatric wards. The effect was remarkable and heartening. The glad cries of, 'Come here, my little darling!' and 'Don't miss me, you pretty boys!' rang out from most of the beds, though of course there were some patients who didn't know what was going on. You might think the little boys would have been put off by old crones cackling through toothless mouths and clutching at them with eager hands, but they weren't. They didn't, of course, like being kissed, because boys of that age don't like being kissed by anyone, but they ran happily from bed to bed, standing politely just out of reach where possible, and answering the flood of questions directed at them. The old women enjoyed their visits more than the old men, but I was surprised at how many of the old men were charmed by them. I didn't take them to the acute wards, where saying prayers or conducting a service for the whole ward was a better way to help the patients.

If you've got the impression that at this period I was as busy as a one-armed juggler, you won't be far wrong. Indeed, the Parochial Church Council began to feel that I should have some help, and I offered a Title to a young man who had gone from Cambridge to Wells Theological College, Roland Clark. He and his wife Norma were a great help in the parish. I can't have done him too much harm, for he went on to be a successful clergyman in Somerset, became a Prebendary, and retired in 1988.

One really needed an annual holiday in those days. In 1949 I took my holiday touring Yugoslavia by train. It had recently been opened to visitors, but nobody much wanted to go. Susan and I had always had our holidays together, but she had no wish to go to Yugoslavia and was not very happy about my going. I've no space to tell you about my adventures there. When you have a young family, holidays are difficult to arrange and also likely to be expensive. We parsons can sometimes overcome both these difficulties by doing a 'locum', short for the Latin *locum tenens*, where you 'take the place' of another clergyman and do his work and live in his house. One such 'busman's holiday' we had in the summer of 1953, when I took charge for a month of the English church at Knokke on the Belgian coast. The congregation, of course, was either English or Belgian wanting to improve their English, so I didn't get much opportunity to speak Flemish, but the children thoroughly enjoyed their taste of Abroad, a less common experience for children in those pre-package holiday days than it would be now.

6

WHILST I was in Knokke I had a cable from the Worshipful Company of Grocers of the City of London, inviting me to apply for the benefice of St Stephen Walbrook, which had been in their gift for centuries. At that time the City was almost the only part of London I didn't know well. Susan was unenthusiastic about leaving a parish on which we were just beginning to make some impact, and which was in the diocese where she was in a very responsible position in the Mothers' Union. I, too, felt that it would be a wrench to leave Clapham Junction for the City, just as it had been to leave Blackburn for Clapham Junction; but I had a secret reason for believing I must not ignore the invitation or dismiss it out of hand.

In spite of my busy life, I had been doing more sexual counselling and sex therapy in Battersea than in Blackburn, and that summer, before going to Knokke, I had had an unprecedented number of clients writing to me, telephoning me or visiting me, as a result of an article of a 'permissive' character which I had written for a widely circulating magazine. Indeed, the number of contacts arising out of that one article eventually came to 235, and I kept very careful records of the first 100 (not knowing at the time there were going to be more than twice as many) because then the numbers would be equal to the percentages of the various types of problem. To my astonishment, I found that no fewer than 13 per cent of my clients were seriously suicidal. Knowing very little about suicide in those days, I unthinkingly adopted the attitude of most people that life was such a tremendous blessing, on which all other blessings depended, that you would have to be mad to fling it away even if things were temporarily going badly for you. And when I say 'mad' I mean literally insane, psychotic, a suitable person to have psychia-

149

tric treatment. It did seem to me to be obvious that the suicidal 13 per cent of my clients should be steered gently towards a psychiatrist, or at least their family doctor.

I soon discovered that this was easier said than done. Only one of them was willing to see a psychiatrist, and he was also the only one who appeared to me to be a psychiatric case. I was astonished to discover that the other twelve, who resolutely refused to have anything to do with any 'headshrinkers', also appeared to me to be emotionally distressed rather than mentally ill. They insisted on being dealt with by me, and I was amazed to discover that I could meet their needs and that none of them *did* commit suicide. I had to rethink my whole attitude to suicide. I didn't then know what I know now, namely that potential suicides who are psychiatric cases are outnumbered by potential suicides who are not psychiatric cases, but I was learning that there were suicidal people who were capable of being helped by someone like me.

It wasn't long before I had begun to say to myself, 'If saving life is so easy, why don't I do it all the time?' The answer was obvious: I had my hands more than full with my parish, the hospital, my scriptwriting, my counselling, and the never-ending burden of what the postman brought, which has oppressed me all my life and which at that time was all the more difficult because my secretary, Vivien, had left me (amicably, of course) to go to Paris as an *au pair* girl, or whatever the French for *au pair* is. (Don't laugh: I can tell you that the French word for brassière is *soutien gorge*, for matinée coat is *brassière*, for cul-de-sac is *impasse* or *route sans issue*, for encore is *bis*, and so on.)

It was clear that suicide-prevention wasn't something I was going to be able to do, so at odd moments my mind busied itself with the question, how would I set about it? It seemed that if I were in touch with a suicidal person the chances were about 12 to 1 that I would be able to help him or her (actually, as it turned out, 8 to 1 was more realistic). But how could I get in touch with the people who were planning to kill themselves? Nobody knew who they were until they were on a slab awaiting the pathologist, and then it was surely a bit late for suicide prevention, to put it mildly.

I did a bit of what Mr de Bono has since called 'lateral thinking'. I hadn't then heard of him, but I'd been *doing* it most of my life. I said to myself: 'I can't know who they are, but they can know who I am, if I make sure that *everybody* knows who I am, and what I am for, and only those whom the cap fits need come to me.' In other words, I would want to advertise that I was specializing in trying to help those who were suicidal, and if the advertising was sufficiently prominent, persistent and persuasive, some at least of those who were contemplating suicide might be willing to ask, 'What have I got to lose?' when wondering whether to come to me or not.

Did I say, 'Come to me', I asked myself. Depression and suicidal thoughts are more common in the wee small hours than at any other time, and public transport is difficult or non-existent at such times. Besides, 'suicide' was (and to a surprising extent still is) a taboo word, and although we no longer buried suicides at a crossroads I had myself buried the body of a little girl in unconsecrated ground, for the Church condemned suicide as *felo de se* or self-murder. (I am ashamed to say that I had on one occasion preached against suicide.) The point was, that the suicidal person might wish, at least at the beginning, to be anonymous, as well as not to have to travel many miles to see a person with whom he didn't have an appointment and who might turn out to be a *dis*appointment.

Then light dawned. Suicide is an emergency, requiring immediate attention. What does the citizen do in an emergency? He reaches for the telephone, on which it says – and here I looked at my own – POLICE, FIRE, AMBULANCE DIAL 999. What was needed was a sort of 999 for potential suicides.

Having worked this out to my satisfaction, I realized that it was simply an intellectual exercise, like solving a chess problem, because I just did not have time to attend an emergency telephone day and night, even with help. So I said to God, 'Don't look at me. Surely you can see I am busy? This mission to save people from suicide, if it's done at all, will have to be done by one of those parsons who has a church in the City with no parishioners to speak of, and the possibility of spending the whole time in some specialization.' And so, having kindly instructed God how to proceed further if He wished to do so, I set off for my holiday in Knokke.

The cable from the Grocers' Company in the summer of 1953 unsettled me. I felt that I was making progress at Clapham Junction, but I felt also a powerful pull towards the work to which God seemed to be impelling me. I have never believed that vocation is a matter of the Archangel Gabriel bawling at one through an ear-trumpet but the general direction in which one's aptitudes, experience and (let us not be ashamed to say) inclinations impel one. You are likely to do something well if you like doing it. Once back in London, I let the Grocers' Company know that I was seriously considering their invitation, and awaited a summons to meet the appropriate committee.

I was received very courteously, as you might expect, and asked what I should do at St Stephen Walbrook if they decided to appoint me rector. I told them about my hare-brained scheme for setting up what would now be called a 'hotline' for potential suicides, and also a drop-in centre for those who preferred to come rather than telephone, and when I had finished my spiel they began to ask very penetrating questions. I answered as best I could, but you will realize that at that period nobody knew many of the answers because the concept was an entirely new one. I had to go in for a lot of what are called 'educated guesses'. When I retired to allow them to consult together about me, I felt I had sounded like a charlatan, so I was most surprised to discover, on being called back, not only that they were going to appoint me, but that they were going to do so because they wanted done what I proposed to do – they thought the experiment well worth trying. After some months of uphill work, I became at times a bit discouraged, and it was good then to remember that a body of distinguished City gents, successful businessmen, had thought my idea worth putting into practice.

As soon as I entered St Stephen Walbrook, I fell in love with it. It has been called 'the most beautifully proportioned interior in the world', and I would not quarrel with that description. It had recently been restored by the firm of Duncan Cameron under the architect Gilbert Meadon, who died just before the work was finished. His successor Godfrey Allen completed it.

The church had not been hit by high explosives, though a landmine, dropped not far away, had done the structure no good, but on 10 May 1941 incendiary bombs had fallen on the dome, part of which had come crashing down in flames and destroyed the seating and part of the choir stalls. It did not destroy the magnificent wineglass pulpit, whose canopy had been taken off and put beside it and the whole bricked in to protect it. I think the altar and font cover had been taken away to a place of safety. Certainly nothing important was lost, except the half of the Victorian choir stalls which contained the rector's stall – this was badly charred. By the time I first saw the building, thirteen and a half years later, it was restored all but the vestries, on which men were still working.

On my way to visit the church, I had been pondering about the most appropriate telephone number to ask for, one which would be easily memorized and give a hint of emergency. I knew the exchange would be MAN, short for Mansion House, and I wanted it to sound something like 999, so I hesitated between 9999 and 9000. Eventually I settled on MAN 9000 as being the ideal emergency number on which to get in touch with a man i.e. a fellow human being.

In the vestry, I found two workmen doing something with rubble, the ceiling having not yet been repaired, and I asked them whether there was a telephone. They assured me that there was, and that it had been reconnected to enable them to get in touch with their firm. After a certain amount of comic cross-talk – after the style of "ave you seen it anywhere?', 'No, Bert, not this morning, I 'aven't', 'Well, it must be somewhere', 'Can't 'ave walked off by itself, Bert,' – they eventually found it under a pile of broken timber and rubble. I lifted it gingerly, as it was covered with dust, and dialled the operator – in those days you dialled 0, not 100. I asked whether the number could be changed to MAN 9000 and was told that it was most unlikely, since nobody having such a good number would be willing to part with it for love or money.

I mentioned that I had no money but plenty of love and could I please be informed who at present *had* the desired number.

'What number are you speaking from?' enquired the operator.

I replied that the dial was covered with dust, and was tersely advised to wipe it clean. I licked my thumb, cleaned off the centre of the dial, and there it was: MAN 9000. 'Don't worry,' I said to the operator, 'I've got it already.' Then I addressed God: 'Very well. I get the message. You had it waiting for me since the telephone was first installed. Now please stop, because it's getting eerie.'

I took it as a sign that God wanted me to do the work I had contemplated doing from this church, and any doubts about the rightness of leaving my parish at Clapham Junction were dispelled, though the parishioners were understandably reproachful, and Susan, when she discovered there was no rectory house because land was about £500 a square foot in the centre of the City, could see that there was going to be no parish life of the kind she had become accustomed to and was very good at. I would have to buy a house, and decided that in order that Susan should still be near her family, and still be in the diocese of Southwark where she was established in her Mothers' Union work, I would buy it in the south-west corner of London. Still a countryman at heart, I looked for a place that was rather like a village, even though within half an hour of Piccadilly

Circus, and found it at Barnes. Susan and I both liked a house on the corner of Hillersdon Avenue, which was a lot smaller than we had been accustomed to, but at least would involve a little less work to keep clean and a little less expense to keep warm. I've always been glad I bought it. I wouldn't be able to afford it now.

At Holy Trinity Blackburn I took over from a predecessor who had been there for thirty-four years, and at St Paul Clapham Junction I succeeded someone who had been there for twenty-eight. At St Stephen Walbrook I succeeded no one at all, because the damage by incendiary bombs meant that the church was not usable by my predecessor, the Revd Frank Gillingham, who had played cricket for Essex and England and who transferred to St Margaret's Lee. The restoration was almost complete when I was appointed in the autumn of 1953: the organ was being rebuilt by George Sanders.

I was happy to know there was no congregation. A congregation would have elected a Parochial Church Council and churchwardens, and one's freedom of action would have been limited by the need to carry these pillars of the church with one. In fact, there had been no election of churchwardens for several years, so that the only person who officially belonged to St Stephen Walbrook was the parish clerk, Mr H. McClintock Harris, who informed me that he had 'a life appointment'. 'I'll be with you a long time, yet, Rector!' he averred. He was ninety-seven at the time, and very sprightly, so I wasn't surprised that he lived to be 102, and indeed welcomed his friendship and his amazing memory for details of the church and its history – he had become parish clerk at an early age. I once asked him about the Victorian mosaic floor. He was having a day in bed, and brightened up remarkably, sitting up with a gleam in his eye and crowing, 'Are they having trouble with it? I told 'em they would!' I made a mental note that if you are going to warn somebody in 1888 that they'll have trouble with something, it's as well to live to be 101 if you want to live to be proved right.

'It's sagging,' I told him, 'and has a dangerous structure notice served on it. What *was* there before they put down this expensive, beautiful and very unsuitable mosaic?' Harry told me there had been square flagstones, presumably Wren's originals (though many must have been lifted to pop a body under, and then replaced), as shown in engravings of the period.

I myself never believed that the floor was unsafe, because on the occasion of Billy Graham's first visit to England he had wanted a 'prestige' church in London in which to preach one of his sermons, and I had agreed to let him use mine, even though I was dubious about the desirability of his type of evangelism. We took all the movable furniture out of the church, managed to pack in 2,300 people shoulder to shoulder, and relayed the service to another 800 outside. If the floor hadn't collapsed then, I didn't believe it ever would.

I wasn't able to be instituted as Rector in November 1953, because a Bill was going through Parliament to set up the new arrangement for the forty or so surviving City churches dreamed up by the Ven. Oswin Gibbs-Smith, then Archdeacon of London. This provided that the number of parishes should be reduced to twenty-four, of which St Stephen Walbrook with St Bene't Sherehog would be one; and then there should be fifteen or sixteen Guild Churches without any parish whatsoever, and with a priest-in-charge entitled by courtesy 'Vicar', appointed for five years renewable for a further three at the most. The City of London is the only place in the country where it makes a difference whether you are a Rector or a Vicar, because only the Rectors have a freehold. It was important for me to be there as long as I wished to stay, if I was going to embark on a life-saving work which, once started, must obviously continue.

I told the Archdeacon that the scheme was daft, because the Guild Churches would be left without any visible means of support – they could only solicit funds by 'poaching' contributions from businesses situated in their former parish but now belonging to some other parish. Furthermore, the idea that the Guild Churches would be for specialists and the parish churches would look after their populations bore no relationship to the reality, which was that some of each had a specialization – mine was to be suicide-prevention – and some of each ministered to the day-time as well as the night-time population. There was also the question of patronage: the Guild Church within what was to be my parish, St Mary Abchurch, had been united since the Great Fire with St Lawrence Pountney, and St Swithun London Stone had been united with St Mary Bothaw. The upshot of it all was that St Swithun London Stone and the attached church of St Mary Bothaw were added to St Stephen Walbrook and *its* attached church, so that the new parish was St Stephen Walbrook and St Swithun London Stone with St Bene't Sherehog and St Mary Bothaw with St Lawrence Pountney. The sad thing about this was that whereas the Grocers' Company had had the patronage from time immemorial, they now had to alternate with Magdalene

155

College Cambridge, who had been patrons of St Swithun London Stone; and it is the latter who will make the next appointment when I die.

The Bill establishing the Guild Churches and the new parish boundaries came into effect in February 1954, and I was able to be instituted as Rector of the five united parishes in March by Bishop J. W. C. Wand. We held a service of thanksgiving for the restoration of the church, at which I insisted the guests of honour should be those who had actually worked on the restoration in their various crafts and functions. I listed on the back of the programme all the names in alphabetical order, and I still remember with pleasure that this put Leslie Abercrombie, electrician's mate, above Godfrey Allen, architect. The men were invited to bring their wives, and the proudest of them was Mrs Cork. Wren's great dome had been rebuilt strongly on a series of hollow inverted saucers of timber in place of Wren's umbrella spokes, by the architect Gilbert Meadon; and the prefabricated coffered panelling was made and put into position by Jim and Fred Cork, father and son.

The money had run out before the repairs to the outer vestry had been completed, and bits of plaster kept falling from the broken ceiling, so I bought some rep cheaply and looped it in such a way as to catch any droppings. This was important, because apart from the church itself, the only spaces available to me were the inner vestry, (which was and still is my study) and the outer vestry. This was accessible at that time only through the church, and there the first volunteers, who came and offered to help me with suicidal callers, attended on a roster basis, with Vivien typing as unobtrusively as possible in one corner. She said the purple rep made it look like a Turkish harem, though I never discovered how she had acquired such an intimate knowledge of these seraglios. They presumably didn't have a builder's window roughly fixed into a hole in the asbestos which covered the place where bombing had removed Stoneham's Bookshop.

To my mind, the most important date in the history of The Samaritans was not 2 November 1953 but 2 February 1954. On the former date I was alone except for Vivien, and imagining that all the people who rang or came or wrote wanted counselling. By the second date, there were about fifty survivors of the larger number of applicants to help me with my chosen task. Those who could were accustomed to meet on Mondays at lunch-time for instruction from me and discussion of the problems of clients (as we then called them – it was the usual Social Service word). In those days I selected the volunteers by the simple expedient of asking myself of each one (a) did I like him or her, and (b) if I had done something of which I was dreadfully ashamed, would I be able to tell it to that face? I rejected all who were pious, preachy or prudish, or who were politicians by nature or parsons by profession. Doctors, psychiatrists and psycho-therapists were listed as consultants working from their own premises.

The only way people could get to me was through the outer vestry, where my volunteer helpers were lying in wait. They thought of themselves like Lepidus, 'a slight, unmeritable man, meet to be sent on errands'. I can't say I disagreed with them at that time: I thought their function was to make me coffee, fetch me sandwiches, and keep the clients from becoming too impatient while waiting for the big event, which was an appointment with me. The volunteers knew only what I could teach them, and as I myself was learning how to do the job, this teaching could hardly be called definitive at that time. However, during the first three months the number of people who came in person increased, but the number penetrating to the inner sanctum for an interview with me decreased.

I asked Vivien to explain this phenomenon: what were the volunteers doing, I enquired, which prevented people from coming to see me? Her opinion was, that they were doing a great deal of nothing. People would come in demanding to see me, and saying firmly that no one else would do, whereupon the volunteers would drown them in tea or coffee and sit with them while they waited their turn. I seemed on the whole to have chosen the volunteers well, because while waiting to see me the visitors gradually poured out their troubles, and most of them left happily an hour or so later, having received what they really wanted, which was not counselling, but what we now call befriending – our name for the listening therapy which is still our hallmark.

Thus it was that on 2 February 1954, I called the little band together, and pretended to scold them for having muscled in on my mission without invitation, and having apparently met the needs of the clients better than I could in the majority of cases. I told them that their punishment would be severe: the whole thing would be handed over to them, the volunteers, because I should never again pick up the emergency telephone, nor be the person to say 'come in'

157

when somebody tapped timidly on the door. I would, however, deal with all the mail, since I had a secretary and they hadn't.

They were flabbergasted, and all spoke at once, asking how they could possibly manage, and what I would be doing. I then made it clear that what I would be doing would be selecting them, deploying them, instructing them, disciplining them, and if necessary sacking them. In addition, I would see, or speak with on the telephone, any client with whom they could not cope. This meant, *inter alia*, that those who needed counselling or expert help from a psychiatrist, for example, would be referred to me – about one in eight. The rest would be coped with by 'befriending'.

We did well to get it right after only three months' trial and error, and the arrangement has continued ever since. All who call up or call in encounter a volunteer who attempts to befriend them, and only the 12 per cent or so who need more expert help are passed on to someone more competent or, rather, with different qualifications.

Once again I was as busy as a one-armed juggler. The Samaritans (the name had been conferred on me by the *Daily Mirror* on 18 December 1953, and I had passed it on to the volunteers) was the 'speciality' of my City church, but I was also expected to operate it *as* a church, and with my usual propensity for overdoing things, I tried to have something every day. I have already mentioned Monday Meeting, for the Samaritans, but in addition I had Tuesday Topic, when I spoke in a lunch-hour about current events; Wednesday Worship, when I celebrated the Holy Communion; Thursday Theology, when the lecture of ancient foundation called St Antholin's Lecture was given by somebody appointed for the purpose, giving me a welcome break; Friday Favour was an organ recital; Saturday Sightseeing allowed me to have a day off while the Samaritans opened the church for tourists; and Sunday Service was the 9.15 Parish Communion, for which there was at that time a small demand.

As soon as I possibly could, I engaged a professional quartet to sing sixteenth- and seventeenth-century Masses in English at the Sunday Eucharist, and soon built up a repertoire of fifty different Masses with the aid of Frank Webb, the baritone who was also choirmaster. I had appointed a young medical student, Joanna Fraser, as organist, and she and I and the choir were only slightly outnumbered by the average congregation. I justified spending most of the church's income on a professional quartet by pointing out that 'worship' meant 'worth-ship', giving God what He is worth, and I considered that He was worth the most beautiful singing to be found anywhere, as well as some £14,000 worth of plate (as valued at that time). In any case, I needed the spiritual strength obtained from wonderful worship in my beautiful church. I still do, though it is on a Thursday instead of a Sunday now.

The media were very good to us. My own name and the name of The Samaritans were constantly in the press and on the radio, and I think this must have been resented by some of my fellow clergy in the City, because they would never back me up on anything I said in Chapter. The worst instance was when I introduced to the City the 'Church Rate' which had been moderately successful in Battersea and could be expected to be much more successful in a parish with hardly any residents, consisting entirely of business houses which could pay the Rate at little cost to themselves because, being 'levied and demanded', it could be deducted from their gross income before tax. As soon as I had churchwardens and a Parochial Church Council, we decided to levy a Church Rate at a pre-decimal penny in the pound per half-year and we appointed someone at a small salary to collect it. It soon became obvious that there was at least £70,000 (which in the '50s was a lot of money) per annum just waiting to be picked up if we could all agree to employ my Church Rate Secretary to collect for the whole City and share out the proceeds. I put it to the Deanery Chapter. All they had to do to obtain sufficient income to remove all their worries about making up the shortfall in the grant each received from the City Parochial Foundation was to raise the right hand. They did not do so, and the matter was dropped. They continued to *appeal* for funds from their parishioners (or from someone else's, if they were Guild Churches), and constantly grumbled about how difficult it was to raise the necessary sums. You will not be surprised that they got no sympathy from me. I don't want to name any of them, and they are mostly dead now. A few years later, two or three parishes *did* adopt the Church Rate, but I gather didn't manage it as efficiently as the splendid secretaries we were able to recruit from a retired officers' association had done.

As my own method of financing a good cause at that time was to sign cheques and hope there would be something in the bank to cover them, it was fortunate that two partners in Scrimgeours, next door on the east, offered to form a finance committee. They were the late Tom Enthoven and Colonel 'Tread' Strettle, who bought me for the Samaritans' use the house at 40 Marney Road, Battersea which was first occupied by my assistant, John 250, and his family,

159

and later by my daughter Felicity, whose husband (now Chief Probation Officer for Hampshire) was needing to live in London for an extra course of study. Apart from providing accommodation for full-time workers, the possession of a hostel was a mistake. It was intended to allow us to accommodate overnight someone in a great crisis whom we were dealing with on one day and wanted to continue dealing with the next and possibly the one after that, but not much longer. It didn't work out that way. Instead, Samaritans wanting to get home after an Evening Duty, and having already handed over to Night Watch, might find themselves with an awkward customer they didn't know how to cope with, and if they'd had plenty of time they probably still wouldn't, because nearly all these were inadequate personalities bordering on the psychopathic.

Now, Samaritans are exceptionally nice people, but I often wished they had all had whatever it takes to say to themselves, 'If I am rather unhappy being with this demanding and difficult person for an hour, what would it be like to have him or her [usually him] in my own home for the night and for God knows how many more nights before I could get rid of him or her?' The unkindest thing Samaritans ever did was more often than not to use Marney Road as a dump for people who should never have come to us in the first place; who could not be helped by our methods; and who simply filled up the few beds we had so that when they were wanted for their proper purpose they were not available. I guess this was my fault. I did arrange that the volunteers should check with Home Service before sending someone for the night, but I should have insisted on authorizing every single one myself. I suppose the reason why I didn't was because by bedtime I was too tired to give instant counselling to a volunteer unwilling to shut the door on one of these characters at turning-out time if he or she pretended to have nowhere to go.

For several years we doubled up the number of clients each year: 100 the first year (which looked silly when we were getting 100 a *day* many years later), 200 the second, 400 the third, then 800, 1,600. Obviously, this geometrical progression could not continue: however, our numbers did go on increasing, and happily the number of volunteers also increased, though not as rapidly, because unlike the clients, the volunteers were rigorously *selected*.

I think while we are still in the '50s you will like to hear about the very first call I had on MAN 9000. I took it before Vivien arrived, and it led to my doing something which subsequently I never

160

allowed, namely leaving my post and going to the person who had called. The result was, that when Vivien arrived I wasn't there, and a call she took, from a very distressed homosexual, she assumed was the first. It was quite a long call, because male homosexuality was a crime in those days, and even those who restricted themselves to consenting adults in private were liable to be blackmailed under threat of exposure, which might lead to the loss of their job and certainly of the esteem of their family and neighbours.

We both had many such calls as time went by, but I think I never had another call to compare with the first one which led me to take a journey on the tube and visit a flat in which was a young woman with four children by three different fathers, who was destitute and about to be thrown out. It wouldn't have been by any means the first time she had been evicted, and she had reached the point where she couldn't take it any more and had decided (as she told me over the telephone) to kill her four children and then kill herself. The means to be used was domestic gas, which was a very common method in those days: coal gas contains carbon monoxide, and is lethal. I suppose she would have had to knock out the two older girls before gassing them, but the details were not important: what was important was the note of genuine desperation in her voice, which I have heard in many people since then and find pretty well unmistakable. However much I have subsequently learnt about the difference between histrionics and genuine despair, I can assure you that my very first call astonishingly led to the prevention of four murders and a suicide. You can't ask for a better start than that.

I was able to get her a week's extension by undertaking that I would find her alternative accommodation. I had no funds except my own, but I was able later to move the poor lady into a cheap room in a small hotel, where she had her fourteen-year-old daughter to help her to look after a toddler, a boy. That left a nine-year-old girl and a baby. I was able to persuade my wife to take the nine-year-old girl temporarily into our home, and that left only the baby to be placed. I shall never forget being driven around all the likely and unlikely people that I knew in a taxi, and not finding anyone able and willing to take a baby even for a few weeks.

'Where to now, sir?' enquired the taxi-driver at last. I told him I didn't know. He said, 'In that case, if you don't mind, sir, I'll just go and tell my wife why I'm late.' He then drove to a side street near Olympia and when he re-emerged from his house, his wife was with him. He hadn't gone to his home in order to tell his wife he would

161

be late; he had gone to his home in order to ask his wife if *she* would take the baby, and she naturally wanted to have a look at it before deciding. It was a sweet little thing, less like Winston Churchill than most babies, and when she took it into her arms I could tell that my search was over for the time being. When Vivien heard about this happy ending, she insisted on paying a weekly sum for the baby's fostering. I hope it warms your heart to read about this as it warmed mine at the time. There are many good, kind people in the world, and because they don't make headlines we tend to forget this. I constantly thank God for the simple goodness of ordinary people.

I won't tell you any more about Case No. 1, because I don't want it to be possible to identify any of the people I mention, unless I have had their express permission to tell their story. Suffice it to say that the whole family was eventually reunited, and passed out of my ken, until thirty-five years later a young woman sought me out to thank me for letting her live in my home for a while when she was nine years old. Her elder sister was almost the only person I have literally snatched back from the jaws of death. While visiting her mother, I noticed that the old-fashioned lift was very unsafe in that there was no gate on the lift itself, only on the opening on each floor. The mother was being very difficult and the toddler was screaming the place down, and this girl was sitting on the floor near the door looking pale and tense. Out of the corner of my eye I saw her slip out of the room, and remembered the dangerous lift shaft. I slammed the screaming toddler into the arms of his hysterical mother, which astonished them both, and dashed out and was just in time to catch the girl as she went down the lift shaft. It was fortunate that her brassière was so strong. I feel sure it is no longer legal to be able to open the gate into a lift shaft when the lift isn't there.

At our Monday meetings the volunteers and I discussed every kind of human problem that had come to us in the previous week. We were thankful not to need to be experts on a thousand and one problems: we needed only to be good at listening and comforting and encouraging. I made it clear that we did not go in for problem-solving, and did not give advice, but listened patiently and discussed the situation with the client until he or she was able to advise himself or herself. The only advice which is any good is that which you give to yourself, knowing all the circumstances and your own capabilities.

I must confess that my belief in befriending, our listening therapy, was stronger in relation to the volunteers than it was in relation to my own work. I knew I was good at counselling, and felt that I was rather wasting my time if I was doing what the volunteers could do equally well or better. However, one day a lady to whom I will always be grateful came into my study, having refused to speak to the volunteers lying in wait in the outer vestry. She was talking when she entered the room, pursued by a Samaritan bearing a cup of tea for her, and didn't stop talking for about three-quarters of an hour. At the end of that time she stood up, took a swig of her by now cold tea, shook me warmly by the hand and said fervently, 'Thank you! That's the best advice I've ever had in my life. I shall go away and do exactly as you say, and I'm sure everything will work out well. Goodbye.' I shared her confidence, though I could not claim credit for giving good advice, or even any advice at all, as I hadn't spoken throughout her time with me, except to say 'oh' and 'mm' from time to time, to show that I was still paying attention, because the woman told her story five times.

However, if you have an enquiring mind you don't need to get bored. I began to ask myself why she had told her story five times, in what way these successive recitals differed, and whether five times was the exactly right number of times for her to tell the story if she was to reap the maximum benefit from our interview. The conclusion I reached was fascinating: it was that five times was exactly the right number of times for her to tell the story, and that each time the story changed. The first time was chaotic, including everything, relevant or irrelevant, just as it occurred to her, in no particular order. The second time was even longer but in more or less chronological order except when she forgot something and had to backtrack, and with a few real irrelevances cut out. The third time was much shorter, as she concentrated more rigorously on essentials. The fourth time amounted to the same admirable précis of the situation which I had myself arrived at half-way through the first telling – but what was the good of *my* arriving at it? And the fifth telling of the story was a repetition of the fourth with commentary, as she advised herself what to do. It appeared to *me* to be very sound advice, but that didn't matter – what was important was that it was what she wanted to do and felt able to do. I don't think she could have managed it alone. My looking at her with rapt attention, great approval and no sign of impatience, made it possible for her to work out for herself what was the best way forward for her.

It rarely happened that someone got to see me who only needed befriending. Most of the time I was doing counselling or psycho-therapy, or deciding to which therapist to send the client. In the early days we had several consultants who were willing to see people for us free of charge. We had a neo-Freudian, a Jungian and a strict Freudian, trained in Vienna, and also a psychiatrist specializing in alcoholism and drug addiction. Later we also had a psychotherapist who was eclectic like myself. The interesting thing to me was, that when deciding which therapist to send a particular client to, I did not relate the client's problem to the school the therapist belonged to. Instead, I related the client as a person to the therapist as a person, imagining them together and getting on well. 'Ha,' I would say to myself, 'I can imagine this person being very stimulated by Paul,' or, as the case might be, 'feeling very cosy with Rowena,' or it might be 'being really straightened out by Ilse.' It usually worked out as planned.

From the very beginning, I ran the organization (as it had now become) with great firmness, and a degree of discipline which possibly would not be entirely appropriate nowadays, but was essential when a bunch of amateurs was trespassing on a very professional field, that of suicide-prevention – angels rushing in where fools feared to tread. I think it was possible for the degree of approval and recognition we obtained from the medical profession in only two years to be granted because the volunteers were known to be selected and supervised by a professional, and their efforts and mine were backed up by other professionals. We were always careful not to get into conflict with any client's doctor, and if a GP was opposed to psychiatry, and the client wanted and needed psychiatric attention, we tried to arrange this through his own doctor if we possibly could. To jump ahead again, our most treasured accolade came when some years later the Maudsley Hospital decided to accept referrals from us as if we were GPs (I am speaking of the London Branch in the late '50s), and I was thrilled to be told that our referrals compared very favourably with those from GPs in that we did not send psychopaths and other untreatable people, but only those who could benefit from psychiatry, and most important, were anxious to co-operate with the hospital. Another landmark, a few years later still, was when some psychiatrists began referring patients to *us* for befriending.

*

164

It was six years before anyone else took up my mad idea, by which time we were already receiving a great deal of publicity in the media. Those first six years were different in character from all subsequent years when there were other centres, and especially different from the period after 1963 when the then twenty-one Branches at home and four overseas joined together formally.

Those first six years, 1953–9, when 'The Samaritans' meant just my work at St Stephen Walbrook, were not only a time of discovery, but also a time of consolidation once the most important discoveries had been made. By 1959 we knew how to deal with suicidal and other despairing clients in the most effective way. Befriending not only worked instead of more expert attention in the majority of cases, but in those cases which *did* need expert attention it was the means of leading the callers to it. For instance, people who had begun by saying that under no circumstances would they see a psychiatrist because they were not mad, after being befriended were asking us to find them a psychiatrist whom we could recommend.

It was easy to convince the medical profession that we were doing no harm and might indeed be doing some good. GPs were not happy about someone telling his or her life-story at great length while they had thirty coughs and sneezes waiting in their waiting-room – patients deserving to be relisted as impatients. If this baring of the soul could be done to Samaritan volunteers, who could be trusted to see it and admit it if the person's situation was beyond them, their load was lightened without putting patients at risk.

All the volunteers except the most recent knew from their own experience that it was right to encourage the client to talk about his or her feelings and to refrain from giving any advice, and of course from stupidities like saying that if the person hadn't done something ill-advised some time ago they wouldn't now be in that situation. Problem-solving would be counter-productive, as would any sort of preaching or exhortation or recommendation that the person should pull himself together when his problem was that he couldn't pull himself together. I warned the volunteers against any sort of probing into the client's childhood experiences, so that they were aware of the dangers of transference and counter-transference.

Above all, everything that was told us was to be totally and absolutely confidential, under no circumstances to be revealed to anyone except to me or an experienced Samaritan deputed by me. When we had contact with Social Service departments, these often expected us to share with them what we knew about the client, and

I'm bound to admit they were usually willing to tell us what *they* knew. However, we remained firm and built up a reputation for being unco-operative which we were very happy to have. Of course, if the client permitted us to release certain information in his or her own interest, we would do so, but even then we felt it better that the client should tell his or her own story rather than have it summarized by us. Confidentiality was particularly important when we were dealing with matters which might interest the police or other authorities. People would confide in us things which could have got them into trouble with the law, or with their employer, relatives or colleagues. Children would confide in us things which they didn't want their parents or teachers to know. Wives would confide things they did not wish their husbands to know, and *vice versa*. Our unswerving trustworthiness enabled us to help many people who could not otherwise have been helped. The City of London has its own police force, separate from the Metropolitan Police. The former almost immediately, and the latter gradually, came to understand that it was in their interests not to know who came and went.

Reports in the English press were copied all over the world, and within the first few months I had a letter from Cuba, a telephone call from Copenhagen and an unemployed baker hitch-hiking to see me from Salonika. The Cuban wanted advice on a fairly recondite sexual problem, which I was able to give him. The Dane began by saying he could only afford a short call: how could he prevent his secretary from committing suicide? I replied that he should stay with her; he objected that she might want to go to the lavatory; and I said firmly, 'This is no time for prudery. Stay with her wherever she goes – do not let her out of your sight.' The call was abruptly terminated, and I never discovered what happened (one became rather used to that). The unemployed baker I managed to get sponsored by a church in Canada, where he not only prospered exceedingly but sponsored I think seventeen of his relatives. I once visited him when I happened to be in Montreal, and he sends me a Christmas card every year.

You may be surprised that it was only clients seeking help who began to get in touch from all over the world. I had myself expected that concerned people would ask my advice on how to set up a similar service in their own countries, but on the whole people seemed to believe that it is more blessed to receive than to give. An honourable exception was The Revd Professor James Blackie, who with my help started a Branch in the northern capital, Edinburgh

166

and secured the telephone number Caledonian 3333.

That was in 1959, and, the ice having been broken, other Branches were formed in 1960. The first of these was Liverpool, formed by the Rector of Liverpool, Christopher Pepys (later Bishop of Buckingham); then followed Glasgow, Aberdeen and Manchester. So you will see that when there were only six Branches, three of them were in Scotland. Next followed Derby, Bournemouth, Ware, and Jersey, and then our first Branch in Ireland, Belfast.

In the autumn of that year, 1960, I travelled via Istanbul, Athens and Rome to Geneva and Vienna: conferences were being held in the last two places, the first organized and paid for by a Paris businessman, the late Georges Lillaz, and the second organized by Dr Erwin Ringel of the University Psychiatric Clinic. I could never be sure whether the Continentals who were determined to set up church-based services instead of The Samaritans were using M. Lillaz to pay for them to defeat The Samaritans, or whether M. Lillaz decided to put his money behind those who didn't share The Samaritans' philosophy. We, of course, were running on a shoe-string and not even at that time united together. The only authority I had was the recognition by Samaritans who were not power-seekers that I was likely to know more than anyone about how to do the job. This was not accepted by the ministers of religion assembled near Geneva who set up an international information centre for telephone emergency services with a Swiss president and a paid Swiss secretary, the latter apparently determined to keep The Samaritans out of Europe in order to have an evangelical crisis-intervention service instead. From that seemingly innocuous information centre there developed a so-called federation designed to swallow up and outvote The Samaritans. For an interminable time it seemed as if they had almost succeeded, but as I write this we are happily free and independent of all other organizations – though there are still very few Samaritan centres in continental Europe and large numbers of church-based ones, and in other continents many centres which do not observe our principles and practices and have not at all reduced their suicide rates.

The other conference held in September 1960, in Vienna, had more beneficial consequences. It was predominantly for psychiatrists, and our Turkish representative, Nuran Ulupinar and I were almost the only 'lay' people present. There was founded the International Society for Suicide Prevention, of which I became the for-tieth member and The Samaritans later became a corporate member, which did not compromise our principles at all, for the ISSP did not work by setting up suicide-prevention centres with emergency tele-phones, but by holding regular conferences and stimulating research into suicide.

By this time I knew for certain that neither religion nor even psychiatry was what the majority of suicidal people needed, but the 'listening therapy' we called 'befriending', performed by a lay person selected for aptitude at this. To preserve the purity of the concept, I selected certain volunteers whom I knew well enough to be sure of their Samaritan nature – not to make the others feel inferior, but in order to have around me a trusted band with whom I could share the burdens of responsibility in the utmost confidence, and at the same time have a little group who, if I died or became incapacitated, could be trusted to carry on in the way we had discovered was the only right way. I called these selected volunteers my 'Companions'.

Many people were driven to suicide because they were too gentle and lovable for the rat race. And where could they find refuge? Who would understand them, and not make them feel inadequate? Not, on the whole, the Church. In fact, in a different way, the Church's standards were as destructive as the world's standards. Church people were all too often narrow-minded, censorious, judgemental, intolerant, conventional. And they did not say with Christ, 'Come unto me all that travail and are heavy laden, and I will refresh you.' There were, of course, honourable exceptions, but the point is that these *were* exceptions, a tiny minority. So the people for whom the world was too harsh would never think of turning to the Church, and if they did, they would be likely to feel worse as a result. The attitudes expressed in the papers read by the millions of ordinary people were inhumane, and this was not pointed out by the papers read in their thousands by the clergy. More and more I felt at home with the desperate, unhappy people who came to The Samaritans, and with those volunteers who proved apt at accepting, understand-ing and befriending them. I was quoted at the time as saying that our object was to create oases of humanity in the desert of man's inhumanity to man.

It won't surprise you, therefore, to know how angry I became when people wanted to introduce worldly or churchy standards into crisis-intervention for the suicidal. By worldly standards, no one could be considered a better Samaritan than anyone else, and no one could be disciplined or sacked without the right of appeal to somebody or other; neither of these was acceptable in a movement dedicated to serious matters of life and death. By worldly standards, the longest serving member should be in charge of a duty. By our standards, seniority counted for nothing, and suitability for the position counted for everything. It would never be Buggins's turn: in fact, Buggins would either not be in the organization at all or would work very humbly and devotedly at whatever the Director thought he or she would do well.

Churchy standards would have us suppose that a Christian, especially a regular communicant, was bound to be a better Samaritan than an agnostic or adherent of some non-Christian religion. This is just not true, though it is the basis of most of the rival organizations to The Samaritans which have proliferated in many parts of the world. Churchy standards would require moral judgements to be made, especially in matters relating to sex, and would label the fact of suicide itself a mortal sin. It took *me* some weeks to shake myself loose from the sophistry that self-murder was worse than the murder of another person in view of the fact that the suicide died in the act of committing a mortal sin and therefore had no opportunity to repent, whereas the murderer of someone else might later die repentant (as, in fact, had the only two murderers to whom I had ministered before their hanging). But you can't be in frequent contact with suicidal persons, including those who have recovered totally unexpectedly after a suicidal act of a most severe nature, without knowing that the characteristic suicidal act is not motivated by hateful cruelty but by an ill-conceived desire to find 'the only way' to end intolerable pain and distress. Just as in cases of murder our law recognizes the doctrine of diminished responsibility, so in cases of suicide it must almost always be possible to plead diminished responsibility, which is why the coroner's verdict so often added to the word 'suicide' the words 'whilst the balance of the mind was disturbed'.

It was, however, in the realm of sexual morality that what had for generations been regarded as the almost unchallenged teaching of the Christian Churches was an obstacle to the task to which we, The Samaritans, had committed ourselves. You could not draw a person back from the brink of suicide if he or she was suffering from intolerable guilt, by confirming or increasing that sense of guilt. But we had to remember that just as we could not impose upon the caller our own beliefs about what was wrong, so we could not impose our own beliefs on what was not wrong. We had to respect his or her convictions whilst trying to lead people to be gentler and kinder towards themselves. One occasionally came across someone with deep religious convictions who had grievously transgressed them, like a certain schoolmaster who had regularly interfered sexually with little boys and summed the matter up by saying, 'I didn't want a psychiatrist to tell me I hadn't sinned, but a priest to tell me I had, and could repent and be forgiven.'

On the other hand we have to remember that in many matters less reprehensible than that it was some priest who had inculcated inappropriate feelings of guilt which one day perhaps some psychiatrist would have to try to remove.

I had considered from boyhood that the Church had 'got it wrong' about human sexual morality. It didn't take many months of working in suicide-prevention to have this opinion confirmed again and again. If you were an adult in the 1950s you will know what I mean, but if you were born since you may not realize what an enormous change has taken place in the attitudes both of the Church and of the general public in the past third of a century. The change has in almost every case been for the better, in that the number of sex-related situations driving people to suicide has decreased. For instance, in the early days of The Samaritans a frequent cause of a suicidal intent or attempt was that a male homosexual had been discovered to be such by some ill-disposed person who was blackmailing him, threatening to reveal all to his family or his employer unless large sums of money were regularly paid. Now that homosexual acts between consenting adult males in private are no longer illegal, even though still disapproved of by certain persons, such blackmail no longer happens, or at least does not create such distress as leads people to seek the help of The Samaritans.

In my youthful years, we had to be careful not to get a girl pregnant because there was nothing for it but to marry her, if possible sufficiently quickly for the resulting baby to be proclaimed premature, that is, seven months. By the 1950s, things weren't quite so bad: it was sometimes possible to obtain an abortion (other than the back-street variety) or, especially in the case of Roman Catholics, to go away and have the baby in secret, and rely on a sympathetic clergyman such as myself to arrange a third-party adoption. At one time I nearly always had one or two babies in the pipeline,

170

ready to be entrusted to some couple who I considered would be suitable even though they had been turned down by some adoption society on grounds I considered insufficient, such as that they didn't attend church or were over forty and might die before the child was self-supporting. Nowadays abortions are much easier to procure. Also, people's attitudes have changed, so that it is much more possible than it used to be for an unmarried girl to bring up her baby if she wishes to do so, or for *her* mother to take charge of her grandchild so that her daughter can still go out to work and perhaps still have a chance of making a marriage.

Long after a pregnancy whilst unmarried had ceased to be a reason for turning a girl out into the snow in England, it was an even greater disaster in certain other countries, particularly Roman Catholic ones. Within a few years the fame of The Samaritans had spread throughout the world, and we had cries for help from people of many nationalities. I well remember one seventeen-year-old girl from a rich family in Central America who became pregnant on a visit to this country, and was so distraught when the pregnancy was confirmed that for some time she could not move hand or foot. When she got over the first shock, she began searching for ways to kill herself, and someone brought her to The Samaritans, where I saw her. She told me that in her country her father would have no choice but to turn her out with nothing but the clothes she was wearing, and get the chauffeur to drop her in the red-light district of the city to earn her living as 'the prostitute she had proved she was'. It made no difference that her father was rich and influential and that she herself was his 'pet': the pressures of society and the Church were too powerful to resist, and she would rather die now than face that shame and degradation. There were two possible ways of helping her, and the one she chose undoubtedly saved her life.

Talking of prostitution, The Samaritans have from the earliest days naturally had a considerable number of calls from prostitutes. The life of the average prostitute is a very hard one, even if she is working for herself and not for someone who takes most of her money and perhaps regularly beats her up into the bargain. There are, of course, a few expensive call-girls who live a life of luxury and comparative ease, but the life of a girl at the other end of the scale is almost unbelievably miserable and squalid. Like most other clients of The Samaritans, the majority of prostitutes want to talk about their woes to a sympathetic listener, in a befriending relationship of one human being to another human being into which sex does not

171

enter. Few men, and perhaps even fewer women, can do this without careful conditioning. One of the subjects dealt with in our preparation classes was, for men, how to shut out from their imagination the work the woman did, so as to avoid all prurient interest and intrusive questions, and for women, how to avoid even the slightest hint of moral superiority because they themselves had most likely never straightforwardly rented their body for a man's gratification – though they might of course have less explicitly granted sexual favours to a man who had spent money on entertaining them or giving them presents. The reasons a girl takes up prostitution as a career range as widely as the reasons a girl decides to accept a particular proposal of marriage: in either case it may be more or less calculating, more or less forced, more or less avaricious, more or less confused.

Most of the prostitutes coming to us were fairly soon referred to me for counselling, but almost invariably I found myself doing befriending: helping the woman to feel good about herself, to accept herself, to accept praise for any claim that she did her job as honestly as possible. It was strange to find some prostitutes telling me of their regular customers – commercial travellers, lorry-drivers and other lonely men moving from place to place all the time – who usually, though not always, wanted sexual gratification, but who invariably wanted a woman to listen to them while they spoke of their joys and sorrows, their small triumphs and their disappointments. 'You know,' one of them said to me, 'a lot of the time I'm a fucking Samaritan.'

It took me a moment or two to work it out, then I said, 'Yes, it's what The Samaritans do, apart from the fucking.'

One thing I had to learn from the prostitutes who came to me was that my hatred and contempt for the men who lived on the prostitutes' earnings was sometimes misplaced. There were indeed evil, cruel men who exploited girls they had trapped into prostitution and who could not escape from their clutches because they were watched and beaten up if they tried to escape; but some of the girls loved the pimp for whom they worked. They had a psychological need for a man with whom they had sexual love-making and regarded totally differently from the punters, with whom they did not allow themselves to become at all emotionally involved and whom they tended to despise. Lavishing expensive presents on the man for whom they walked the streets, and who might upon occasion be needed to protect them from some drunken or violent

172

punter, gave them a satisfaction which humanized their situation in life.

I was given to understand that the prostitution scene in the United States was very much more violent, being part of organized crime, than that in this country, and that in many parts of France the pimps were far more vicious and far more likely to be protected by the authorities than those in Britain. I learned a great deal about this some years later when I visited one of the most admirable women I have ever met, in the south of France. She went by the nickname of 'Colibri', which means 'humming-bird'. She ran a refuge for prostitutes who had managed to escape from their *souteneurs*, some of whom would stop at nothing to keep their source of income enslaved to them. They sometimes had the help of police whom they bribed to help them to get girls back; and it was said that they had prominent politicians in their pockets, too. Colibri was not afraid of any of these, though she was frequently threatened. The chief difference between her refuge and that at Chiswick for battered wives was that these non-wives would *never* let the side down by going weakly back to further punishment. Also, of course, the Chiswick wives didn't include girls whose pretty faces had been slashed to make it more difficult for them to earn their living in the only way they knew. There was no one I admired more than Colibri, and I am ashamed to say that I have not been able to keep in touch with her nor have I heard anything about her, as I would have done if she had been doing something 'respectable' like ministering to the destitute dying on the streets of Calcutta.

In our own country, prostitutes are persecuted. We English are not in all ways as hypocritical as we are commonly held to be, but in the matter of prostitution we most certainly are. It is, quite properly, not illegal to be a prostitute, but our laws, and the way the police interpret and implement them, make it almost impossible legally to encounter potential customers and to entertain these in a place which is inviolate. Life is far, far harder for the prostitute than for her customers, who mostly run very little risk unless they accost and annoy women who are not 'on the game', or engage in persistent kerb-crawling in an area which the police have earmarked for attention.

But, you may say, surely prostitution is forbidden in the Bible, being either fornication (if neither of the parties is married) or adultery (if one is or both are). You may be asking yourself, 'Is this a parson writing? Does not one of the ten commandments explicitly forbid adultery? Is not St Paul in the New Testament constantly condemning fornication, not to mention homosexuality?' On the other hand, you may know nothing about the Bible, and care less, but I have to make my position as a Christian priest clear.

The ten commandments of Moses do not apply to Christians. They, and other Old Testament rules and regulations, do apply to those who follow the Jewish religion. We Christians judge the Old Testament and the Apocrypha by the standards of Christ. We find certain passages inspiring or edifying, and others cruel, misleading or irrelevant to our needs. We see the Old Testament as the progressive revelation of God to a people whom He chose for this purpose, who come gradually to an understanding of something of His nature and will and purpose; and as a preparation for His coming to earth Himself as the Messiah, the Christ, in the Incarnation. In my belief, those who have held that every word and thought in the sacred scriptures is divinely inspired and as valid for all time as if it were dictated by God and taken down in Hebrew shorthand, are grievously mistaken and have caused enormous unnecessary suffering to believers. In Christ's words, 'they lay on men burdens grievous to be borne.'

By now you may be thinking, 'I've read a lot about what this man *doesn't* believe; isn't it about time he told me what he *does* believe? Then I can consider not only whether it justifies him being a Christian priest, but also whether I myself am at all convinced by it. To be told adultery isn't a sin is surprising, to say the least of it.' I sympathize with you, if that is what you are feeling, but I am bound to say, 'Hold on a minute: I have not stated that adultery is not a sin.' I am not a believer in a certain version of the Bible known as 'the Wicked Bible' because the printer inadvertently (?) omitted the word 'not' from 'Thou shalt not commit adultery.' I do not accept either 'thou shalt' or 'thou shalt not' as *absolute* requirements when applied to adultery. The only command I recognize is the command of Jesus Christ to love God with all our heart, mind, soul and strength, and our neighbour as ourselves. The command to love is absolute and binding and cannot be superseded by anything else because it comes from God who *is* Love through Jesus Christ, incarnate Love, finding a response in our hearts where His Holy Spirit, Love, dwells, recognized or unrecognized or partly or intermittently recognized. As the hymn 'Immortal love' puts it, 'Love only knoweth whence it came, And comprehendeth love.'

All our thoughts, words and deeds are to be subject to the law of

174

love. Where love is, there God is – you can find the expansion of this thought in the first epistle of St John in the New Testament.

It is so simple that a child can understand it. But it is also very profound and can be complicated: as the late C. E. M. Joad constantly reminded us, 'it all depends on what you mean by . . . love.' We use one four-letter word where the Greeks used three words, for friendly love, sexual love and altruistic love (what Christians would call Christian love). Not only do we use 'I love' to mean 'I like', 'I lust', and 'I seek to bless or benefit through loving-kindness', but we also make confusion worse confounded by using 'I love' to mean 'I hate'. This may express itself by seeking to enslave, dominate, exploit, harm, devour or destroy the object of the so-called 'love'. A familiar example is what the French call *le crime passionnel* where the jealously possessive 'lover' kills the object of his or her desire. It is equally clear in the case of the parent who will not permit his or her child to develop as God intended, but forces the child to conform to his or her own ideas. A less obvious but more horrifying example is that of the religious teacher who inculcates a belief in a person who is described as 'God' but is cruel and arbitrary, in fact a devil.

Let us be clear then, that the command of God to those who believe in Him – not only Christians but any human being who will pay attention – is to live by the law of loving-kindness. By that law, we may suppose that adultery is, in a majority – perhaps a large majority – of cases, unloving behaviour; but in some cases it may be more loving than the alternative. What I want to make clear to you is that whether it is sinful or not is determined not by whether it is adultery or not, but by whether it is loving or not.

As I understand it, Christians live by grace. That is to say, they rely on God within them to guide them in every situation so that they may act in accordance with the law of love and may understand what love demands in any particular case. Those who are not Christians are well advised to follow a system of rules and regulations such as the Ten Commandments and other parts of the Old Testament, or I suppose the Upanishads or Sutras. Children, of course, have an easier choice: all they have to do is to obey their parents. Even so, they are not excused obedience to God's prompting if their parents should command them to do something totally unloving.

Many Christians find it difficult to believe that Christ did not give other commandments beside the commandment to love. They point,

175

for instance, to the Sermon on the Mount, where they find a number of injunctions, such as if someone pinches your jacket, give him your overcoat too; if someone forces you to labour on clearing a path for a mile, do it for two miles; if somebody hits you on one side of your face, offer him the other. Taking these to be commandments has misled many people – particularly the last, which has led the foolish to expect nations to be pacifist and unresistant when attacked by an aggressor. Christ was not giving commands, He was giving illustrations of how far the law of love might carry you. There *are* situations in which a mugger may be forced to think in an unaccustomed way by giving him what he had not demanded (and in any case by giving him something as a free gift you change yourself from being a victim to being a benefactor; you retain your human dignity, and allow him an opportunity to show his by repentance). As for 'turning the other cheek', there *are* situations where an overwrought and perhaps immature person lashes out at you and then is terrified at what he has done, where the most loving thing is to invite him to hit you again. But there are also circumstances in which the most loving thing, for example with a bully, is to beat the living daylights out of him if you are capable of doing so.

Once we have it in our heads that there is no law other than the law of love, our only problem is to make sure we do not deceive ourselves when we are applying it in our own lives. Self-deception is very easy, as the devil well knows, and the temptation to twist the facts to allow us to do the naughty thing we want to do is very strong. *Gnothi seauton* – know thyself. It is wise to look at ourselves with the same critical eye that we may turn on other people and their hypocrisy. When a drunk goes on drinking neat spirits 'purely for medishinal purposhiz', we know that this is a false excuse, and if some psychotherapist says he can help his glamorous female patient only by having sexual intercourse with her, so that it is a really loving thing to do to exploit her in this way, you know that he is deceiving himself but (you hope) not the girl.

Some people advise consulting with other Christians before deciding to do something contrary to conventional behaviour. I think you should be careful about this, particularly in matters related to sex, because the Church has become so polluted by false puritanical values that you are likely to be made to feel guilty for acting in accordance with the law of love.

It wasn't long before The Samaritans had to confront the problem of unwanted pregnancies and the possibility of a client wishing to have a termination. The subject of abortion has attracted more single-issue fanatics than any other I can think of. Not all of them were Roman Catholics, but the Roman Catholic Church has been particularly fierce in its condemnation of abortion. Samaritans whose private convictions were against abortion were reminded that this was entirely permissible as far as they themselves were concerned, but that their views must not be imposed upon, or even mentioned to, clients. Callers must not be pressurized into having, or not having, a termination of pregnancy, and any who asked for the address of the nearest clinic where they could obtain counselling and an abortion, if that were the medical recommendation, were to be given the address without any persuasion one way or the other.

One of our Roman Catholic members to whom I explained this in the early days was sad that her Church was less humane than the one to which I belonged, or at least than those in the Church of England who thought as I did. She was surprised to discover that we did have auricular confession in the Church of England (though not all priests were willing to hear confessions), and that this was in most parishes not a regular weekly routine but for the great events and crises in one's life. In the course of the discussion she decided that many priests in her own Church increased the penitent's feeling of guilt in the confessional, and knowing that I myself did my best to reduce guilt in the confessional and make absolution a source of joy and relief, she brought me a list of the Roman Catholic clergy known to her and her friends who did the same, and who would not, for instance, make youngsters feel guilty about normal adolescent masturbation.

When I tell you that the number of names on her list was five, I am not meaning to imply that that was the total number of humane priests in the London area.

In the 1950s I had quite a number of clients coming to make a formal confession. For some reason this hardly happened once we got into the '60s. A fair proportion of these clients were teenage boys worried about masturbation. I am not speaking at the moment about the far greater number who had consultations with me in my study, but about those who asked for absolution in church. At that time I sometimes used to remark that I must hear more confessions than any other priest from people who had never made one before and would possibly never make one again.

177

The pattern became distressingly familiar: the penitent was obviously unfamiliar with the procedure. I would sit inside the communion rail and he would kneel on the outside near me, and I would say, 'God Almighty bless you and give you grace to make a good confession,' whereupon he might reply, startled, 'Eh?' I would know then to leave out the bit about 'since my last confession, which was such and such a time ago'. 'Say the following words after me,' I would command, enunciating clearly, and giving him a few words at a time. '"I confess to God Almighty, Father, Son and Holy Spirit, in the sight of the whole company of heaven and of you, my Father, that I have sinned in thought, word and deed, through my own grievous fault. Especially I accuse myself of the following sins."'

There would follow an awkward pause. I would say, 'Especially I accuse myself of the following sins colon dash: that means you have to tell God in your own words what your sins are.' Again an embarrassed pause.

I would say, 'You wouldn't have come seeking absolution unless you felt that you had some sins. Please say what they are.' After a lot of fidgeting and throat-clearing there would come out some muttered word or expression indicating or hinting at masturbation. 'Are you talking about masturbation, tossing off, wanking?' I would enquire with mild surprise, and on receiving an affirmative grunt I would say, 'Oh, that – all boys do that – you'll find something much more satisfactory before you are much older, with any luck, but please don't waste my time, tell me now about your sins.'

The youth would then, of course, be speechless, his prize exhibit having been ruled inadmissible. Eventually after some rummaging around in his mind he would produce something like, 'My dad asked me to clean the car for him, and I said I would, but I didn't because I wanted to go out with my mates, and I then told him I forgot, and when he scolded me, I was rude to him and he hit me.'

'Very hard, I hope!' I would say sternly. 'You really are a miserable little bugger, aren't you? How ungrateful can you get? If your mates were *real* pals, they'd help you clean the car, wouldn't they? And then being rude to the father you should respect! You really are a sinner who should truly repent and receive absolution. Now say after me: "For these and all my other sins which I cannot now remember I am heartily sorry, firmly determined to amend, and I ask God to forgive me and you Father to pray for me and grant me absolution."' This would usually come out gaily, in a sort of sing-

178

song of relief, and I would then give him the absolution. I would then say to him,'For your serious sin you must have quite a heavy penance. Before you leave the church, find the hymn book, look up the hymn whose first line is "For the beauty of the earth", read it through slowly to yourself, thank God for the absolution you have had and then for the next two weeks offer every day to clean your father's car, and whenever he accepts the offer, do it very thoroughly. And now, go in peace with the blessing of God, and pray for me also, a sinner.'

I would then go back to my study, and put away my cassock and surplice and purple stole (but didn't have to change my shirt, because I hardly ever wore a clerical collar in those days, even for services). It would sometimes happen that the delirious young man would come and tap on my study door wanting to reassure himself that it really was possible for him to go at it hammer and tongs, so to speak, and he would get short shrift from me. 'Making a confession is not a social occasion,' I would snap. 'I am not Chad Varah and you are not whatever your name is, I am a priest and you are a penitent, and we have finished our business, now piss off.'

'I only wanted to ask, if you don't mind, sir,' he would burble, 'how many times is all right?'

'As many times as you can manage,' I would growl. 'Nature is self-regulating in this regard.'

'Would five times be all right, sir?' he might persist, without saying whether he meant per week, per day or per hour.

'Not if you want to get in the *Guinness Book of Records*!' I would tell him through my teeth, adding, 'Now will you 'op it, and let me get on with my work?' and he would go away walking on air, the weight of the world lifted off his shoulders. Sometimes I would discover in later interviews that he was doing it less and enjoying it more now that it had ceased to be sinful and compulsive.

Of course, it wasn't only young men who were distraught about masturbation, believing it to be not only a sin but their chief sin, blotting out from their consciousness all the sins against the law of love which they constantly committed, so that it might occasionally happen that the only virtue they displayed in a period of many hours was loving themselves in masturbation. Older men were sometimes more extreme in their feelings of guilt and unworthiness: the worst cases were those who had deep religious convictions bordering on the fanatical, and the more they studied the Bible, the more they found that condemned and depressed them. It was by no means

179

unusual to have a man believing that masturbation was 'the sin against the Holy Ghost which cannot be forgiven'. It was often quite difficult to convince them that if God was infinitely loving and forgiving, then there could not be any sin which could not be forgiven except one which by its very nature made forgiveness impossible. God's forgiveness is the restoration of the loving relationship of father and child between God and the human being, and so God proffers forgiveness to all who repent, the instant that they repent. (I guess God is never bored, otherwise He would have a miserable time listening billions of times a day to people beating the breast because they had enjoyed the gift of sex which he gave them to enjoy.) Now, what sin cannot be forgiven because it cannot be repented, so that the proffered forgiveness cannot be accepted by the sinner? Obviously, only diabolical pride which, like Satan's, prevents the soul from recognizing that good is what is pleasing to God, and evil is what is displeasing to God, so that the person whose sin is overweening pride refuses to accept that God is the judge and, denying the light within him, will say in effect, 'Who are You to forgive *me*? I do not accept Your so-called forgiveness!' Such a person has committed the sin against the Holy Ghost, and it is important to know that we cannot say God *will not* forgive it, but that He literally *cannot*.

With matters of such moment to consider, is it not a tragedy that a large part of the Christian Church, instead of concerning itself with the massive intellectual and philosophical structure which has been built up into Christian theology over the centuries, should demean itself into becoming an international conspiracy against human beings' carefree enjoyment of the pleasures of the senses, including sex? It is using a steamroller to crack a peanut to call down the wrath of the creator of the universe to prevent boys from masturbating.

And girls, of course. Females have been fortunate in one respect, in that their sexuality hasn't been taken seriously enough for them to have been exposed to the same threats of madness, blindness, sickness and damnation as were directed against their brothers. It wouldn't have been considered nice in Victorian days to suppose that girls could regard sex as anything other than submission to a lawful husband, so that it was unthinkable that they could wish to pleasure themselves sexually, and actually do so. It isn't often in this cruel world that women have an advantage, and of course the unspeakable nature of female masturbation also had its disadvantages, in that those who enjoyed it had no way of knowing that they were not freaks. (The same inability of the Victorians to envisage females masturbating also led Queen Victoria, when a Bill criminalizing homosexual behaviour, making it a felony, was put before her for signature, to cross out the passage referring to 'female with female', genuinely believing that some inattentive man had thoughtlessly put in the other half of the human race, much as if, in drafting some law about pregnancy, he had said 'he or she should be attended by a midwife'.)

Although it is in general true that, because of their physiology and psychology, men are spontaneously sexed, requiring very little stimulus to arouse their sexual desire, and women are responsively sexed, being aroused chiefly by the attentions and caresses of some acceptable male (or female), this is only a general tendency and not a strict rule. Males manufacture very much more testosterone than females (indeed, the hormone is named from the testes), but females do create in their bodies sufficient for them to experience spontaneous sexual urges, and if this did not happen they would never have the impulse to masturbate. Males masturbate much more frequently than females, but cannot have as many successive orgasms as some liberated females can achieve.

Female masturbation does not seem to produce nearly as much guilt as male does, perhaps because its lower incidence, the fact that it might be considered indelicate to refer to it, and the lack of any tell-tale marks on nightwear or bedclothes, lead to few or no terrible warnings to girls, of the type encountered by boys. Girls did not, however, completely escape feelings of guilt about their masturbation. For instance, a girl I was counselling many years ago and whom I suspected of being troubled about masturbation, flatly and convincingly denied it in spite of all my efforts to make it easy for her to seek help in coming to terms with it; but meeting her much later when serving in my next parish but one, she again sought my help with her psychological problems, and this time admitted to having been a frequent and compulsive masturbator and worried sick about it at the time when I had suspected that this was the cause of her distress.

Another example from thirty years ago is that of a young woman who told me that she had been educated at a convent school where she had been lonely, homesick and unhappy, and often cold in bed. In her narrow cot, she sometimes cried herself to sleep (sobbing under the bedclothes tended to warm things up), and sometimes

181

masturbated for the same purpose, and for comfort. However, in the morning she would see the framed text above her bed, 'Thou Lord seest me', and would feel guiltily that God had been watching her and was disgusted with her. She had never confided this in anyone until she told me, and this was a mercy, because you cannot rely on 100 per cent of clergymen to assure a girl in such a situation that the meaning of the framed text for her was, 'Lord, my loving heavenly Father, waking and sleeping You are watching over me, You know how unhappy and cold I am, how desperately I need to be loved. Thank You that You created my clitoris as a source of pleasure and let me learn to use my fingers to give me comfort and to make me relaxed and sleepy.'

Of course, attitudes in the '90s are much more open and permissive than in the '50s and '60s, and I must have contributed as much as anyone to this improvement, but it is still comparatively rare for women to announce to all and sundry that they pleasure themselves by masturbation.

You must not suppose that the *theological* basis for my ideas about human sexual behaviour formed any part of the instruction I gave to potential volunteers in my own and other Branches of The Samaritans, where I was accustomed to take the classes on marital problems and on other sexual problems. In the seminar on marital problems I would discuss the mental and emotional differences between men and women, the physiology of the male and female sexual organs, the comparison between the stem of the penis and the vagina, and between the glans penis and the clitoris, the techniques of masturbation and 'petting' in the two sexes, the importance of both parties being concerned about the woman's orgasm seeing that the man's was hardly ever difficult to achieve, the different speed of arousal of males and females, what positions for sexual intercourse were best for different purposes and physiques, how to deal with premature ejaculation, and any questions raised by the class. I would point out how difficult it was for the two sexes to be tolerant of the other's contrasting attitudes and desires, and even to be willing to say, '*Vive la différence.*' I would warn them that many husbands' complaints about their wives added up to 'she is a woman' and many complaints of wives about their husbands added up to 'he is a man'. Married couples had to learn that a man is not a woman with a prick, nor is a woman a man with a cunt.

It was my policy to accustom the potential volunteers to the honest, explicit Anglo-Saxon words for the male and female organs

182

and the conjunction of them, all three of which derived from the Sanskrit and are found in most Indo-European languages in similar form. They would not necessarily be expected to use these words but they must at least understand them and not be offended if clients used them. I would rebuke those who used to 'sleep with' to mean 'have sexual intercourse with' or 'have coitus with', telling them that it is not only a mealy-mouthed evasion expression but also an impoverishment of the language, because we need sometimes to be able to say 'slept with someone' meaning precisely that. The other euphemism at that time was 'to jump into bed with' someone. It was always 'jump', never 'get' or 'slide', so a visualizer like myself had a mental image of a sexually aroused male doing a long jump at a cowering female across the length of an Olympic-sized bedroom.

In the class on sexual problems, I would explain masturbation, male and female homosexuality, male impotence, female supposed 'frigidity', and sexual deviations such as fetishism, exhibitionism, voyeurism, transvestitism, trans-sexualism and sado-masochism. The purpose was not to turn the volunteers into counsellors on sexual problems, but to enable them to befriend more intelligently those clients whose sexual preferences they had at least encountered in my class even if they had not previously encountered a case in real life. At the end of the class on sexual problems, some volunteers would emerge bemused and others apparently relieved and liberated. The only people who withdrew or were told not to return were those who found it impossible to accept homosexuality as normal for some 10 per cent of the population.

This is probably a good point at which to inform you categorically that it never happened, not even once, that some Branch at which I had taken a class on sexual problems reacted so negatively as to want to leave the movement, or that someone had to be sent to soothe them down or to persuade them not to resign in protest. Any allegation to the contrary is a calumny totally without foundation and is in fact the opposite of the truth, which was that many Branches invited me to give 'the sex talk' because they did not have anyone who could do it sufficiently explicitly, calmly and without embarrassment, and make sure that any potential volunteer who was going to be shocked was going to be shocked by me and not by a client who might then feel rejected and condemned.

*

183

The only dispute there has ever been on a matter of sex between myself and some members of some Branches has been on the question of what our response should be to sexually aggressive or sexually demanding calls. As early as 1955 an entry appeared in the log book: 'What do we do about all these obscene callers?' and underneath, in my writing, 'What do you think? Befriend them, of course.' When I questioned the volunteers about the nature of these calls, I discovered that some of them were pathetic, from rejected or frustrated men begging for some kind of sexual acceptance from a woman, and some were aggressive, expressing various degrees of rage and resentment against women for real or imaginary slights by one or more of the sex. Most of the female volunteers saw no difficulty in befriending the first group. The second group divided again into two, those who with skilful handling could be helped not to think of all women as being tarred with the same brush, and those who by reason of psychopathy were determined to manipulate the volunteer to their own purposes, being adamantly determined not to be diverted from this by the establishment of any kind of human relationship. Perhaps because of having gone through my class in sexual problems, very few of the women volunteers were uncomfortable with sexually demanding/sexually aggressive calls. Being thoroughly familiar with the terminology used by many callers, they were able to concentrate on what was being said without worrying about how it was said. Also, of course, they were basically sympathetic to the sense of grievance of the frustrated male callers. They did not expect gentlemanly restraint from men who for the most part had no experience of affection and understanding from a woman, let alone acceptance of their sexual nature.

It was not, therefore, as in some Branches, unwillingness on the part of the women volunteers to try to cope helpfully with such calls which led to the setting up of the 'Brenda' system whereby selected volunteers were given special training for this work. From the beginning, we had made it clear that the volunteers were there to serve the needs of the clients as far as they rightfully could, and that the clients' feelings took precedence over the feelings of the Samaritans. All decisions about our policies were arrived at after discussion in which everyone might join, but which ended by my summing up the feeling of the meeting (without ever taking a vote) in the words, 'The needs of the client dictate that we do (so and so).' The needs of clients who wanted to talk about their sexual needs to a woman volunteer, whether while masturbating or not, dictated that the woman who took the call should be competent to deal with it calmly and constructively, and should not be someone resentful, nervous or manipulable. 'Brenda' was conceived not in order to protect women volunteers from calls they found distressing or disturbing, but to protect the callers from women who would be distressed or disturbed by their very natural impulses. It is no criticism of such women – many of whom were excellent with callers that others of us found exasperating, such as alcoholics – that their upbringing and life experience rendered them vulnerable in this field.

Women volunteers who felt a concern for these callers were given special training by me, so that they would both feel confident in dealing with the calls that came, and also discover, in consultation with one another, how best to help each individual. They formed a sisterhood which constantly exchanged and updated information on the callers and prepared such a useful card-index that after a while it hardly mattered which of them a caller happened to encounter when he rang. At first, this specialized service for a certain type of caller operated within the Branch simply by a caller of this kind being asked to hold on for a moment whilst a Samaritan permitted to take such calls was summoned to the phone. There was almost always at least one on duty, but if ever there wasn't, the caller would be asked very politely to call back at a certain time when there would be a young woman available to take his call. (One of these 'young women' was a charming great-grandmother.) I should emphasize that the other volunteers were expected to deal, and did deal, with all kinds of sexual problems except this special kind where the caller did not recognize that he had a problem but was simply seeking gratification of one kind or another. If such callers heard a male voice, they would almost always hang up, though they would sometimes ask if they could speak to a woman, and male volunteers quickly learned that a succession of silent calls might sometimes be ended by getting a woman volunteer to answer on that line.

The name 'Brenda', which is now world-famous, had not yet been conferred upon those women Samaritans who had had extra training to enable them to go a little beyond befriending into a form of counselling. Brenda was christened some years later when in the late '60s a Branch was formed at Brent in north-west London. The Samaritans there were able to attend their phones from 7 p.m. to 7 a.m., but for the rest of the twenty-four hours they asked the London Branch to cover for them. That meant we had to put in an extra telephone line with a handset clearly marked BRENT, and when it rang, the nearest Samaritan would pick it up and say 'The Samaritans of Brent, can I help you?' He or she would then try to persuade the caller to call after 7 p.m., but if the matter seemed too urgent to be left until then, one of the Brent leaders would be rung at his or her home and asked to take over.

It wasn't long before Brent were able to manage a twenty-four-hour service, whereupon we found ourselves with an additional telephone with a peculiar number, and I instantly decided to hand it over to the sisterhood. Now we were really in a position to make some progress. The number was kept secret, and only given to callers who were judged by the women volunteers taking their calls on the ordinary lines to be helpable by our methods. Each such selected caller was given not only the secret number and its hours of 'womanning', but also two Christian names: a masculine one for himself, and a feminine one for the girl he was to ask for. When he rang that number, the woman who replied would say simply, 'Who is that? And whom do you wish to speak to?' In case of a wrong number, nothing was betrayed, but an invited caller would say, for example, 'This is Edward for Caroline.' There were alphabetical lists of boys' and girls' names available, and the date each was used was pencilled against it. Even before looking up his card or folder, the Samaritan answering would know when 'Edward' had first called (and the choice of name might also be significant). There would be an agreed policy for Edward which every volunteer would scrupulously follow, and any variation had to be discussed at the regular meetings of the sisterhood and agreed. Consistent handling was most important for the caller's progress. It would, for instance, have been counter-productive to have one young woman more permissive than the others about frequent masturbatory calls, because instead of being equally happy with any interlocutor, the caller would then ring incessantly in the hope of getting the respondent he felt he could manipulate.

If one of the sisterhood was chatting with a client over a coffee and was needed to answer the Brent telephone, she would naturally not be asked in front of the client, 'Will you come and suppress your yawns whilst listening to a chap wanking?' but 'Excuse me, could you come and take a Brent call?'

This became known to the Samaritans of Brent, and instead of being honoured, they were horrified. 'Very well,' I said. 'We'll use "Brenda" instead. All the members of the sisterhood will be called

Brenda, and those who use this service will be called Brenda callers.'

From reading Brendas' notes, I suspected that there were several instances of Brenda callers getting themselves listed under more than one name, in order to ring more frequently, so I appointed my then secretary, Suzan Cameron, to spend a month taking all the Brenda calls, with other Brendas on duty with her in turn for company and experience. It proved to be true that when each separate caller was restricted to asking for one name only, the total number of such callers declined to one-fifth of the previous inflated number.

The first thing Brenda had to learn was that she was on duty to befriend the sexually frustrated caller in his imagined relationship with someone other than herself, and never, never to permit herself to be the object of his lust. She was to be his elder sister or young aunt or 'platonic' friend, with whom he could speak about anyone else in whatever language he chose, and never herself his 'target for tonight'.

Befriending is beautifully aimless. It does not seek to change, reform, improve people. Those exposed to it often make changes in themselves, but that is because *they* want to, not because *we* are dissatisfied with them as they are. They have a right to be themselves. Counselling, on the other hand, seeks to effect changes in the client which the client desires, with the client's consent and cooperation. The counsellor is trusted because he or she knows how. Brenda is only a semi-counsellor, because she does not know how in any field except that of dealing intelligently and constructively with sexually demanding or sexually aggressive callers. In that field, she is unequalled. A famous psychiatrist was asked for advice on how to deal with such callers, and his reply was, 'Ask Brenda – she knows more about it than any of us.'

Sad to relate, the Branch concerned did *not* do so, but set up its own scheme, which did it all wrong, caused havoc and rebellion in the Branch, and led to their joining others who, having tackled the matter entirely the wrong way, informed all and sundry that 'the Brenda system didn't work'. The few Branches which followed London in learning from years of experience of Brenda's predecessors discovered some important things. First, and most important, that the majority of the callers were depressed, lonely, and woefully ignorant of how to make a good relationship with a woman; and not a few were suicidal because of this. Secondly, Brenda's Samaritan acceptance of them at every stage allowed a gradual improvement towards the goal set (oh, the interfering hussy!) by Brenda,

187

with at times reluctant co-operation from the caller, namely gradually and patiently to set the caller free from dependence on often angry masturbation with fantasies of violence towards or humiliation of women, with no interpersonal relationship, and help him to approach the opposite sex as human beings and make friendly relationships with them which might or might not lead to some sexual gratification eventually.

So many men needed this type of rehabilitation that those Branches which did not have a Brenda system began to feel overwhelmed by the callers who rang one Branch after another trying to find a Brenda and tended to become more and more aggressive. The Branches' response in too many cases was to try to discourage such calls by such heartless expedients as asking the caller to ring back when he had finished masturbating, and then speak to a man. There was even one period when the Executive laid down a policy of trying to block what were prudishly described as 'M-calls', responding (understandably, if not with much understanding) to the widespread anxiety of female volunteers about calls they felt incapable of dealing with comfortably. Small wonder that some of them would cling to calls from harmless, non-suicidal old ladies, slightly lonely and always game for a gossip, as a safe refuge against the Brenda caller. The ridiculous situation arose where The Samaritans were willing to listen calmly to tales of murder, massacre, mayhem, matricide and any other M except masturbation. Fortunately the instinct of well-selected Samaritans began to reject this as 'un-Samaritan', and Branches were allowed to do as they liked, which, in the absence of nationwide Brenda training, meant the problem was swept under the carpet and Branches somehow muddled through.

You mustn't suppose that I am unsympathetic to the problems of Branch Directors in recruiting and retaining volunteers. They know that if they accepted only Brendas they would be unable to maintain a twenty-four hour service, so they have to accept some, perhaps a majority, of volunteers who, perhaps because of their personal insecurity about sex, would never be able to cope with a Brenda call and might resign rather than do so. It is a real dilemma for Directors, who don't want to lower the standards but also don't want to be unable to carry on the service.

Small wonder that in the '70s and '80s, services began to spring up, advertised in magazines like *Forum*, where for a fee you could ring a number and speak to a girl, advertised as eager to talk sexually to you, whilst you masturbated. Now, I am not decrying this form of semi-prostitution. There are girls willing to talk sexually to any man on the telephone from the safety of a booth, who would not be willing to be gazed at lustfully, let alone touched, let alone permit coitus. Girls who need the money and feel comfortable with any stage from the most uninvolved to the most intimate, find what suits them best, and if what suits them is talking sexily on the telephone to an unseen stranger for a handsome fee, they will naturally hope to get their clients hooked, so that the stream of lucrative calls does not dry up. You can see how this is the opposite of Brenda. Brenda is trying to do herself out of a job by making her ministrations unnecessary to the caller. Samaritans who have not scrupled to apply the term 'prostitute' to Brenda are guilty of complete misuse of the term, as well as being so uncharitable that one wonders how they got accepted as volunteers.

The problem is not confined to this country. Wherever in the world I lecture on suicide-prevention to Branches of Befrienders International and other crisis-intervention services, when the time comes for questions one of the first is sure to be, 'Please will you tell us how to operate a Brenda system.'

7

T HIS is my story, not the story of The Samaritans, but the two
are so inextricably intertwined that I must share with you
some landmarks in the growth of the movement. November
1953 to February 1954 was a period of discovering that befriending,
not counselling, is what seven out of eight of the callers want, and
that it is something lay volunteers, if carefully selected and supervised, can do better than anyone else. 1954–59 was a period when
The Samaritans and I were learning how to do the job of helping the
suicidal and despairing to which we had dedicated ourselves.
1960–63 was a period of expansion to other towns and cities in the
UK and overseas, culminating in the establishment of a Company
Limited by Guarantee, registered at the Board of Trade, and licensed
to omit the word 'Limited', so that our Association was known as
The Samaritans, or The Samaritans Inc.

During the period 1956–62 I enjoyed a grant from the Calouste
Gulbenkian Foundation, which enabled me to take on some paid
staff. The Revd John Eldrid and Miss Mary Bruce, a psychiatric
social worker at St Bartholomew's Hospital, joined me in 1958 and
the Revd Eric Reid from the Church of Ireland the following year.
Mary Bruce left in 1965 and shortly afterwards took charge of the
London Council on Alcoholism and later still returned to Scotland
and married. Eric Reid went into the Hospital Chaplaincy Service in
1967 and became Secretary to the Hospital Chaplaincy Council in
1975 until his retirement in 1987. John Eldrid left in 1963 to
become Director of the Portsmouth Branch, and returned again as
my Deputy Director eight years later. On our twenty-first anniversary, 2 November 1974, he took over from me as Director of the
London Branch and I became Chairman (and President) of
Befrienders International, The Samaritans Worldwide. I remained,

of course, Rector of St Stephen Walbrook, and my being on the premises must have been awkward for John at times, loyal friends though we were and are. He was a very popular Chairman of The Samaritans Inc. and was re-elected for a second three-year period, the only one to be so honoured. When The Samaritans moved from St Stephen Walbrook to 46 Marshall Street, Soho in October 1987, he went as their Director until his retirement in 1988, and still remains a consultant.

There were times when I needed to discuss the case of a client with psychological problems with someone who knew more than I then did, and after a couple of years Dr Basil Merriman, a specialist in alcoholism and drug addiction, volunteered and was a great help. After Mary Bruce's arrival, I turned more to her, and later to Dr Richard Fox, at that time in charge of the emergency clinic at the Maudsley Hospital. He accepted my invitation to become psychiatric consultant to the London Branch, and in 1963, when the Association was formed, he became consultant to The Samaritans Inc. and continued after he transferred to Severalls Hospital, Colchester. He was a genius at explaining psychiatric problems in layman's language, enlivened by much-appreciated humorous asides, though these were fully appreciated only by English speakers – at international conferences his persiflage sometimes left parts of the audience uncomprehending the laughter of the remainder. He and I made several trips together to Poland and Czechoslovakia to make contact with psychiatrists there who were interested in suicide prevention, but no actual Branch of The Samaritans resulted at that time except in Gdańsk, where Professor Dr Taduesz Keilanowski (phthisis, not psychiatry) was able to set up a Branch. Participation by churches in those countries was, of course, out of the question, and this was no great disappointment to me after the experience I had had in Western Europe, where churches wanted to take over for their own purposes what I knew must be a purely humanitarian movement.

The other psychiatrists who were important to us at that time (there have been many since) were Dr Doris Odlum and Professor Dr Erwin Stengel. Dr Odlum when I first met her was already a famous child psychiatrist and a campaigner against attempted suicide being a felony under English law. When she was given the job in 1961 of helping to draft the Suicide Act, she discussed the subject with me. I told her that in the metropolitan area the police took a very humane view of suicidal acts which did not prove fatal, and

191

hardly ever engaged in a prosecution which led the person to imprisonment, except in a few cases where they thought it necessary for the protection of the person concerned and the avoidance of a public nuisance – as for instance in the case of a man who regularly swallowed an unbelievable assortment of cutlery and took up a lot of hospital and operating-theatre time. The normal police procedure, I told her, if they thought the person was still a danger to himself or herself, was to urge the person to see their doctor with a view to psychiatric treatment, or, latterly, to come to The Samaritans. Only when the person proved recalcitrant would they prosecute, not in order to get the person sent to prison, but so that they might be inclined to accept as an alternative being put on probation with a condition that they received psychiatric help.

Dr Odlum told me that unfortunately the situation in the provinces was totally different, and many miserable wretches were exposed to the increased misery of prison. Of course I agreed with her that attempted suicide should be removed from the Statute Book, as it was that year. I invited her to become consultant psychiatrist to her home Branch, Bournemouth, and she was so invaluable there that she was asked to be consultant to the whole movement. In 1974 she was elected President, and hugely enjoyed the annual conferences, where she always gave the closing address and beamed delightedly at the standing ovation always accorded to her. Her death from angina at the age of ninety-seven was felt as a personal loss by a large proportion of Samaritan volunteers in the British Isles.

Dr Stengel, who never lost his Austrian accent and was for many of us the archetypal psychiatrist, spoke at our second annual conference at St Mary's College, Durham in 1963. (The first had been at Balliol College, Oxford in 1961). His excellent lecture was marred by a passage which totally misunderstood what was meant by 'befriending' in a Samaritan context. When I explained to him afterwards that the listening therapy practised by Samaritan volunteers involved much more than just 'being friendly', he grasped the point at once, wrote out a revised version of the passage for me to approve, and promised to include it in his Penguin book, *Suicide and Attempted Suicide*. Unfortunately, his secretary or someone at his publisher's got the papers mixed up, and the original faulty version appeared in the book and did us a lot of harm by seeming to damn us with faint praise. It also gave our enemies on the Continent the opportunity to disparage our work by quoting from an obviously authoritative book on the subject of suicide. He tried to make amends by becoming our President until his death, when he was replaced by Dr Odlum.

I laid it down very early that every Branch should have a psychiatric consultant, or failing that a medical consultant with some psychiatric knowledge. The Director of a Branch, which was a non-medical organization, needed to have someone with whom he could take counsel when having to make decisions about clients with psychiatric illnesses.

I myself received a great deal of instruction from our various consultant psychiatrists and from interviewing mentally ill clients and then discussing their cases with a consultant, especially those I have already mentioned. It was particularly useful when they asked me to give my opinion, and then discussed at length whether they agreed with it or not, and why. After the first ten years, I noticed that I was hardly ever needing to obtain a psychiatric opinion on someone, though of course I still had to refer to a psychiatrist those who needed medical help, such as endogenous depressives. Without the discipline of a degree course and professional qualifications and clinical practice, any knowledge one acquires is theoretical, and however useful, does not qualify one to give any treatment or to prescribe.

In the early days, it was important for me to be with my Samaritans every day and as much of the day as possible. People like 44 Roger Martyn, 75 George Millington and 219 Jean Burt, who were capable of taking a little responsibility and even of doing what we called a 'special interview' (getting as near counselling on, for example, marital problems as an unqualified person could rightly get) were on duty normally only one day a week, so even if they had all joined by that time they would not have been able to take responsibility if I were away ill (which fortunately hardly ever happened) or was on holiday. Clergymen in the Church of England were accustomed to having a month's holiday every year, modified perhaps in war-time, and if they worked a six-day week, as most of them did, they really needed it. Once I had started The Samaritans it was more difficult to be absent, but thanks to my secretary, No. 2 Vivien Prosser, I was able to get away for a month in 1955, though it wasn't exactly a holiday. I was second-in-command of a delegation of five Anglican priests to the Soviet Union, to be guests of the

Patriarch of Moscow and All Russia.

The delegation was nothing to do officially with the Church of England. The Archbishop of Canterbury was left perfectly free to repudiate it or take notice of it on its return. The invitation had come from the Moscow Patriarchate. The reason for it was simple: there had been a Pan-Orthodox congress in Romania, at which, because of political pressures, Anglican Orders had been declared invalid. This meant that the warm and friendly relationship between the Church of England and the Russian Orthodox Church and other Eastern Orthodox Churches in Communist countries could not possibly continue.

Although we did not have full intercommunion as we had had since 1934 with the Old Catholics, we had hitherto tended towards the Eastern side of the schism of 1054 AD, when Western Christians backed the primacy of the Bishop of Rome and Eastern Christians that of the Bishop of New Rome (Constantinople) which the Emperor had made his capital. Since that date, the churches of the East, each with its own Patriarch, owed allegiance to the Ecumenical Patriarch of Constantinople; and because his authority was not centralized or oppressive, there was no phenomenon in the East comparable with the Reformation in the West. Never having been oppressed by the Patriarch of Constantinople as we were by the Pope before the Reformation, many of us felt warmly towards our Eastern Orthodox brethren with their tradition going back almost unchanged to the time of the Apostles.

The lengths to which the Reformation went differed in different countries, and in different factions in our own country, where at one end of the scale there were those who did not wish to be reformed at all (the Recusants), and at the other end of the scale those who wished to make a clean break with the past, sweep away everything reminiscent of the old religion, and make a fresh start on the basis of nothing but the sacred Scriptures, disowning all tradition and Christian history up to that time. It was typically English that most of us did not wish to go to either extreme, and after a somewhat chaotic period it became fairly clear that most of us wanted to reform the One, Holy, Catholic and Apostolic Church, not to destroy it or replace it; and we wished to have our own national church, free of interference from or domination by Rome. So, whilst the Church of England is Protestant in the sense of protesting against the abuses of Rome, in a positive sense it is a Reformed Catholic Church, modelling itself upon the early church before the politicians and power-

194

seekers corrupted it. Whenever Rome was being particularly arro-
gant – as happened in 1871, when Pope Leo XIII declared Anglican
Orders invalid – it was a comfort to know that the great Eastern
Orthodox Church looked down upon the Roman Church as being
schismatic and heretical, and was kindly disposed to Reformed
Catholic Churches which repudiated the Pope of Rome.

The question of the validity or otherwise of Anglican Orders in
the eyes of Rome came up only because the Pope had appointed a
Commission to investigate the subject. This Commission consisted
of learned Roman Catholic church historians. The conclusion these
scholars came to after all their investigations and disputations was
that Anglican Orders were valid, but 'irregular' – presumably their
irregularity consisting in their not being in communion with the See
of Rome. The Pope and his advisers prepared a Papal Bull on the
subject, but before publishing it thought it courteous to inform the
Cardinal of England, Cardinal Vaughan, the one who would
obviously be most affected by it. Cardinal Vaughan practically had
apoplexy when he read it, and expostulated to the Pope in no
uncertain terms, pointing out that if Anglican Orders were declared
valid, however 'irregular', the Roman Catholic Church in England
could no longer claim to be the only true, Catholic and Apostolic
Church in the kingdom. The Roman Church was already sneered at
by Anglo-Catholics as 'the Italian Mission', implying that there was
something unEnglish and hardly respectable about being RC. This
was unjust, as I discovered when I worked in Lancashire, where
Roman Catholics were descendants of those who had fled there at
the time of the Reformation, and only in Liverpool were they Irish
immigrants.

Faced with the assertion that the proposed recognition of Anglican Orders would render the Roman Catholic Church's claim to be
the only true church untenable, the Pope instructed his scholars to
rewrite their report in such a way as to arrive at the opposite
conclusion. This is not the best way to make a dissertation convincing, and the resulting Bull was child's play to demolish, to such
admirable scholars as the then Archbishops of Canterbury and
York. When the Pope read it, as he could because the Archbishops
had written it in very elegant Latin, he must have wished the subject
had never been raised. You used to be able to get from SPCK an
English translation of the Bull and of the Archbishops' demolition of
it for half a crown. I rashly lent my copy to a Roman Catholic, and
not surprisingly never got it back, but I still remember the principal

arguments on both sides. Let me give you just one example.

One reason given for declaring Anglican Orders invalid was that in the consecrations of Bishops there had not always been a ceremony called *porrectio instrumentorum*, a formal handing over of certain instruments of office. This didn't come in until the sixth century, therefore if *porrectio instrumentorum* is held to be necessary, the Pope's own predecessors were not validly consecrated so that he is not a Bishop, let alone Bishop of Rome. In effect, what Cardinal Vaughan caused the Pope to do was to sit on a branch and saw it off at a point between himself and the trunk.

I am sorry to say that this was the kind of behaviour on the part of the centralized dictatorial papacy after 1870–1 which did not surprise or alarm us. But a declaration by a Pan-Orthodox congress that Anglican Orders were invalid, without reasons given which could as easily be demolished as were those adduced in Apostolicae Curae, was a different matter. We felt betrayed. The Orthodox knew this, and were unhappy about what they had been forced by political expediency to do. We could not appeal to them to change their minds (when would there be another Pan-Orthodox congress?) and they could not tell us why they had acted as they did and beg our pardon. The idea then occurred to the Patriarch of Moscow and All Russia, Alexii, that communication between our two Churches might be re-established without risk of a rebuff, which he did not dare to take, if he invited a group of Anglican priests to be his guests and to be made aware of the situation. They could then come back and invite the Archbishop of Canterbury to pay a visit, and if the Archbishop refused he could be told that the delegation was not only unofficial but had not been authorized to convey any such invitation. (Yes, I know this sounds disgustingly like politics: that's what it was.)

The only Anglican priest the Patriarch had met was the Revd Stanley Evans. He had been to Moscow as part of a trade union delegation, and was generally regarded as a fellow-traveller. He was able to find only one person to go with him, whose name I cannot remember and who when we were there never said anything I thought noteworthy. Because of my interest in the Russian Orthodox Church, Evans invited me to join the delegation, and I agreed on condition that I should be second-in-command of it and could choose the other two members of it. The two I chose were the Revd Roland Clarke, who had been my curate at Clapham Junction, and the Revd Christopher Bourne who used to travel to Bolton with me to give lectures during the war.

July 1955 was a relatively prosperous period for the Russian Orthodox Church. Stalin had rewarded it for the way it had helped to keep up morale during the Great Patriotic War, and had died before he could revert to his normal nastiness and paranoia. Malenkov was now in charge, not for very long, and the Church was flourishing as much as was possible in an atheist state where evangelism was forbidden and anti-religious propaganda was encouraged. Russians, however poor, were madly generous to their church, and the Patriarch had huge funds at his disposal. Giving VIP treatment to five of us for a month was no problem, nor was the procuring of visas for us. We flew to Prague and changed planes there. A lavish spread had been prepared for us in the VIP lounge at the airport and we were greeted by Czech Communist officials as well as by Orthodox priests, who were not necessarily fellow-travellers but simply obedient to the Patriarch.

We took off in an old Dakota for an eight-hour flight to Moscow, during which there would be no refreshment other than occasional glasses of tea served by a surly woman in civilian dress who appeared to be pregnant. About half-way we ran into a tremendous thunderstorm, the clouds of which stretched both high and wide so that we could neither go round it nor over it nor under it. Each time we were struck by lightning it was rather exciting, and evidently the pilot thought so too because he turned round and took us back to Prague. The VIP lounge in which we had been entertained was deserted and squalid and there was no possibility of getting anything to eat or drink. The staff regarded our clerical collars with suspicion and hostility. After an interminable wait we took off again, and eight hours later arrived in Moscow. There we were met by high-powered ecclesiastics and Communist guide-interpreters, and taken to an hotel, used only for VIPs, called Sovietskaya Gostinitsa.

We didn't get any opportunity to wander round on our own. Indeed, the amount of sightseeing we did was fairly limited: we seemed to spend most of our time having huge meals, with lashings of caviar, sturgeon and other delicacies, with indifferent Russian champagne and *wonderful* Georgian wine – I'll never forget the one romantically named No. 22 – and enough vodka and brandy to keep on drinking toasts until we were not likely to have much judgement of what we were told. The Russians preferred the brandy to the vodka because it was more expensive, but the vodka was better.

We did, of course, see all the usual sights, including some you can't see nowadays, and we went to Lenin's tomb in which at that time Lenin's embalmed corpse and Stalin's were on either side of the visitor. As I looked down on the body of Stalin, knowing more than most of my hosts about the atrocities he was guilty of, I muttered, 'Better a living lion than a dead dog.' (Yes, I know the Book of Proverbs had the animals the other way round.) We were taken of course to Zagorsk and also to one or two small monasteries in the countryside. There were at that time sixty-three seminaries for training candidates for the priesthood, and a large number of nunneries, one of which we visited near Odessa, on the shores of the Black Sea. (That was where the KGB tried to entrap me, as I shall tell you in detail shortly.) Before we went south we went north, by the famous Red Arrow train to Leningrad, where they were already in 1955 drenching visitors for a joke with the various remote-controlled fountains in the Winter Gardens. (They didn't catch me again when I was there thirty years later on a four-day tour from Helsinki, where I had been attending a suicide-prevention conference.)

The chief interest for me was the wonderful services in the great cathedrals with the Metropolitan and other dignitaries, and the marvellous Orthodox singing for which I have always had a passion. We became very friendly with the Professor of Music, Professor Pariiski, whom we also met in Moscow. On my Finnish package tour those many years later, I was distressed to find that none of these great cathedrals was still used for worship, and, wanting to go to a Russian Orthodox service, I found that this was the only religious denomination not mentioned on the notice-board in Hotel Leningrad. However, I leapt on to the first tram that came along on the Sunday morning, and for surprisingly few kopeks I came within sight of the green dome of the great church in which the poet Lermontov had been married. I got off the tram and walked towards it but every road or path seemed to lead away from it or round it – a very cunning and presumably expensive way of preventing worshippers reaching it. I persevered, however, and found a sapling growing through the great keyhole of the main door. Refusing to be deterred, I went round to the other side, where a surly fellow pretending to sweep the courtyard tried unsuccessfully to chase me off. I then went down some steps into the crypt, and found myself in a sort of holy Aladdin's cave, with golden icons gleaming in the light of lamps and candles, and the worshippers repeatedly crossing themselves from right to left (not, as in the West, from left

198

to right) as they listened to the choir singing the Kiev melodies and other music I found so worshipful. But let me not confuse you: the contrast between 1955 and thirty years later in Leningrad was that the Church was no longer rich and powerful and the great cathedrals were shut, just as the contrast between 1955 and my visit to Moscow in 1989 was that the Church's influence was immensely reduced and the number of seminaries had fallen from sixty-three to about three.

We didn't return to Moscow by Red Arrow: the Patriarch had hired a plane to take us via Moscow to Kiev, and after visiting Kiev to Odessa. (Again the contrast between the magnificent services in Kiev in 1955 and the dreary place to which I made a day trip from Romania when on holiday there in the '80s was depressing.) My youngish guide-interpreter, who was a captain in the KGB, had at last discovered that I understood some Russian, which I had kept from him in order to learn things they didn't want me to know, and while circling Kiev in preparation for landing there, he suddenly addressed me in Russian, calling me 'Mr Varyagh'. Pointing at the golden domes beneath he asked whether I was still claiming them.

The significance of this was that St Vladimir, Prince of Kiev in the ninth century was a Varyagh, and he affected to believe that *I* believed I was descended from one of the Varyaghi (in our history books Varangians) after they were defeated and scattered by a Scandinavian pirate called Oleg (Pushkin wrote a poem about it). I suppose it is barely possible that one of them reached Yorkshire before our first trace of the name there in 1480, but I replied that I wouldn't wish to live anywhere in the Soviet Union, not even Kiev. He then sneered at my posh accent, saying 'And what little Prince taught you Russian, Mr Varyagh?', to which I replied, dead-pan, 'Prince Leonid Lieven.' I think that was probably the point at which he decided that I was an enemy of the Soviet Union. Stanley Evans and the delegate he chose were seen as friends and the two I had invited as neutral.

There were two things that happened in Odessa, a great port on the Black Sea about twenty miles from where the River Dniepr debouches into it. One of these was worrying, the other heart-warming beyond belief. I have already told you that the KGB tried to entrap me in a nunnery on the outskirts of Odessa and I promised to tell you how. We had all of us heard stories about how the KGB used *agents provocateurs* to try to put possibly useful visitors in compromising positions which would then be photographed and the

199

photographs used to blackmail the victim into spying on behalf of the Soviet Union. This was particularly effective if the victim was a practising homosexual, because at that time exposure was a far more serious matter than it would be now or at any time in the post-Wolfenden period. Of course, heterosexuals were also enticed, and like many visitors to the Soviet Union at that time I had had fantasies of being seduced by Mata Haris indistinguishable from Greta Garbo or Merle Oberon, so that when confronted with the incriminating photographs I could pretend to be shattered and promise to do anything, anything – and then betray my Controller to MI5½. (Another fantasy was the one in which I showed my contempt for them by pouncing on the photographs with eager delight, requesting spare copies to make my male friends envious.)

It was a blistering hot day when we set out for the nunnery, and I decided to wear nothing whatever underneath my double-breasted cassock. We were kindly received by the good sisters, who laid on a special entertainment for us in the shape of a quartet of singers of liturgical music, one of these singers being tenor, which was just credible, and another being baritone, which was hard to believe – perhaps the bass sound came from her stomach, since I could see no male organs (I refer of course to the Adam's apple). While being conducted around the nunnery we had noticed a couple of flighty-looking nuns who, though wearing the appropriate garb, did not seem to fit in and were always giggling on the next corner we were coming to. It was very cleverly managed that I was separated from the rest of my delegation and led by my interpreter to a staircase at the top of which there was alleged to be a music room.

Arrived there, I was aware that one of these two suspect nuns had followed us and was now bearing a violin. My interpreter said that she was anxious to show the distinguished visitor her progress in learning to play on the instrument, and without more ado she began to produce the most excruciating sound from it. She asked me in Russian how I liked her music, and I lied, and she then asked whether I thought she was attractive. I tried to explain that one did not look at nuns with this kind of assessment in mind, but my Russian was inadequate to the task of explaining this without hurting her feelings, so I turned to my interpreter, only to find that he had vamoosed. The girl then opened her habit to reveal that, like myself, she was wearing nothing underneath. I just had time to take in the evidence that she was a synthetic blonde when the plot dawned on me, and I made a dive for the stairs. Half way down I ran into my interpreter and the photographer (not the one employed by the Patriarch who followed us around everywhere) coming up, and I pushed back past them, calling out to my interpreter that the fiddling was so excruciating I had to get out into the fresh air. I didn't stop running until I had rejoined our group. I do hope the girl didn't get into trouble for failing to entice me.

Stanley Evans wasn't with us on this occasion. I hope I didn't do him an injustice in assuming that he had been told to stay away. His excuse for not being with us all that day was that he had engaged unwisely in a competition with his interpreter to see who could eat the greater number of green peppers, and he had won but had been quite ill as a result. This was such an unlikely story that it may well have been true. His illness, whether genuine or diplomatic, meant that not only did he miss the nunnery but also was absent from the service of welcome in Odessa Cathedral laid on for our delegation by Archbishop Nikon. He was a venerable and charming man, and Christopher and I thought that he was probably a genuine Christian. All of us, attired in cassocks and accompanied by a couple of interpreters, were received into the sanctuary behind the iconostasis, and the cathedral was packed solid with what I was later told were 4,000 worshippers standing shoulder to shoulder.

I had been warned that at an appropriate point in the service Archbishop Nikon would introduce me (in the absence of Stanley Evans) to the congregation as 'a priest of our sister church, the Anglican Church of England', and I was to give an address. My interpreter stood beside me when the time came, but I foxed him by speaking Russian, so that he would know that he must translate what I actually said and not what he thought I ought to say. '*Nadyéos*' *chto nash priyést pomózhet ooprazhneniyoo mira*,' I shouted. ('*Dyelo mira*' would have been better.) It meant, 'I hope that our coming may promote the cause of peace.' Immediately there was a roar from the entire congregation, and I couldn't help recoiling a little, wondering whether I was going to be lynched. What had I said wrong? I continued with my address, but each time I paused this roar was repeated. After the fourth time I was able to make out the words: '*Spasee vas Góspodjee!*' (God save you!)

This frantic approval, I later realized, arose from tremendous relief: these people had suffered appallingly during the Great Patriotic War, and had been told by their lords and masters that we in the West were fascist plutocratic capitalist oppressors of the toiling masses, armed to the teeth and likely to attack Odessa at any time without warning, so a representative of these, unarmed and less than eight feet tall, introduced by their revered Archbishop and beaming at them and speaking to them *in their own language* about *peace*, had them sobbing in the aisles. When my Russian ran out I used my interpreter, but this was a bonus, because speaking gibberish, i.e. English, I was obviously a genuine English plutocrat (how could they possibly know how difficult I had sometimes found it to manage on my stipend?).

When the service, with its wonderful singing, came to an end, we had to make our way out of the church through this packed congregation. I had never had such an experience before, and I have never had such an experience since, not even when surrounded and embraced by loving Samaritans at annual Conferences of 1,200 or more. It took me forty minutes to get out of the church, and my companions only a little less, because it seemed that everyone, men, women and little children, wanted to kiss my hands or failing that the hem of my cassock. (Don't worry, I now had trousers on underneath.) All of us felt humbled and subdued for the rest of the day. I was angrier than ever with the Soviet authorities who had taught those good, simple people to hate and fear their fellow Christians in my own country, and was ashamed that in our own thinking about the Soviet Union we mostly forgot about the ordinary people who suffered far more from their rulers than we ever would.

From Odessa we went to the Patriarch's summer palace on the shores of the Black Sea at a point where a fairly high cliff separated the palace from the part of the beach belonging to it and reserved for it. Access to the beach was by a funicular, hand-operated by large, gentle, bearded monks. It was wonderfully relaxing there, and the Patriarch was able to spare time for many conversations with us. He asked whether any of us was personally acquainted with the Archbishop of Canterbury, and I told him I was. He asked me on my return to tell the Archbishop that he, the Patriarch, would very much like to welcome him to Moscow, and on receiving a message that it would be accepted, a formal invitation would be sent to him.

Back in Moscow, where our rooms had been reserved all the time at Sovietskaya Gostinitsa, we were given time to spend the 2,000 roubles each of us had been given as pocket money and which we had hardly needed to touch. There wasn't much to buy, but I spent 1,500 of my 2,000 on a Zorkii 3 camera with an f2 Jupiter lens, which I gathered was a rather rough Russian version of the Leika 3c. Its great disadvantage was that you had to load the cassette in a

202

dark-room, though I later discovered you could use normal cassettes once you were back in England and could get them. I did some quite good work with it. But, probably deliberately, it was almost the end of our stay when I acquired it.

There weren't many shops, even on the main street, Ulitsa Gorkova, and I shall never forget dear old Professor Pariiski pointing out with great pride some handbags in a shop window which would not have entirely disgraced a shop in East Cheam High Street. 'Splendid workmanship, don't you think?' enthused Professor Pariiski.

'Er – very nice, very nice indeed, Professor,' I replied politely, not wishing to hurt his feelings, but of course a brilliant musician could pick up the tone of tactful insincerity, far more disparaging than any sneer.

'I realize you must have much better in your own country,' he murmured wistfully.

'Some things are better here, some things are better there, that's natural,' I assured him; but I fear he was not comforted.

I was able to get away from my minders only twice, once at the beginning and once near the end of my stay. On the first occasion, our delegation was going to be taken to see a small factory where candles and other ecclesiastical requirements were made, presumably by nuns. I pleaded a headache, and went up to my room to lie down. As soon as the party had left, I nipped down the back stairs in case the front were watched, made my way to the nearest metro, dived into it, took a ticket to a moderately distant suburb, and came out into the open air there, feeling wonderfully free. The feeling did not last: I was still in what at that time was the world's biggest prison, the USSR.

I went and knocked on the door of one of a row of similar houses, and said to the astonished middle-aged lady who opened the door, in Russian, 'I am an English priest from London visiting the Patriarch of Moscow and All Russia as his guest. May I come in and meet your family?' Instead of hissing through her teeth, 'Begone, capitalist running-dog and fascist lackey!', she beamed and took me into the small, overheated living-room, and introduced me to several children and what I took to be her next-door neighbour, while she made tea. All was pleasant for about five minutes, whilst I told her about my children, but then the neighbour sent out the oldest of the boys with a message I didn't hear, and pretty soon a workman came in without knocking, and sat down and began to question me. This overbearing fellow was the monitor of the block, who had to report everything to the police. He didn't like it that *I* had the nerve to question *him* on why it was necessary for him to interrupt a friendly visit by a member of a foreign delegation. Was it, I asked, forbidden for Soviet citizens to receive such a visit? Would the lady of the house get into trouble for letting me in, when it was purely by chance that it was her door I knocked at? All this was straining my Russian a bit, and when he made some placatory remark I still didn't know whether my visit was or wasn't illegal but decided to bring it to an end.

Outside, in the bright sunshine, I got one of the gathering crowd to take a photo of me with the family I had visited, and I made a note of their name and address. I never received any reply to the picture postcard I sent them from London on my return. The busybody insisted on walking me to the metro, asking which station I was going to and which hotel I was staying at. He had a young man following him at a discreet distance, who followed me into the underground, doubtless to see whether I really *was* staying at the Kremlin and getting off at Red Square. I managed to lose my 'tail' and get back unobserved to Sovietskaya Gostinitsa in time to greet the party on their return from the candle-factory. As far as I know, they never discovered what I had been up to.

The other occasion when I escaped was a day or two before we were due to fly back to London. We were walking with our guide-interpreters along Ulitsa Gorkova for some reason I now forget, and whilst my minder was engaged with somebody else I nipped down a side street, turned left and right and hurried for about 200 yards, then stopped and looked around. To my amazement I was in what could only be described as a slum – 200 yards off the main street. There were tumbledown little houses built of timber which obviously hadn't had a lick of paint since 1917, and it looked as if each was divided between four families. A grimy little girl of about eight addressed me, but I didn't understand what she said. I stared at her in disbelief, because it was the first time in my life that I had seen rickets, except in a photograph.

Suddenly there appeared a man who seemed like a soldier – he was armed – but I later discovered he was a policeman. This young man sternly bade me to follow him, and would take no notice of my explanation that my friends were waiting for me on Ulitsa Gorkova and would be alarmed at my disappearance. We walked for a very long time until we came to a grim building in a sordid street which was the local police station. '*Podozhditye zdess*'!' bellowed the policeman, who obviously thought foreigners would understand Russian only if it was very loud. I could sympathize with him, because I had the impulse to bawl at him, 'Now look here, my good man!' A ragged fellow whom I took to be a tramp was lounging on a seat and picking his nose, and after a while I was summoned to an inner room. 'This gentleman was first,' I demurred, pointing at the tramp, but my willingness to wait my turn was ignored.

The man of moderately high rank who sat behind the desk had a hard face and cunning little eyes, but he was no fool. I had decided to speak only English, and he understood enough to know that his policeman had boobed. He got on the telephone and jabbered away – I couldn't follow what he said: I was getting tired of the Russian language, anyway, for that day – and after an interminable wait a battered old jalopy arrived at the door of the police station and the superior officer insisted on shaking hands. The over-zealous idiot who had arrested me tried to ingratiate himself by calling out '*Do svidaniya*' (au revoir), and was not comforted when I replied that I would not be seeing him again as *I* would not be going to Siberia.

The jalopy dropped me at Sovietskaya Gostinitsa and drove off, and my minder was very reproachful indeed that I had given him the slip. I told him all that had happened, and later that evening two well-dressed gentlemen presented themselves and were introduced to me as the Chief of Police and the Governor (surely not of the whole of Moscow? I never found out). These gentlemen apologized profusely for the inconvenience to which I had been subjected, whilst at the same time making it clear that it hadn't happened. Double-speak, as in 1984, was obviously not just an invention of George Orwell but was alive and well and living in Moscow in 1955. I accepted their apologies and agreed it hadn't happened, and more importantly, that I would not make a scandal story about it in the press on my return to London. I said that I had greatly enjoyed the Patriarch's hospitality and would not think of embarrassing him with lurid press criticisms, but would carry the secret to his grave. Nobody noticed my choice of pronoun, and now that the dear man is in his grave, I feel free to reveal to you what happened.

As soon as I could, I sought an interview with the Archbishop of Canterbury, and was courteously received as always. The result was that relations with the Eastern Orthodox Churches were re-established and it was indicated that an invitation to the Archbishop from Moscow would be accepted.

The Revd Stanley Evans was killed in a car crash with a lady friend soon after our return. I have no reason whatever to believe there was anything sinister in this. A death that *did*, however, seem to me sinister was that of my friend Pyotr Struve in Paris, when a lorry carrying a projecting steel girder backed into his car and smashed his windscreen and his head. I came to know Pyotr because of his marriage to Tatiana Lebedev, who years before had been *au pair* to us at Blackburn, and most evenings helped me to bath the triplets. Like most other Russians in Paris, Tanya knew that I was regularly visiting priests on the outskirts as Secretary of the Orthodox Churches Aid Fund, and I was often invited to their house. At that time Pyotr was a doctor of medicine, but later on he was ordained to the priesthood. He had many contacts with the Soviet Union, and took a special interest in compiling a list of those priests and bishops who were believed to have been infiltrated by the KGB either to undermine the Church or to spy upon it. He told me he had a more accurate list of metropolitans and bishops who were KGB atheists than anyone else. I did not tell anyone this, nor did I mention my suspicions to anyone at the time, least of all to his distraught widow, who was left without means of support.

It was a relief to get back to my children and take their photographs with my new camera, and to get back to The Samaritans, who had managed well without me, as I had expected they would. The reason why I was not surprised was that my conviction had grown that in a crisis the *urgent* thing that is required is befriending, supporting the person who *has* the problem, and not the counselling or other expert treatment to deal *with* the problem. The big exception to this was the person suffering from a clinical depression, that is, one caused by hormonal changes in the brain, which would respond only to treatment by a doctor; but of course, only very good befriending could usually get these people to agree to see their doctor, and any Samaritan volunteer encountering a depressed person who didn't seem to have obvious reasons for his depression would, as a matter of common sense, concentrate on wheedling the person into seeing a doctor. Over a period of a month, therefore, the work had suffered less by my absence than it would have done by the absence of a dozen reliable volunteers. Over a longer period things would have begun to come apart without firm direction, and there were of course many people awaiting counselling on the premises who had not been able to be referred to one of our psychotherapists.

It is difficult in the '90s to remember how prudish and impermissive society was in the '50s, whether you lived through the period or not. I was very glad indeed to be back on the job when a man was brought in to see me who had agreed to speak with me but not with anyone else before committing suicide. The man, in his thirties, had lived in the north of England with his mother, a long-time widow in indifferent health who was very demanding. He had no social life whatever. He was well thought of at his work, but made no friends there: as soon as his work was done, he pedalled home on his bicycle. 'Now, mind you come straight home, Sidney,' his mother had admonished ever since he was a small boy. (His name wasn't Sidney.) The only occasion on which he didn't come straight home, Sidney, was when there was a party after work at his firm for a young man who was going to leave. Sidney was distressed at the thought of this young man leaving, as he was very much attracted to him, and often glanced at him when he was sure he would not be observed. He told his mother he would be staying for the party, and for the first time resisted all her objections.

He had never drunk alcohol before, and naturally it had a powerful effect upon him. It also made him urgently need, on his unsteady way home, to relieve his bladder. He propped up his bicycle, and went into a public lavatory, where he observed a young man vaguely resembling the one he had been attracted to at work and now would not be seeing again. This young man smiled at him, and to Sidney's astonishment began masturbating. Sidney had never seen an erect penis before. His own instantly sprang to attention, and he began to imitate the young man's movements. Then the young man 'adjusted his dress' (as the notice by the door bade you do before leaving in those days) and arrested Sidney for importuning.

At the police station, Sidney was in a daze, but was aware of being photographed by a reporter from the local newspaper. He pleaded with the man not to submit the photograph to his editor, but in vain. Sidney said the story would kill his mother. The reporter laughed. When Sidney was allowed to go, he got on to his bicycle and made for the newspaper office, where he lay in wait. Alcohol, injustice and callousness had turned this mild, inoffensive man into an avenging fury: he knocked the reporter out cold, and took his camera and removed the film. He rode home, put his bicycle into the shed, and went to say good night to his mother. Then he took all his money, made sure the kitchen fire was safe, left the house, posted the keys through the letter-box, and walked to the station, where he bought a ticket to London.

On the journey, he removed all identification from his pockets and clothing, and on arrival waited for the underground to open, and made his way to the part of the platform nearest to the point where trains emerged from the tunnel. He was planning to fling himself in front of the train in such a way that the wheels would go over his face, and make him unidentifiable. As he heard the roar of the approaching train, he braced himself for the desperate act which he hoped would prevent his mother from knowing, ever, the shame of his arrest and the manner of his death. At the police station he had given the name of the colleague in whose honour the party had been held, which had been responsible for his downfall.

A carpenter on his way to work at that early hour, with his bag of tools over his shoulder, noticed the tense behaviour of Sidney, who because of the roar of the approaching train did not hear the approaching carpenter. Sidney was snatched back at the last moment, bundled on to the train when the doors opened, and severely admonished by the carpenter. Mention of the dreaded police forced Sidney to agree to accompany his rescuer to The Samaritans, he having been promised that he would have to see no one but me.

In an incoherent way he gave me the account of what had happened which I have now given to you. He was surprised and pleased by my indignation at the unscrupulous behaviour of the *agent provocateur*, and at my unconcern about his mother or any person except himself.

I explained to him why homosexuality was normal for about a tenth of the population, and that it is not wrong to be what you are, nor to do what you want to do if you can meet a grown-up who also wants it, though not in a public place like a lavatory. (You will realize this was a pre-Wolfenden way of saying 'consenting adults in private'.) Obviously his next question was going to be, how do I ever meet such a person? I ran through my mental list of homosexual men outside London who had cause to trust me, settled on one who lived in Sussex, sent Sidney off for a couple of days with a Samaritan volunteer who was living happily with his boyfriend, and was glad to be able to tell Sidney next time I saw him that a friend of mine would find him a job and somewhere to live, and look after him until he met the partner I felt sure he would find one day. He

208

was very ambivalent towards his mother, but I was able to persuade him to leave with me a blank sheet of paper on which he had written: '*Dear Mother, I had to leave. Not your fault. I shall not be coming back. Forgive me.*' And then after his signature, '*I am alive and well and living in Scotland.*' I arranged for this to be posted to his mother from Scotland – well, Scotland and Sussex both begin with S, do they not? Before I saw him off at Victoria, he told me I might use his story for publicity purposes for The Samaritans, but the only part I told a reporter began with the carpenter seeing someone about to jump in front of a train, his bringing him to me, my finding that homosexuality was the cause of his despair, and my introducing him to homosexual friends. After all these years, I have told *you* the full story, which I think will be more instructive than giving you snippets about many different clients.

Some stories are short to begin with: one such was the young man who burst in in great distress, and as soon as the door was firmly shut, tore open his fly buttons and produced his erect penis. It looked as if it had a tight band between the stem and the glans, which was bare and purple, and he moaned, 'Help me, sir – I can't get it back.' I realized at once that what he couldn't get back was the foreskin. It was too tight to be pulled back to expose the glans during tumescence, and he had pulled it back while his penis was flaccid, and then tried to stretch the prepuce by stroking his penis to erection. Whether this had been days, hours or a few minutes ago, I didn't ask; I just said that I thought I could help him but I must first wash my hands. I went into my little washroom, filled a plastic bowl with cold water, came out and hurled it at his crotch, then grabbed his penis and pulled. To my great relief, the cold water had shrunk it, and the prepuce now covered the glans. 'You've ruined my trousers!' he complained. 'Such gratitude!' I thought to myself, but I don't know what I would have done if it hadn't worked. I lent him a cassock to wear whilst his trousers dried.

It must seem to you as though I am always the hero (or villain, as the case may be) of the stories I tell you, but this is because I don't always know in sufficient detail what happened in cases where I was not personally involved.

I think you may be interested in one episode of which the heroine was Jean 219, who, alas, died in 1990 after thirty-three years' service. We did not in the '50s allow clients to come to us in person at night, and most Branches still don't: if we couldn't deal with them satisfactorily on the telephone, we would send someone to see *them*. For this purpose we had a Flying Squad: the name was ironic, because it wasn't a squad, but just one apparently timid but really intrepid damsel. (A few years later, Edinburgh Branch really *did* have a squad, of four strapping Scotsmen, no doubt armed with dirks.) The volunteers on Night Watch (the name inspired by Rembrandt's painting) were not allowed to send out Flying Squad. They first had to ring Home Service (apologies to the BBC), because the Samaritan in charge of Night Watch was not actually present in the Bunk Room but was at home and able to be objective about the necessity to send out Flying Squad. To do them justice, Flying Squad never complained about being sent on wild-goose chases, since they regarded the occasional false alarm as part of the job, but I was very protective towards them, knowing most of them had to go to work the next day, as did the people on Night Watch. Volunteers on a particular Night Watch didn't necessarily know callers who regularly took us for a ride, or rather tried to *get* a ride, so leaving it to Home Service to call out Flying Squad was a wise precaution. I remember one time when I was doing Home Service, as I did about once a week, the volunteers on Night Watch were most insistent that I should give the benefit of any doubt to that poor Mr Smith, who was stranded at Piccadilly Circus without money for a taxi, and had swallowed thirty-one aspirin and refused to have an ambulance. (We wouldn't ever send an ambulance without the caller's consent.) 'Give Mr. P. Honey my compliments,' I said, 'and tell him if he wants a taxi home, he should hail one.'

'But', protested Night Watch, 'his name isn't Honey, it's Smith!'

'234,' I pronounced firmly, 'do as I said, now.' In an organization dealing with matters of life and death, you have to have a signal which means don't argue, just obey orders, any discussion must be later. This signal was to speak the volunteer's Samaritan number very clearly (I can't remember what it was, but probably not 234). When she came back to the ex-directory line on which she was ringing Home Service, she was subdued. She reported, 'He said it was worth a try, or maybe not, as he never pulled it off nowadays. Sir, how did you know he was a P. Honey?'

'He always uses a phone box in Great Windmill Street,' I answered, 'and he always claims to have taken thirty-one aspirin. I might believe a round number – ten, twenty, fifty – but even the first time I didn't believe thirty-one. Now if you don't mind, I'm going back to sleep.'

I wouldn't be on Home Service for another six nights, but then I'd remain on until I was woken up, and would then be replaced, so that I never had two disturbed nights in succession. The same applied to Flying Squad. On the night I want to tell you about, a young woman with an American accent had rung to say that she had just been about to go out on her beat when she smelt gas; she had gone into another room on her floor, the third, and pulled the young man who inhabited it out of the gas oven. She said he was a homosexual whose boyfriend had ditched him, and she couldn't wait any longer as she had to get to work. She gave the address, which was in Soho. Night Watch rang me, and I rang Jean, the 'intrepid damsel' who was Flying Squad. Like me, she didn't drive, but there were always taxis near where she lived. I told her what had been told me, and she replied, 'I am on my way.' I went back to sleep, sure that she would cope well, and would wait until morning to tell me about it.

Sure enough, she reported the following morning that she had taken a taxi to the address given, and the cabby had said to her, 'Don't like the look of this, Miss, I'd better come up with you.'

'No need,' said Jean, but he followed anyway, until they ran into two desperate-looking characters coming down the stairs, whereupon the cabby turned and fled. 'My brave protector!' murmured Jean, and plodded on up to the third floor. She opened the door, and there were two naked Chinese fighting one another with knives, watched by a naked red-headed girl lying on a *chaise longue*. 'Was it you who rang The Samaritans?' enquired Jean politely.

'Neaouw, musta bin the American girl on the second floor,' replied the redhead with a strong Cockney accent.

'What are they fighting about?' asked Jean.

'Which of 'em shall 'ave first go at me,' answered the redhead with a yawn.

Jean turned to the two Chinese. 'Stop that at once,' she commanded, quietly but firmly. There was something very aristocratic about Jean, which led people to do as she said. She took out half a crown, said to the combatants in turn, 'You're heads, you're tails' and tossed the coin. She pointed to the one who had won, saying, 'You first,' and the loser obediently sat down while the other approached the *chaise longue*. Jean then went to the floor below, realizing that to an American third floor means second floor, found the grief-stricken homosexual and befriended him until it was safe to leave him.

211

'You were very brave, Jean,' I said to her, 'especially as I guess it never occurred to you that Chinese are inveterate gamblers and couldn't possibly have resisted a tossed coin.'

Talking of Flying Squad reminds me that at that period I was often driven around by a young man who had been a client and was begging to be accepted as a volunteer. I didn't feel quite sure he was ready, but his prayers must have been heard, because one evening I received a call from a man who said that he didn't want to be helped not to commit suicide, as he had firmly made up his mind to do so; he simply wanted somebody to talk to him whilst he died. He didn't want to die alone if this could be avoided. If I tried to talk him out of it, he said, he would hang up at once. I had no choice but to agree. I did not of course tell him how difficult it was for somebody dedicated to saving life to refrain from making any such attempt, because that was my problem, not his. I won't bore you with what we talked about – inconsequential matters, nothing to do with life and death and where do we go from here – but although he kept swallowing whatever it was, he seemed to take a long time to become unconscious. At last his speech became slurred and intermittent, and when I judged that he was about to topple over, I said casually, 'If you should by any chance change your mind, now would appear to be a good time, if you will excuse my mentioning it.' He murmured something to the effect that 'thash aw ri'', and then I heard an almighty crash as he fell to the floor.

He seemed to take the telephone with him and not to damage it too much, because I could clearly hear his stertorous breathing. I bellowed through the mouthpiece that I was still there, and willing to help if he wished me to and would give me his address. After an interminable time he seemed momentarily to recover consciousness and grunted a mangled form of address. Fortunately, my hearing was a lot better then than it is now. Then there was nothing more. My driver came in just then, but I was unable to leave the shop and go with him, so I gave him careful instructions as to what he was to do. He managed to find the house; he could get no answer from the doorbell or his knock, and there were no lights, but he knew the man was in the first-floor front because I had told him so, so he drove his car on to the pavement and climbed on to the roof of it, and managed to get on the windowsill. He was struggling with the fastening of the sash window when a voice enquired amiably, 'Can I be of any help to you, sir?' When he looked down, he saw a burly policeman standing there.

212

'I – I am not a burglar,' he burbled.

'I can see that,' said the policeman. 'Do you mind telling me what you are trying to do?'

'I'm a Samaritan,' said the not-yet-Samaritan proudly, 'and I'm trying to get a man to hospital who may have taken an overdose.' He then climbed down and gave the policeman a hand up, and watched with awe to see what clever method the police had for breaking in. He was disillusioned when the policeman stood on the ledge with his back to the window, and kicked backwards with his heel. Then he reached through the broken glass, turned the catch, pushed the sash up, and climbed in, and put on the light.

The two of them managed to get the man into the car (my postulant was so terrorized by me that he wouldn't call an ambulance because he thought we hadn't had the unconscious man's consent, though we had), and drove him to the hospital and stayed with him in Casualty until he was out of danger.

'Can't make you a liar, Fred,' I said. 'You told that policeman you were a Samaritan, so I suppose I'll have to let you be one.' Like most volunteers, he thanked me effusively for letting him slave away at all hours under a strict taskmaster, for more kicks than ha'pence.

Somewhat perilous situations weren't confined to Night Watch. One day a young man rang up and insisted on speaking to me, so of course he was allowed to do so. He said that he was a deserter from the army, and seemed a little disappointed when I said, 'Oh, yes?'

'Is that all you have got to say?' he demanded.

'Er – you must find life on the run very difficult,' I ventured.

He agreed that life on the run was indeed very difficult and he was getting fed up with it. After a long pause, I asked whether he'd like to come and see me.

'You'd have *them* waiting for me,' he accused.

'Them?' I enquired. 'If you mean the police, they *never* come here. They know that it is in the interests of crime-prevention that they should leave it to us to be a good influence on those who come to us, and people wouldn't come if they thought the police were observing who came and went. I assure you, the police just don't bother us.' He seemed unconvinced, but agreed to meet me in the pub opposite; just before I set out to cross the road he rang again to change the rendezvous to another pub.

I went there, but nobody accosted me, so after a while I

approached a young man and said to him, 'I've come – why don't you speak to me?' He asked how I knew he was the one, and I said I just picked the one who was looking guilty and furtive – and that if he looked like that he was likely to be arrested even if he hadn't done anything.

'Don't you dare follow me!' he hissed. (Yes, I know you can't hiss a sentence with no s's in it but he did say it through his teeth as he backed away.) I thought it likely I should see him again, because before fleeing he had learned what I looked like and would recognize me if our next rendezvous was on a street corner. It was. I won't weary you with all the time-wasting he put me through before eventually he agreed to come and see me in my study.

Once there, he sat down, refused a cup of coffee (doubtless believing it would have a Mickey Finn in it), and told me that he was a homosexual. He could see I was unimpressed, so he went on to explain that he was the only homosexual in his army hut and the other men picked on him. I suggested mildly that what he meant was that he was the only one who *admitted* to being homosexual, because there were likely to be half a dozen in his hut. Anyway, he had found life intolerable, and had decided to desert. He had brought with him a revolver, which he showed me, saying that if I had betrayed him and the police came he would blow a hole first in me, then in the policeman, then in himself. 'I told you,' I reminded him, 'the police never come here.' At that moment, the door behind him opened, and there stood a huge policeman in uniform. 'Bugger off!' I said angrily. 'Can't you see I'm busy?'

'Sorry, sir!' he said and shut the door just as the deserter turned to look. I guess that policeman never knew how close he'd come to having a hole blown in him. And, what was more serious, in me.

'Who was that?' asked the soldier, half rising and waving his revolver.

'Nobody important,' I fabricated, 'just a chap who's got a crush on my secretary, but he's never tried to get at her through that door before.' (I later discovered that the policeman *was* looking for my secretary, but whether he was after Vivien's feminine charms or a mug of coffee, I didn't enquire.)

After a long conversation, during which I slowly recovered from the shakes, I was able to persuade the deserter to let me ring up his commanding officer at Aldershot, without saying that he was with me, in order to ascertain what would happen to him if he did give himself up. The person who answered the telephone didn't want to put me through to the commanding officer, but when I told him my name he agreed to do so. It was very heartening the way this happened more and more often, as the general public began to appreciate the work of The Samaritans. The CO sounded charming, but I had to lie to him. I told him that I had been rung up by a deserter whose name I gave him, but that I was very doubtful about whether the man would come and see me, though I felt it likely he would ring me again. I said he wanted to know what would happen to him if he gave himself up.

The CO asked why he had deserted, and I told him. He said that normally a deserter would spend as long in the glasshouse as he had spent AWOL, which in this case was two years, but that he felt sympathetic towards the soldier who had obviously had a miserable life in the army and a miserable time since he deserted. 'Tell him from me,' he said, 'er – that is to say, if he *should* get in touch with you again – that he should go with you to the nearest police station, and wait there for a military escort. On arrival back here, he may be asked questions, including whether he wants a court martial or not. It is important that he should say nothing except, "I throw myself on the mercy of my Commanding Officer."'

'Thank you very much,' I said gratefully. 'I'll tell him what you say, and I've no doubt he will agree – that is, if ever I see him.' I don't think the CO was fooled.

A few minutes later, the soldier and I were walking down to Cloak Lane, where there was a police station in those days though there isn't now, and I had stopped shaking because the gun was in my pocket and not his. The police were very nice to him, and he didn't blow holes in any of them, of course; I shook hands with him and wished him luck, and told him I was convinced the CO would be very kind to him. Then I handed the gun over to the police and went back to the church.

The CO very kindly let me know what *did* happen. The deserter got two weeks instead of two years in the glasshouse, followed by a dishonourable discharge, which was precisely what he had wanted.

People often used to accuse me and other Samaritans of being heroic, constantly dealing with dangerous assignments. Gratifying though this might have been in other circumstances, we had to point out that the clients were almost all victims rather than desperadoes, and that even the few who were mentally deranged were not usually a danger to us, their only friends. I remember one paranoid schizo-phrenic who had been described by an eminent psychiatrist as the most dangerous man he had ever met, who on one occasion when he thought I had said something which implied a mild rebuke, dug his clenched fist deeply into his trousers' pockets, and said through his teeth, 'I'm leaving now, because I don't want to tear you limb from limb when you've been like a friend in the past!' He then rushed out, and when I saw him a few weeks later I thanked him for not tearing me limb from limb when I had said something I ought not to have said.

I don't think any of us minded dealing with the psychotic, but the psychopaths were a real bugbear. We knew the psychotic were pretty incapable of insight, because a good part of their thinking was withdrawn from reality into a world of delusion, but we didn't find them totally unbefriendable, as a rule, and were often successful in creating a relationship with them which allowed us to wheedle them into going for psychiatric help. Unfortunately, at that time there was little that could be done to cure any of the types of schizophrenia we encountered, but the country was blessed with a considerable number of long-stay mental hospitals where people who because of their psychiatric problems were unable to cope in the world outside were able to live under supervision and even regard the hospital as a sort of home and the nurses and some of the other inmates as their friends. This has now alas been changed by the closing down of such hospitals and the turning out of their inmates into 'the community'. The snag is, of course, that mostly there is no community that wants to be bothered with them or knows how to cope with them, so we find them amongst people who are homeless for different reasons, sleeping rough and generally giving the impression that ours is an uncaring society. I cannot state that that impression is wholly false.

When people *can* live in the world outside the mental hospital, that is obviously a good thing, and with Samaritan befriending a large number of people were enabled to do this even in the '50s, when you'd have needed both hands to count the mental hospitals within reach of Sutton, Surrey alone.

We had at that time a Samaritan whose number was 181, but I won't tell you her name, because I'm going to mention the opinion of some of her fellow Samaritans at the time I decided to take her on, and I wouldn't want to hurt her feelings. All agreed that she was sweet, gentle, and possibly even some sort of a saint, but they also considered that she was confused, vague, and lacking in common sense. As one of the brusquer Samaritans put it to me, 'She's a dear, but seems rather proud of knowing nothing at all about psychology, says about sexual problems that she's never had any experience – this without a trace of self-pity, admittedly – and although very devout, can't talk about it without talking heresy; so what use is she?'

'No use at all,' I replied, 'except . . . that anyone you put with her – anyone whatever – seems to get better.'

I was vindicated when one day I was taking a class of Samaritans on psychological problems for a change (you will realize I mean a change from sexual problems), and had arrived at the subject of paranoid states. I pointed out to the class that people with paranoid delusions of persecution could not be helped by proving logically that the things they alleged were unlikely to have happened or even couldn't possibly have happened. Irrational delusions, I told them, could not be dispelled by rational argument, and any attempt to deal with them in this way would mobilize all the often above-average intelligence of the person concerned in defence of his or her delusional system. The net effect was to deepen and extend it. Thus, by arguing with a paranoid person about his or her delusions, you were making them worse, and that was not what Samaritans were for, was it?

What then, the class wanted to know, *should* we do?

Remember, I said, that to us Samaritans nobody is mad all through: there must be some areas of their personality and thinking which are not affected by their madness, and what we have to do is to concentrate on these areas, and ignore the ones that are deluded. I gave as an example a man several of them had encountered who was followed everywhere by a seven-foot tall Chinese called Riley. Fortunately, nobody had been so uncivil as to ask him whether he didn't mean Li-lee (on the analogy of flied lice) but only one of them had discovered that he was a devotee of steam engines and was very knowledgeable about them, and had had the sense to engage him in conversation on this fascinating subject.

At this point, 181 came in, tripping over the people in the back row, flustered, and apologizing for having got on the bus going in the opposite direction to the place where this particular meeting was for some reason held. 'Typical!' someone muttered – I have never suggested that Samaritans are invariably as tolerant of their fellow Samaritans as they are of the clients. When 181 was seated I said

217

that she had arrived opportunely, because I happened to know that she was befriending a client in the category about which I had been lecturing. 'Tell us,' I said to her, 'about Mrs Whatsername. You've been visiting her once a week for about six weeks, haven't you?'

'Er, well,' said 181 apologetically, 'I hope it doesn't matter, but I sometimes go more than once a week. She's a very nice lady. We get on well. I quite enjoy going to see her.'

'Does she have any crazy ideas?' I asked.

'Well,' replied 181, 'I wouldn't say *crazy*, but she does have some rather – er – funny ideas, sometimes.'

'What ideas?' I persisted mercilessly.

'Well,' said 181 reluctantly, 'she thinks the woman next door is stealing her hot water. But most of the time –'

'Do you mean going into her house with a bucket and drawing it from the tap?' I interrupted.

'No,' admitted 181 uncomfortably. She was now pink with embarrassment. 'I mean, she thinks the woman next door – er – you see, one of my friend's big pleasures in life is to soak in a hot bath, and she builds up the fire to heat the back boiler, and then when she draws the water for her bath it's stone cold.'

'Has she any explanation for this, 181?' I asked.

Shifting uneasily, 181 muttered, 'She – she thinks the woman next door – er – took it.'

'How?'

The man who had commented 'typical' on 181's late arrival volunteered, 'She had got a plumber to tap into next door's pipes!'

I glared at him. 'No more interruptions, please! Continue, 181.'

Almost inaudibly, miserable at the exposure of her friend's weakness, 181 mumbled, 'She thinks the woman magicks it away . . . But', brightening, 'it's only the neighbour on that side! She's got nothing against the old man on the other side!'

I let a pause ensue, shaking my head at any who raised a hand. 'So, 181,' I enquired, 'do you tell Mrs Whatsername there would have to be pipes for the woman next door to steal her hot water?'

'Surely that would be very discourteous,' replied 181, looking shocked. 'No, I simply say to her, "Shall we go and make some jam? I found a good recipe in a woman's magazine and I've brought the fruit." Or perhaps I might say, "I've got my knitting into an awful tangle, can you sort it out for me, please?" She's a marvel at knitting – do you know she can do Fair Isle and read or talk at the same time?'

'Thank you, 181,' I said. 'Please continue to deal with Mrs What-sername in the wise, correct, and courteous way you have employed hitherto. And now, would you be kind enough to pop into the kitchen over thataway, and make me a cup of milky coffee? No sugar.'

As soon as she was out of earshot, I addressed the class. 'Any of you who have been wondering why I hold our wispy, vague, bashful 181 in such high esteem should now know the answer, if you have been paying attention. You will note that 181 was the only person who didn't hear my lecture. Purely out of her Samaritan disposition and innate courtesy, she intuited the correct way of befriending a paranoid client. As I explained to you before she arrived, you do not try to counter irrational statements with rational arguments: you simple change the subject, if necessary making repeated attempts to do so, until you arrive at something on which you know she is perfectly sane, such as jam-making or knitting.'

I pointed at the man who had suggested the need for plumbing. 'You,' I thundered, 'if I had been foolish enough to entrust Mrs Whatsername to you, would have taken on a lady who was para-noid about the woman next door stealing her hot water, and soon you'd have had her paranoid also about the plumber who "helped" her by constantly putting in and removing hot-water pipes, and the plasterer who equally frequently made good so you couldn't see any sign of their depredations; and before you'd finished you'd have had her paranoid about half the neighbourhood as you forced her to use her not inconsiderable ingenuity in inventing ways of combating your attacks upon her delusional system, which you would have deepened and extended to such a point that not even 181 would be able to steer her gently into her sane areas of thinking.'

The object of this tirade looked a little subdued, but not for long. My coffee arrived, borne unsteadily by 181, who enquired sweetly, 'Did you say one lump or two?'

'Typical!' commented the one who had been rebuked, and grinned at me. I grinned back approvingly. I liked the affectionate teasing between Samaritans when there were no clients present.

The 'villain' of that episode became the 'hero' of the next, about a year later. Though not a born Samaritan like 181, he was capable of acting like a Samaritan when on duty, and our need for different temperaments and talents is demonstrated by the fact that 181 could never have had with a GP the conversation of which I overhead our end. The part I heard went like this:

219

'Oh, no, Doctor, she didn't have any complaint at *all* . . . no, she said you were most kind to her and prescribed some tablets for her . . . Oh, no, Doctor, we'd never imagine *we* can do better than a doctor in cases of depressive illness. No, we always try to wheedle such people into going to see their doctor . . . Well, she only came to us because she said the tablets didn't work . . . Well, of course we said that she should tell you herself, but she didn't like to . . . No, no, she didn't suggest you wouldn't be willing to listen, she just thought it wouldn't be right for a woman from a poor neighbour-hood to tell a clever gentleman like you that his pills were no bloody good . . . Well, she said she was still depressed, and the pills made her mouth dry . . . Yes, Doctor, you know and I know, though as a Samaritan I'm not supposed to know, that imipramine does take some days to work and that a dry mouth is one of the side effects, but *she* didn't know that . . . No, Doctor, I'm afraid she can't start taking them now, because she flushed them down the lavatory – I asked her whether the lavatory was depressed, but she didn't laugh: she *is* very depressed, as you know . . . Oh, would you? That's very kind of you, Doctor . . . Five o'clock this afternoon?' At this point, I tapped him on the shoulder. He caught my eye, and I nodded, and he continued: 'I'll see she gets to you . . . I'll bring her myself, to make sure. Thank you very much, Doctor!'

No, he wasn't a student. He was a retired railwayman, who had left school at fourteen.

You will remember that I said that although Samaritan befriending does have some usefulness with the psychotic, it is no help with the psychopathic? Neither of the Samaritans in the previous two stories could have effected any improvement in a psychopath. I'd better tell you what a psychopath is.

Let's oversimplify by dividing the human being into three parts, brain, heart and body. In most people, these parts develop more or less side by side, so that as we get older, from birth up to our prime, we get cleverer, and better able to make relationships, and become physically developed. Some people shoot ahead of their stature in brain power or emotional maturity, whereas others lag behind in one or the other. Those who lag behind in bodily development are called midgets, dwarves, or persons of restricted growth, and it doesn't matter, because they may be, and usually are, intelligent and loving human beings. (The same is of course true of many people

220

with various kinds of disabilities. In the case of children with Down's syndrome, the parents know that they won't live much beyond twenty or be able to earn their own living, but that they will be affectionate and lovable. Anyone who would rather have a psychopath with a high IQ and a perfectly formed body wants his or her head examined.)

People whose mental power does not develop used to be listed as morons, imbeciles or idiots, according to the severity of the handicap. Nowadays classification is more likely to take into account the educational standard reached at a particular age – for instance, you might say that someone of fifteen reads as well as an average child of five. A similar use of 'average age' can be applied to emotional development, or lack of it. At one time we used to classify the egocentric near-heartless in descending order of severity as: grossly psychopathic, psychopathic, somewhat psychopathic, inadequate personality bordering on the psychopathic, markedly immature. Nowadays, we try to be more precise by giving the age at which we would expect the emotional development, or failure of development, exhibited by the particular person whatever his or her chronological age. This is quite useful for Samaritans and other lay people faced with the necessity (being unqualified to diagnose) of making some sort of assessment of whether they can relate usefully to the person in question. When confronted by a psychopath, whether aggressive or manipulative, one has to learn not to be influenced by the image of the apparently adult body in front of us, but ask oneself at what age the behaviour of the person would seem not inappropriate. If what the person says or does is characteristic of a person below the normal age of puberty when the person has in fact come 'of age', it is going to be useless to attempt to befriend – that is to practise the listening therapy which is what Samaritans have to offer to people in crisis. The psychopath won't come needing emotional support to get through a crisis, but rather demanding things to be done for him or her which are either impossible or highly undesirable.

Once you have seen a six-foot man of twenty as a rather nasty little boy in a rather horrid prep school, you will not be surprised at his bragging and blustering and attempted bullying, but neither will you blame him for behaviour he cannot help. You will concentrate on getting him to give you up as a waste of time and go away without hitting anyone or breaking anything, and without making it unavoidable to call the police, which Samaritans never do except as a last resort – if then. When once you have seen a physically developed girl of twenty, with or without noticeable sex appeal, behaving like a baby in a cot having a murderous tantrum, you won't suppose that she would accept you in any other role than that of slave, which is not what Samaritans are for. It is sometimes difficult to convince male heterosexual Samaritans that if the hysterics are succeeded by flattery ('You are the only one who understands me, I know *you* can help me,') the best that is likely to happen is that they will be accused of rape, and the worst is that they will have to change their address and perhaps their job, because she has found out about both and pursues them relentlessly. A person of eighteen whose emotional development is that of an infant, a toddler, or a very young pre-pubertal boy or girl is not capable of forming the other half of a befriending relationship, and is no more capable of being a husband or wife, father or mother, than someone from eight downwards would be.

You will probably be beginning to understand why we don't accept soppily sentimental people as Samaritans. They would be likely to claim that *everyone*, without exception, is capable of being befriended, and because we are dedicated to the serious business of saving lives, and are not an educational institution, we do not let them learn the hard way how wrong they are. If we did – and I am ashamed to say that sometimes people have crept into the organization with this fatal defect – they would lumber the Branch with the burdensome results of their ineptitude. The nationwide (and more and more nearly worldwide) movement was very nearly strangled in infancy by people who hadn't yet learnt how to bounce off the wilier psychopaths, or who, after speaking to them on the telephone, had unwisely invited them to come in, believing that the volunteers on duty after they themselves had left would be better able to cope.

Out of a depressing collection who afflicted us in the early years, I will single out one whom we called New South Wales. He was middle-aged with the emotional development of a toddler. Chief among the people he hated was his mother, who lived in a caravan on the outskirts of London which she moved to a different location whenever he tracked her down. I never met her, so I have no means of judging whether the psychopathy was genetic or the result of reprehensible neglect in infancy. On one occasion he came in almost in a good mood, chortling that he had crept up to the caravan, tipped it over, and that the cooking stove had exploded and set the whole thing alight. He didn't know whether his mother had been

222

burned alive or not, and wasn't sure whether he wished her to have gone, however painfully, beyond his vengeance or not. In fact, it seems that she recovered and, as he had boasted of being the perpetrator, he was brought before the court and sent to a mental hospital for 'treatment'.

There is, of course, no 'treatment' for psychopaths, and certainly not at the lower end of the scale, but courts in those days seemed to be reluctant to send them to prison, which was the only place where they were reasonably content, even though of course they grumbled very much about it, not being able to get at unlimited tobacco, booze and women. Much later, their untreatability was definitively demonstrated by the late Dr Maxwell Jones, who had the theory that they could be cured, or at least improved, by having a special hospital staffed by himself and other dedicated people, where the psychopaths would (as he once put it to me) 'knock spots off one another instead of off the general public'. The ratio of patients to staff was something like 3:1; every act of misbehaviour was discussed by staff and patients, and it was hoped that something resembling a conscience would develop and the inmates would see the error of their ways. He wasted eight years of his life on this before realizing that it just didn't work. He would not have laboured in vain if everyone had accepted his conclusion – that psychopaths can only be contained and not improved, except that the condition tends to mellow in middle age.

This didn't happen in the case of NSW: he was middle-aged when he first began to make impossible demands upon us, and for seventeen months he tried to clog our telephone lines by ringing them alternately throughout the night. This he did even when he was in mental hospital, when he would break into Matron's office and use the telephone there free of charge. On one occasion, when he was either let out for the day (would you believe it?) or had been discharged because the staff were understandably fed up with him, he lay in wait for me in the church with an iron bar with which to bash out my brains. Now, I beseech you not to say that he wouldn't have done that because he would have swung for it. Psychopaths not only have no conscience, they also have no prudence; like a spoilt baby, they want what they want when they want it, and are not deterred from immediate gratification by considerations which would require them to see beyond the end of their nose.

One of the Samaritans saw him lurking there and, without my knowledge, called the police. We had always had a good relation-

223

ship with the police, even though what we mostly wanted of them was to keep out of our way, and a plain-clothes officer soon came round. He arrived just in time to observe NSW rushing towards my unsuspecting back with the iron bar raised to strike: he grabbed NSW and disarmed him. I was asked whether I wanted to charge him. If he had been neurotic or even psychotic, I should have said, 'No,' but I had no hesitation in this case, and said, 'Yes.'

I might as well have spared my breath to cool my porridge, because when this dangerous character appeared in court at the Mansion House next door, he managed somehow to look like a poor, harmless, downtrodden little creature, shabby and pathetic. Somehow he shrunk himself from his normal six feet to a bent, crumpled, five foot two or thereabouts, and denied that he had had any intention of harming me. He was in my care, he alleged, and had the iron bar to protect himself in case I should attack him, because I had told him to go away and not bother The Samaritans any more. The beak, who may not have been anti-Samaritan but was probably anti-clerical, treated me to a lecture on Christian compassion and forgiveness, and suggested that NSW and I ought to make it up and be good friends from now on. I prayed very hard that this twit might say something to NSW which would cause him to fly into a rage and leap at the beak's throat but, alas, my prayers were not granted.

There are still judges and magistrates who don't understand, or don't want to understand, the nature of psychopathy, and defence lawyers sometimes make it appear as though a dangerous psychopath is mentally ill. They can sometimes even find a psychiatrist – whether incompetent or venal is not for me to say – who will back them up in this, so that the psychopath is inflicted on some long-suffering mental hospital instead of being sent to prison.

I hope you haven't been manipulated into believing that anyone who thinks prison is the best place for them is inhuman and un-Christian. If you have, I shall try to forgive you and to refrain from hoping that you may learn the truth the hard way. The only people who have done more damage to The Samaritans than psychopaths are those who have urged us to try to help psychopaths by 'befriending' them.

I mentioned that not all psychopaths are of the extreme, aggressive and dangerous type. Leaving aside the so-called 'intelligent psychopaths', who are the cunning and unscrupulous politicians, businessmen, and conmen, I should like to tell you about some

Left: Vivien, Samaritan No. 2, after her marriage in USA. Right: Monica Dickens Stratton, MBE, 1222/1/1 and 12/1/12, Founder of US Samaritans, after retirement to England

Left: With Samaritans' President Dr Doris Odlum, York 1985. Right: With Jacques Conchon, Founder of CVV (The Samaritans of Brazil)

With secretary Ann 606

With Girl Friday Pam at York

With unofficial Samaritan (a missionary had affiliated Buddhist Taiwan to hardline Christian 'Life Line' without their knowledge, but they wouldn't make him lose face by joining BI.)

With Indian Samaritan

With welcoming party of Samaritans, led by Jacques, in Sâo Paulo

...thor at tenth anniversary of Love-Line, Seoul,
...h Founder Shim Chul-ho and Akira and Yukiko
...m Osaka

In Beijing 1991 with 'hotline' members

Left: With Samaritan Odana at Brazil Conference. Right: With Samaritans of Manawatu, New Zealand

I arrive unobtrusively in Hong Kong (on my left, next but one Elsie Elliott CBE, next but three Andrew Tu, Founder)

I leave Bahrain unobserved, at twice the speed of sound

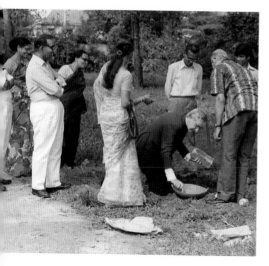

Laying foundation stone of Colombo centre

TV interview in Dutch in Surinam

TV interview in French in Mauritius

TV interview translated into Portuguese in Brazil

Old Vicarage, Barton upon Humber

John Donat's photograph of St Stephen
Walbrook

Henry Moore shows his altar to Lord Palumbo

Left: Becoming a Banauq Dyak. Right: My wife, Mothers' Union Central President, becoming an OBE

With children and their spouses (Felicity's missing)

In Kalgoorlie using molten gold as
illumination

On my way to post cards 'love from Chad
from Chad' I catch Chadians off guard in
Ndjamena

With rare buffalo in Torajaland

Dance of Death in Kalimantan

inadequate personalities bordering on the psychopathic. I took on one of these, a butch, aggressive girl, as a favour to a psychiatrist who had done a favour to The Samaritans, and wasted on her an hour once a fortnight for six years with very few breaks, during which time there was at the most a 3 per cent improvement. I don't entirely grudge the time I spent on her, because I had my reward one day when, exceptionally, she came to see me when very drunk. Her attempts to seduce me on that occasion were abandoned when I told her that girls hoping to produce a usable erection in a male should not grab his tender parts with fingers like steel claws, whereupon she settled down with a black coffee to treat me to a fascinating lecture on my defects as a 'sucker' – that is, a useful victim of a confidence trickster. In telling you about it, I will cut out not only the most lurid language but also the incoherences and digressions.

Tidied up, what she said was: 'You think we [she meant psychopathic personalities] are stupid, pathetically obvious, laughably transparent and naïve. You think that way because we go the whole gamut of acting-out from A to H, without any logical connection, just jumping from one display to the next, irrationally. What you don't realize is that all this is for a purpose, that of discovering the chinks in your armour. While you are thinking, "The stupid sod doesn't realize that I am not impressed when he/she goes in rapid succession from rage to whining, from threatening to pleading, from screaming to sobbing, from blackmailing to seduction," all the time it is you who don't realize what is happening. Some people can be frightened, some can be blackmailed, some can be flattered, some can be made to feel guilty. As you are well aware, we don't have what's called a "conscience", but we know how to get the better of those who have. Some can be seduced, if not sexually, then into playing the role of a mum or a dad – oh, there's no end to the possibilities. And all the time we are rabbiting on we are watching you. We find your weak spot, and then we attack it until we have you where we want you. But you, you hard bastard, you haven't got anywhere we can get our knife in. Well, there's only one conclusion: you are one of us! I shall warn all my pals to keep clear of you!' Even though I didn't trust her an inch, I couldn't help liking her, and I'll always be grateful for what she taught me.

A girl I hoped was neurotically rather than psychopathically manipulative committed the unforgivable sin of telephoning me at my home on my day off, saying that if I didn't agree to see her that day instead of Tuesday she'd kill herself and leave a note blaming me. 'You do that, sweetie,' I told her, 'and I'll find out where you're buried and come and piss on your grave.' There was a shocked pause, then she said, 'You *do* love me . . . See you Tuesday.'

If you are a Samaritan, you have to be wary of your friends, or rather those you thought were your friends, otherwise they will sick on to you any inadequate personalities they want to get free of. One such wonderfully illustrates the lack of prudence even in those who are not grossly psychopathic. He had been in Borstal, which is the best place for such characters, and there he had been a model prisoner, as they mostly are. They are too immature to cope with freedom to do as they like, but within the limits set by a Borstal institution they find the choices which face them narrowed to a point where they can mostly cope with them.

Claud was no exception. He had been so highly regarded by the chaplain that he had been appointed chaplain's dogsbody – I don't know what the proper name is – which got him off all kinds of exhausting activities and allowed him various perks, including the possibility of watering the Communion wine by a third and drinking or flogging what was saved thereby.

I had a long talk with him when he was discharged, and came to the conclusion that he would be very difficult to help, because he was lazy and would rather spend money in the pub, boasting, telling tall stories and standing drinks in exchange for admiration, than earn it. In those days, many people, including landladies, had pre-payment meters for gas, which was used for gas-fires and cookers though no longer for lighting. Every time Claud broke open a gas meter and stole the contents, it was fairly easy to discover that he was the guilty party in the house, but as an over-indulgent relative always paid the landlady back, the only inconvenience Claud suffered was that of having to change digs. At last, however, the time came when a landlady refused to let Claud get away with it even though the money was repaid. He had to appear in court, and I was asked to appear to plead for him.

I hadn't realized how much weight my name already carried: I was careful not to give any false witness, but the mere fact that I appeared on Claud's behalf gave the impression that I would personally keep him out of trouble and would be capable of doing so. I was far from sharing this opinion. Afterwards, I said to Claud, 'Claud, you know that if you do this again, you will go back to Borstal.'

'Oh yes, sir, I know that. I was very lucky to get away with it this time.'

'You don't want to go back to Borstal, do you, Claud?' I asked.

'Oh, no, sir,' replied Claud. 'That's the last thing I want.'

'Why don't you want to go back to Borstal, Claud?' I persisted, speaking as if to a child (which is what, for all practical purposes, he was).

'No girls,' he replied succinctly.

'You do *believe* that if you break open one more gas meter, or steal in any other way from your landlady, you *will* go back to Borstal, and that I wouldn't be able to save you even if I were willing, which I'm not?'

'Yes, sir,' he assured me. 'Just one more gas meter, sir, and I'm back inside. Not even you would be able to save me.'

'Good,' I said. 'I'm glad you realize that.' I repeated this conversation to the relative who had always, foolishly, made good the money Claud stole, and he asked me what I thought were the chances of Claud keeping out of trouble for a while. I evaded the question, though privately I thought the correct answer was 'nil'. Two weeks later, Claud broke open the gas meter in his digs, at a time when no one else could possibly have done it.

8

1960 was an important year for me, because it was the year I had the opportunity to try to expand our work not only in Great Britain, but also overseas. In that year not only had Liverpool and later Manchester started up, but the recently formed Edinburgh Samaritan Centre had been joined by Glasgow and Aberdeen. Three of the pioneers of those days are now dead: James (later Professor) Blackie of Edinburgh, the Rector of Liverpool, Christopher (later Bishop) Pepys, and the Revd Basil Higginson, who rescued Manchester from a chaotic beginning and was later Joint General Secretary of The Samaritans when we had an Association. Stanmore would have been Branch No. 5 but folded when its Director left.

London now having Deputy Directors made it possible for me to travel both at home and overseas, though I did not at that time travel to the four overseas Centres. The one in Hong Kong had been started in 1958 by a brilliant schoolmaster, Andrew Tu, a refugee from Red China who, being Mandarin-speaking, had had to learn Cantonese in order to set up the first of his series of schools. He started suicide-prevention in 1958 with the aid of the United Nations Association and a crusading member of the urban council, Elsie Elliot, protector of the poor, now his wife. They adopted befriending in 1960, the same year in which the late Gonville ffrench-Beytagh, Dean of Salisbury, Rhodesia (now Harare, Zimbabwe), understandably known to his friends simply as 'French', started the first Centre in Africa. He was later Dean of Johannesburg; when expelled from there he became a neighbour of mine in the City as Rector of St Vedast, Foster Lane.

A Samaritan who, like Jennifer 200, Jean 219, and Caroline 235, had become a personal friend, was Nadir 352, a member of a renowned Parsee family in Karachi who had married a member of an equally prominent Parsee family in Bombay. He mostly lived in Jersey, but when in the West spent most of his time in London, where he had many friends. He was responsible for financing the people who wanted to start Samaritan Centres in Karachi and Bombay, the latter of which still operates under the guidance of our friend Dr Sarah Dastoor.

My foreign tour in 1960 was not to Africa or Asia, but to Europe. In order to attend conferences near Geneva and in Vienna, I was to visit the three ancient capitals in the opposite order to the usual one, taking the Tauern Express from Ostend to Istanbul, a train journey of three days, to visit Nuran Ulupinar, founder of Canyoldoşlar Cemiyeti (Comrades in the Spirit). Then I was to fly to Athens to try to persuade Archbishop Damascinos to allow one of his deacons to start a Branch of The Samaritans in Athens (it didn't come off, and still hasn't), and then to Rome (where we *do* now have a Branch) on the way to Geneva. I had expected to like Athens better than Rome, but found its pale beauty less attractive than the glowing ochres and other rich colours of Rome.

The Tauern Express (like the Orient Express, which started from Paris) was a bit of a swizz in that you thought that the immensely long train you got on in Ostend was going all the way to Istanbul. At many of the important stations we came to, we lost one or two carriages which were going to destinations other than Istanbul; we were joined by carriages bound for Istanbul and other places such as Budapest or Athens, and carriages from places other than Ostend, such as Warsaw or Prague, which were also going to Istanbul. I chose a carriage which was going the whole way, but nobody in it was going to accompany me for the whole journey. Very few people braved a couple of nights in the train, for unless you were well provisioned and a devoted student of Cook's Continental Timetable (as I was) you would suffer when the restaurant car was taken off in Belgrade. You would arrive at the Bulgarian frontier, see people having a breakfast of omelettes, bread and tea at the frontier station, and be unable to participate because it was forbidden to change money into lei except at a bank, and no banks were open at 5 a.m. Is it any wonder that hungry people risked breaking the law, as I did myself? The Bulgarian alphabet is practically identical with the Russian, so I could read the notices, but when challenged pretended I couldn't. 'Where ignorance is bliss . . .'

Things were not much better in Sofia, and after Bulgaria the train wiggled in and out of Greece, Turkey, Greece, Turkey again. When, unconcerned by hunger but crazy with thirst, we stopped at a Turkish town where an enterprising little boy was offering huge water melons, the kind that are red inside, at an unbelievably low price, I bought enough to keep me going for the rest of my journey. The swanky Tauern Express had been getting less and less like an international express as we went further east, so that first we were stopping at quite small towns, and then at villages, and from about fifty miles outside Istanbul, the final indignity: peasants by the side of the track would wave us down as if we were a tram.

For the last thirty miles or so we acquired a powerful new locomotive and rattled into Istanbul in great style, pretending we'd been going like an international express all the way from Ostend. Nuran met me at the station and her chauffeur took us to her flat in the suburb of Şişli, where she lived with her husband and two daughters. Her husband spoke some French but her daughters spoke only Turkish.

I soon discovered that Canyoldoşlar Cemiyeti was not patient of being turned into a Samaritan Branch, because it was essentially a small collection of psychiatric clinics for the poor. Nuran's founding of them showed how good-hearted she was, and I readily agreed that she should join me in Vienna later for the conference of psychiatrists which I would be attending there.

My most moving experience in Istanbul was when at my request Nuran took me to pay a courtesy call on the Ecumenical Patriarch. She had never been to this centre of Orthodox Christianity, but as I speak no *modern* Greek she introduced me in Turkish, and I was allowed to sign my name in the great Visitors' Book. A young Greek bishop on the Patriarch's staff, passing by, peered idly at my signature. Then he asked me if I would be kind enough to wait for a while: he would return shortly. Nuran and I sat and waited, and eventually he came back and conducted us through more and more magnificent reception rooms until finally we arrived at a small, cosy study like my own library, where the Patriarch, Athenagoras, was writing at his desk. He rose and came towards us beaming, and I knelt and kissed his hand. He spoke kindly to Nuran in Turkish, and fed us a sticky sweet substance from a jar with a spoon. He then addressed me in excellent English, telling me that the young cleric who had escorted us had recognized my name as being the same as a name on his, the Patriarch's, prayer list.

I was astonished and humbled by this information. It seemed that he had read about my work in an article in *The Reader's Digest*, by

230

Charlotte and Denis Plimmer. I protested that he must have hundreds of names on his prayer list so that it was very clever of the young cleric to have spotted mine. The Patriarch replied that he had intended hundreds of names on his monthly list and dozens on his weekly list, but not very many on his daily list. I was overwhelmed by the knowledge that the man I regarded as the senior Christian in the whole world, Pope and Patriarch of all the Orthodox, prayed for me every day. I still feel blessed beyond my desserts when I think of it. I cherished the knowledge in times of difficulty very often, until his lamented death. The Plimmers' article had been entitled 'Love from a Stranger'. I felt that was what I had had from the Ecumenical Patriarch.

In the Street of the Coppersmiths I bought Susan a tall copper water-pourer which she still has, from a smith called Alexander. I was luckier than St Paul (see 2 Timothy 4: 14). I learned a wonderful Turkish word from Nuran: *boşver* (pronounced 'boshvairrr'). It means roughly, keep calm, take it easy, don't get your guts in an uproar, *festina lente*, *mañana*, softly softly catchee monkey, God's in His heaven all's right with the world, everybody loves you, it'll be all RIGHT! A most useful word, containing a whole philosophy.

Sadly it was not *boşver* in Athens, where I failed to impress the Archbishop. I guess he only agreed to see me because the Patriarch urged him to. The plane that was going to take me to Zurich and Geneva was unaccountably delayed, so I took a plane to Rome instead and had a day there before flying direct to Geneva. There I took a train to Nyon, and arrived at the Château de Bossey about half an hour late for the start of the conference of representatives of 'telephone emergency services' arranged and financed by M. Georges Lillaz. I gathered that three out of the four great department stores in Paris were owned by companies or syndicates, but the fourth, Bazar de l'Hôtel de Ville, was owned by M. Lillaz, who sold it, and on the proceeds did whatever interested him, including spending some time with gurus in India. (He died in 1990.) Crisis-intervention services with a superficial resemblance to The Samaritans but without any contact with us had been started, or were about to start, in Paris, Brussels, Amsterdam, Zurich, Stuttgart and possibly other places in Germany, with a strong church connection everywhere (in the case of Paris, strangely enough, the Protestant church, represented by M. Jean Casalis). M. Lillaz had heard about

231

this, and arranged the conference for the representatives of those countries to get together with representatives of The Samaritans, six of whom attended. In addition to myself, the only one who continued for long was David Arthur, a schoolmaster from Scotland who later became Chairman of The Samaritans Inc. I suppose there were twenty-five to thirty people present, all told. In the Chair was the Revd Ernst Schwyn of Biel/Bienne (a town evenly divided between French- and German-speakers), who was almost equally fluent in German, French and English. This very lovable man (now dead) was prevented from contributing his own thoughts because his whole time was taken up in translating for the Revd Otto Kehr, the German representative who knew no other language.

As I told you, the meeting had started when I arrived, but Ernst interrupted it to say, 'Welcome to our beloved Founder!' I had never met him, but I had by then been photographed in periodicals all over Europe. Everyone stood and applauded, and I begged them to continue with the meeting, which they did. I was in a quandary. From the little I knew of those present and the services or would-be services they represented, I definitely hadn't founded them and was unlikely to approve of them. Nobody from the Continent seemed to know anything about suicide and certainly nothing about befriending, and much of the discussion turned on theological points and the utilization of social services. It was decided to set up a Centre International des Services de Secours d'Urgence par Téléphone, with an office in Geneva and a French-Swiss Protestant minister as its Secretary. The President was to be the Chairman of the work in the country in which the conference was held, and it was agreed to hold the next conference in two years' time (i.e. 1962) at Bad Boll near Stuttgart, when Otto Kehr would take over the Presidency. An international centre for the exchange of information seemed to me relatively harmless, but I didn't foresee that it was the thin edge of a most destructive wedge. In 'Great Britain v. The Rest', The Rest had money from M. Lillaz and from the German Church Tax as well as the machinations of the paid Secretary, and Great Britain had effectively only me, other Samaritans being too busy with their own Centres. Not that I wasn't busy myself, but I did have three deputy directors.

At the same time that I was trying to keep the Church and politicians out of suicide-prevention, I was having to try hard to make a go of my own church *as* a church. The City was then, as now, pretty well deserted at weekends, so we didn't get many at our 9.30 Sung Eucharist on a Sunday, but it was the highlight of the week for *me*. After it, I used to take the underground to Westminster Abbey and put on a cope and read the Epistle at *their* Sung Eucharist, where a big choir with organ was a different musical experience from the quartet singing SATB unaccompanied at St Stephen Walbrook – wonderful as they were. When the Abbey didn't need me any longer, I transferred to St Paul's Cathedral, which was more convenient.

The Mansion House had come within the bounds of my parish in 1954 when St Mary Woolnoth became a Guild Church and lost its parish, but it was in 1960 that I decided that the Lord Mayor ought to hold in his own parish the highest office a layman can hold, namely the ancient office of churchwarden. I approached Sir Edmund Stockdale, who was happy to accept the honour but doubted whether he could attend very often. I urged him not to attend at all, as he had to attend so many services in his official capacity and we did not wish to turn him into an atheist by over-exposure to religion. Besides, weekends are the only time when a Lord Mayor gets a bit of peace and rest during his year. Each Lord Mayor has been churchwarden of St Stephen Walbrook from the Easter after his taking office, ever since.

In that same year, the Aldermanic Sheriff, Sir Richard Studholme, did me the honour of inviting me to be his chaplain. That meant that I rode with him in his coach at the Lord Mayor's Show, attired in The Gear, and lunched with him several times at the Old Bailey with the judges. He should have become Lord Mayor three or four years later, but unfortunately was taken ill with cancer, and as his chaplain I ministered to him in hospital and on his deathbed. He was a dear, good man. As the stretcher-bearers were carrying him into the Gordon Hospital, he was dictating some legal notes to his secretary (he was a solicitor) and the nurses could not make him comfortable until he had finished this. Was this work for some very rich and influential client? No – it was for a poor widow who was unable to pay him for the work he did for her.

Most of the Continentals involved in suicide-prevention were more interested in the Church than in the callers' suicidal tendencies. In the United Kingdom we were fortunately free of this tendency almost everywhere, even though we had to make considerable use of ministers of religion. When we were able to start a Centre for The Samaritans in Belfast in 1961 – and it is this which allows me now to speak of 'the UK' instead of 'Great Britain' – the miracle was that we were able to get the Revd Bill Thomson, Presbyterian, the Revd Jimmy Musgrave, Church of Ireland, the Revd Sidney Callaghan, Methodist and the Revd Hugh Price, Roman Catholic to work together on something they all passionately believed in and had in common, namely a purely humanitarian service to the suicidal based on befriending.

Only Manchester and Birmingham made false starts: Manchester because a minister whom I will not name, and who had been at Château de Bossey, thought it a good idea, when people rang up for help, to persuade them to allow their home telephone numbers to be published in the papers so that other unhappy persons could ring *them* up. Basil Higginson sorted out the ensuing chaos, and his being a priest did not invalidate him. In Birmingham, Canon Bryan Green at St Martin's-in-the-Bull Ring considered that suicide was too narrow an interest, and advertised for distress of all kinds. I told him that if you advertised for suicides you would get everything else as well, thrown in, but if you advertised for general distress, you wouldn't get any suicides. It took some time for the truth of this to emerge, which explains why Birmingham is only Branch No. 25. I am not disparaging this famous preacher: it was a mistake anyone could honestly have made.

These two instances showed clearly that as the number of Centres increased, it would be necessary to have a National Association to band together the existing Branches and promote the creation of new ones, and this was achieved on 11 April 1963, when The Samaritans became a Company Limited by Guarantee. The Memorandum and Articles of Association were drawn up with the aid of Roger Martyn, 44/1, who is still active in the Central London Branch. The Secretary was my own secretary at that time, Daphne Morriss, and the Honorary Bursar her friend Leslie Kentish; in that same year Dr Richard Fox was appointed Consultant Psychiatrist and not long afterwards Professor Morris Carstairs, who died in 1991, began to give invaluable help north of the border. Until 1963, our headed paper simply said:

The Samaritans
to befriend the suicidal and despairing
St Stephen Walbrook, London EC4

With the formation of the Association, it became the London Branch. More recently, with the proliferation of Branches in Greater London, it became the Central London Branch, usually acronymed. The Founding Branches joining with London were Aberdeen, Belfast, Bombay, Bournemouth, Brighton (closed down, and later restarted), Cambridge, Dundee, Edinburgh, Glasgow, Hull, Jersey, Karachi (discontinued), Kowloon Hong Kong (expelled, replaced by Wanchai Hong Kong), Liverpool, Manchester, Portsmouth, Reading, Salisbury Rhodesia (now Harare Zimbabwe), Stoke on Trent and Woolwich (discontinued). These were full, voting Branches, though the four overseas could never attend. There were also sixteen Probationary Branches and fifteen Preparatory Groups striving to be accepted as such.

As Chairman of The Samaritans Inc. I had a good deal of travelling to do, in my own country and on the Continent, and was fortunate to have such good assistants to look after the London Branch between my absences, and when I was keeping engagements with newspaper reporters, radio and television. In the following year, 1964, I was going to be even busier, because the third conference of the International Information Centre was to be in England, and I as Chairman of The Samaritans Inc. was to be its President for the next three years.

We Samaritans had already had three conferences, at Balliol College Oxford in 1961, at St Mary's Durham in 1962, and at Sheffield (where our colleague Dr Erwin Stengel was Professor), in 1963, where we met for the first time as an Association. I chose Christ Church, Oxford for both the international and the national conference, with a separate national conference at Dundee for those who found it more convenient. The Oxford conference was splendidly organized by Daphne Morriss and Leslie Kentish, who had never done one before, and everyone was impressed with the arrangements and the beauty of Oxford. But that was almost all they did agree upon. I cannot remember a single Continental delegate from the countries affiliated to the International Information Centre who accepted our basic principles, nor do I remember a single Samaritan who was not utterly loyal to them. The only ray of hope from the Continent came from beyond the Iron Curtain:

Dr Frantiska Martonová from Prague represented Linka Duvěry (Confidential Line). This consisted entirely of psychiatrists and psychiatric nurses and was based at the Charles Hospital at 11 Ke Karlova. She and I were kindred spirits almost immediately, and Dr Richard Fox and I visited her and her colleagues later in Prague, where the service was at that time run by Dr Miroslav Plzak. I still don't know what her religion was, if any.

The Oxford national and international conferences in 1964 ran from 6 to 13 September, and the alternative national conference at Queen's College Dundee from 18 to 20 September. As I have mentioned, I was doing a lot of travelling inside the country at the time, and after the Dundee conference went to Wolverhampton; Harrow; London for the Executive Committee; The Samaritans' Weekend at Keele; Havering to talk on sexual problems (preceded by a meeting with the Patriarch that afternoon at Lambeth Palace); Newcastle; Hampstead (where Richard Harries, now Bishop of Oxford had started a befriending group); London for the Europe Committee of SPG and a Samaritan meeting; Lochearnhead; Hampstead to talk on sex; St Mary's Hospital to address the London Medical Group; a new volunteers' class; spent a weekend in Jersey in Nadir's house; visited Orpington Branch; Leatherhead to talk on sex; Sheffield; Manchester; Wimbledon; the City Temple; Torquay to talk on sex (back on a sleeper); Croydon; St Martin-in-the-Fields; Cheltenham College; Port Talbot; Cardiff; Trinity College Dublin (my friend George Simms was no longer there, having gone to Armagh to be Primate of All Ireland – he died in November 1991); Hull; Northallerton; Durham; and Lincoln – all before my birthday on 12 November.

Around this time, Daphne 505 progressed from being my secretary to that of the Association, and Ann 606 became my secretary. She and I worked fifty-five steps up my helical staircase, which gave us good practice in remembering my mother's dictum, 'Use your head to save your legs.' She worked in Room C, I in Room D, separated by a partition, and when I arrived she would already have opened and sorted my mail and laid it in three piles, More Urgent, Less Urgent, Too Difficult. The third one she wouldn't let me tackle until she had made my coffee, and I had recovered from the climb. On her own desk would be other piles: No Answer Required, File, Pass On to Someone Else, Your Devoted Secretary Can Deal With. She had a wonderful temperament, always good-tempered, and with the admirable quality of zest: as I got more and more tired I used to think I lived on her energy and youthful enthusiasm. Down below us, reached by a perilous ladder, was Room B where Daphne and Leslie worked, previously divided by a partition into A and B for John 250 and Mary 260; and below *that* the bunk room, before we moved it down to the crypt.

All this time, and ever since, the work of The Samaritans has gone on twenty-four hours a day, seven days a week, 365 days a year, except in leap year. Any clergyman who has arranged an all-night vigil of prayer with one or two people every quarter or half-hour has probably had difficulty in filling the roster through the night, and must surely be amazed that The Samaritans of the London Branch already at this time had four or five on duty every morning, four or five every afternoon, ten or eleven every evening, and two all night, plus Home Service and Flying Squad.

The unhappiest task I had to perform during the next three years was to go several times a year to Waterloo (not the railway station – the place in Belgium) for a meeting of the International Committee of the International Information Centre. The only agreeable thing about this was that we were accommodated by the Smiling Nuns, a missionary order whose rule was to smile at everyone they met. There was nothing else to smile at during those bitter meetings with the representatives of Switzerland, Germany, France, Belgium, the Netherlands and the paid Secretary from Geneva who behaved as though *he* were the President and took no notice of my reminders that he was to take notes of our discussions and decisions and to put them into effect if he could. The chief subject on which we wrangled was the proposed international norms, which were to guide the behaviour of all the Centres including The Samaritans. You won't need to be told that this was an impossible task, because if the 'norms' were acceptable to The Samaritans, they wouldn't be to the rest; and vice versa. I sometimes got a little support from the Belgian, Fr Parée, or from Peter Noden from Holland, but never from both at once, and we were always outvoted.

We Samaritans had our own set of Principles (twenty in my original and revised versions, Seven Principles and Seven Practices in the even better current form) which were much more stringent, of course, and included 'Samaritan volunteers are forbidden to impose their own convictions or to influence callers in regard to politics, philosophy or religion.' Other members of the Committee were determined to make the 'norms' sufficiently vague on this point to allow the Germans and others to restrict their membership to Church people chosen for their evangelistic prowess. (There has recently been some improvement in this regard, in some centres.)

There is more agreement on principle between Mr John Major and Mr Neil Kinnock than there was between me and the other members of the International Committee, whose Secretary was already plotting with others to convert the International Information Centre into a Federation, which would incorporate, swallow up and outvote The Samaritans. This was to happen in 1967, when I ceased to be President. That was the year in which I not only ended my Presidency of the International Information Centre with great relief, but was also persuaded by Dr Richard Fox to resign as Chairman of The Samaritans Inc., although I had been re-elected by twenty votes to four. As a good friend he was worried about the effect upon me of the negative ambivalence of many influential people in the movement. If I had known that I was not only going to be replaced as Chairman by the excellent Bill Thomson but also be excluded from the Executive Committee, I probably would have heeded the advice of a wise City gent who had been distressed by the way in which Richard Carr-Gomm, founder of the Abbeyfield Society, had been ousted by that Society. I had known and admired him.

You mustn't think all my gallivanting around took up most of my time. It didn't. Although I had good help and *could* get away when it seemed important to do so, I always grudged the time when I was doing something other than what I felt called to. Whenever I returned from an absence, long or short, John 250 or one of the others would report on everything that had gone on in my absence and seek my decision on anything that had waited for my attention. Enabling the volunteers to do their unique job was to me the most important thing, but second only to that came the continuation of my counselling on sexual problems. This had now become more interesting because Mary 260, Jean 328 and others took over most of the psychological problems, and I had trained a few volunteers to do 'special interviews'.

When I was relieved of male homosexuality and most straightforward marital problems, I was able to concentrate on lesbians (of whom I had several hundreds on my books eventually), pre-orgasmic women, and male 'deviants' as they were called in those days without any pejorative intention – simply meaning that fetishists,

238

for example, were a departure from any meaningful norm in a way that homosexuals weren't. (It was common at that time amongst sex therapists to classify deviations as being 'of aim' or 'of object', sado-masochism being an example of a deviation of aim and fetishism an example of deviation of object. Naturally, to turn one's attention lovingly towards a person of the same sex in a sexual relationship was neither kind of deviation.) Also reserved for me were prosti-tutes, whom I was very glad to try to help, and heroin addicts, whom I could mostly have done without but didn't have many volunteers I could trust with them, because addicts are manipulative and exploitative and very plausible. The normal tendency of volun-teers is to believe what the client tells them, which is good in most instances, but is quite disastrous in the case of addicts of heroin and other drugs of dependency, alcohol, nicotine and gambling.

It is understandable, even if reprehensible, that some Church representatives should pinch a new idea and stand it on its head in trying to turn it to their own purposes, which they sincerely believe are 'to the glory of God'. You'd think quite a small child would understand that you can't convert a listening therapy into a means for forcing religion down people's throats (I borrow the cliché, though of course it's down people's ears that high-pressure evangel-ism forces its way), but then the world would be a much happier place if we didn't do what offended little children. What is inexcus-able, in my opinion, is to pervert the nature and purpose of an organization that has realized someone's vision, to attach the carica-ture like a parasite to the original organization, to try to diddle that organization into recognizing the caricature as being equally valid, and then, like a virus infecting a living cell, set about taking over the original organization and replicating itself with it. This is what was planned at Geneva in 1960 and came nearest to being achieved in 1967 when it was proposed that the Information Centre should be converted into a Federation, the International Federation of Tele-phone Emergency Services (IFOTES). I strongly opposed this, but had just been replaced as President by Fr Rémi Mens of Antwerp (with whom I had no quarrel – we always teased one another affectionately in Flemish) and as Chairman of The Samaritans Inc. by dear good Bill Thomson. So I had lost all authority and was outvoted.

The men who planned and executed this act of piracy were, of course, sincere in their belief that *I* was the renegade, the apostate, depriving the Church of a fine means of publicity and kudos, and they persuaded their dupes, including some Samaritans on the Executive, that 'internationalization' would not affect The Samaritans in any way but simply give them an opportunity to influence all Western Europe. This was not true: the cheekiest thing proposed was a voting system rigged so that The Samaritans, who outnumbered all the others put together, would always be outvoted. They must have been surprised that the Samaritan representatives either didn't notice this or didn't think it mattered. For the record, the federating organizations in each country concerned would have votes according to the number of Branches in the country.

For	1 Branch,	3 votes
„	3 Branches,	5 „
„	10 „	7 „
„	50 „	9 „
„	100 „	11 „

Thus a country with one Branch could join with a country with 10 Branches and muster 10 votes against our 9, we having between fifty and a hundred Branches. The tail would always wag the dog. There was nothing I could do for seven years, and what I did then provoked a rage and fury which destroyed several precious friendships.

Alas, I have once again got far ahead of my story. Back to the early '60s: at Bad Boll, Stuttgart in 1962 those who attended were asked to affix to the notice-board a list of the problems presented to the respective organizations in order of frequency. Depression was at the top of The Samaritans' list, and spiritual difficulties at the bottom. It was the opposite way round on the German list and most of the others – in fact, you could have turned the whole German list upside down and found the British list.

9

IN 1967 I took what could be called a one-eighth sabbatical: a sabbatical is one year off in seven, and I took three months off in my fourteenth year with The Samaritans. Marcus Morris had wangled me a single ticket to Hong Kong by British Airways, on a plane that ended up in Tokyo and therefore had a stunningly beautiful Japanese air-hostess among the English roses. By arrangement with Andrew Tu, I was to work for a month with the Hong Kong Samaritans, and then make my way back by any route I fancied. I stayed at Hotel Fortuna in Nathan Road, on Kowloon side, and went every day to the Centre at Lok Fu to work with The Samaritans, our oldest Branch outside the British Isles. I made no attempt to learn Cantonese, but relied on interpreters.

I think I was only moderately successful in befriending Chinese clients, because straightforward translation of their words into English did not at all convey the way they thought and their general philosophy of life, so totally different from ours. It soon became clear to me that we English live in a 'guilt' culture, where as individuals we need to feel at peace within ourselves, with a quiet conscience; and we pride ourselves on not worrying too much about what other people say or think if we are convinced that we are right. Orientals, on the other hand, seem to live in a 'shame' culture, not trusting their own judgement but submitting to the judgement of the community in which they live, so that the worst thing that can happen is to 'lose face', in other words be held in less respect by neighbours than they formerly were.

I was not on the strength of the Lok Fu Centre as a befriender, but as a counsellor, and I soon realized that I would never be able to help the clients to the kind of insight which I thought made sense in their particular situation. For instance, there was a young couple,

241

both of them teachers, who had been engaged for many years, but could not live together and could not make love because that would not be acceptable in their community. So each lived with ageing parents whom they supported, but they could never amass sufficient money to be able to have a slap-up wedding with 100 tables of guests, or whatever the number was which they reckoned would allow them not to lose face over the whole procedure. Examining their options for a way forward was very frustrating, because there weren't any that were acceptable to them, except to continue trying to save up enough money for a wedding until both sets of parents died. None of the solutions to their problem that would have been feasible in the West could even be considered. I soon abandoned all attempt at counselling except in matters of private behaviour, and with that couple I fell back on befriending, namely listening and sympathizing and hoping that their burden shared was a little alleviated.

Befriending is, of course, applicable in any culture whatsoever, as I discovered when a lady from a remote part of the new territories came in, speaking a barbarous dialect of Hakka which not even our few Hakka-speaking volunteers could easily understand. Eventually a couple of them who spent an hour with her managed to comprehend what she was on about, and translate this into Cantonese (they didn't speak any English). Then a very beautiful damsel translated the Cantonese into English for me. All the time the woman was talking and the Hakka-speakers consulting and then producing streams of Cantonese and my interpreter was whispering the English equivalent into my ear, the old lady was squatting there with her eyes fixed unswervingly on mine. Lord knows how she had come to hear of me in her remote fastnesses. Because I was frequently interviewed by the Chinese press which doesn't use Latin characters, Andrew had bestowed upon me a Cantonese name sounding as nearly like Chad Varah as he could contrive, Chan Wah-Lok (in Mandarin this becomes Chen Hua-Loh). What rumours about me had reached her remote village I don't know, but she came saying that she wanted to consult Chan Wah-Lok.

Even when her problem was translated into English, I couldn't make out what was the point at issue. Some village custom which was totally meaningless to me had been breached, I think inadvertently, by her, and she seemed to be afraid her neighbour would find out about it and think badly of her. I asked her, through my series of interpreters, what possible courses of action were open to her. It

242

turned out that the first one involved bringing her husband into the matter, and I felt her reluctance to do this. The second one, which attracted her slightly more, involved some participation by her son, but there were practical difficulties because he lived at a distance. The third possibility was unthinkable, namely that she should demean herself by appealing to her neighbour directly.

I divined that the third possibility was the least objectionable even though very difficult, and decided to go all out for it. She objected that her neighbour, whom she named, would think badly of her and furthermore would spread the tale all round the village. I said how strange it was that she should think this, because this was precisely what Mrs Hoo Flung Dung thought about *her*. Yes, I said, by a strange coincidence Mrs Hoo Flung Dung had been to consult Chan Wah-Lok about a very similar situation. 'There is something she wanted to confide in *you*,' I told the old woman, 'but she hesitated to do so because she thought you would think badly about her, and repeat the story all over the village.'

The old lady was indignant. 'How dare she suggest such a thing!' she cried. 'I should listen to her confession with understanding, for we are all weak at times, are we not? And I would never divulge it to a soul! She ought to know that — we have been neighbours for fifty years!'

I looked at her sternly and pointed my finger at her and asked, 'Why should she know that about you, if you don't know that about her?'

She gaped at me in astonishment and there was silence for a long time. Then she said, 'She didn't come to see you, sir, did she? You made it up, to teach me a lesson.'

'No, she didn't come,' I confessed. 'And yes, I did make it up. I am glad you have learned the lesson.' She then sprang forward, kissed my hand, and bounded out of the room.

Every evening Andrew would call for me and take me out to dinner at one of the thousands of Hong Kong restaurants he knew. I have never eaten so well in my life. Sometimes Elsie Elliot joined us — an elected member of the Urban Council, she was the one who cared most about the poor, and defended the hawkers from harassment and the refugees in the 'bird's nest' villages on unproductive hillsides from persecution. (They were called 'bird's nest' because they were built of any odd scraps of material in the way a bird builds its nest.)

About half-way through my time in Hong Kong, I fell ill. I

suppose it was some sort of 'flu. A Chinese 'doctor' was summoned and gave me some pills to take. Soon after taking them, I began to suffer from hallucinations. My room was on about the seventeenth floor and had a narrow little balcony outside the window. I couldn't get rid of the idea that I would sleepwalk in the night and fall off this balcony and be killed. It's wise in such situations to tell someone. I rang up Andrew and told him, and he came round at once. His solution was simple: he would sleep on the floor between me and the door that led to the balcony. He assured me that he was a light sleeper and that I wouldn't be able to get past him. Then he went and had the luxury of a hot bath, which I suspect was not available where he lived at the time. I don't know whether he slept at all that night, but I slept like a top. The next day he brought someone to see me who may or may not have been a proper doctor but had a diploma from some society of 'Apothecaries'. This chap took one look at what I'd been prescribed, shuddered and threw it away, and gave me something else. He said that what was wrong with me was accumulated exhaustion; which made sense.

I was very anxious before returning to England to get a glimpse of life in Red China. Visas were not being issued, and no Westerners were getting in except diplomats, because it was the height of the cultural revolution. The Red Guards were everywhere and neither the police nor the army could protect anyone from them if they decided to dislike them. All my Chinese friends begged me to give up the idea of going to Canton, the nearest big city, but when I remained obstinate they reluctantly told me how to set about getting a visa from Mr Chan, Red China's representative in Hong Kong at that time. I won't weary you with the detailed strategy and tactics, which I didn't always understand myself: I will simply summarize it by saying that by visiting Mr Chan every day and saying what they instructed me to say, we eventually reached a situation where he would lose more face if he didn't procure me a visa than if he did – though he'd be briefly unpopular with the authorities in any case.

When my month in Hong Kong expired and my visa became operative, a sad little band of Chinese Samaritans saw me off at the railway station, convinced that I was going to my death. I had an uneasy feeling that I ought to have listened to them, but as soon as I crossed the border I began to be fascinated by what I saw from the window of my train. I call it 'my' train because Mr Chan had made me pay through the nose for a first-class carriage, a room at the Oriental Hotel, and a guide-interpreter and a driver and car. My carriage was on the front of the train, immediately behind the engine, and always stopped beyond the platform, so that I couldn't visit the other part of the train and the other passengers couldn't visit me. There were often crowds of Red Guards at the stations where we stopped, and I snapped away with my camera: as soon as they saw me, most of them turned their backs, but some rushed towards the train, shaking their fists and snarling.

The time passed very quickly as I ran from one side of my compartment to the other, looking out of the windows but not taking many photos because we were going too fast. Eventually it got dark, and then very dark, and then the train pulled up with a great grinding and screeching, and from my window on the left I could see that we were at a level-crossing and there were jeeps with headlights blazing and a spotlight playing on the door to my carriage. Men in uniform got on, and although they didn't speak English they made it plain that I was to accompany them. We drove away along the road and the train went on without me.

Eventually we arrived through streets in what must have been the suburbs of Canton at the Oriental Hotel, where I was unceremoniously dumped with my bag and the uniformed men drove off. I was quite glad to get to bed, in an enormous room furnished with huge examples of Victorian furniture, and with a floor highly polished but with a dead cockroach in the middle. The following morning, I woke wondering where on earth I was, because I could hear monks chanting their office outside my door. 'I am in the Oriental Hotel in Canton, fool that I am,' I told myself. I padded across the room in my bare feet, remembering to avoid the cockroach, opened the door a crack, and peered through. There, in the broad corridor, was a circle of young men and women who were obviously waiters and chambermaids, and in charge of the chanting was a better-dressed man who must have been an under-manager. They all had little red books of the thoughts of Chairman Mao, which they were chanting antiphonally. I hastily unpacked my own little red book, which was in French because I hadn't been able to get one in English, and joined the circle in my pyjamas, somewhat to their surprise.

After breakfast, my guide-interpreter, Mr Wu, arrived and said my car and driver were waiting outside, and where would I like to go. I had been asked by Bishop Baker in Hong Kong to see if the

245

English church was still functioning and if the priest was still at liberty, because Canton came within his diocese but he hadn't been able to visit. 'There is no English church in Canton,' Mr Wu assured me, leading me out to my battered vehicle. I told him I knew there was one, and suggested perhaps he wasn't willing to take me to it because the government disapproved of religion. He assured me that wasn't the reason, but simply that if such a building existed, neither he nor the driver knew where it was (he hadn't asked the driver).

'What's the use of asking me where I want to go, if you've already made your mind up where you will and will not take me?' I snapped. Mr Wu was placatory. He put on a sincere expression and went into a long spiel about how, if he or the driver *had* known where the English church was they would assuredly have driven me to it, allowed me to stay there as long as I wished, and even to take *photographs* of it, if that was my desire.

'Very well,' I said, 'I accept your kind offer.' I then produced a map of Canton's main streets which Bishop Baker had kindly drawn for me on a large piece of paper, with the street names in Chinese characters which I couldn't read but Mr Wu could. I pointed to the English church, and he shrugged his shoulders and told the driver where to take us.

Arrived at the church, I crossed the broad road to inspect it, and found it was all boarded up and no sign of life. It was covered all over with Chinese characters on boards and placards; I photographed all these, and then went back to the car and took a couple of photos of the whole building. Mr Wu was observing me closely, and appeared relieved that I was satisfied. He probably hadn't realized that I wouldn't have the faintest idea of the meaning of the Chinese placards, which, when Bishop Baker saw the photos, he told me were most opprobrious slogans about Christianity.

I then let Mr Wu take me on a general tour of the city, but he was very nervous and the driver frequently turned down a side street in order to avoid crowds of Red Guards. I noticed that many streets had arcaded pavements so that shoppers were under the projecting part of the upper storeys, which were supported on pillars of square cross-section. These pillars were all covered with Chinese characters. I had seen the same sort of thing in parts of Hong Kong, where the inscriptions related to the nature of the business carried on in the shop adjoining, but these inscriptions were different in that they all seemed to be the same in colour and size and layout. My suspicions were confirmed when I asked Mr Wu what they said.

They were all quotations from Chairman Mao. There wasn't, in fact, anything whatever to read except the thoughts of Chairman Mao.

The rest of my time in Canton appeared to be spent solely in trying to drive around where we wouldn't encounter any Red Guards. Sometimes we saw them camping by the roadside, and if we got downwind of them we could sometimes smell them. They were dressed in what I took to be Mao uniform with red armbands, and the boys were dressed like the girls – at least, I could see no difference between the sexes but Mr Wu assured me that at least one-third of them would be girls. Knowing how attractive Cantonese girls are in Hong Kong – nine out of ten pleasant to look at, one out of ten beautiful, one in a hundred unimaginably stunning – it was difficult to understand how the same Cantonese people in Canton could look so uniformly *un*attractive. Once when we passed a group of Red Guards on a strip of grass who appeared to be behaving like normal teenagers after a disco, I told Mr Wu that it cheered me up to see that some of them had normal desires and impulses. Mr Wu was shocked.

'They are exploring revolutionary attitudes and enthusiasms,' he explained austerely.

'That's what I meant,' I murmured.

On my last day, Mr Wu had run out of innocuous places to take me to, and suggested we go for a walk in the Martyrs' Memorial Park.

'*Christian* martyrs?' I asked. Alas, I was again shocking poor Mr Wu.

'Communist martyrs!' he corrected me virtuously.

We strode out across the patchy grass, passing the few empty flowerbeds. At last he pointed to a hill on top of which was some kind of monument and said, 'There's the Martyrs' Memorial.' It wasn't at all like the one at Oxford on top of which undergraduates regularly placed jerries after a quite difficult climb. 'We could go up and photograph it,' suggested Mr Wu, who had previously tried to sabotage my photos by instructing the driver to drive quickly and jerkily whenever I produced my camera. He was evidently living for the hour when he would see me off at the airport.

At this point, a crowd of Red Guards which I was later able to estimate at fifty appeared from the other side of the hill and some of them pointed down at us. 'Alack!' exclaimed Mr Wu quaintly. 'We must get back to the car!'

He began to run but I caught him by the collar and dragged him back. 'I used to be a runner, Mr Wu,' I told him, 'and I can assure you we could not get to the car before they reached us. If we run, they will most certainly lynch us. If we stay here, and you translate exactly what I say to them, we may get out of this alive, possibly even uninjured. Do you understand?' He began b-but-ting and I said firmly, 'Mr Wu, I am a psychologist and I have spent a lot of my life dealing with tough working-class youths in youth clubs. Up to now you have translated not what I said but what you thought I *ought* to have said. I assure you our only chance is if you do and say exactly what I tell you.'

'Yes, yes!' he assured me, his teeth chattering.

'Right,' I said. 'Now we walk slowly towards them, looking quite unconcerned and smiling welcomingly.'

This tactic was successful in one respect: the avenging horde stopped charging like a herd of bison, and slowed to a quick walking pace; but their faces when they were close enough for us to see them remained grim, angry and suspicious. Soon we were surrounded by jostling, elbowing, shoving, snarling Red Guards, and I had difficulty in holding on to Mr Wu, whom I needed to have within earshot to interpret for me.

My aim was as far as possible to separate the mob into individuals with whom I could relate on some level. I constantly turned from one to another of the Red Guards surrounding us most closely, asking where they came from, how many days they had walked to join with their comrades in Canton, and such-like questions. If a sullen face didn't answer, I swiftly turned to another. I remember the first who *did* answer — I think it was a girl, but can't be sure — and said he/she came from Nanning. I answered brightly, 'Nanning? What a coincidence! I'll be going there tomorrow, on my way to Vietnam.' In fact, I was due to fly *over* Nanning later that day, if we ever got to the airport. 'You walked eighteen days!' I exclaimed to another. 'I guess you must have walked further than anyone else.'

'No, no,' shouted a couple of others, giving their own journey times.

I had been looking round to try to find the leader, and I must have been correct in my identification, because when I said to him, through Mr Wu, 'You seem to me to have qualities of leadership — are you in fact the leader of these Red Guards?' he agreed that he was. I asked if he would mind telling me his name.

'What's *your* name, and where do you come from?' he shouted rudely.

'My Cantonese friends call me Chan Wah-Lok,' I replied, 'and I come from England, to study the achievements of Chairman Mao and the Red Guards.'

It felt like an hour before the atmosphere of suspicion and menace changed, but perhaps it was only about ten minutes. I was very relieved indeed when the leader, in response to my request for permission to visit the Martyrs' Memorial, started to lead the way towards the hill, and the rest straggled after him with me and Mr Wu. When we got to the Memorial, I asked if I might take a photograph of it. Everybody seemed to want to be in the photograph, so I asked Mr Wu to take a group photograph with my camera, with me in the middle of the group. Then many of the Red Guards crowded round with their little red books, asking me to write in them. I thought they wanted my autograph, so I began signing in Chinese characters Chan Wah-Lok. Nobody objected until Mr Wu looked over my shoulder and exclaimed indignantly, 'Don't write your name, write "Glory to our wonderful helmsman and leader Chairman Mao".'

'Mr Wu,' I said firmly, 'I have just saved your life, so don't you dare tell me what to write and what not to write. *Ho gegrapha gegrapha*!'

Eventually we parted amicably, and Mr Wu and I went back to our car, he worrying all the way about the meaning of the words he didn't know, *ho gegrapha gegrapha*. How could he? It was a quotation from the Greek New Testament of Pontius Pilate's words, 'What I have written, I have written.'

When we got to the airport, Mr Wu said that it was not permissible for me to take undeveloped film out of the country. I must therefore give it to him to be developed. 'Certainly,' I said. 'I am most grateful to you, because I doubt whether in Phnom Penh they have facilities for developing colour-negative film and making colour prints. You, of course, under your great helmsman, Chairman Mao, will be able to do this splendidly before my plane leaves in an hour from now. If it takes a little longer, and I miss my plane, I guess I can count on you to get my visa extended . . .' Mr Wu was most magnanimous in allowing me to take the undeveloped film with me, since, although I was right that they could do it very swiftly and well, he had personally observed every shot I had taken and therefore he knew there was nothing objectionable.

Before leaving, I paid him and the driver the huge sum agreed, and thanked them both, and said that had tips been allowed in their society, I should have been glad to give each of them a little present. Mr Wu indicated that tips were in fact not acceptable in a socialist society because they would be demeaning, but it was standard practice that satisfied customers should pay double the agreed fee. This I did without a murmur. You will probably understand that, like St Mark in the Garden of Gethsemane, I should have been prepared to slip out of my clothes and flee naked if only I could get on that plane and out of Chinese air-space.

There were not many passengers for Phnom Penh on Royal Air Camboge, but I found myself next to two interesting ones: young North Korean soldiers on their way to join the Viet Cong. They each gave me a North Korean cigarette, which I saved 'to smoke later', and in exchange, I drew on my table napkin a map of South-East Asia. They asserted that they had never seen a map of any kind, which I found hard to believe, until I saw how tenderly one of them folded it up and put it away. They knew no English and I no Korean, but we were able to converse in Russian, which I spoke slightly better than they did.

Because of hostilities, our plane, after flying over Nanning, turned southward and flew along the coast of North Vietnam and didn't turn west until we would be crossing South Vietnam on our way to Phnom Penh. Looking out of the window, the North Koreans said how beautiful the country was below them. They would be proud to fight for it. I told them I was sorry to disappoint them, but it was *South* Vietnam we were flying over. 'Oh, what an ugly country it is,' they exclaimed.

There cannot have been any French colonial capital more charming than Phnom Penh was in 1967. I found myself a delightful hotel, and gave the cycle-rickshaws lots of custom as I explored every corner of the place. No one could have imagined the devastation that was due to be caused to it when the Khmer Rouge arrived.

The country was governed by Prince Norodom Sihanouk, who had changed from monarch to prime minister but was still totally in charge and was obviously the right person to keep his little country from being crushed between the Americans and the North Vietnamese. His policy seemed to be to try to offend the North Vietnamese less than he offended the Americans, on the ground that the Viet Cong actually had large numbers of their soldiers on his side of the Mekong River and were also more ruthless than the Americans. He denied to the Americans that there were any Viet Cong in Cambodia and for a considerable time he prevented American bombing-raids to prevent the North Vietnamese from using the west side of the Mekong as a safe route along which to go before crossing into South Vietnam.

The chief thing I wanted to see in Cambodia was, of course, Angkor Wat and the other temple ruins north of Siem Reap, which itself was north of the great lake, Tonle Sap. Before the flow of tourists was stopped (I was able to get a visa only because friends in Hong Kong knew the Cambodian consul there) people would fly to Siem Reap and spend half a day seeing a couple of temples and then fly back, but this wasn't my style at all. I decided to go to Siem Reap by bus, which was scheduled to take fourteen hours, and (glutton for punishment) to break my journey at Kampong Cham and take another bus to Kampong Thom, on the Mekong, and see for myself whether the Viet Cong were there in force. They were. Fortunately they didn't taken any notice of me during the short time before the bus went back to Kampong Cham, and I was quite relieved to be once again with the charming Cambodian people who joined and left the bus all through the day (I was the only one going the whole way). It was a wonderful way to get an insight into the life of the ordinary Cambodian, as we trundled slowly and unsteadily past their farms and villages; who could help loving the gentle, beautiful Cambodian people? All day their mascot (me) was handed by departing passengers to newcomers, and we shook hands and smiled and shared our provisions.

When we eventually arrived in Siem Reap, I was exhausted and happy to flop down in a rather bleak hotel. The following morning I engaged a cycle-rickshaw. I chose a very sturdy, stolid fellow from amongst the applicants, because I wasn't just going to Angkor Wat for a few hours and then back again – I wanted to explore as many as possible of the temples which covered sixty square miles, and especially wanted to go to Angkor Thom. I have done a lot of useless things in my life, but I suppose the most useless was to learn how to tell at a glance the century in which any of the temples was built. When I was a boy I had read Richard Halliburton's account of his adventurous journeys, all of which I have now emulated, and the one that appealed to me most was his exploration of the temples and the jungles of northern Cambodia. I was thrilled by the account of the French entomologist in the nineteenth century who, at a time when the temples were lost in the jungle and only a half-believed legend, suddenly came up against a stone wall of great height while

251

chasing a butterfly. However far he went to the right or to the left, the wall continued. Angkor Wat is surrounded by a wall a mile square, i.e. you could put the entire City of London within it. What *is* in it is the biggest, most elaborate of all the temples, with innumerable carvings telling, among other things, the history of the Khmer people. How their civilization came to an end is a mystery. Having this enormous temple all to myself was an experience I shall never forget. If ever the Khmer Rouge are driven out, and the mines cleared, I should like to go there again.

I paid my sturdy cyclist handsomely, and he told me he was glad to have improved his English during our long days together. It was wonderful to be as free as a bird – whenever I was travelling on behalf of The Samaritans I always had some objectives, however devious the route I took between them. On this one-eighth sabbatical, I could go more or less where I pleased – or so I thought. I had no intention of going back to Phnom Penh the same way: at the very least, I would travel back on the other side of Tonle Sap, and take the railway from Battambang; but I had a more ambitious plan, namely to go to Poipet on the Thai frontier. This frontier used to be crossed by a railway at that point, but I gathered a couple of miles of track had been torn up. I thought that if there wasn't too much barbed-wire, and if any frontier guards were bribable, I might be the first person to cross at that point since the frontier was closed, and could get to my next stop, Bangkok, by this unusual route. Alas, when I got there, the barbed-wire coils seemed endless and I was warned of mines.

Sadly, I made my way to Battambang and checked into an hotel, where I was shortly visited by the most inscrutable character I have ever met in my life. He looked Cambodian, if one assumed that they had a small proportion of very villainous types, and was dressed in a navy-blue suit. He gave his name as Henry, but his English was so bad I was never able to ascertain precisely who he was or what he wanted, except that he desperately wished to be my friend, and kept shaking my hand and smiling ingratiatingly. He was very anxious that I should accompany him to some place not far away where they took photos so that he and I could have our photos taken together. I invited him to have dinner first, but he had no time for that. It appeared that he would treasure all his life a photo of me with himself, and he actually went on his knees to persuade me to accompany him.

Needless to say, I was deeply suspicious of the whole thing, but decided to find out where he wanted to take me, keeping behind him if possible when he entered any building. We came to a shop in the main street which advertised itself as a photographic studio, and I naturally thought we would be going in there; but no, our destination was the ramshackle, apparently boarded-up shop next door, to the right. We went up some rickety stairs, and arrived in a room where there was indeed an old-fashioned camera on a tripod, with a taciturn fellow in charge of it. Henry and I posed together in front of this camera, and thinking it would show his friends, whoever they might be, what bosom pals we were, I linked arms with him for one of the photos, and for another put an arm across his shoulders. He was rendered most uncomfortable by this. He then asked if he might have a photograph of me by myself. The photographer proceeded to take what I can only describe as mug shots, after which we went out into the street and Henry disappeared. I suppose he was in somebody's secret service, but whose, or for what purpose, I never knew. Perhaps I had been observed trying to 'escape' from the country via the closed crossing at Poipet. I guess by the end he was convinced that I was a harmless lunatic.

I really enjoyed the train journey from Battambang to Phnom Penh, and was affectionately greeted by the staff of my hotel. Remembering that I had an introduction to Liz Broatch, secretary to Prince Norodom Sihanouk, which I had done nothing about, I telephoned the palace, and she invited me to go and have drinks with her that evening. I did not meet the Prince.

I learned that Liz had almost completed her eighteen months' service and was leaving the Prince's employ in a week's time – in fact, the next day, a Sunday, I was to take the Air France flight to Bangkok, and she was to take the same flight the following Sunday. We agreed to meet in Thailand, but this was a bit difficult to arrange as I did not know where I would be staying. I knew I would be staying with a Mr and Mrs Rainsborough, that he was a manufacturing chemist, a German Swiss who had taken the name Rainsborough when he had joined the RAF, and his wife was German. They were going to meet me at the airport. I told Liz I would leave a note for her at the airport giving my address and telephone number; but the following Sunday, in the Rainsboroughs' comfortable home, we waited in vain for a call.

Although the Rainsboroughs were not Roman Catholic, they

worked very hard for a Roman Catholic charity. In the north-west corner of Thailand, adjoining the Burmese frontier, there were many villages inhabited by Karens fleeing persecution by the Burmese, who had established a unitary state dominated by them instead of a federation of the six nations who inhabited the country. Most Karens are Anglican, but some are Roman Catholic and it was these who were offered education in a boarding-school at Mae Hpon, high in the mountains above Chum Tong, where eighty little boys were looked after by two French Basque priests, and sixty little girls were looked after by three Spanish Basque nuns. The Rainsboroughs kept them supplied with pharmaceutical needs and items of clothing and other necessities, and they needed someone to go up there to take the consignment that was overdue because they had both been too busy.

I offered to take the consignment, as I was most anxious to visit the Karen, a nation in which I had always taken an interest. I booked a first-class sleeper on the train to Chieng Mai, since it was a nineteen-hour journey; I was to be met by a White Father at Chieng Mai and taken by car to Chum Tong, where a Karen guide would meet me to guide me on the stiff three-hour climb up the mountain to Mae Hpon.

When I boarded the train on the Tuesday, whom should I find in the next sleeper but Liz, who had not been given my note and had imagined that we would not be able to make contact again. It turned out that she had an invitation to stay in Chieng Mai with a cousin of her bank manager, but when she heard where I was going she was keen to come with me, and felt sure her hostess would understand. It's a good thing we ran into one another, because she was very ill during the night, and I nursed her. On arrival in Chieng Mai, when she was well again but still pale and shaky, we got out on to the platform and spied my White Father. Liz went to talk to him, but I delayed following her because I had noticed among the people waiting to greet their friends the most beautiful girl I had seen since the Japanese air hostess on the way out from England. How, I wondered, could I possibly make some excuse to talk with her? I assure you that all I wanted to do was to feast my eyes on her beauty for a little longer – on a journey like that, one doesn't expect to make deep and lasting relationships.

I busied myself getting Liz's and my luggage out of the train, and then saw that the girl was shaking hands with Liz – she was her hostess. It turned out that her name was Keskanök Lee, or something similar. Although she was in her early twenties she seemed to be a clever businesswoman, who owned three sawmills and had just bought a large piece of land where she thought the university would wish to expand. She readily agreed to Liz's coming with me to Mae Hpon, and invited both of us to stay on our return 'at one of my hotels'. The White Father then drove us to Chum Tong where our Karen guide was waiting, and I think I arrived in better shape than Liz after our long steep climb up the mountainside. It was arranged that I should stay with the two priests and Liz with the three nuns. The next few days were amongst the most unforgettable of my life, for we had arrived in Shangri-La.

The staff communicated with one another in Basque, with me in French, with Liz in Spanish, and with the children in Karen, in which all teaching was done, though they were also taught Thai as a second language. Each day began and ended with an act of worship in Karen, and between lessons and meals there was plenty of time for play. The most noticeable thing was that the children played together without any of the roughness or spite one is accustomed to seeing in children at play in any country. We discovered that these children appeared not to have any original sin at all: they were never violent, they did not steal, and they could not lie. I had taken with me huge bags of boiled sweets, and often produced these when I saw a crowd of children. They would come and take a sweet and thank me prettily, and if I offered one to a child who already had one, he or she would show me the sweet and be unwilling to take another, but would point to some child who hadn't got one yet. 'Thy kingdom come, on earth as it is in heaven,' I thought; but of course there *was* a less happy side to the Karen character. The priests told me that in the villages around, the rate of suicide was very high. They attributed this to the timidity of the Karen, and their inability to bear frustration and hardship. Yet they were brave enough to prevent the Meo and other tribes that traded in opium from bringing any drugs into their villages or carrying them through their territories. Outside every village was a sign saying 'We are Christians, we do not allow opium on our territory.'

The two priests unfortunately did not get on at all well together. Each had his own very powerful radio, and they would sit at opposite ends of their long living-room, each playing his radio as loudly as possible to try and drown out the other. Yet they were dedicated men: one of them took me to see the graves of their predecessors on a nearby hillside, and showed me the plot where his own body would lie when the time came.

I asked him what I could do to help with the work. He said the best thing would be to adopt one of the children, and send what seemed to me a ridiculously small sum each year via the White Fathers to cover its education and keep. I asked whether I might choose the child to adopt, and he said yes, provided that he or she was not already adopted by people who had never been to Mae Hpon but had seen photographs of the children in Chieng Mai or in Bangkok. I had been watching the children all the time I was there, and had been particularly struck by one little girl who seemed to me to have a grace and dignity which set her apart from the others, though she wasn't apart when it came to playing with them or joining in the work of washing-up in the stream. When I told the priest which one I had chosen, he said she was the only child in the school who would be likely to go to university, so it would be expensive if I adopted her. I said I would pay for her until she finished university and asked if I could be introduced to her.

Her name was Nau Bei Hpau which I was told meant 'the girl who gathers flowers'. She owned nothing except her shift which she wore by day and night, a red headdress for special occasions, and a little Cross of what looked like aluminium. I asked what I should be permitted to give to her, and was told she mustn't be made too different from the other children; limited to three items, I chose a blanket to keep her warm at night, flip-flops to protect her little feet, and a gold Cross and chain. Liz also adopted a girl.

When the time came to go, I was very sad at parting from my little one, but promised to go and see her whenever I was in Thailand. Unfortunately, it was some years before I was in Thailand again. The Rainsboroughs were no longer there, and when I rang the White Fathers and was able to speak to one of the priests I had met at Mae Hpon, who happened to be visiting the house, he begged me *not* to come and visit my little girl. She hadn't after all gone to university, but had got married, and her husband would not at all understand an elderly 'farang' going to see her. I had had a progress report in Spanish from one of the nuns a couple of years earlier, but a further letter telling me of the latest developments never reached me.

Liz and I had several delightful days as Keskanök's guests, but Liz had an engagement in Malaysia, and faced as long a train journey from Bangkok as the journey *to* Bangkok. Although Keskanök begged me to stay, and I longed to do so, Liz was nervous about travelling without me, so we went together back to Bangkok where I took her to the station for the train to Malaysia and reported back to the hospitable Rainsboroughs.

I desperately wanted to go to Rangoon, to see the Shwe Dagon, but the country was closed at that time and no visas were being issued. I thought if I could wangle my way into Red China, surely I could wangle my way into Burma? I studied the airline timetable, and then booked a flight to Rangoon on Union of Burma Airways, and a connecting flight to Calcutta on Thai International. The first flight arrived in the early evening and the connecting flight didn't depart until the following day. I then stormed into the Burmese Consulate in Bangkok, complaining bitterly about having to change planes in a place called – what's its name again? – Wrong Goon or some such? – when I only wanted to get to Calcutta. Now, I supposed, they weren't going to give me a visa for that one night, so I'd have to stay in an airport without any facilities miles from anywhere! Bloody silly way to run an airline, bloody silly way to run a country! I put on such a fine show of righteous indignation that the tiny Burmese behind the counter went to consult someone, and came back and said that in the circumstances I could have a visa for one night. As I left, bearing my precious passport and visa, I saw that he was grinning to himself, and I later discovered why.

The flight from Bangkok to Rangoon was memorable. I was glad to note that the plane was a Viscount, with Rolls-Royce engines, but the chief attraction was the pilot, who hardly stopped talking to us the whole way, with a powerful Scandinavian accent. Here is a sample: 'This is Captain Hanson speaking. You will guess that I am not myself Burmese, though this is Union of Burma Airways, in fact, very few Burmese are called Hanson, but all Danes are called Hanson, unless of course they are called Rasmussen . . . You will be wondering why is Captain Hanson going left and right and left and right instead of straight ahead. Well, if you will look out of the window, you will see enormous piles of cotton wool. These are cumulus clouds. If we were to go through them we should go bumpity bump, bumpity bump, which wouldn't bother Captain Hanson at all, but might be found unpleasant by the passengers; therefore Captain Hanson avoids them by going left and right and left and right . . . In a minute you will hear a sudden change in the sound of the engines and you will think oh my God. Do not think oh my God, because change of sound of the engines has been produced *on purpose* by Captain Hanson for technical reasons which would be beyond your comprehension . . . In a moment, you will hear – indeed, you will *feel* – an almighty THUMP under your seat. Do not be alarmed: you wouldn't want us to land without having the wheels down, now would you? Trust Captain Hanson! . . . There, you see, we landed safely, in spite of Captain Hanson chattering away and not paying attention to what he was doing!' The other passengers were all Burmese, and I don't know whether they understood Scandinavian English or not.

At Immigration, I showed my passport and pointed to my visa. The Immigration Officer sniggered, in much the same way as the tiny clerk in Bangkok had done. 'It is perfectly true that you are entitled to enter the country,' he explained, 'but we are a very long way from the city, and there is no transport, and if there were you would not be able to pay for it, because the banks are shut and it is forbidden to change money into kyats except at a bank, so you had better make yourself comfortable for the night.' As I lugged my case towards the street, he added, 'It's no use your trying to walk to the city – you wouldn't get there in time to get back for the plane to Calcutta tomorrow!' I ignored him, and greeted Mrs Coombes as she got out of the Rolls, apologizing that Bill couldn't come because of his duties at the Embassy. What the tricky Burmese didn't know was that I had sent a cable to the Ambassador.

We dined in state, and after a good night's sleep my hostess took me to the Shwe Dagon, of which I can only repeat the famous words of the Guide Michelin, '*vaut le voyage*'. It must be the most impressive religious building anywhere in the world. That's not gold leaf on the main pagoda which you can see pointing to the sky from miles away: it's solid gold. We naturally went barefoot, and when we descended, the chauffeur produced bowls of water and towels. We then went to the British cemetery about twenty miles north of Rangoon, which was immaculately kept. In the visitors' book there were several years without signatures, and my signature was preceded by that of Lord Mountbatten. It would be followed after an interval by a royal Princess. I don't suppose they've torn the page out.

My flight to Calcutta left on time: I was able to assure Customs that I hadn't handled a single kyat during my time in Burma.

My arrival in Calcutta gave me a shock from which I have never quite recovered. I do not recommend anyone visiting India for the first time to let Calcutta be their first port of call. You get out of the plane at Dum Dum Airport and go out to the rickety bus which (at least in those days) bounces you slowly through mile after mile of bustees. A bustee is a group of low-grade houses belonging to a particular landlord, and some are sewered and some are unsewered. In the sewered bustees, the human waste is more or less confined to open channels. In the unsewered bustees it spreads everywhere. You think you will never come to an end of the sea of dung inhabited by people the colour of dung who smell of dung.

It wasn't quite as bad the next time I was there, but on this occasion I asked myself, 'Where does one begin to make a place fit for human habitation?' The answer came to me with shocking force: 'Anywhere. Stop the bus at random, and get off, and spend the rest of your life in the spirit of the young Victorian doctor whose father had a Mayfair practice that paid him richly for holding the hands of hypochondriac old ladies, and who refused to inherit the practice but went to China as a medical missionary. "And what do you think you can do for five hundred million Chinese?" enquired his father sarcastically. The son replied, "When the sun goes down, I do not complain of darkness, I light my candle. It will not illuminate the world, but it will illuminate my surgery."'

I had to remind myself that I already *had*, back in London, a vocation for the relief of human misery which I could not abandon and for which I was better fitted than the one to which I felt drawn on that dreadful journey. Suddenly I felt an urgent desire to be back in my spiritual home – I'd had a fascinating holiday, but it had served its purpose of making me ready to get back to work. However, I reminded myself, my work was no longer in London or even in my own country, but was something valid anywhere in the world. By the time I reached the impressive centre of Calcutta the urge to sow the seeds of a Samaritan service in as many places as possible before I died, was stronger than the yearning for my familiar place.

I remember preaching at St Paul's Cathedral on Chowringhee at the crowded 8 a.m. service, and then being taken by car to St Andrew's Presbyterian Church, with sandwiches and a thermos of coffee provided by ladies of the congregation. The driver stopped outside the church so that I could have my breakfast, and as I lifted my sandwich to my mouth I became aware of a little face at the window staring at me, or rather at the sandwich. It was a tiny little girl. I rolled down the window, and gave her the sandwich. She didn't eat it. She took it to an even tinier girl sitting on the steps of the church, doubtless her small sister. She did not share the sandwich with her. She gave her the whole sandwich. I got out of the car and went across and gave *her* the other sandwich. Then I went back and drank my coffee, and thanked God that in poverty and squalor there was still love. (I also told myself that if I lived there, I should have to get used to eating when surrounded by people who hadn't anything.)

From the Caravelle which took me on to Bombay I had the great joy of seeing Everest on our right-hand side. In Bombay, ignoring the hole in the ground made by the previous Caravelle, I was able to spend a lot of time with our second oldest Branch, founded and maintained by my friend Nadir Dinshaw and directed by a wonderful psychiatrist, Dr Sarah Dastoor, a Parsee like Nadir himself. She was assisted by three Parsee social workers and a number of volunteers who included Hindus and Muslims. The Parsees are Zoroastrians from Persia who fled at a time of persecution and were given sanctuary by the King of Gujarat – to this day Parsees speak, as well as English, their own form of Gujarati. They are known for their generosity. I stayed with Naju Bhabha, sister of Nadir's wife Hilla, and her husband Khursedji, a distinguished lawyer, on Cuffe Parade, Colaba. In the next flat lived her sister-in-law Dr Amy Bhabha, FRCP, the leading paediatrician in Asia married to Coovedgi Bhaba.

Naju was secretary of The Samaritans at that time, and did much Samaritan work herself. One evening in the middle of dinner, a telephone call came which led her to say she must go at once on an errand of mercy, and I begged to be allowed to go with her. As we drove along Nepean Sea Road, I thought we would be going to Mount Nepean, the big house inhabited by her and Hilla's mother, Dinoo Dubash, where I had several times been entertained, but we turned off into a side road and stopped. We waited in silence for some time, and then another car came, and stopped behind ours, and an Indian gentleman got out and Naju got out to speak to him. Then his car followed ours into a compound with lots of small houses, which I realized must be the servants' quarters of Mount Nepean. Many quiet, sorrowful people gathered around our car, and led us to the arched hall of a simple dwelling where, lying back in a wooden armchair, was an elderly woman with an enormous swelling on her neck. The top half of the half-door was closed whilst the Indian gentleman went in and examined her, and when he came out he gave a piece of paper to Naju, who gave it with money to one of the young men standing around to fetch the medicine. Then the Indian gentleman drove off, and Naju whispered to me, 'Mother's servants are all Goanese. They are Christians. They would like you to say a prayer for the old lady.' This, of course, I did. Then we drove back to Colaba to finish our dinner, and I learned that the Indian gentleman, who could only make the old lady's death easier, was the leading cancer specialist in India.

Nothing so moving happened again the rest of the way home, though there were *amusing* incidents – for instance, in Doha, capital of Qatar (to pronounce it, say 'gutter' with a finger pressed firmly on your Adam's apple, if you have one), I was put in quarantine because I hadn't recently had a smallpox vaccination, and on the flight to Shiraz, in Iran, for the first time in my life I had in the adjoining seat to me a fairly large goat, whose seat-belt I had to fasten for him.

Arrived in Shiraz, I was making my way to the terminal building when I saw a young couple sitting precariously on top of an archway, and as they looked English I shouted up to them, 'You look pretty silly, sitting up there,' and the girl, who turned out to have been at school with my daughter, shouted back, 'Not as silly as you, lugging that enormous drum.' I had obtained the drum in Burma to amuse my children, and regretted this many times, but it justified itself by getting me an invitation to supper and bed.

In Isfahan I was fortunate to stay in an hotel run by Assyrian Christians, and was able to tell them that their Mar Shimun, then living in Chicago, was a friend of mine. They were wonderfully kind to me, and when I had seen enough mosques, took me to the airport for a flight to Tehran. Incredible as it may seem, the aeroplane which should have landed to take passengers from Isfahan to Tehran just didn't stop at Isfahan – it flew right over us. We later learned that it had trouble with its undercarriage, and its pilot, not knowing whether it would work more than once, decided to get it to Tehran, where there were workshops. This proved to be a blessing in disguise, because my Christian friends booked me a seat in a 'taxi' going to Tehran for a ridiculously small sum, and I shall never forget that wonderful ride across the desert. I found in Tehran that I wouldn't have enough money to fly home all the way, but would be able to fly to Istanbul and take the train from there. I sent Nuran a picture postcard, telling her the time of my arrival and asking her to meet me at Yesilköy, and after my name I wrote '*Boşver!*' When the postcard arrived at her flat, Nuran was at her house on Bugada in the Princess Islands in the Sea of Marmara (an earthly paradise, I thought it was, when I was there), and at that time her daughters knew no English. Seeing the word *boşver*, they rang up their mother who knew the card must be from me and hastened back to Şişli just in time to get to the airport to meet me. *Boşver*!

10

I want to share with you a story I made up for the instruction of Samaritan volunteers and continued to use very often in preparation classes and other talks.

There was a remote village surrounded by flat meadows and approached by a road straight as an arrow. Around the meadows were thick woods. One day a flying saucer landed in one of the meadows, and Martians descended from it. Being such a remote village, where nothing ever happened, everybody rushed out to have a look. The Martians had a robot which spoke the language of the villagers, very loudly. It commanded all the men and boys to go and hide in the woods, and all the pre-pubertal girls and post-menopausal women to go back to their homes. The remainder of the females, that is to say those between menarche and menopause, were to line up along the straight road in order of height. The tallest beanpole of a girl was to be furthest from the village and the smallest girl nearest to the village and the rest were to range themselves according to their height at intervals of an eighth of an inch. This was supervised by the Martians with measuring rods, who also ensured that where there were two or more girls of exactly the same height, they should stand in line behind the marker. When they were all arranged, the ladies at either end stood alone, but next to them were two, and next to them three, and the numbers standing in line increased as you moved towards the centre, where there were fifty in the exact middle, with forty-nine on either side, and so on. 'Do not dare to move!' barked the robot. 'We shall be returning.' Then the flying saucer took off and hovered about a hundred yards above the collection of females and took photographs. They returned, and presented an enormous enlargement of one of the photographs to the village, posting it up outside the village church.

Then another flying saucer appeared in the sky, and the Martians muttered something in an incomprehensible language and took off in the opposite direction. The women and girls milled around but did not go back to the village. When the next flying saucer arrived, Venusians descended from it, and were pleasantly surprised to find that they had all the females from the village between menarche and menopause. They had a robot speaking the language of the villagers very audibly but sweetly and persuasively, and it begged their co-operation in conducting an experiment. The Venusians would stand and embrace each of the damsels in turn, and take a reading for each with a gadget that each of them had. They would then assign to the girl or woman a number, which they would paint on her forehead. When they had done this they told the women and girls to arrange themselves in such a way that the highest number was furthest from the village and the lowest number (which was in fact a minus number) nearest to the village. Any of them who had the same number as someone else was to stand behind the marker, in line. They ended up not at all in the same order as before: tall and short and medium height were all mixed up together indiscriminately, because the Venusians had not been measuring their height. What had they been measuring? They were kind enough to say, when it was too late for the females to be embarrassed or seek to change their position. The Venusians were measuring the strength of sexual attraction of each of the women and girls for someone of the same sex, that is to say, the degree of their lesbianism compared with the most lesbian in the village. The one with the biggest minus number was a woman considered by her fellow villagers to be a nymphomaniac, insatiable for male sexual partners.

The Venusians asked them sweetly not to go away, as they would be coming back. Then they went up in their flying saucer and took photographs from the same height as had been used by the Martians. They came back, and said that they were going to present an enlargement of one of the photographs to the village, with many thanks for the kind co-operation they had received. Followed by excited girls, they made their way to the village church, and stopped in amazement. 'Why,' they said, 'you already have the photograph we have just taken! How is that possible?'

One of the ladies took it upon herself to enlighten them. 'Just before you came,' she said, 'we had a visit from Martians, who arranged us on the road in much the same way as you, but according to different measurements from yours. They did not measure our

...' She broke off and blushed prettily.

'What did they measure?' enquired the chief Venusian.

'Our height,' she told him. The Venusians pinned up their photograph next to the Martian one, said goodbye, and took off in their flying saucer. The men and boys came back from the woods, but life in the village was never the same afterwards. Nobody called the insatiable girl 'the town bike' any more, and several ladies who had looked longingly but secretly at one another in the past now felt able to declare their love, with complete tolerance from the other females. Of course, there were some males who could not bear to think that there were females who did not need them.

The shape that was photographed from both space ships was what is known as the 'distribution curve'. It shows how varying characteristics, of any kind whatever, are distributed according to the number of examples of each. The shape of the curve does not change, though its steepness may. You will realize now that the same curve would have been obtained had the extra-planetary visitors conducted their experiments with males, or if they had measured IQ, or if they had measured bust sizes of women and penis sizes of men. The thing I want you to grasp is that when arranged for the Martians, the lady in the middle of the rank and those in the file behind her, who were of exact average height, could not claim to be morally superior to those an eighth of an inch taller or an eighth of an inch shorter. And when arranged by the Venusians, the corresponding 'average' females could not claim to be morally superior to those on either side of them. The conclusion is, that where you are on the distribution curve is where you are. It is not where you have chosen to be; there is nothing deliberate about it; and therefore there is no question of sin or wrongdoing. Where you are on the spectrum of human sexual behaviour is where your genes, your upbringing, and your life experiences and opportunities have placed you.

The majority of lesbians who came to see me did not know this or did not believe it. They felt guilty or freakish. They were not able to accept themselves, and of course they were aware that many people, including their families, would not accept *them*, if they knew. I am happy to say that I have seen a gradual change in this matter, and hope I have contributed towards it. More and more lesbians are now able to be accepted by their family and even by their colleagues

265

at work. The situation still isn't as it should be, but I am not often nowadays in the position of suffering from helpless pity for a girl who had just told me her sad story.

A girl came to see me whose best friend was another girl with whom she had been at school. This is, of course, usual. The other girl moved a few miles away, but they continued to meet regularly – in fact, they seemed inseparable. Let's call the one who came to see me Lorna, and let's call her friend June. Lorna knew that she was in love with June, but had never shown any sign of it, because she was afraid June would be shocked and would reject her. Nevertheless, she allowed herself to hope that one day it might be possible to express her love, because like herself, June seemed to take no interest in boys. The only physical contact the two of them had was to walk arm in arm, and to give a brief hug and kiss on the cheek when parting. One day they were both invited to a party, and as the party was going on late it was agreed that Lorna should spend the night at June's house. They had had a few drinks at the party, but not enough to be tipsy. Lorna's heart beat very fast when she realized that June's mother had put her in June's room, to share a three-quarter size bed. She undressed very quickly, in order to be able to watch June undressing without seeming to do so. She felt powerful sexual desire towards June, but decided that it would be unwise for her to make the first move. Eventually they were both in bed together, chatting sleepily about the party, and then June put out the light and snuggled up to Lorna. Lorna had never felt so blissful in her life. After a while she leaned over and kissed June on the mouth. Then she slipped her hand gently between June's thighs, kissed her mouth again, and said, 'I love you, June.'

At this, June sat up straight in bed, switched on the light, looked at Lorna with horror and disgust, told her to get out, said that she never wanted to see her again, and called her opprobrious names. Lorna was paralysed with shock. June pushed her out of the bed and turned her back to her. Lorna slowly got dressed, went downstairs, let herself out, and began the long walk back to her own home. On the way, she tried to throw herself in front of a speeding car. The driver braked and swerved and managed to miss her, screamed abuse at her, and drove on. She was able to get into the house without being heard, but didn't know what she would say to her mother in the morning, or on all the occasions when June would be expected to come and see her. She also didn't know what, if anything, June would say to *her* mother, and to all who were accustomed to seeing her with Lorna. I think you will realize that here we have an example of a suicidal girl who is not in the least mentally ill and does not need psychiatric help. What does she need? She needs the kind of befriending The Samaritans offer, but it's going to be a long time before she gets over the shock of rejection and contempt.

I think the reason why so many young lesbians came to me was because they needed someone old enough to be their father who, unlike their real father, did not disapprove of them being what they were – quite the opposite – and was not a male chauvinist resenting their unavailability to the predatory male. Being a parson was a great help too, because if they belonged to a church, or cared at all what church people might think, it was very reassuring not to be labelled a sinner because of something they could no more help than a brown-skinned person could help having a brown skin. I have no patience with those who say it's all right to accept that a person is what she is, but not to condone her doing what she wants to do in consequence, because I know very many examples of loving sexual relationships which are as permanent as the average marriage. It's no good telling me that the child molester is what he is, and there-fore accepting that is equivalent to giving him permission to go on molesting children. It should be clear to anybody who thinks at all that his situation does not come within the definition 'consenting adults in private'.

Male homosexuals are far more active sexually than female. This is partly because they produce much more testosterone. If two men are living together as lovers, when one doesn't think of it, the other does; but if two women are living together, when one doesn't think of it the other often doesn't either. Let me introduce you to Pat and Pat. Pat was one of those names that were found convenient because they could belong to either sex. The two I'm thinking about were accustomed to call one another Patrick and Patricia. I had enabled them to overcome their difficulties in accepting that their love for one another was legitimate and permissible. One day I was very happy to receive a picture postcard from them from Majorca, say-ing, '*Having a lovely time. We are here on our honeymoon, and it's all your fault. Love, Pat and Pat.*' Then one of them had added, '*Wish you were here,*' and the other had crossed it out.

Seriously, they did still need me from time to time, because of the testosterone deficiency I have referred to. I remember one of them ringing me up to say how happy they were and that they had just moved together into a new flat. The following dialogue ensued. 'Still going all right in bed?' 'Oh yes, yes, of course.' 'Do you still make love regularly?' 'Yes, well, fairly regularly.' '"Fairly"?' 'Well, you see, we've both been working very hard lately, what with getting the flat ready and so on, and we get very tired . . .' 'So when was the last time?' 'Oh, not long ago.' 'When?' 'Er – mm – oh, about a month ago.' 'Pat, will you do something for me?' 'You know I would do anything for you!' 'Then make love to Pat tonight. This very night. Without fail. Whether convenient or inconvenient. Will you do that?' 'Yes.'

The next morning I was rung up by the other Pat. 'Oh, Chad, we are so happy together. I had to ring you up to tell you how wonderful it is with Pat. I was beginning to think she'd gone off me, but she hasn't. She most certainly hasn't!' I expressed gratification, and did not say that the two of them appeared to be living on *my* testosterone.

I once had a letter from a lesbian in the Republic of Ireland, who had never admitted to anybody before that her orientation was towards her own sex. I never discovered how she knew that she could trust *me*. I invited her to come and see me, and with some difficulty she made the long journey, and found it a great relief to speak for the first time about her deepest feelings. I had deliberately put on a clerical collar and black suit that day, but didn't, of course, pretend that I was RC. She imagined that she was the only person in her town who experienced these desires. Her guardian angel must have been working overtime, because I was not only able to tell her the usual percentage of the population which was like herself, but was able to add that I actually knew of one person within easy reach of where she lived. I explained that nobody can ever introduce two people to become lovers, but one can introduce them to become friends, knowing that they have a certain secret in common. I said I would ask the other young woman's permission to enable the two of them to meet. I'm happy to say it became a wonderful friendship, and I did not enquire whether it became anything else.

As I said earlier, I believe it may interest you if I recollect an example of each of my particular categories at this period. I'll tell you about a trans-sexual – that is to say, a person who felt he or she was in the wrong-sexed body – a bit later, but first I'll tell you about a transvestite. You mustn't confuse trans-sexuals with transvestites, who are in my opinion merely a variety of fetishists who like to dress up in the clothing of the opposite sex; the term is in practice applied only to men wishing to dress up as women. A common fallacy is to suppose that these are homosexuals wishing to be attractive to men, but the vast majority of transvestites are heterosexuals getting a kick out of wearing garments belonging to the sex they lust after.

The young man was, like most transvestites, heterosexual, dressing or posing as a woman in order to feel sexually close to women. Although he enjoyed dressing up as a woman, his chief pleasure came from surveying himself naked in a full-length looking glass. He had had hormone treatment to enlarge his breasts, and had a feminine hairstyle, but when his eyes panned downwards towards his carefully shaved legs and his pubic tuft trimmed so as to appear like a neat triangle pointing downwards rather than a straggly triangle pointing up towards the navel, he was abruptly reminded of his masculinity by a penis which became more and more prominent as it became more and more aroused. He did, of course, masturbate while looking at himself narcissistically in the glass, but kept toying with the idea of having his penis cut off and a clitoris substituted for masturbation purposes. He asked me whether this was possible, and I told him that it was; that a sliver of the glans penis with its connection to the body could be placed by the surgeon at the top between the artificially created labia. But wouldn't it, I suggested, be more sensible to bring one hand through between the legs from behind, grasp the penis and scrotum and pull these backwards, then close the thighs so that the view in the glass showed only the pubic hair pointing downwards to the meeting of the thighs in a Y?

He thought this was a brilliant idea, kicked himself for not having thought of it himself when he was the intended beneficiary, and rushed off to the loo to try it. He came back with this enthusiasm slightly diminished because, he said, as soon as he became sufficiently aroused his erection could not be held back between his thighs without discomfort. 'Wait here!' I commanded. I nipped up my helical staircase to another room and rummaged in the desk there until I found what I was looking for: a gadget which fitted round the 'neck' of the penis, was attached by a spring to the back of a belt and had a cord leading away in the opposite direction, tied to a piece of wood which could be held between the teeth. I did not, of course, tell him about the person for whom it was originally designed, but I will tell you.

It was many years before, in fact soon after the war, and before I had actually started The Samaritans but was fitting in sexual counselling at home. A girl came to see me who was working as a nurse in a hospital with a ward for amputees. I don't know whether they were all war-wounded or not, but they were all male in her ward. She was particularly sorry for one young man who had lost both his arms. I think he was the only one in the ward in this situation, but certainly he was the only one who after she had got to know him, made an explicit request that *as* a nurse she should help him sexually. All the other men in the ward, he said, were able to masturbate if they wanted to, and most of them did as far as he could judge; he alone had to suffer the frustration occasioned by his erections being much more frequent than his nocturnal emissions (which she, of course, had on occasion had to clean up, and thought nothing of it). All he was asking was that when she was on night duty she would use her hand to give him relief. She said she would not give him an answer until she had consulted someone she trusted. I felt humbled when she told me that that someone was myself, though I had never met her before. She had read something I had written, and decided that here was a priest who really believed in the Christian faith *and* who was not negative about sex. (You will notice that 'and': as I wrote it I remembered that the famous David Livingstone, in ordering a gravestone for his father, had included in the inscription the words 'of poor and honest parents'. When the stonemason objected that 'but' was the accepted form, Livingstone replied that he found it insulting.)

I questioned her gently about how she felt about the matter and it was clear to me that she was quite happy about refusing or complying if I would take upon myself the burden of instructing her in what was the right thing to do. I was to give her her orders, and she would carry them out. 'There needs to be somebody, sir,' she pleaded, 'that a girl can turn to in a tricky matter like this, and get a straight answer.' I could only agree, remembering the little girl who had killed herself and whom I had buried on my first day in the ministry: 'there ought to have been someone she could have asked.' These are the instructions I gave her.

'You must tell the man that your relationship with him is that of nurse and patient. It is not, and never will be, and must not appear to be, a personal relationship, let alone a sexual one. He did not ask you to make love to him – he may have wanted this but he didn't ask for it – he asked you simply to be hands for him, because he hadn't any. So you say to him that you will help him on your terms as long as he sticks to what you have laid down, but if he does not observe the conditions you will cease to oblige. The conditions are: he must never ask. You alone will decide when to go to him, relieve him. You will only do this at times when you know you will not be disturbed. Whilst you are doing it, he must not look at you and must not speak. When you have finished, you will clean him up, cover him up, and go, still without any word from him; and he must not speak to you about it at any other time. You yourself must not speak of it to anyone, and if *he* does, you must calmly deny it, and desist from then on, lest you should be under observation. If he has any sense, he will give no hint of your kindness to him.'

She replied that she was entirely happy about the conditions I laid down, and it relieved her mind a lot to think that she could show pity simply as a good nurse. She would under no circumstances tell anyone else, and especially not her boyfriend.

I haven't spoken of this before, but it is now forty years ago. It is unlikely that the nurse to whom she handed over when she left will be shocked to learn that the gadget she taught her how to affix to the man's penis, and take away again when he had finished, had been invented by me when the nurse knew she was leaving, and that she herself had used her hand.

Talking of gadgets reminds me that a couple who had been to SPOD (Sexual Problems of the Disabled) were referred to me, and I devised for them a contraption which allowed them for the first time to have sexual intercourse. It was a Heath Robinson affair, but it worked. I trust you will feel that there needs to be somebody who *cares* whether disabled people are helped to get the sexual satisfaction they cannot hope to get without someone's ingenuity. Or, of course, someone's kindness. The only two organizations of which I am Patron are the Terrence Higgins Trust for Aids sufferers, and the Outsiders Club, for disabled and handicapped persons of both sexes who are given opportunities of getting to know one another.

An interesting example of someone you have to think about before deciding which category they belong in was one I will call Ramona, a mild-mannered, middle-aged person who normally dressed in unisex shirt and trousers but at home wore a dress. Certainly the face looked more feminine than masculine to me, but then as you look around you in the underground you will see many men who would look quite credible as women if they were dressed as women. Ramona was in fact homosexual and enormously enjoyed anal intercourse, which she fairly often managed to get

271

herself invited to in spite of being not at all 'pretty'. The reason why she came to me was that she had heard that I had been known to recommend a person for a sex-change operation, even though of course the decision could only be made by the surgeon concerned. 'I never thought', she confided, 'that I should be consulting a clergyman about whether to have the embarrassing and useless thing between my legs cut off or not, but everybody says you would be the best person to ask.' I told her that when dealing with questions like that I was not being what most people think a parson is for, and after a long discussion I gave her unequivocal advice that she should retain her small, never-erecting penis and testicles, because the loss of these wouldn't make her a woman but would neuter her. She was, strange as it may seem, a woman *because of* her male organs, or, to put it another way, she was a sexual being because of those organs, and was with their aid emotionally a woman.

Though technically male, because of having this penis which never erected and these rather undeveloped testicles, Ramona wanted to be thought of as a woman, so I shall use the feminine pronoun for her. She wanted to be able to dress like a woman and have a woman's job: her dream was to be a lady's maid, but she would settle for the job of a girl in a cigarette kiosk. But what would she do if challenged, or arrested for making use of a ladies' public lavatory? I gave her a note on my headed writing-paper stating her name and address and that she was a patient of mine, and that she could not possibly be in a public lavatory for any other purpose than to make water. I invited the police to get in touch with me at any hour of the day or night for confirmation of this, and I signed it. Armed with this, she was able to come *literally* out of the closet, and go out and about, wearing a dress. A year or so later, I had the pleasure of giving her a character reference to be taken on as a lady's maid by someone living in Belgravia.

A very different case was that of a neat-looking little fellow with a will of iron, whose name was Albert. He, like Ramona, wanted to be made love to by men, but there the resemblance ended. He was determined to have a sex-change operation, and he had been saving up the necessary money for years. He had failed to get recommended for the operations on the National Health Service, and had even gone so far as to write to Saudi Arabia to a contact he had found there, to enquire about the possibility of being castrated by someone accustomed to making eunuchs. It turned out to be a non-starter. When he told me of all the various means he had tried to get

272

his genitals removed and imitation female ones created, I felt that he was too one-track-minded about it to be able to listen to reason.

Nevertheless, I tried to reason with him. I told him that his sexual responses to men were possible because of his sexual apparatus, and that if it was removed, he would not become a woman, however convincing-looking a vulva some surgeon might manage to fake up: he would, in fact, be neuter, having no sexual desire for either sex. He wouldn't believe me. He was going to be, he said, an irresistibly sexy woman who, because of his knowledge of the male, would be able to seduce any male who seemed to him, or as it would then be to 'her', to be sexually desirable. I told him I wished he had more reasons for wanting to be a woman than to have an endless succession of male sexual partners, but all to no avail. I only saw him again once, when he told me he had contracted for a series of eleven, or it may have been thirteen, operations in Belgium, for which he was to pay £600 – a lot of money in those days. My last words to him were, 'If you want to be a woman, Albert, at all costs keep your balls.'

A couple of years later, I had a girl come to see me whose appearance and attire were calculated to provoke wolf-whistles. She gave the name of Charmian MacHinery, and spoke about what a delight it was to go shopping with other girls, and buy lovely clothes, and compare them. The only snag was, her girl friends wanted always to talk about the effect the new clothes would have on their men friends, and she, Charmian, had no wish to talk, think about, or be acquainted with men. 'I think sex is disgusting,' she confided, with a moue and a pretty, simulated shudder.

I said, 'Forgive me, Miss MacHinery – I don't want to offend you, but I must confess that – er – I don't feel myself to be in the presence of a woman.' At first she bridled, and tried to pull her skirt to cover her knees, but then gave a little laugh and confessed, 'I thought you hadn't recognized me; before my operations, you knew me as Albert.'

I hadn't, in fact, recognized her: it was my instinct which told me that she was not a woman, but come to think of it, surely not a man? 'I am very happy, now,' she said, 'as long as *men* will keep away from me. My only regret is that I went through so much to have an artificial vagina as well as the – outer parts. But I like the company of other women, and above all, I like shopping, and dressing up.' At this point, I was assailed by a terrible temptation, namely (I'm ashamed to admit) the temptation to say to her, 'I told

273

you so.' I didn't *yield* to it, but I did experience it, which Samaritan No. 1 shouldn't do, because we exist to make people feel better, not worse. My reminding her that I'd warned her that she wouldn't become a woman but would become a neuter, could only have distressed her and made her feel that I was disparaging the woman-hood of which she was so proud. So I simply said, 'I'm so glad you're so much happier than you were when I saw you a couple of years ago.'

Privately, of course, I was interested to note this example of the truth of my theory, and was thankful that Ramona still had her shrunken male genitals and thus was able to enjoy the occasional anal intercourse when it came her way – though not, of course, as much as she enjoyed being a lady's maid.

If your organs are in the right places and working reasonably well, give thanks for this, and do not despise those who are forced to all sorts of contrivance in order to get any sexual pleasure at all. You can criticize *me*, if you like, for aiding and abetting the sexually handicapped, but the only result will be that I shall continue to believe that I am doing God's work and that you are heartlessly opposing it.

One day a girl came in who seemed upset and distressed, so one of the Samaritans tried to befriend her. However, she seemed to be impatient of this, and said she wanted to see *me*. The volunteer knew that I had a full appointments book that day, but shouldn't have said, 'I think he hardly sees anyone except lesbians, these days.' The only result of this was that the young woman stated firmly that she was a lesbian, so now could she please see me? The volunteer went to another room and buzzed me and said cheerfully, as if offering a great treat, 'I've got a lesbian for you!'

'I'd rather have lunch,' I replied. She was shocked, so I said, 'Very well, wheel her in, and ask the SiC [Samaritan in charge] if a sandwich could be brought to me – ham, with not too much English mustard.'

The damsel sat with me whilst I ate my sandwich and I sipped my coffee and she her tea, and she answered my questions about her sexual feelings. By the time I'd finished my sandwich, I was able to say to her, 'Young woman, you are in luck; I have good news for you: you are not a lesbian.' (I didn't say this because there is anything wrong with being a lesbian, but because life is easier for those who aren't.)

'I know,' she rejoined. 'I only said I was because I couldn't think of any other way of making sure you would see me.' I didn't see the point of reproaching her for wasting my time, so I simply asked her what her sexual problem was. She began to squirm with embarrassment and wring her hands. Blushing deeply, she said, 'All my life, ever since I was quite small, I have wanted to . . .' She buried her face in her hands and broke off.

I won't weary you by telling you how many times she began that sentence and how many times I tried to get her to complete it. We tried her taking a deep breath and rushing at it; we tried *me* saying the first bit and waiting for her to carry on; but eventually I had to say to her, 'In five minutes precisely there will appear at that door my next client, who happens to be one who would get into a state if kept waiting for even a minute. So, it's really now or never. You can write it down, if it's any easier for you.'

She shook her head. Then she took a deep breath, and said rapidly, 'Ever since I can remember, ever since I was a small girl, I have wanted to piss on the carpet.'

Equally rapidly, I said, 'Be my guest.' She gaped at me. 'We are now down to three minutes,' I said. 'There's the carpet.'

She stood, hitched up her skirt, and I suppose lowered her drawers (I don't know because I was looking into her eyes), squatted down, and did for a very long time what she had wanted to do ever since she was a little girl. I reasoned that if she had wanted me to watch what she was doing, she would have lowered her eyes, and she didn't, so I continued to look at her with beaming approval. She straightened up and sat down and heaved a tremendous sigh. 'I feel wonderful,' she said.

'I'm glad,' I told her, 'but we now have less than a minute, so I'm afraid I have to push you out.' She tried to persuade me to let her pay for cleaning the rug, but I reminded her that I had invited her to be my guest. At the door, she turned and said, 'You will never guess what.' I know it's going to make me sound insufferable, but why should I mind? I knew exactly what she was going to say.

'I can't imagine,' I lied.

She stood as if in a trance, in the open doorway, and said wonderingly, 'I won't ever have to do it again.' Then she was rudely pushed out of the way by my next client.

A few days later I happened to be meeting our consultant psychiatrist, and asked him to explain the case to me. 'What does it matter?' he asked. 'Some of us would have had her on a couch for weeks, trying to find that out. What I like about *you*, Chad, is that you are so practical. Please don't change. She probably never *will* need to do it again.

I've told you that from February 1954 I never picked up the emergency telephone unless called to it by a Samaritan. There was the occasional exception, when the SiC had all his or her team either befriending face to face or answering the increasing number of telephones, and one day I was roped in to answer a call nobody had responded to before me. 'I am going to throw myself off Waterloo Bridge into the Thames,' stated the voice of a young man.

'*Waterloo* Bridge?' I complained. 'How non-U can you get? Don't you know London Bridge is the accepted one for suicides?'

'Is that The Samaritans?' the voice asked disbelievingly.

'The Samaritans, can I help you?' I amended, this being the standard Samaritan reply.

'You're supposed to stop me committing suicide,' said the young man, 'not advise me which bridge to do it from!'

'I agree, and I apologize,' I said; 'my only excuse is that I thought you were going to ask me for money – people who *threaten* suicide tend to attach some sort of little "unless" to it.'

'Um,' he murmured.

There was a long silence. Then, afraid he would simply hang up, I continued, 'How much do you want, and what do you need it for?'

'A thousand pounds, to pay my gambling debts, otherwise I get my legs broken, and then my wife would know, and I promised her I would never do it again,' he said in a rush.

I told him, 'I don't have £1,000, and if I had I wouldn't send it to a gambler, but I'm willing to see you if you'd like to come and talk to me.'

'What's the good of that, if you aren't going to lend me any money?' he demanded.

'Better, I should have thought, than catching your death in the Thames, either from cold or from some nasty disease.' (This was before it was cleaned up and had salmon in it.)

When he arrived, I saw a pleasant young man who seemed to me to be not an irredeemable gambler, because the excitement of gambling didn't mean as much to him as his marriage, and the debt was an old one – he hadn't gambled since he got married, and would rather die, let alone bet, than lose his dream girl, whose views on gambling were emphatic. I asked him to give me a list of the people he had approached or could approach, and we worked on it together. 'You see,' he groaned, 'I've tried everyone possible who wouldn't tell my wife about it.'

I informed him that he was a silly ass to say that it was no help to come and talk to me if I wasn't going to give him any money: only by talking to me had it become plain that he hadn't included on his list the most obvious person.

'Who?'

'The boss who employs you,' I said.

'I couldn't ask him!' exclaimed the young man. 'I'd lose my job!' I stared at him scornfully until he got the point. 'Oh, I see,' he said. 'Why worry about losing your job if the alternative is to lose your life.'

It turned out that he was employed by a multi-national corporation which I won't name. The head of it was a power in the land of whom even I had heard. Let's call him Mr Big. The young man gave me permission to telephone Mr Big.

Getting to talk to the Misters Big of this world is not as easy as you might think. I found the number of the building in which he worked in some executive suite, but was ages being passed higher and higher until at last I reached the dragon whose duty it was to prevent people like me from bothering him. She was immovable. She wouldn't even tell me whether he was in the building, but invited me to write and ask for an appointment. She would not, however, commit the discourtesy of hanging up on me, so I persisted in pleading that it was a matter of life and death which required (as Winston Churchill memorably put it) 'action this day'. Eventually she told me to hold on a minute. I held on, for much more than a minute. If she thought I was going to let her off the hook by hanging up, she had another think coming. Then a charming young feminine voice spoke into the telephone enquiring, 'Did my colleague say that you were Chad Varah?'

'Yes,' I assured her. 'May I know who you are?'

'No,' she replied succinctly. 'I don't want you to know who I am, and you evidently don't recognize my voice. Please don't try to find out. A couple of years ago you saved my life.'

'The Samaritans . . . ' I interjected.

'You personally.' It didn't often happen that I personally saved somebody's life, because by the time the Samaritan befriender passed a person on to me for counselling the danger was pretty well past. 'Perhaps you didn't realize,' she continued. 'I never came back to thank you. But I am glad to have the opportunity to say to you now, whatever you want that it is in my power to give, you may have.'

I couldn't imagine who she was, whether she ranked above or below or alongside the dragon, whether she was Mr Big's personal secretary, wife or mistress; and I didn't care. 'Thank you,' I said, 'you are the answer to my prayer. All I want is two minutes on the telephone to Mr Big.'

'That won't be easy,' she murmured, 'but you shall have what you have asked, even if I have to . . . don't go away.' I suppose it was only three or four minutes until the silence was broken by a confident male voice.

'Mr Varah,' it said, 'you have demanded two minutes of my time. Here I am.'

I mentioned the name of the young man on whose behalf I was ringing, and asked him if it meant anything to him. He said that it did, because the young man was one of his most promising young fellows, destined to go far. 'Only as far as from London Bridge into the Thames,' I told him. He told me I was talking nonsense, and I told him he hadn't got to his high position by not listening to experts. 'Very well,' he said, 'what's the trouble?'

'Old gambling debts of £2,000,' I said.

'You are sure he's stopped?' asked Mr Big.

'One can never be certain, but I think so,' I replied.

'Tell him to see the chief accountant,' he decided. 'Anything else?'

'No, thank you, sir,' I said politely. 'Your two minutes is up.' I then replaced the receiver. Looking back on it now, I think it was rather ungracious of me, but I had been looking at my watch, and even one more sentence of thanks would have taken me over the two minutes, which had taken me about half an hour to organize.

The young man gaped at me and said, 'I don't believe it!'

'You should,' I said, 'because they don't want to lose the amount they've spent on your training so far.'

'No, I don't mean *that*,' he said. 'I mean, how did you know that it was £2,000 and not £1,000 that I owed?'

'Hard-won experience,' I told him. 'Addicts always lie.'

For once, I did hear something further from a satisfied client. It seems the accountant granted him an immediate £2,000 and had him sign a bit of paper saying that it would be deducted quarterly

278

from his salary for I forget how many quarters. Six months later he was given a rise which wiped out the quarterly payments. The young man abjured gambling to such an extent that he wouldn't even buy a raffle ticket.

My gambler-with-the-rare-happy-ending I acquired by having to pick up an emergency telephone call for once. I am reminded of an occasion when I was 'on reception'. The dreaded 'flu had struck, and the SiC, going spare because of a shortage of volunteers, eventually buzzed me and said would I 'take the desk'. This meant, sit behind a kind of bar counter with a shelf underneath it on which one could write, and receive those who came for a personal visit. When they came in at the new entrance we had had built, No. 39 Walbrook, they could either go up a few steps on the left to the room then called Gulbenkian, where in the old days the Samaritans on duty would congregate but which was now used as the administrative office, or downstairs to the right, where I joked that we were 'lautrec' (we had two loos). To be faced with these unisex loos was very reassuring for the callers, because anxiety and nervousness often make a person feel he or she must make water. If you ignored the loos and turned right, on your left would be the desk and only by passing this could you either turn right into the bunk room or left under Humility Tunnel (tallish people had to bend their heads) where a corridor the whole width of the building at right angles to the tunnel gave, at that period, on to the room called Vivien, after Samaritan No. 2, the room called Mary, after Samaritan No. 3 (the first Samaritan to die), the Common Room, where attached to one of the pillars was an urn called Ern – this room was reinstated in 1991 and named the Lord Palumbo Room – and two rooms corresponding with Vivien and Mary. At the end of the passage was a fire escape. (In case you are puzzled by the word 'reinstated', increased busy-ness made it necessary to divide this room into four and open up the two end rooms to accommodate seven telephone 'positions'. Three of the little Befriending Rooms were named after George 75, Godfrey 585 and Diana 600.)

You will realize that as there was normally no one in the basement bunk room except at night, I was isolated from all the activity of the skeleton staff beyond Humility Tunnel that evening, answering the original 9000 line and four additional emergency lines on 626 2277, and befriending clients face to face in one of the small rooms or at the end of the Common Room furthest from Ern. I was thankfully scribbling away at arrears of correspondence when a girl of about eighteen with straight blonde hair came unsteadily down the steps and confronted me at the desk. With olde worlde courtesy, I stood up, and she said, 'You've got to give me £6.'

'Young lady,' I said, 'I am afraid you are mistaken. I don't have to give you £6, and in fact I couldn't if I wanted to, because I don't have £6.' (Ever since Barry 13 left to become a parson, I had had no help with expenses, and three times had had to transfer my over-draft to another bank.)

'But I've got to have it!' protested the girl. 'I need it for a fix. Maybe you don't even know what a fix is?'

It was foolish of me to answer as I did; one shouldn't be sarcastic with clients. 'We parsons lead very sheltered lives,' I claimed falsely, 'but even I know that a fix is an injection of some prohibited drug, usually heroin.'

'Well then,' she exclaimed impatiently, 'you must *know* that I've just *gotta* have the money.'

'I agree, I agree,' I assured her. 'Our only disagreement is about where the money is to come from, as it can't come from me.'

She took up a dramatic pose, and proclaimed, 'If you don't give me the £6, I shall have to get it by prostituting my lily-white body, and it will be all your fault.'

'Big deal!' I commented. 'You're surely not going to tell me it would be the first time? It's the usual way that reasonably pretty girls whose fathers or boyfriends are not millionaires sustain their habit. Be thankful you aren't revoltingly ugly or male: if you were, you'd probably have to do dangerous things like robbery. And by the way, it is not *my* fault that you have a habit you can hardly hope to support except by prostitution.'

She looked really shocked and pointed a finger at me. 'You mean you don't *care*?' she accused. 'All the other parsons I've been to couldn't bear it, and gave me the money to prevent my falling into sin.'

'I can only apologize for my foolish brethren,' I replied. 'Conning poverty-stricken clergy is some sort of sin, no doubt, but I differ from them in having far more respect for you when you are earning your heroin by your own efforts rather than pandering to clerical prudishness.'

'You', she informed me, 'are a hard bastard!' – and she swept out, before I could ask for that useful testimonial in writing.

280

I felt desperately sorry for her, trapped as she was, but knew she would have no chance if everybody was sentimental or prudish. I went and got myself a cup of coffee from Ern, which was why I was standing at the foot of the steps sipping it when she came back. She projected herself towards me, and I quickly put my coffee down on the desk as she threw herself into my arms and laid her head on my shoulder and started sobbing. I gave her a slight pat or two, but didn't make a big production of it. 'I've been looking for you,' she sobbed.

I'm afraid I was still suspicious. 'It's the seduction bit, now, is it?' I suggested.

She beat my chest angrily with her fists. 'I know you can't or won't give me the money,' she said, 'but you can't refuse to help me to kick it. I'll never do it by myself, and I never met anyone I can't con. I need a hard bastard like you.'

My heart sank. I didn't know how I could refuse, but I knew what it would involve if I took her on. At least, I thought I did. I grievously underestimated. 'Do you realize,' I asked her, 'that I shall have to learn to love *you*, a total stranger, as much as if you were my own daughter, and go through God knows what for God knows how long? It's a lot to ask!'

'I know,' she said humbly.

I handed her my coffee and she drank it. Then I said, 'I'll take you on on one condition. You can lie, cheat, steal, but you must never under any circumstances tell the slightest untruth to me. You and I can't get you free of this terrible slavery unless you have no tiniest secret from me. The first time I catch you out in even the smallest fib, I shall stop wasting my time on you.'

She looked me straight in the eye, shook hands and said, 'Agreed.'

'Then you will meet me', I commanded, 'at 10 o'clock tomorrow morning outside the Drug Addiction Clinic in Vincent Square.'

'But if I register there,' she wailed, 'they'll start cutting me down: from six jacks a day to five and one ampoule of physeptone, to four jacks and two ampoules, and then three of each . . .'

'How else are you going to get off it?' I demanded. 'You have to cut down gradually, and I'll be giving you my support.'

'I suppose so,' she replied dismally, and turned to go up the steps. Then she came back, and put on a performance which would have rivalled Sarah Bernhardt's. She clutched her brow, she bit the back of her hand, she pressed her knuckles against her cheeks, she rolled her eyes, and eventually groaned, 'My God, I forgot! My fix for

281

tonight! I can't go on till 10 o'clock tomorrow without a fix!'

'I know you can't,' I replied reasonably. 'I understand that you have to have a fix for tonight.' And I put my hand in my trousers' pocket. A peculiar expression came over her face. I drew out a coin and handed it to her.

She gawped at it, and asked, 'What's this?'

'Surely you've seen a shilling before?' I said. 'It's your bus fare to Gerrard Street. I'm told the Chinese are quick, clean, and honest – they pay what they say they will, but it's not much. I guess you'll have to take on three, so I wouldn't want you to tire yourself out by walking there.'

She laughed so loudly that the SiC darted through Humility Tunnel to peer at us, and quickly withdrew. 'Oh, thank God!' cried the girl. 'For one dreadful moment I thought you were going to give me the £6. If you had, you'd never have seen me again. You really are a hard bastard! See you in Vincent Square!' With that, she bounded up the stairs.

I didn't know whether or not to hope she'd be at Vincent Square the next day, but she was. I won't weary you with the agonies I went through with her, or the number of times I had to go out in the middle of the night to rescue her from some dreadful dive, or the unsavoury characters I had to have dealings with. About three months later I was lecturing to The Samaritans at a Branch on the south coast when I was called out to take an hysterical call from someone the local Samaritans were sure I would want to speak to. She was incoherent, but at last I managed to grasp that she had lapsed and was feeling utterly hopeless. She had 'scored' and had had a huge fix, which was already wearing off. I tried to project massive calm down the telephone. 'We're just having a little relapse,' I assured her. 'I was expecting it about now – perfectly normal. Have you got any of the stuff left?'

'Yes,' she sobbed, 'but I'll throw it away to prove to you that I do love you.'

'Don't throw it away, sweetie,' I ordered her. 'Fix it, and have a good night's sleep, and come and see me in the morning. God bless you!' And I went back to my lecture. I thought to myself how many people who would despise this girl wouldn't be capable of such a sacrifice as throwing away – if indeed she could have managed it – a few precious grains of heroin.

I am sure you will be delighted to know that eighteen months and three more lapses later, she was free.

Life for a former addict is by no means easy. She has lost all her friends except fellow-junkies, and *they* are such poor friends that they will constantly try to tempt her back with offers of free fixes. Her life is likely to be so lonely and empty that she can easily be dragged down into the underworld again. But I'm happy to tell you that twenty years later that girl was still free – and married.

All the time I was being either intrigued or exhausted, the volunteers were plodding along faithfully, befriending sad or desperate people, and listening patiently to endless tales of woe. You mustn't think, however, that I had *all* the excitements: let me tell you about the one which you will understand better now that the layout of the crypt in those days has been made clear to you. I was not in any way involved. I can't remember whether I was on the premises or not, but if I was, I wasn't in the room furthest from reception which I shared with my then secretary Anna 700, but up in my study, isolated from the action but able to keep an eye on the church. Our intercom system allowed the SiC to get in touch with me if he or she needed to do so, but nobody did on this occasion.

The particular duty I'm going to tell you about was exceptionally full of men. Whether this had anything to do with the fact that Liz 874 was SiC, I don't know. I do remember that one of the men on that duty had expected to be chosen by me, and when I chose Liz, hinted that it was because she was young and very beautiful. I am all in favour of girls being beautiful, but I care too much about the clients of The Samaritans to inflict upon them any sort of dumb bimbo. (The word wasn't in use at that time.) As it happens, both the heroines of this story were personal friends of mine; Liz still is; Dorothy 716, who was in her late 70s at the time, has since died. I had invited her to be SiC but she had declined, and I then appointed Liz for the simple reason that she was the most suitable, as was proved when a man came furtively down the steps waving a hand-gun. Liz, sitting at the desk, heard his footsteps and turned her head and thus saw his shadow before she could see him. Instantly, in a low but carrying voice, she enunciated, 'All men vanish – Dorothy come here.' I hope no Samaritan will be amazed that all men instantly made themselves scarce, and not even the one doing some filing in the bunk room (you didn't think we could spare it *only* for bunks, did you?) popped his head out to ask, 'Why?' I believe lives were saved by Liz's instant command and her shift's instant obedience.

By the time the gunman was level with the desk, there was nobody to be seen – unless you count the schoolgirl bent over her homework, which is what Liz looked like at that moment – except a doddering old lady giving her celebrated imitation of *Arsenic and Old Lace*. 'Good afternoon,' quavered Dorothy. 'How kind of you to come and see us. Do please follow me to where we can sit and have a chat.' She then tottered off through Humility Tunnel into the room called Mary. The gunman followed her, looking round and seeing no one else. 'Do please sit down,' invited Dorothy, still looking and sounding decrepit. 'May I offer you some refreshment? We have excellent tea, rather horrible coffee, and of course cocoa ...?'

'I've got a gun,' rejoined the man, waving it.

'Oh, so you have!' exclaimed Dorothy delightedly. 'They do make them very realistic these days, don't they? If you will tell me where you got it, I should like to buy one for my little great-grandson – '

'It's real, and it's loaded,' interrupted the man, pointing the gun at Dorothy.

'Didn't your nanny teach you, young man, that it's very *rude* to point a gun at a lady?' Dorothy had an endearing habit of addressing people as though they were all upper class like herself, brought up by nannies and accustomed to ringing for Hudson.

The gunman didn't know what to make of her, especially when she stopped dithering and suddenly moved like a cobra striking. Before he knew what had happened, the gun was under her voluminous skirts and unimaginable underwear. 'Give me that back!' blustered the man.

'Later, perhaps,' said Dorothy mildly. 'I'll just take care of it for you for the time being. Do you mind telling me why you were carrying it? You were not afraid of *me*, I take it?' She gave a thin deprecatory laugh, as if to deny how formidable she could be.

To summarize the story as recounted to me later by Dorothy, the man had escaped from a mental hospital, where he was convinced that one of the psychiatrists was responsible for all his troubles and ought to be eliminated. He had procured the gun – she never discovered whence – in order to effect the elimination. At this point, Dorothy enquired with a puzzled frown, 'Is he armed to the teeth?'

'Eh?'

'This doctor – is he armed to the teeth?'

'Of course not,' said the man.

284

'In that case,' pronounced Dorothy reprovingly, 'surely you must see that it wouldn't be *cricket* to attack him with a gun? Surely your nanny told you – '

At this point, looking as if he thought he'd come to a madhouse, the man got up and ran towards the exit. Too late, Dorothy shouted, 'Mind your head!' He gave himself an almighty whack at the entrance to Humility Tunnel, staggered up the stairs and was never seen by us again, though a little later men in white coats came and asked for the gun.

As soon as he'd gone, Liz called, 'All men come here!' They all came running, and she told them, 'Hug Dorothy until she stops shaking. Then sit her down and make her a cup of tea. In a teapot. Warmed. Served in a cup and saucer.'

Other friends of mine from the same period were Mary 683, probably from the class before the one at which Dorothy was accepted, and Godfrey 585. Mary was the church treasurer and also drove me around in her Mini. When she got fed up with trying to teach physics in the East End to large classes where the majority did not want to listen, she took up remedial teaching, and found half a dozen disturbed children much less exhausting and more rewarding. One incident she told me about sticks in my mind – I don't think she'll mind my telling you about it, because it illustrates how being a Samaritan tends to affect one's vocation. She noticed immediately that her new charges' limited vocabularies included all the four-letter words, which they used with boring frequency, and she asked them if they knew what these words meant. (You will realize how this took my mind back to 1935!) When she told them the meaning of the words, they hardly ever used them except to mean what they mean, and she was delighted. But one day, while she was in the loo, a telephone call came for her from (I suppose) County Hall. The small boy who answered the telephone said to it, 'You'll have to wait – she's in the toilet, having a wank.'

Mary emerged just in time to hear this. 'Dear little boy!' she said through her teeth as she took the telephone. I was shocked to discover from her that as a remedial teacher she was given a black mark for this. I myself would have given a black mark to the inspector, or whatever bureaucrat it was, for having failed to notice what an easy relationship she had with her little charges, and how one of them supposed to be backward had replied with spontaneous wit. It's a depressing thought that the higher you get in any profession, the more humourless stuffed shirts you are likely to find.

Godfrey Gooch was a big, forbidding-looking man with a heart of gold, but unfortunately not a heart of strength. Like many people whose appearance doesn't do them justice, he had found his metier in The Samaritans. He asked to see me one day, and said, 'Chad, I'm going to leave you half my estate.'

'No, Godfrey,' I told him. 'I don't want your money. I want you to go on living.' He told me that it wasn't his decision, nor his doctor's opinion. Then he said, 'Well, you can't stop me leaving it to The Samaritans, and that's what I shall do, though I'd have liked *you* to have a bit of comfort.' The dear man died soon afterwards, and his estate was so complicated it took ten years to clear it up, but the money became available in the nick of time to allow us to buy No. 3, Hornton Place as a West End Annexe. Even though we had a land-line connecting the two premises of the London Branch, it was rather awkward having half our volunteers five miles away, but it was worth it while it lasted, and when Hornton Place was eventually sold, the sale price went towards the new and presumably permanent Centre in Soho, to which The Samaritans moved in 1987.

You will remember that volunteers' numbers were issued consecutively so that you could tell by the number how long someone had been with us. I juggled it just a little to get round numbers for my staff, such as David 1000 Moore and Michael 1100 Butler. The former stayed with me longer than the latter, and was very friendly with our Bursar, Bill 990, the only person I have ever known who has presented accounts in a way that kept me entertained and also enabled me to understand them. David, who married a volunteer called Corinne, left to go back into church work, and for a period illustrated books written by Bill in the latter's inimitable style, explaining difficult subjects, such as economics, to the general reader with the aid of drawings by David of a character he invented called Fred. David used to doodle all the time he was listening to clients on the telephone, and volunteers began to collect these doodles for their artistic interest.

It was at about the same time that Norman 1005 became a volunteer; he was one of a tiny handful of Samaritans who became social friends, and with whom I regularly stayed in France, Switzerland and Kent until our beliefs and attitudes diverged and communication ended.

11

IN 1971 there came to see me Harry Junkin, a Canadian who had made his fame and fortune by scripting *The Saint* for television. Like many people who have become successful a little bit down market, Harry wanted a prestige project on which to employ his impressive talents as a scriptwriter. As I have always believed that publicity is our life-blood, I made it clear that I was anxious to co-operate with him if I could. However, what he wanted as a writer was something I could not possibly grant, namely access to all our records and files, which are totally confidential. Most of them are shredded after three months, anyway. He got up to go, but I told him to wait a minute, and said that we weren't story-tellers, but he was. What he could do would be to make up stories, including characters in distress of various kinds, and bowl them at me, so that if I felt that the situation could lead to the person getting in touch with The Samaritans, I could tell him how The Samaritans would respond. He was immediately interested, because this was obviously a less laborious way of doing the job. He asked me whether a successful businessman, who had an invalid wife to whom he was devoted and an increasingly possessive mistress who was constantly urging him to put his poor wife into a home and marry *her*, could become so desperate that he might ring The Samaritans. I told him this was indeed very possible. 'Right,' said Harry. 'I am that man. You are . . . a middle-aged Samaritan in Charge called Janet.' So began the collaboration which was to culminate in the series for television entitled *The Befrienders*.

Most of our meetings were in his handsome apartment in Albert Court, where he had his electric typewriter and tape-recorders. He and I would play the parts and discuss the possibilities until we had the basis of a script, which he would then either write himself or

287

farm out to another recognized scriptwriter for television. I insisted on being allocated one of these eleven scripts, and when Harry protested that I had no experience as a television scriptwriter, I countered that by telling him that strip cartoon was a much more visual medium than television, and my experience on *Eagle* and *Girl* (I didn't mention *Swift* and *Robin*) made film- or television-writing child's play by comparison. I showed him some examples of back numbers, and he was sufficiently convinced to let me do No. 6, *Nobody Understands Miranda*, a story of a depressed girl who thought she was depressed because she had lost her boyfriend, her best friend, and her job, but in fact had lost these *because* she was depressed, that is, was suffering from a depressive illness ('like what doctors are for'). Miranda was played by Jean Marsh, later to be famous as Rose in *Upstairs Downstairs*, Janet was played by Megs Jenkins, and Miranda's befriender by Jane Wellow. The other two Samaritans were played by Michael Culver and Peter Armstrong. That dear man the late Gordon Jackson played a police inspector who utterly failed to get any information out of Janet.

Harry Junkin's reputation and contacts ensured that the series of eleven fifty-minute dramas was accepted by the BBC, whose artistic people were so ravished by the beauty of the crypt that they made an exact mock-up of it in the studios, except for having holes to poke cameras through. We couldn't possibly have disrupted our work by having filming on the premises. Naturally, I read all the scripts and attended all the rehearsals. Although the 'creator' of the format had the last word, we hardly ever differed and the series in my opinion presented The Samaritans in their more dramatic aspects accurately.

The eleven episodes were shown from February to May 1972 on BBC 1 at a peak viewing-time, usually 9.15 on a Saturday, and attracted an average of over eight million viewers. In order not to drive the London Branch crazy, I had not used a real Samaritan emergency number but had obtained from the Post Office the special number 790 3456 with fifty lines on it, which I had installed in a disused school, the Greencoat School, Hamlet of Ratcliff, which is in Stepney not far from Stepney Station on the Fenchurch Street line (790 is a Stepney exchange). I furnished the school with bunk beds and old carpets and desks and chairs, and lived there myself in the former headmaster's study for the eleven weeks. It was bitterly cold, and there was little comfort for the volunteers, who were from Branches all over the country, plus two, Willou Wagner and Maryel

Sauter, from Bienne, Switzerland. Only one person turned straight round and went back home to the Channel Islands, not because of the squalor, but because the two dormitories were not male and female, but smoking and non-smoking.

I set up an old TV set in the ops room, and we were able to watch the programmes as they were televised. We knew that the minute one of the 'Samaritans' said, '790 3456, can I help you?', *all* our fifty phones would ring. We would rush from one to another saying, '790 3456, The Samaritans, can I help you?' and in almost every case the person would hang up, having satisfied himself or herself that the number was a real one, but not wanting to receive Samaritan befriending or indeed to miss any of the programme. Occasionally, however, the person ringing needed The Samaritans, and my little *ad hoc* teams managed in most cases to put them in touch with their local Branch, though some had to be dealt with by our temporary 'East End Annexe'. The log book and records were eventually transferred to the London Branch, which took over all clients not otherwise accounted for.

No publicity we have ever had has had such an immense impact. The work of the busy Branches was doubled, of the medium Branches trebled, and of the smallest Branches quadrupled, and we also had a considerable number of applicants to become volunteers.

The BBC were delighted with the success of the series, and we had every hope that it would be repeated on BBC 2 and even of a further series. All this was, however, knocked on the head by a volunteer in the Reading Branch, a Quaker who started an unofficial magazine called *The Samaritan* (with permission) and included in the first issue a condemnation of the series *The Befrienders*. The result was that all my efforts and those of Harry W. Junkin (now dead) to build on our success were rebuffed by the BBC, who said coldly that, 'The Samaritans didn't like it.' In those days 'Ampex' tape was very expensive, so when the BBC were sure they had finished with a programme, they wiped the tape and reused it. *The Befrienders* had cost £60,000 per episode, which was an enormous amount of money in those days, and I haven't yet ceased to mourn that they were wiped. The offending magazine continues to be published quarterly, and, although it frequently gives a platform to malcontents, it has over the years published some useful material. I have never thought it right to give to any volunteer power greater than is afforded to the Founder or the elected Chairman.

We retained the school at Stepney as long as the trustees would allow us to do so, and used to hold preparation classes there. When we were granted royal patronage, Her Royal Highness the Duchess of Kent was suggested as our Patron, and I respectfully requested that Her Royal Highness might submit herself to our normal selection procedure, but individually and not in class. The Duchess readily agreed to this, and I had the privilege of doing her preparation in the squalid surroundings of the disused school. I am happy to tell you that Her Royal Highness passed with flying colours, proving to be a natural born Samaritan. We agreed that she should work for a limited period as a volunteer in the London Branch, before her many other engagements made such regular fortnightly sessions impractical. The Duchess did not, of course, befriend callers face to face, but answered only on the telephone, and then by the name I had myself bestowed upon her, 'Miranda 1500'. Her Royal Highness has been a wonderful Patron, and whenever she addresses large or small groups of Samaritans – and there are over 1200 each September in the Central Hall at York University where she has several times spoken to us – everybody feels that Her Royal Highness is 'one of us', and knows what it is like to be a Samaritan volunteer, because she has 'been through it'.

Before being destroyed, *The Befrienders* was shown in Malaysia, Singapore, New Zealand and Zambia. You could of course see Malaysian television in Singapore, and one Monday when I happened to be in Singapore I saw the Malaysian broadcast of episode No. 1. The next day I was invited by The Samaritans of Singapore (who at that time still belonged to us, we believed) to address all the Samaritans at the YMCA on the subject of depression. When I arrived at the hall, I found two enormous television sets on the stage, and was told they were going to watch a little television before hearing my talk. I went to the back, sat next to Janet Lim, one of their Samaritans who had worked with me in London, and whilst talking to her I recognized familiar music. I looked up, and there on both television screens it read 'NOBODY UNDERSTANDS MIRANDA by CHAD VARAH'. Everybody clapped and laughed. After the showing, I was able to base my lecture on depression on my television play.

Our three branches in Malaysia are all owing to that showing, and are all called The Befrienders after the programme. Malacca will make four and Cameron Highlands five.

*

My life was becoming more varied and interesting, including lots of foreign travel. It would be tedious for you as well as for me to tell you everywhere I went and everything I did, so how would it be if we were to do a 'lucky dip'? I've kept many of my itineraries, so let's see where I was on our twentieth anniversary, 2 November 1973. H'm, it seems I was in Bloemfontein, South Africa, but how did I get there? I remember I stayed at the Deanery and I spoke at Eunice Girls' School, but you will want to know how I *got* to Bloemfontein – a rather unlikely place to start our first Branch of The Samaritans in South Africa, because it was the heart of Afrikanerdom. But, as always, it depended on there being someone there who shared our concerns and was prepared to work.

1973 was the first year we had our annual conference at York, where nowadays we always have it. Sir Keith Joseph told me that his minions had told him that we saved the country £2 million a year by keeping people alive or keeping them out of hospital, so I cheekily thanked him for his 'generous offer' but said we couldn't possibly accept so much and would he ask the Bursar how much we were short? We've always used the resulting grant to pay for our members to go to our conferences. At that conference we had a debate at which I had to propose the motion that suicide is always preventable, and I also had to do a demonstration interview with a Samaritan from Rochdale, Sara Heap, who identified so perfectly with a client she had befriended that you could have heard a pin drop but for the occasional sound of a sob or two. I found it very moving myself. Then I had to get back to London for a wedding and a baptism and a dinner, and the next day have a lot of inoculations, and then fly back to Lusaka and change there for Ndola, where my son Andrew and his wife were living. They had gone out to teach in a secondary school at Chingola on the copper belt. When, for the first time, pupils began to get O levels and A levels in woodwork, President Kaunda gave a Danish furniture firm permission to make furniture in Zambia provided they employed Andrew as manager and his pupils, some of whom were in their twenties, as the workers.

During my week's holiday I visited Livingstone with Andrew and his little daughter Tamsen, because that was where my mentor Bishop Hine had been based when he was the first Bishop of Northern Rhodesia. I had wanted to go to Zimbabwe by crossing the frontier there – it's only about a two-mile walk through no man's land, and my case wasn't very heavy – but Andrew wouldn't hear of it. Nor would he take me across into neighbouring Zaire in the Opel (for which I had sent him parts by airmail from London) because soldiers always robbed travellers, stole their cars, and told them they were lucky to be able to walk back alive. I never *did* get to Zaire . . . yet.

So on the 28th I flew to Blantyre, Malawi, with no time to visit the island cathedral of Likoma in Lake Nyasa, where Bishop Hine had also been Bishop, because I had to go the next day to Salisbury, Rhodesia. You can imagine the use The Samaritans of Salisbury made of me, but they also gave me some time off. My outstanding memory is of Great Zimbabwe, those amazing stone buildings of peculiar design and debatable purpose which astonish all who imagine that Africans in time past built only thatched huts. I was driven to Umtali (now Mutare) via Moody's Pass, Birchenough and Skyline to visit the Branch there. On the Sunday I had to preach three times before lunch, but it's the first occasion I shall never forget. This was at 7.15 a.m. (in the tropics even I am an early riser) at Zita Rinayera, Sacubva, a huge church in a black township, which was packed to the doors. My host and I were the only white-skinned people unless you count one poor girl who was an albino. My interpreter into Shona, one of the churchwardens, had only elementary English, which suited me because it would force me to speak simply to that simple congregation. I can still remember my sermon, though I doubt if anyone else can. Here it is, leaving out the pauses for translation.

'There is a woman here I want you to meet. What? You don't see her? *I* can't see her with my eyes but I can see her in my mind. She looks like the woman standing near you. She lives in a *rondavel*. She is married. She has five children. Her husband does not work. He sits around all day with his friends. They talk. They boast. They grumble. They gamble. They drink too much beer. Where does the money for this beer come from? It comes from this woman. How does she get it? She gets up early in the morning, whilst her husband is still snoring. [I imitate the snoring and get a laugh.] She washes and feeds the children and gets them dressed. The older ones go to school, the younger ones go to the fields with her. The smallest she carries on her back. She works hard all day in the field. Sometimes she takes what she has grown to the market. Anything she does not sell she takes home to feed her family. By the end of the day she is very tired. She feeds and washes her children. She mends their clothes. She tells the little ones stories. She puts them to bed. When her husband comes home, he is drunk. The food she has prepared for him is a bit spoilt. He grumbles, and beats her up. She tries not to scream so as not to upset the children. When at last she is able to go to bed she is in pain from her bruises. She hopes she will be able to do her work the next day. Her husband steals the money she has made in the market. He beats her because it isn't enough. She has managed to hide a little for her children's needs. She is glad when he is so drunk he falls asleep and does not force her to make another baby.'

At the end of this sermon, I could hardly bear the expression on the faces of some of the women. In the oppressive heat of the church the silence was almost palpable. I broke it, by saying through my interpreter, 'If you know this woman, please put up your hand.' Almost every hand in the place went up. 'Right, hands down. Now, if you *are* this woman, please put up your hand.' At first there was no hand put up, then hesitantly there was one, then another two or three followed suit. Eventually half the people in the building had their hand up.

Then I asked, 'What can we do for this woman?'

The congregation all shook their heads. There was nothing to be done – it just had to be borne.

'Is there nothing we can do to help this woman?' Not so many heads were shaken this time as people looked expectantly at me, wondering if I knew of a miracle.

'Would it be any good to beat up the husband? No, he would only beat his wife more. Would it do any good for the woman to leave her husband? How could she leave? Where would she go?'

A stout woman in the front row spoke up, in English: 'We can pray for her.'

'Yes,' I said. The woman next to her, who I later discovered was the Enrolling Member for the Mothers' Union (how pleased Susan was when I told her about this!) said in Shona: 'We have to teach our boy children to be different from their fathers.' I agreed with this but then said that it wouldn't help the poor woman *now*.

After a pause, I said, 'There is something that can be done for her now, if we are willing.' They all pricked up their ears, and seemed a little disappointed when I told them what it was.'We can listen to her when she tells us about her troubles. We can share her unhappiness. We can feel for her.' (My interpreter hadn't known the word for sympathy.) 'We can make her feel that somebody cares, that we admire her for being such a good mother and for working so hard and for being so brave. We can give her love.'

I then told them as simply as I could about the work of The Samaritans, and asked if any of the congregation were willing to be taught how to be Samaritans and listen to people's troubles, even if they could not change the way they had to live. About forty people, mostly women but with some men, volunteered on the spot.

Although in African countries it was usually white citizens (or expatriate workers) who took the initiative in starting a Branch, it was always the intention that there should be black members. I can't say that Sacubva township was the first to have black members (Bulawayo had, for instance), but I'm sure it was the first to be entirely black and to work only in Shona. (In Bulawayo they mostly speak Ndebele.)

After a public meeting in Salisbury, I took the night train to Bulawayo and had lunch with David Broomberg, who is still the guiding spirit there and is now Africa representative. They had a very full programme for me including speaking to the Rhodesian Christian Council and to the National Co-ordinating Council of The Samaritans, taking a volunteers' class, and doing an early-morning celebration of the Holy Communion for the Sisters of the Community of the Resurrection, where the door was opened to me by Stephan Hopkinson in drag. This turned out to be his sister Mary.

Apart from The Samaritans, the most exciting thing I came across in Bulawayo was Jairos Jiri, a wonderful piece of black initiative for black blind and disabled people, mostly men, to which I was taken by Samaritan Len. I have never forgotten the patience and compassion shown by the staff towards the inmates. I should have liked to stay and work with them, but was disqualified by lack of pigmentation in my skin. I had made friends with Jackie Beattie, who next day drove me to the airport to catch RH717 to Johannesburg, where I was met by my wife Susan's friend Jo Emery and introduced to another wonderful organization, Black Sash, composed almost entirely of upper-class English-speaking (not Afrikaner) ladies dedicated to helping black people with such things as difficulties created by the Pass Laws.

Next day I took the 6.15 p.m. train to Nelspruit, Eastern Transvaal, arriving at 4 a.m., and getting myself with difficulty to Mataffin by 7. This was an estate owned by Susan's friend Thelma Donaldson, which had on it a village of several thousand black workers, an orange-juice plant, and every kind of local fruit, including to my astonishment eighteen different varieties of avocado.

Thelma most generously gave up her own bedroom to me and slept in a spare room. I was able to celebrate Holy Communion at the family service at 9. Thelma was a model Mothers' Union member – she spent all day working in a mother-and-baby clinic she had set up on the estate, at her own expense, of course. She managed to take time off to take me round the Kruger Game Park before I went on to Mbabane, Swaziland. After five days exploring Swaziland, I went to Durban, where the Life Line was much more like The Samaritans than in any other place in South Africa except Welkom and perhaps Port Elizabeth. I tried to make myself useful to the Durban volunteers, but it wasn't all work: one day I was dressed in very old clothes and taken right inside the Sugar Terminal, seeing what tourists don't see, and emerging stickier than I have ever been. I still remember how shocked I was to discover that the 98 per cent pure sugar brought to the Terminal, which could almost have been used without any refining at all, had to be officially dirtied in order to be refined in the same way as sugar produced elsewhere. This was *before* the EEC bureaucracy which, among other things, forbids us to grow Brophy's non-burping cucumbers in our own country.

My next engagement was to spend five days with friends of my wife on an estate near Kroonstad, Orange Free State, belonging to Oubaas (old boss) Naudé. It was much smaller than Thelma's and for cattle rather than fruit, but had a village and a school for the workers. I got on very well with Oubaas, not expecting him to be anything more than paternalist, which he was. It was fun driving around in a jeep at night hunting, looking for gleaming eyes in the dark, but more fun driving around in the day and laughing at the *korhaan*, which we didn't deign to shoot because it was too easy. They were slow and incompetent fliers, and even when landing tended to fall over and get up, looking embarrassed: I told Oubaas God invented them to put us in a good mood. He looked a bit disapproving when, after addressing the schoolchildren, I shook hands with the black headmaster, but I said, 'I'm a *korhaan*,' and he laughed. He died last year. To be good according to one's lights is the most we can expect of anyone, isn't it?

If you have looked at a map you may wonder how I got from Durban to Kroonstad. We rang up Anna, Oubass's wife, sister of Susan's friend Donvé Leach (then Mothers' Union President for the Republic of South Africa, but now living in Richmond) and arranged a meeting point half-way. My generous Durban hosts took me to lunch in Little Switzerland, then we went via Oliviershoek to

Witzenhoek, in the shadow of the beautiful mountains of Lesotho, where I was handed over.

So *now* I can tell you how I got to Bloemfontein on our twentieth anniversary, 2 November 1973: I travelled by train from Kroonstad, and stayed with Aidan Cross at the Deanery. They kept me very busy, and three days later it was decided to start The Samaritans of Bloemfontein, which is still going strong, now under the exemplary direction of Pam Williams.

On my way to the Cape from there I took a train to George. You wouldn't believe how slowly it chuff-chuffed across the country, but it was an express compared with the train from George to Knysna, to which I changed after only three-quarters of an hour's wait. It was very rash of me to take these trains, because there was no way of getting from Knysna to Cape Town. I had been warned that hitch-hiking was almost impossible. However, I enlisted a girl with admirable legs, who kindly thumbed a lift for me with a pleasant young couple who didn't mind me substituting for the girl. We arrived in Cape Town after midnight in good time to stay (not for the first time) with Cynthia Howard and her husband.

That weekend of 17 November had more coincidences than any I can remember in my life. Euan, whose sister Anna was one of my Samaritans, asked me if I'd like to see an apple farm at Elgin. I said I would, and wasn't it funny that if he and Cynthia hadn't been able to have me, I had an introduction to Andrew and Anne Brown at Elgin. 'But,' he said, 'those were the people we were intending to take you to!' When we got there, we found they were nursing their vicar back to health, he having hit his napper in a fall from his motor-bike. The curate was visiting him, and bemoaning the fact that he couldn't do all the services required of him because he couldn't be in two places at once. 'If only,' he wailed, 'a Samaritan in Anglican Orders would pass by, not on the other side.'

You can guess the rest. I found myself celebrating and preaching at 8 a.m. at St Thomas Rondebosch. The day's biggest service in that climate began early. After the service, I found myself in conversation with a charming lady whose name I didn't know. Euan, who wasn't a churchgoer, was waiting for me outside, and demanded, 'Why were you talking to Audrey Theron?'

'I didn't know I was,' I said.

He told me that he had once wanted to marry her daughter but that she had married a chap called Malcolm. 'Funny,' I said, 'the only *other* introduction I have in Cape Town is to a girl called

Jacqueline Malcolm.' So the next day I was dining with her and her mother. I visited Life Line in Cape Town and found it the most preachy Life Line I'd ever encountered outside Sydney.

On the 21st I took SA763 to Windhoek via Upington, where I remembered the words of 'Sarie Marais' which I'll translate for you from the Afrikaans: 'Then fled I to the sand of the Upington strand, down there by the great river.' Windhoek was then capital of South West Africa, now called Namibia. The next day I spoke to the Rotary Club and on the Sunday preached in the Cathedral and two other places; the day after that I spoke to the Lions and the Ministers' Fraternal. A morning meeting and later dinner with the Dean led to a successful Samaritan class at 8 p.m. on the Tuesday, and for the first time I was able to conduct role play in Kwanyama, the language of the Ovambo people, with the aid of an English girl whose father had been a missionary. She had grown up speaking Kwanyama and in fact spoke it better than any of the Ovambo volunteers. I was able to supervise the role plays in English and Afrikaans myself.

Apart from Ovambo volunteers befriending beautifully in Kwanyama, the two things that stand out most in my mind are my getting lost in the Namib Desert and my heart-to-heart talk with an Ovambo Anglican priest.

South West Africa was originally a German colony, and much German influence remains in the architecture and in the culture of Windhoek. I had an introduction to a German called Paul Bohlsen, whose girlfriend Evica Cooke offered to drive me sightseeing wherever I wished to go (I was taking the Saturday as a day off). I asked her to take me to the edge of the Namib Desert, leave me there, and come back for me at 6 in the evening. This desert has the world's highest sand dunes, and as I struck out on foot into it with a few provisions on my back I realized that keeping more or less on the level I would soon be hopelessly lost. I don't know to this day why I persevered and plodded on, whilst the sun beat down. I'm sure I wasn't trying to commit suicide, though it sounds as if I were: I just could not resist the emptiness and the awesome silence. I felt I was discovering myself. You will have realized my life was so busy dashing from place to place and meeting innumerable people that I hardly ever had any opportunity to get to know *me*.

I walked on until half the time I had allotted myself had elapsed, and turned round to come back just as I found a small branch of a tree, about twenty inches long, dry as a bone, silver in colour, polished by sand and wind, and looking exactly like a dragon. I tucked it under my arm, and took it back to England with me (so you now know that I *did* get out of the desert alive). I eventually presented it to Henry Moore (who exclaimed delightedly, 'Why, it's a dragon!') to go amongst his collection of *trouvailles*. Some years later, when he wasn't well enough to visit his exhibition in the Calouste Gulbenkian premises in Lisbon, I offered to go and photograph it for him as I would be visiting our Branch in Oporto at the appropriate time. He professed to be delighted with my informal photos to add to the professional close-ups of the individual items, and I myself was overjoyed to see my dragon in the middle of the showcase of his *trouvailles*.

Navigating by the sun isn't as easy as I thought it would be, and as 6 o'clock approached I felt I either wouldn't get out of the desert, or would miss the rendezvous and have a very long walk back to Windhoek. Eventually I climbed the highest dune I could see and looked in the direction where I thought Windhoek might be. Perched on the top of another dune was what looked like a hurricane lamp. I realized it must be the top of the television tower, so made straight for it, walking downhill and clambering up, and downhill and clambering up, without daring to go round by the level valleys. I arrived at the rendezvous just as the girl was about to give me up for lost.

When I wandered around a black township (I think it was called Khomasta) with their priest (let's call him Father Ovambo) he pointed out to me a prison-like building which housed the black migrant workers from countries to the north and east. It was guarded, and they weren't allowed out much. Father Ovambo told me in a shocked tone that some of the women in his congregation were in the habit of going into these barracks and having sexual relations with the inmates, who were either bachelors or separated by many weeks' journey from their wives. 'Some of them do it for money,' he told me, 'and I suppose it does help to feed their children, but others do it for – for – '

'For love?' I suggested.

He looked nonplussed. 'I have often had to preach against it,' he said. I took him by the arm, and walked him the whole length of that ghastly block.

'My dear Father,' I said, 'I have met your affectionate wife and your lovely children. Put yourself in the place of these men, who have not only no sex but also no feminine companionship, no tenderness. Shall we not, as priests, forgive those who do it for money, and bless those who do it for love?'

There was a long silence. He then embraced me, and said, 'Father Chad, there shall be no more of those sermons. You have opened my eyes and heart.' I don't suppose he realized that he had been the means of opening mine.

On the way back I had a night in Kimberley, and was able to see the world's deepest man-made hole and to meet the *most* 'Samaritan' Life Line I had encountered anywhere, though unhappily it was on the point of fading away through lack of volunteers due to deaths and removals. It does my heart good to know that there is now a Branch of The Samaritans there. Then I went via Bloemfontein to Johannesburg, where the charming Anne Hughes met me to take me to the Community of the Resurrection in Rosettenville, which you will associate with the name of Trevor Huddleston. On Advent Sunday I preached at a 'coloured' church at Riverlea and in the evening I attended St Mary's Cathedral where, after the service, Anne Hughes pointed out to me David De Beer. He was chatting to somebody, but I walked across to introduce myself to him, for he was well known for his opposition to apartheid. Before I could reach him, somebody did a rugby tackle on me. The person then picked me up, dusted me down and said apologetically, 'You evidently don't know that David is banned. This means, amongst other things, that he is not allowed to talk to more than one person at a time. Don't look now, but that man over my left shoulder behind the pillar is a policeman watching him.' It was an unforgettable reminder of the injustices of that period.

I was kept busy in Johannesburg both with church contacts, with a visit to Benoni Life Line (redeemable, I thought, if I'd had more time with them), and having lunch with the Methodist minister in charge of the Johannesburg Life Line, who seemed to me almost as dyed-in-the-wool as the Cape Town chap. On my last day I spent the day working with Black Sash, whose members seemed to me to be the nearest I had encountered in the whole of Africa to first-rate born Samaritans. Businesslike upper-class English ladies were sitting behind trestle tables on the other side of which were black individuals, couples or families. I took a vacant chair next to one of these

299

ladies, who didn't stop scribbling as she said, 'Who are you?'

'A friend of Jo Emery,' I said.

'Name?'

'Chad Varah.'

'Good,' she decided, 'take that seat over there, get a history from that couple, and write out an appeal for them. In triplicate.' I did as I was bidden, feeling very privileged to be accepted, and more and more enraged by the Pass Laws system as I worked. I discovered that the name of the person who set me to work there was Elizabeth Roe. The next day, before taking the evening flight to Nairobi, I visited the Baragwanath Hospital, and reminded myself that however much I despaired of Christians intruding their evangelism inappropriately into the work of crisis-intervention, what the Church had done in promoting worship, welfare, human rights, education and medical care deserved the highest praise.

In Nairobi, where I had excellent introductions, including to doctors and other persons of influence, and the Kentmere Club, I embarked on one of three attempts to get a Branch going there, each beginning with enthusiasm and promise, and petering out. We still haven't one.

My next attempt was to be in Khartoum, so I went to the Sudanese Consulate in Nairobi and asked for a visa. The two chaps in charge were annoyed at having their football on television interrupted, and assured me that I could get a visa on arrival at Khartoum airport. I flew to Addis Ababa, where the Anglican chaplain took me to see the Coptic church of St Stephen, and put me up for the night. Then I took an Alitalia plane, which had started its journey in Mogadishu and was destined for Rome via Khartoum. There was also a large party of American Presbyterians, all labelled, booked for Khartoum on an Ethiopian Airlines plane, bound for Cairo via Khartoum. You will see why I mention this in a moment. On arrival at Khartoum, I presented my passport, innocent of any visa, and was screamed at by an angry little Major who told me that President Nimeiry himself had given orders that no one was to be admitted without a visa. How dare we colonizers assume we could trample on their laws and customs? I knew it would be no good telling him what his Consulate in Nairobi had said, so I apologized for my ignorance of the latest visa requirements, and hoped that I might be allowed in for a couple of days as I was due to stay with the British Ambassador.

This enraged the little Major further, confirming his erroneous view that I was a colonizer. I saw Charles Roach, chaplain at the Embassy, waiting for me on the other side of the barrier, so I went to ask his help, but he said it was useless. I then handed him the bottle of duty-free whisky I had brought and while the little Major was getting a boy to intercept my baggage, I found the Ethiopian Airlines representative and got him to change my ticket to that day's flight instead of one two days later. The advantage was that it was going to Cairo, where I was due next, rather than Rome. The angry little Major tried to hustle me back on to the Alitalia plane, but I pointed out that I was booked on the Ethiopian one which was going only ten minutes later. If he would permit me to board that plane now, he would be rid of me sooner than if I had to change my ticket to go out on the plane I had come in on.

Before he could work this out, and whilst he was engaged with the boy carrying my baggage, I bounded up the steps of the Ethiopian plane and was met by a charming Ethiopian lady in sumptuous Amharic robes, who crooned at me, 'Oh, Mr Varah, we are so *sorry* that you have been incommoded by the *uncivilized* Sudanese, and are happy to have you on board. Please *ignore* what it says on your ticket, and make your way to the *first* class.' Steerage was full of those Presbyterians I had seen in Addis Ababa, all of whom turned and looked at me disapprovingly; I heard whispers of 'tossed out of the country' and 'international crook'. At the entrance to the first class stood a stunningly beautiful Ethiopian girl holding a glass of champagne which she passed to me with a welcoming smile. I used it to toast the Presbyterians with the words, 'As you see, crime pays.'

I have hardly ever enjoyed a journey more, because the very few people in the first class were not interested in Maryam's hospitality, so she kept bringing me drinks and all kinds of Ethiopian titbits. Although she was not allowed to sit down beside me, she stood near me for most of the journey, and our conversation passed the time most pleasantly. At one point I was bold enough to tell her she was the most beautiful Ethiopian girl I had ever seen, and I thought she ought to be Miss Abyssinia. She hung her head bashfully, began wearing a hole in the carpet with her toe, and eventually muttered, 'I am.' She then let me take her photograph. When we arrived in Cairo, I was loth to leave her, so by the time I said farewell to her at the top of the steps, the bus was already full of Presbyterians waiting impatiently. I made to shake hands with Maryam, but she put her hands behind my neck and pulled my head down and gave me a tender kiss. Dizzy with the excitement of being kissed by Miss Abyssinia, and perhaps a little with the liquid refreshment she had provided for me, I staggered down the steps unsteadily, and clambered aboard the bus, where the assembled Presbyterians regarded me balefully. 'I told you crime pays!' I snarled at them.

So there I was in Cairo, two days before I was expected. I decided to catch the train to Luxor which took the rest of the day and all night, and was the bumpiest train ride I have ever had, worse even than one from Krakow to Prague. One really needed seat-belts, which were not provided. Sleep was impossible. Arrived in Luxor, I booked a bed at the hotel for that night but set off after breakfast with a guide I hired. I was his only customer, but he took me across the Nile on a boat big enough for a party, and discussed the details of our day, so I didn't have any time to look around. Then suddenly, in the blazing sunshine, I saw with a shock of recognition a building ahead of us. I realized that, Egypt's civilization having lasted so long, most of us have had one incarnation at least in Egypt. Having presumably had several since, I couldn't get over the fact that I was coming back to a dear familiar place, though one much changed by time. Throughout the day I kept feeling that I knew the way. After a much needed night's sleep, unable to face that bouncy train again, I flew back to Cairo. After seeing the pyramids and the Sphinx, I was anxious to get home to London, to spend Christmas with my family. I arrived back on the third Sunday in Advent.

The very day I got back from Cairo I had to see an old friend who, whilst I was away, had become part of an eternal triangle; and shortly thereafter I had to cope with the distress of another corner of it. I'm glad to say it ended without murder or suicide, but it was hard work tidying it all up before fleeing the country again a couple of days after my thirty-fourth wedding anniversary. There were also special friends to see, just because we had missed one another: Peter Palumbo, Monica Dickens, Roger Pilkington and his childhood sweetheart Ingrid, Martin and Betsy Rosen (whose baby I was to baptize a couple of weeks after my granddaughter Heidi), and a sweet devout call-girl for whom I will borrow the name 'Bree Daniel'.

There was the Branch Committee of the London Branch to be fitted in, and the Overseas Committee of which I was now Chairman. Lunch at Broadcasting House, lunch with the Master of the Grocers, lunch with Bruno Burger of the Italian Voce Amica, a broadcast to Germany, a debate at the Cambridge Union, several clients, and a very important meeting with Mrs Robertson (of my travel agents, at that time) who was happy to have me work out my own complicated journeys from the ABC airline timetable, leaving her only to write out the tickets. (One of her proudest possessions was a photo of me taken in Adelaide, holding up both hands above my head and making an arch which reached to the ground on both sides, composed of a great number of airline tickets stapled together which took me round the world in five months and sixty-five stops.)

Mrs Robertson spent the weekend making bookings and writing out tickets so that I could go to Bombay for three days, Colombo for three, Bangkok for four, Kuala Lumpur for two, Singapore for five, Kuching (Sarawak) for two, back to Singapore for a flight to Djakarta for three days, Denpasar (Bali) and then Darwin. Here there was a snag: the Indonesians wouldn't allow one to travel via Timor, neither Dili nor Kupang, although there were flights. I therefore had to go back to Singapore to get a flight to Darwin. I stayed there three days, and got a Preparatory Group going, before flying down to Perth, where my friend George Appleton, formerly Archdeacon of London, had become Archbishop and had started a Branch of The Samaritans (he was later Archbishop in Jerusalem). The Samaritans arranged for me to stay with Stanley Calloway, the Professor of Music, in the University of Western Australia, and my fellow guest there was André Tchaikovsky, pianist and composer, who had been visiting Fellow. Six days later we travelled together to Adelaide, where he was to give a recital in the attractive town hall and I was to stay with Keith Seaman, who was in charge of a very Samaritan-like Life Line.

He was later knighted and became Governor of South Australia. The only remarkable thing about this was that the powers that be had noticed the calibre of this Methodist minister and had the imagination to let him be a blessing to the whole State and not merely to Adelaide. Keith had not fallen for the sock-it-to-them Christianity of the founder of Life Line, whom in fact he challenged to his face at a worldwide Life Line conference in Hamilton, Ontario. He and a kindred spirit from South Africa proposed there that the organization should recognize two categories of Life Line: one humanitarian like The Samaritans, and the other evangelistic and exclusively Christian. In North America the organization was called Contact Teleministries Inc. and was in the charge of a minister from Nashville, who backed the Sydney Life Line founder's denunciation of the proposition, and after it was voted down gleefully announced the result to the Press. I can still remember the words in which Keith told me about this. 'He announced that Guard (I think he meant God) has spoken through his prophet: 146 delegates have stood up for Jesus! I thought it was a little less than candid of him not to mention that 139 had voted against the proposition that all branches must be evangelistic and exclusively Christian.' But Keith Seaman never took his branch out of Life Line and affiliated it to The Samaritans, so I had very little hope that other Samaritan-minded Methodists would do so.

After Melbourne and Hobart I went to Canberra, where an Anglican was in charge of Life Line and was assisted by a splendid fellow called Ian Milne whose 'Strine' was so broad I could scarcely understand it. He had been sacked from Sydney Life Line for trying to introduce Samaritan ideas and methods there. A couple of days later I was in Sydney for the weekend not, of course, to visit Life Line, but to pay my respects to Ted Noffs, who was minister of the Wayside Chapel at King's Cross. He was the one who had originally wanted a Branch of The Samaritans in Sydney and had been told that his then boss was going to reinvent it as an evangelistic enterprise.

From Sydney I flew to Wellington for a week, where the Dean, the late Walter Hurst, had started New Zealand's first Branch. Walter was a man of vision, who on his retirement to Tauranga started a successful Branch there too. It was wonderful to be with Samaritans again, and to be able to help them with publicity and to take preparation classes and of course enjoy marvellous hospitality.

I did not at that time visit the South Island, where Christchurch had a very preachy branch of Life Line, but had to go to Auckland because I was to fly from there to Fiji. Auckland Life Line was, and continued to be, ambivalent towards Samaritan ideas.

After four days I flew to Nadi (pronounced Nandi) which is the international airport of Fiji and is a horrible place. Arriving at nearly midnight I could only find a squalid hotel with abundant insect life and a bright electric light that wouldn't go off. In the morning I was able to fly in a little plane to the pleasant capital, Suva, where I spent four days including Palm Sunday. Although I had meetings with the clergy in the hope of arousing interest in a Branch, they were rather naturally preoccupied with Holy Week at that time, so I entered into the life of the cathedral as fully as I could, and paid particular attention to the Mothers' Union. I was even more caught up with the life of the church in Papeete, Tahiti, of all places; I hadn't gone there to start a Branch, but to have a little break, staying with François-Bertrand Gérard, and his wife and two little boys. He was the second son of my friends in Paris and Aspet, André and Marie-Thérèse, and was working there for Orstom as an ethnologist. Somehow they discovered that the size-able English-speaking population had no one to take a service for them on Easter Day, so we borrowed a church, Eglise de Bethel, and I celebrated the Holy Communion at 8 a.m. for no fewer than forty-two people, which wasn't bad since it was arranged only on Good Friday.

I had a lovely time with the few French and many Tahitian friends of my host and hostess, who included me in all the many parties that were held in Easter Week, on Tahiti and Moorea. I swam only in swimming-pools because I was nervous of the *poissons de pierre* which abounded in those waters. This ugly 'stone fish' had a sting which was reputed to give the most excruciating pain to the foot of any kind known to medicine, and I had no intention of finding out for myself whether this was true.

I had broken my journey at Papeete in order to take Air France flight 104 to Lima, Peru. This flight in a stretched DC8 was at that time I think the longest flight anywhere; nine hours without crossing a single speck of land. We must have been pretty short on fuel by the time we landed at Lima in fog: I assume the pilot hadn't enough fuel to get to another airport. We did a dodgy landing, and from my window seat on the starboard side I could see one wing missing the ground by about four inches. I was glad when the plane stopped just short of the end of the runway. You can't any longer fly from Tahiti to Peru – in fact, if you want to cross the Pacific to the Antipodes you nowadays have to do it from California, Seattle or Vancouver. Going round the world via South America gets more and more difficult.

After four days in Lima I flew to Quito in Ecuador, arriving on a Sunday morning and therefore badgering my hotel for information about an English church service. There was no church, but there was a place where the English colony met for worship, and I took a taxi there without even unpacking. On arrival, I found that because they had someone to play the harmonium but didn't have a priest or lay reader, they were going to have a hymn-singing service. When I

305

revealed that I was an Anglican priest they were overjoyed, and got out the vessels and vestments. As nobody knew where the prayer books were I did the service from memory. Afterwards, a charming couple and their little girl took me to lunch, and then to the line which marks the equator, which I was able to straddle, thus having one foot in each hemisphere. The next day I flew to Panama for the day and then to San José in Costa Rica and a couple of days later to New Orleans, where in the famous Vieux Carré I was able to sample the most wonderful French cooking.

I had a couple of days in Jacksonville (where Delius once lived) in order to take part in a meeting of the American Association for Suicidology. This conference of the AAS was held in Turtle Beach Hotel, and it was a very special occasion for me, because I was to be presented with the Louis I. Dublin Award 'for outstanding contributions in the area of suicide-prevention', and a certificate signed by Robert Kastenbaum, president that year, and Charlotte Ross, secretary, hangs in my study above a photograph of Louis Dublin, whom I knew. Mine was the third such award, the first having been to Karl Menninger, author of *Man Against Himself*. It was the first to a 'layman' (in medical terms) and I think probably the last, because the AAS is a professional body with high prestige and there are of course enough psychiatrists in the USA to fill it many times over. Dr Richard Fox was there, and told me that I wouldn't have to make a speech (but had apparently told Charlotte that the acceptance speech would be brilliant).

It wasn't brilliant, though I think I was suitably overwhelmed: I simply told a distinguished audience about the last client I had had before leaving England: a man came to see me who wouldn't give his name, which didn't matter at all, but wouldn't say what he wanted to see me about, which did, rather, as I was busy preparing to come here via the Far East, the Antipodes, and South America. He *had* vouchsafed that it was a sexual problem, so I gave him an outline of the sort of problems men had which I had dealt with, whilst his jaw dropped and eyes opened wide at these revelations. I watched him closely and didn't find many clues to what it might be that was troubling him, though by trying to do the Sherlock Holmes bit I came to a tentative conclusion about his occupation. After my beseeching him to tell me what was bothering him, and his telling me he was unable to do so because the ceiling would fall in or the heavens would fall or some such, because of the enormity of what he had been guilty of, I eventually took the risk of saying to him,

306

"Well, as you can't tell *me*, would you like me to tell *you*?" He began to bet millions, which I didn't think he had, but the way he expressed it seemed to confirm my theory. So I took the risk of saying firmly, "I think you can find sexual pleasure only in masturbating a stallion, a male horse."

'He paled, cowered, glanced nervously at the ceiling, then said, "If it had been such an unmentionable thing, what would you have said, sir?" I replied, "I'd have said I hope you won't get your foot trodden on." He asked me what the something I was talking about, and I explained, "Well, stallions are very heavy animals, and fiddling with their genitals is likely to make them restive, so I hope you won't get your foot trodden on. I wouldn't like you to be severely injured by doing something which I gather is not uncommon in stable-hands." "And is that all you have got to say?" he demanded. I pondered with wrinkled brow for more than a minute. Then I said, "Yes, I think that's all I wanted to say to you." He then shook my hand, and went out beaming, walking on air, as the saying is.' There was a good deal of applause from the assembled suicidologists, one of whom (they are a ribald lot) called out, 'Did you get a call from the horse?' Which provoked a lot of unseemly laughter.

After the conference I stayed a night in Baltimore and then arrived in New York to spend a couple of days with Al Freedman and his colleagues on *Forum* magazine and on *Penthouse*. I had met Al, founder of *Forum* magazine, when he was living and publishing it in London. I was first a contributor to the magazine and then a consultant, listed on the inside cover as one of the people who answered readers' queries. I remained a consultant until it changed to *Penthouse Forum*, still serving a useful purpose but not really the right place for the sort of articles I wrote. Al and his dear wife Esther, a true Samaritan until her lamented death, were very hospitable to me, as was Bob Guccione, proprietor of *Penthouse*. Two of the 'Pets' took me to lunch at an expensive restaurant, where they were charming and demure but still the centre of attention. That was a memorable May Day, but the next day I had to go to Boston to spend a week with the second biggest Samaritan Branch in the world, founded by my friend Monica Dickens, great-granddaughter of Charles Dickens and wife of Commander Roy Stratton, USN. She had worked with me in London after researching a book about The Samaritans which was published under the title *The Listeners*, and had caught the bug and never got over it. She used to drive seventy miles each way each day from her home in Cape Cod, where I was to stay with her many times until after her husband's death she moved back to England.

I had only ten days back in London, during which time I had our Annual General Meeting and a weekend at our conference centre at Swanwick, before setting off again for Scandinavia, in which term I include Finland. I was due to give a lecture at 7 p.m. in Helsinki on 20 May, and Susan was driving me to the airport for my Finnair flight ('Going to vanish into Finn air, Dad?' asked my youngest triplet, David), but there had been a bomb at Heathrow and we were held up in traffic until not only did I miss my flight but also the Volvo overheated, and I had to leave Susan to cope with it while I hitched a lift. I used to say my bible was the ABC airline timetable, which like the real Bible has a much bigger Volume I than Volume II, so I knew that I could catch Pan Am 002 to Frankfurt and connect there with a Lufthansa flight to Helsinki arriving at 5, for my lecture to the Finnish Psychiatric Society at 7. I toured the branches of Palveleva Puhelin, as their hot line service is called, visiting Oulu, Kemi and Rovaniemi (the furthest north I got) within the Arctic Circle, where it is bright enough to read in the middle of the night. I flew back to Tampere, where I was to conduct a two-day seminar on sexual problems, and stay with Jouko Sihvo and his wife Marketta who took me to dine at the top of the television tower.

From Helsinki I went to Stockholm and Uppsala on the way to Gothenburg, where Greta Meyersberg was soon to start a Branch, and Lund, where Ninnie Sahlström's Vänskaps Huset (Friendship House) seemed a possible base for a Branch of The Samaritans. (It did some good work, but remained independent.) From Malmö I crossed to Copenhagen, where I celebrated Whitsun Day by attending a service in the Mariakyrkan and managed to meet Irina Grut, Yana's younger half-sister whom I hadn't seen since I was a curate in Lincoln.

The Maria church was in Istedgade, near the station, and as I went along the street I noticed that it was full of shops selling sexy magazines and films. When I had a couple of hours to spare, I went back, chose the biggest of these shops, and spoke to the man in charge. He was at first astonished, because as I saw for myself customers rushed in and out and barely looked at him when they paid him, and then suspicious, which can't have been because he thought I was from the police – Denmark was very civilized in having freedom of speech and publication, and did not censor what could be described as 'pornography'.

I was soon befriending the man in the shop, who was very lonely because no one chatted with him and most people didn't look him in the eye. I explained that I was a sex therapist and a consultant to *Forum* magazine, and asked him what was the proportion of the various kinds of sex-appeal magazines. He invited me to look for myself, which I did later to check his own estimates. Roughly 90 per cent of the magazines were both 'normal' and 'benign' – that is to say, they showed heterosexual activity obviously unforced, being enjoyed by the participants. Four per cent showed male homosexual activity, and 3 per cent female ditto, the two together amounting to less than the proportion in the population. Out of the remaining 3 per cent, $2\frac{3}{4}$ per cent appealed to various deviations – fetishistic, sado-masochistic (principally spanking), bondage, with some transvestitism, and the other quarter of 1 per cent showed activities with animals (these were in a section headed 'bizarre'). There were only two magazines relating to child sex abuse, and I believed the man when he told me there was no demand for them so he didn't have any under the counter. Almost all the magazines were what would be described in this country as 'hard core', which is difficult to define, but seems to mean that erect male and open female genitals are shown, sometimes approximated.

I hope you are capable of thinking clearly about what in our own country is so often condemned and confiscated. The strict meaning of the term 'pornography' is, 'writing about the activities of prostitutes'. It has been extended to mean writing or depicting any kind of material calculated to be sexually arousing. Of course, quite sublime literature may be erotic and may be highly arousing to a minority of readers, which has led to the accusation that there's one law for the rich and another for the poor – though of course appreciation of classics is not confined to the rich, and many of the poor are prudish. The point I want to make is that I do not permit any self-appointed nanny to decide when I may or may not be sexually aroused, or to deprive me of material likely to effect this if I want it and am prepared to pay for it. I hope *you* are equally determined to be in sole charge of your genital apparatus, and solely responsible for any legal use you may make of it.

Realizing how much misery was caused in England to timid souls who quite naturally wanted to peruse sexually explicit material sometimes, but had been made to feel ashamed of this desire and curiosity and were regularly cheated by unscrupulous rogues who sold them shrink-wrapped boring magazines at a high price, knowing that most of them would not dare to complain, I bought a few magazines to give to clients who had suffered this deprivation. I was flying directly back to London and was quite prepared to have a public row at the Customs if they tried to confiscate them. The 'SMAGS' (sex misery and guilt spreaders) rejoice that most people, and especially parsons, are terrified of being publicly accused of approving of pornography, however benign, however educational. I am not one of these.

I strongly suspect that the cowed victims of the SMAGS are far more numerous than the alleged 'moral majority', whom I consider very immoral indeed because they arrogate to themselves the right to make other people's moral judgements for them, which God does not permit. I think this may have been demonstrated when a certain solicitor in the City got together with a certain Area Dean, who happened to have been at school with me but whom I had never been aware of because he was new and not in my house when I was a prefect. You will notice that I do not mention the names of persons of whom I disapprove.

I was informed that I would be arraigned before the Deanery Synod on a charge of conduct unbecoming a clergyman because of my association with *Forum* magazine. I could, of course, have ignored the whole matter – the Deanery Synod had no authority, and if it had voted to express an adverse opinion to the Bishop I doubt if he would have done more than summon me for a discussion. However, I decided to defend myself, and in preparation for this, I went through the articles I had written for *Forum*, and my answers to readers' queries, and picked out paragraphs which referred to morality in general or Christian morality in particular. I made a selection of these, and photocopied them in sufficient number to give every member of the Synod likely to be present one to study and keep. I asked that anyone who took exception to any of the sentiments expressed in these paragraphs should say what his or her objections were, when I would answer. Nobody ventured to do this.

I then suggested that our Lord Jesus Christ would very much wish those things to be said, especially to the readers of *Forum*, most of whom would not, one supposed, read theological publications.

Would anybody contend that there were sentences in these paragraphs which Jesus Christ would not wish addressed to a readership of mostly unbelievers or half-believers? The Area Dean's summing up betrayed the fact that he had been one of the instigators of the arraignment. He then called upon the proposer and seconder of the motion to put it to the meeting: the proposer did so, but the seconder no longer wished to second, and in spite of the Area Dean's urgings, no one else present was willing to second it. I then said to the meeting that I did not wish such a motion simply to fall by default: I felt I had the right to a vote on the matter, and I besought the seconder to second the motion even if he then voted against it. This is in fact what happened: the motion was proposed and seconded and defeated, there being one vote in favour and almost everyone else present against – I think there may have been one or two abstainers.

I guess some of the clergy may have felt that if this sort of hounding could happen to the founder of The Samaritans, it could happen to any of them; I think a certain number present were swayed by my arguments; but I still feel that the majority who refused to condemn me were secretly glad that I defended freedom of speech with regard to sex.

It was in 1974, three months after my return from Scandinavia, when I did that which I told you was going to cause rage and fury in IFOTES. In between I was taking volunteers' classes, seeing clients, attending the centenary of my theological college at Lincoln, attending the Archbishops' and Bishops' Dinner at the Mansion House as the Lord Mayor's Rector, seeing friends: Valerie Jenkins (now Grove), Monica Dickens, André Tchaikovsky, Tom and Marianne Arkell, Phillip Hodson, Ann Hooper, Pat Delbridge, Nadir Dinshaw, Rex Cannon, 'Bree Daniel' and especially Peter Palumbo, with whom I stayed at Buckhurst Park and also went on holiday to Conaglen in Argyllshire. (My wife Susan was in Malawi for the Mothers' Union, where the local members took her on foot from village to village, she leading a goat at each stage wherewith to feast the next Branch.) Whilst in Argyllshire I foolishly rode on gravel one of the two boy-sized motor-bikes Peter had taken up for his son and a friend. I had never been on a motor-bike before, and as I turned sharply to avoid hitting the house, the gadget skidded on the gravel and went off without me. I thought nothing of my twisted knee at the time.

The excitement began when I invited Samaritans from all over the world to come to London for an 'overseas committee' meeting which would consider the possibility of setting up a sister organization for the Branches outside the British Isles. The twenty-two who came represented every Continent (except South America – Jacques Conchon from Brazil had come a month before and could not make a second journey). We were of all ages, both sexes, and every colour of skin. None of those who gathered in the church of St Stephen Walbrook on 3 September 1974 knew one another, but I knew every one of them, because of having visited them in their own countries.

Looking around at the eager souls gathered for that historic meeting, none of us could have guessed what would happen: for instance, one would never have known that it would not be the two Swedish ladies present, but Greta Meyersberg, a Swedish member of the London Branch, who would return to Sweden and start Någon att tala med Samaritans (someone to talk with, Samaritans) in Gothenburg; it recently celebrated its fifteenth anniversary. No one would have known that Vijayan and Premila Pavamani would start an excellent Branch in Calcutta and that with permission from the Bishop (my old friend Lakdasa De Mel, Metropolitan of India, Burma, Pakistan and Ceylon) I would be able to build for them a Branch Centre and home in the compound of the cathedral, paying for it by the very simple expedient of writing to the UK Branches in an aggressive, not at all cap-in-hand way, saying that only the first fifty Branches to send £50 would have the honour of their names on the board in Calcutta, and any larger, smaller, or later amounts would be returned. I had the necessary £2,500 in a fortnight. The fact that, more recently, political differences with the Branch in Delhi created a rift, wasn't entirely a bad thing because the Bengali authorities became very hostile to any kind of help from outside for their suffering people, even obstructing Jack Prager until recently.

Joseph Chipudhla of what is now Harare was the first black African Samaritan, helping the difficult switchover from expatriate to indigenous membership in Africa. Sally Casper ably represented the United States, and became a splendid Branch Director there. One of the New Zealand representatives, John Lloyd, became a Branch Director at Palmerston North, and the Australian one, John McKechnie of Perth, Western Australia, became the youngest Director Perth had ever had; his wife Beth became at the same time

Director of Telateen, the teenagers' line in the same building. The person who did best, however, was the one who hadn't been able to stay for the meeting, Jacques Conchon of Brazil, where CVV-Samaritanos grew by leaps and bounds until at the time of writing it has sixty-seven Branches.

The twenty-two delegates decided unanimously to set up Befrienders International, and to elect me not only as Chairman for three years, but as President for life. (My term as Chairman was eventually renewed three times, before I was able to hand over to Vanda Scott.) We now needed to get the agreement of The Samaritans Inc. to independence for the 'overseas committee', and our meeting had been planned with a view to our attending the annual conference at Manchester University. I took all my pioneers to lunch at Sion College, and the next day to Manchester in a minibus driven by a lesbian client who had become a friend. The then chairman refused to allow us to meet the Executive. Eventually I was able to persuade him that, accompanied by 'our lawyer', John McKechnie, I *should* be allowed to meet the Executive, otherwise I should denounce him at the Council of Management meeting on the Saturday. I couldn't be prevented from attending that, because when I was persuaded to give up the Chairmanship, and not given a seat on the Executive, I *was* made a permanent member of the Council of Management (which I still am).

John and I were coldly received, and were told that the matter could not be discussed without notice, so I gave notice that I would bring it up at the next meeting, on 2 November. We had to let our 'overseas' Samaritans return to their homes, puzzled, rebuffed and above all shocked by the contempt shown to their Founder, whom they considered still to be their guru. If it hadn't been for the ordinary Samaritans, who made a great fuss of them, they might have been totally disillusioned. I did not at the time understand why this had happened: was it simply that politicians instead of Samaritans had got themselves elected to positions of power? I discovered much later that, though that may have had *something* to do with it, the real reason was the machinations of my old enemies.

After seeing off the visitors I had the usual jobs to do: a Psychology and Sex Congress in Bradford; a talk to The Samaritans at Scunthorpe, where my brother Hugh was Director; a London Branch Committee; an overseas broadcast; a lecture to the Royal Society of Health on the Role of the Volunteer; a new volunteers' class on sex; nipping over to Amersfoort in Holland to address a meeting on suicide (HRH Princess Beatrix was presiding and graciously congratulated me on giving my address in Dutch and accepted a copy of my book); an argumentative meeting with the Executive; three days ill in bed (not as far as I remember in consequence); a restorative lunch at Harrods with Rex, where he was then Marketing Manager; another London Branch Committee; the baptism on 20 October of my grandchildren Joel Harding and Alexa Varah, before flying that evening to Spain for a week for Samaritan business; back for radio programmes on Capital and LBC; a Walbrook Ward Club lunch; filming by the COI; on Susan's birthday a concert in aid of The Samaritans at St John's Smith Square by my friend André Tchaikovsky; the next day a rush to get by train to Aberystwyth by 8 p.m.

They were going to start a Branch there, and had booked a room on the pier for the meeting at which I was to speak. They were given a room of the size they normally had for political meetings, and the man in charge of the pier was astonished to have to give the biggest room they had, and carry in more seats, and still have people standing. There was immense enthusiasm, increased when David Evans spoke to the meeting in Welsh. A Branch did result.

But it was my own Branch to which I chiefly owed a duty. Although my Samaritans said that they wanted me to stay as Director indefinitely, and were quite happy to have John Eldrid standing in for me whenever I was abroad, as I so often was (they weren't thinking of Aberystwyth), I had made up my mind that twenty-one years was enough and that I could not combine being Director of the London Branch with Chairman of Befrienders International. We agreed what must be done. On 1 November, All Saints' Day, my friend Lakdasa celebrated the Eucharist at St Stephen Walbrook at 5, and we had our anniversary party from 6 to 10 in Grocers' Hall. My Patrons, the Worshipful Company of Grocers, were always ready to help, and were glad to know that I should still be Rector of St Stephen Walbrook, however many times a year I flew round the world.

The party was not unnaturally a sort of farewell, and many of those present were sad about this, but I wasn't. I should still be in my study, and should still see them all when I went down to the crypt to get myself a coffee. I did not then know how much I should miss being asked to make a decision, or having a difficult client referred to me, or being free to point out anything that seemed to be amiss. I didn't know how bereft I would feel when self-deprived of clients and volunteers, and left with what I found most burdensome – the many letters arriving each day in excess of the number I could deal with. But of course, I would have formal responsibility for the work I had already been doing abroad whilst John 250 loyally covered my absences.

But the die was not yet cast. There had to be a formal resolution of the Council of Management, which was to meet on 2 November 1974, a Saturday, at 10.45 at Church House. I could not be sure what they would decide, because ever since they had ignored my recommendation seven years before that we should not become members of IFOTES, those elected to positions of responsibility did not share the blissful ignorance of the ordinary volunteers of the very existence of this organization, or of the pressure which it was bringing to bear upon their Council. Not content with incorporating The Samaritans Inc. in their 'federation', which to me seemed a perversion of all my past labours, they were determined to claim also any fruits of my future labours if I should be successful in establishing in many other countries Branches which were true to our ethos, methods and principles, and not to theirs. They had even had the nerve to demand that a book of mine be withdrawn from circulation because it contained a couple of pages of hilarious and truthful description of the goings-on at that time in one of their Swedish branches. The Executive did not agree to withdraw the book, or to prevent it from being used in our preparation classes. I found something more edifying to do with the space in the next edition.

When it came to my turn to speak, I said, 'Chairman David, Fellow Samaritans, today is the twenty-first anniversary of the founding of our movement.'

'Oh, is it today?' asked the Chairman in a tone of astonishment. It was my, our, twenty-first birthday; the Chairman neither knew nor cared and nobody had briefed him. ('Did they give you a present, Daddy?' asked my daughter Felicity. I told her it hadn't been that sort of occasion, but that the London Branch had, the previous evening.)

I put the motions, and they were carried; not unanimously, but *nem. con.* From that moment, Befrienders International (The Samaritans Worldwide) was recognized as a sister organization with the same principles and practices, but independent, governed under whatever arrangements were agreed between me as Chairman and the representatives of the constituent Branches. And John Eldrid

315

the representatives of the constituent Branches. And John Eldrid would take my place as Director of the London Branch.

Bruno Burger of Genoa, Italy, was Chairman of IFOTES at the time, and tried very hard to persuade me that because The Samaritans Inc. were members of IFOTES, the Branches of Befrienders International were also members of IFOTES, whether they liked it or not. Doubtless pushed by the evangelizers (of whom he was not one, nor was his successor, my friend Ellen Balaszeskul of West Berlin), he tried repeatedly to persuade me that it was not right to confine IFOTES to Europe by depriving it of Centres in other continents, to which I replied that IFOTES had deprived The Samaritans of the possibility of expansion into Europe, and that most of Australasia and of North America was already overrun by organizations with which the Swedes, the Germans and others would have no quarrel at all.

The Italians were at that time closest to The Samaritans, largely because crisis-intervention was in many towns a work of the young, under such heroes as Lino de Gennaro of Turin. And we had friends behind what was then the Iron Curtain: in fact Professor Dr Tadeusz Kielanowski founded an actual Branch of The Samaritans in Gdańsk, which he called Anonimowy Przyjaciel ('The Anonymous Friend').

None of these was, of course, any help to me in trying to spread The Samaritans around the world. I had no means of consultation with our people far away except by travelling to them – I had no funds with which to pay for them to travel to me. I had no staff apart from my devoted secretary, and many duties still to fulfil for The Samaritans in my own country. I often felt very much alone. I several times read St Joan's 'Yes, I am alone' speech in the trial scene of Shaw's play, and took courage from it.

I wasn't, of course, alone in the sense that no one else was working for what I believed in. If this had been so, my nine years as Chairman of BI would not have seen the number of Branches grow from nine to ninety. But it was no one's *business* but mine to take responsibility for trying to see that any spark anywhere in the world was fanned into flame if possible. I still grieve (when I think about it) for my stillborn children, or those that died in infancy, or fell by the wayside, or defected. Among them are the following: Benidorm, Bucaramanga, Cairo, Calcutta, Cali, Chicago, Darwin, East London, Evora, Fort Victoria, Freetown, Fuengirola, Gdańsk, Geraldton, Greymouth, Gweru, Kalgoorlie, Karachi,

Kitwe, Kowloon, Lagos, La Paz, Luanshya, Lusaka, Manila, Montevideo, Nairobi, Ndola, Peshawar, Port Hedland, Port Louis, Port Moresby, Port Vila, Quito, Rosehill, Santiago de Chile and Singapore. This last, which deceived us into thinking it had joined BI when it hadn't, was listed by IFOTES as being a 'member country'.

Long after Andrew Tu started in Hong Kong in 1958 what became The Samaritans in 1960, and with which I worked for a month in 1967, there was started an English-speaking line in Wanchai, on Hong Kong side. The Chinese line was at Lok Fu on Kowloon side, where Andrew had established his Mu Kwang Schools with the help of Elsie Elliott. The two parts of the Hong Kong Branch were supposed to work together, with the Director of each taking the chair at joint meetings in turn. At that time, the Director of the Wanchai Branch was Vanda Scott, whose husband was building the Hong Kong Mass Transit Railway and who later moved to Singapore, then to Dallas, then to London.

There was a crucial meeting of the Chinese Branch, which a certain person whose name I will not mention had packed with newly recruited members who voted Andrew out and this other person in. From that moment, the dedicated volunteers mostly left, the emergency phones were mostly not answered, and Chinese callers had to ring the English-speaking Branch which did, of course, have members fluent in Cantonese. The worst thing was that the Chinese did not turn up at the joint meetings except when their leader was in the chair, and then they tried to close down the English-speaking Branch. Vanda appealed to me, as Chairman. You would hardly believe it possible for my devoted friend, Isabel Vincent, who was looking after my mail in my absence, to get in touch with me, because I was travelling in Central Africa and at the relevant time was in Burundi, trying to start a Branch in Bujumbura with the aid of missionary friends. But Isabel by some miracle was able to inform me of the situation, and I was able to get a cable to Vanda in Hong Kong, using my authority as Chairman to suspend Lok Fu and using madly efficient Isabel to notify every Branch of Befrienders International in the world. When I could investigate, I had no hesitation in expelling Lok Fu, which stirred up anti-European feeling in most sections of the Chinese-language press and part of the English. I received a lot of racist abuse which I refused to take personally, pointing out that it was not Europeans who were being deprived, but the unhappy and suicidal

317

Chinese citizens, including some of the poorest. The English-speaking line goes from strength to strength under Jessamine Doe, and I haven't recently heard anything of the former Branch which was disgraced.

12

ARLY in 1975 the pain in the torn cartilage of my left knee –
the result of my accident with a motor-bike the year before –
took me to my orthopaedic surgeon Peter French, who
decided it needed a meniscectomy. This would be a nice change
from having frozen shoulders wrenched around whilst briefly anaes-
thetized, tearing adhesions and making one feel one-sidedly cruci-
fied. He fixed on the Catholic Nursing Institute, opposite the Imper-
ial War Museum, because he liked the way they did nursing. I was
glad I didn't have to report until 4 on 3 February 1975 for an
operation the next morning, because I was able to attend a celebration of the Guild of St Bride, founded in the reign of Edward III,
of which Marcus and I were chaplains, so would get to shake hands
with the Prince of Wales who was honouring the event.

I wondered whether it mattered to the Nursing Institute that I
wasn't RC, but I soon discovered I should have been eccentric if I
had been. Let me regale you with an account of the place and of
myself as given by a newly arrived devout Jamaican nurse to her
friend in the corridor outside my door. I won't attempt to reproduce
the accent. 'When I come here, first time in England, I think it's
going to be like a nunnery, ministering all the time to well-behaved
Catholic priests or even Monseigneurs. Instead, they is all Arabs, the
patients, heathen Moh-hamidans if you ask me, and the only priest
on this floor isn't only a heretic, he's downright shocking. What's in
his fridge, I ask you, Sissie? I'll tell you what's in his fridge. Caviar is
what's in his fridge. And champagne, in little bottles. And what does
he have on either side of his bed? Fast-looking girls, blondes, that's
what he has. Well, one of them's a blonde. Actresses, or whores, I
shouldn't wonder.' And they wandered out of earshot.

I was delighted to have brightened her life, but the caviar and champagne didn't come from living on immoral earnings, they came from my generous friend Peter. As to the beautiful girls, one of them was my secretary Suzan Cameron, who *was* an actress, and the other was 'Bree', who *was* a blonde. As soon as I was fit, Peter had me at Buckhurst Park to recuperate, but I didn't convalesce long enough.

An important thing happened on 25 February. I had to go to the Fleet building to have Sir Edward Finniston present to me the five millionth telephone in London, which by a bit of juggling they had made also the twenty millionth in the country. This was to be mine in perpetuity, in recognition of my pioneering a new use for the telephone, or rather the *line* was: the instrument would change from time to time. The line I was allocated was 283 4444, and I'm happy to tell you that when British Telecom took over from Post Office Telecommunications they continued to allow me the rent-free use of this line, which I use only for incoming calls.

I was still hobbling about on a stick, but after a busy week managed to fly to Madrid on 1 March, arriving at 11 p.m. Only later did I discover that my brother Edmund had died two hours later, on his sixtieth birthday, St Chad's Day. I intended the following morning to take the train to Badajoz and across the frontier to Lisbon, and told the taxi driver to take me to the small hotel directly opposite the Atocha station. He stopped at the Mercator Hotel, dumped my bag on the pavement, accepted a backhander from the porter and drove off, yelling that Atocha was just across the road. I got up in good time, but the station wasn't across the road, and there were no taxis. I hobbled what seemed like half a mile, dragging my bag, for the 7.35 train, and arrived just in time to see the back of it.

I went back to the station entrance, sat down on the floor with my back against the wall, and then found I couldn't get up. Everybody was hurrying past, and I knew what it was to be alone, friendless and helpless. 'If I were in England, I'd ring the Samaritans!' I thought wryly. Then I remembered that although it was a Roman Catholic organization, which hated The Samaritans because we gave a truthful answer to Spanish girls who asked whether they could get an abortion if they went to England, there was a hot-line called Telefonos de la Esperanza. I even knew the chap in charge. All I needed was to be able to get up and use a telephone. But no one took any notice of my too-gentlemanly appeals for help.

I had noticed a girl dressed and made up very provocatively, strolling slowly round, obviously looking for punters. When she passed close to me, I called out to her, and she gave me a disdainful look and passed on. The next time she passed, I muttered in Spanish that I couldn't get up. She shrugged her shoulders and passed on. The next time round I said nothing. She passed on, then slowed, then stopped and turned, then came to me and helped me up. Whilst she was supporting me to the telephone on the wall, a client approached her. She told him sharply that she was busy. He accused her of preferring foreigners because they paid more. She told him to carry my bag. He meekly did so. There was no telephone directory, so she sent him to find out the number. I don't know where he got it from, but he came back with it. She produced the money, and didn't leave me until I was speaking to the man I knew, and had received an assurance that they would come and get me as soon as they could. Then, waving away my grateful thanks, she went off to earn her living. Of such, I thought, is the kingdom of heaven.

Half an hour later a car came for me and I was taken to the Centre, and given VIP treatment and booked on a flight to Lisbon and taken to the airport. A week later I changed planes in Madrid for Malaga, and spent the next week with the Costa del Sol Branch, never dreaming that after many visits and much instruction, the person in charge would follow the line of Telefonos de la Esperanza on abortion, and Amigos Internacionales would close down.

It would be tedious to detail my journeyings, mostly abroad and by air. Eventually the number of countries I had visited, at least once, however briefly, added up to 163 (at the time of writing), but we haven't so far been established in more than thirty countries, because unless you can find local people who are willing to work hard and give it a high priority, there won't be a Branch that lasts.

Before the month was out I was in Ottawa, attending the first conference of telephone emergency services for the whole of Canada, arranged by Pat Delbridge, in charge of the Ottawa Distress Centre, formerly of the Orpington Branch of The Samaritans. Pat had arranged for me to be the principal speaker at the Conference, so you may be sure that the cause of befriending by The Samaritans' method was forcefully put and persuasively argued. By the end of the Conference, it seemed that almost all the crisis-intervention centres throughout Canada, except those affiliated to Life Line, were agreed that they should aim to provide the sort of service I had pioneered. A meeting was arranged restricted to the representatives of all the Canadian centres, so naturally I did not attend. I was horrified to learn afterwards that it had been impossible to form a national organization, not, for once, because of the evangelizers throwing a spanner in the works, but because the French question, which so often bedevilled Canadian politics, had intruded itself even into suicide-prevention. French-speaking delegates demanded equal representation for French-speakers throughout Canada, even in provinces where there were hardly any of them.

I was disgusted and outraged, as I always am when irrelevant considerations prevent us from preventing suicide. I had done my best to make the French feel equally valued, even going to the point of joining one of the French-speaking discussion groups myself, lest they should feel neglected. We still have no Branch of our own in Canada except in Lethbridge, Alberta, which I have visited several times, but which didn't then exist. On the way back I not only visited our Branch at Boston but also a branch of Contact at Northfields NJ near Atlantic City, which I had been told was more like The Samaritans than Life Line. Indeed, it proved to be so, but (by now a familiar pattern) it never severed links with Contact and didn't join BI.

In the six weeks before I was off again I had the usual hectic round, including the National Conference held that year at Lancaster; preaching at Great St Mary's, Cambridge; visits from Dr Jozef Hes of Tel Aviv, Jacques Conchon of São Paulo and my friend Elena Pitotti from Milan (one of her Cézanne-like oils hangs in my bedroom). Not much recreation, except when dragged out for lunch or a cinema by 'Bree Daniel', or for dinner with André Tchaikovsky. Then to Gothenburg and many places in Sweden right up to Umeå; then Paris and Nice; then to Vienna by invitation of Prälat Leopold Ungar, head of Caritas and father of suicide prevention in Vienna in that he engaged Erwin Ringel to specialize in it, which led to the foundation of the International Association for Suicide Prevention (IASP). It was an honour to be invited to address Caritas at Eisenstaat, and always a pleasure to stay in Vienna with my friend Maureen Agu, founder of The Befrienders there and married to a Nigerian atomic scientist. I had dinner with His Excellency and Lady Lasky before flying to Tel Aviv to stay with Dr Hes and give a lecture in Dutch which he translated into Hebrew.

Then I went to Jerusalem for the meeting of IASP: a very popular venue, because so many members were American psychiatrists, and so many of them were Jewish. They stayed at the Hilton, but I was kindly put up by Mrs Ruth Broza-Levin in the charming village of Moza Illit. I was happy to spend a day in Ashqelon with David Billig, who had been my doctor and friend all the time I was at Clapham Junction, and his wife Rossi; he is now dead, and so would I be but for him, because over thirty years ago he bullied me into giving up smoking. Then I flew via Tehran to Karachi where, as my friend Nadir was in his Jersey home, I was beautifully looked after by his secretary Peggy Rodrigues.

I flew on via Rawalpindi to my real objective, Peshawar. There a group of Christians, under the inspiration of James Magi Khan, had read my book, had started what was meant to be a Branch of The Samaritans, and had begged me to go and set it on the right lines. In those days Peshawar was very far from being a tourist place, but was about as exotic as you could get, and it was very gratifying to be living with citizens who were ordinary in everything except in being Christians and in wanting to be Samaritans. I stayed in All Saints Vicarage with the Revd Rafiq Wajid, preached at his church, and enlisted Dr Shafique, a Muslim, whom I was happy to appoint as psychiatric consultant. One of the young men took me on a terrifying ride on the pillion of his huge and powerful motor-bike, scattering all kinds of livestock and picturesque conveyances, as we sought an Afghan visa and a ticket on the bus to Kabul up the Khyber Pass.

This was a journey I wouldn't have missed for anything, and I managed to convince myself it was necessary in order to fly from Kabul to Delhi, my next stop, because of bad feeling at that time between Pakistan and India. The person I was to meet in Delhi with a view to starting a Branch of The Samaritans was Kirun (Kitty) Sharma, a young social worker with many friends still in the university. Kitty did eventually get a Branch going for a while, and there is another one in Delhi now, but the group of students to whom she introduced me were a great disappointment.

One evening when she wasn't available I took them to a restaurant they chose, and stood them dinner. As soon as they knew I was paying, they gorged. They did not seem to have any understanding of what I was there for. When we went out into the hot scented darkness a tiny little girl ran towards me with outstretched hand, and suddenly I missed my grandchildren most painfully. I pressed a tiny coin into her hand, and as she ran off skipping with delight, they all scolded me for encouraging begging. 'You were very welcome to my hospitality,' I said coldly. 'There is no need to be so effusive in your thanks. And now you must excuse me.' I then walked quickly away and hailed one of the little vehicles that serve as taxis to take me back to my modest hotel. Once there, locked in my bare room, I suddenly burst into tears, and then began sobbing, and could not stop for some time. I suppose it was the realization that those who had the brains and the influence hadn't the heart. Or perhaps it was just the appalling poverty of India, which I'd first seen even more shockingly in Calcutta in 1967.

I had to go on with my planned journey so I could not afford to stay downhearted for long. Besides, in every country I visited I was usually in the company of the nicest people in that country.

The reason why I don't tell you the continuation of that journey is that it was the longest I ever undertook – it was, in fact, 'Mrs Robertson's Arch', round the world in sixty-five stops, between 15 October 1975 and 17 March 1976. I was away from home for the anniversary of The Samaritans, my own birthday, and most exceptionally for Christmas, which I spent with John and Beth McKechnie in Perth in a temperature of 100°. Perhaps one day I will write a book entitled *My Home was an Aircraft*, about all my intricate journeys and the many adventures I had, but all I want to say about this particular journey just now is that I was worried about going away for so long when my friend 'Bree Daniel' needed my friendship and support more than ever. She had made the difficult decision to marry a man who not unnaturally insisted that she give up her vocation as a call-girl. She assured me before I left that she would be all right provided that I wrote to her once a fortnight, and I gave to her, as well as to my secretary Suzan Cameron, all the addresses I knew of in advance.

I didn't write once a fortnight – I wrote a brief note nearly every day if there was a post office anywhere available; and I received several aerograms from her. But then there was nothing from her in Melbourne, nothing in Sydney, nothing in Canberra, nothing in Brisbane, and I began to be really worried whenever my busy life gave me time for this – naturally, she was included in my prayers for my family and for my special friends. Then I arrived in Townsville, where she and Suzan knew the date of my arrival *and* my address *and* my telephone number. It was, in fact, the Bishop's house, which he had kindly lent to me because he was going to be away in the bush. As soon as I arrived, his housekeeper said that I must ring my secretary, and do so at once because it was the middle of the night in England and she wanted to get to sleep. When I rang, she told me sadly that 'Bree' had killed herself. It was some days before I could simply thank God that she hadn't died without ever having been liked and respected by me as an exceptional human being.

In those days it was quite difficult to get out of Eastern Australia without going back down to Sydney, but I managed to find a little plane that flew from Cairns to Port Moresby in Papua New Guinea. That was the only place on my travels where I had a narrow escape from being mugged: I left my hotel at night to walk to the post office, and was intercepted by a young chap whom I suspected of carrying a knife, who insisted on walking with me. I kept a conversation going with him, and did not let him get behind me. When we arrived at the post office, the mail boxes were inside a doorless anteroom where it was pitch black. I went in and posted my letter and he followed me; I managed to glide out without his noticing – we who were born in the country can see in the dark. Then I waited with my back to the wall. He came out looking to see in which direction I had gone. I called out, 'Here I am, waiting for you – aren't you going to walk back with me?' We walked back together, and I managed to pretend to be more at ease than I was, still keeping slightly behind him. Arrived at my hotel, I stood in the doorway under the eye of the porter. The young man did not dare to enter, but told me that I was very lucky. I might well have been robbed, if I had not had a gun on me, 'as you Americans always do'.

'How dare you take me for an American!' I said. 'I am English, and of course I am armed only with *sang-froid*.'

'What's that?' he asked, but I left him wondering and went to my room.

I was booked on the inaugural flight of Air New Guinea. This was a beat-up old Boeing 720B, with an English crew and attractive New Guinea hostesses in national costume. On the way to the airport, we passed a farm with a notice outside in Pidgin, the official language of the country: MI PELA SABE SELIM PIK. In case you don't get it, it means 'I am the fellow, you savvy, who sells pigs.' I picked up an income-tax form in the post office just to have an example of

325

complicated Pidgin. The flight was to Manila, and we flew the whole length of the huge island of which Papua New Guinea is the eastern half. On arrival in Manila, we got out of the plane, and were instantly thrown to the ground. The earthquake was only about 4.5 on the Richter Scale, but having taken transport into the city and booked into an hotel, I had just taken off my clothes and filled a bath in my little bathroom tiled all over and looking very solid, when the earthquake hit again, this time at 6.5. All the water emptied out of the bath on to the floor, to my amazement.

I went to the phone and rang the desk.

'Yes, sir?' yawned the man on the desk.

'Was that an earthquake?' I enquired.

'Yes,' admitted the man in a bored tone. I didn't like this. *He* was supposed to be the excitable Latin, and *I* the phlegmatic Englishman. 'Will there be anything else, sir?' he asked languidly.

'Yes, there jolly well will!' I answered. 'My bathwater has slopped all over the bathroom floor. Kindly send someone to mop it up.'

'Very good, sir.'

Shortly afterwards there came a tap at my door, and I opened it to find an unlikely-looking maid. 'Are you the maid, come to mop up my bathroom?' I enquired.

'No,' she said, 'I'm the – er – housekeeper for this floor. I've come to see what I can do to make you comfortable.'

'I'll be very comfortable once I've had a bath and some sleep,' I assured her. 'Please tell the maid to hurry up.'

She came into the room and shut the door. 'When I said I wanted to make you comfortable,' she murmured, 'I meant I would do *anything* you wished to – to make you feel – good.'

I was still grieving for 'Bree' – not that she went to hotel rooms uninvited – so I spoke even more gently than usual in such circumstances, and begged to be excused availing myself of her charming services on the ground that I was really exhausted. She departed reluctantly and the maid came. Next morning when I left, she and other girls arrived in a minibus – they evidently didn't sleep in the hotel. I greeted my 'housekeeper' by name and wished her good morning, but she stared straight through me. I guess she was equally unresponsive to any men who *had* availed themselves of her services. How unlike dear little 'Bree' who had been purely like a daughter to me. In my absence she had taken up wine-making as a hobby, and then drinking it as a hobby, and had then turned to barbiturates, and had then taken an overdose. When her husband found her body, he too killed himself, and the two bodies were cremated at the same crematorium and the ashes put on the same rose bed, which you know by now I had no interest in visiting.

During my absence my secretary Suzan Cameron went to Everest with an expedition on which a boyfriend of hers was cameraman, and he was killed. She drove a truck back all the way through Afghanistan, Iran and Turkey, which shows the calibre of the girl. Before his death, this boyfriend had introduced her to 'Bhagwan' Sri Rajneesh, who at that time was in an ashram in Poona, and she left me to go there as this guru's disciple. I didn't think it would last, so I promised her I would keep her job open. When Rajneesh moved to a ranch in the wilds of Oregon, she went with him.

My life continued its usual pattern: when in London, the daily struggle with correspondence, and the satisfaction of dealing with people with sexual problems, mostly coming now otherwise than through The Samaritans, and including many pre-orgasmic women whose difficulties became my chief specialization. One day I may write a book about how such women may be helped – it isn't a thing I can deal with *en passant*. Occasional free time I spent with unchanging friends like Peter Palumbo, Nadir 352, Liz 874, Margie 1219, Louella, and Amanda; and with friends visiting from overseas, Nuran (now Evirgen), Farida Pedder (a wonderful befriender from Bombay), Yana from Portugal, Catherine Kuhn from Switzerland, Maureen Agu from Vienna, Beate Kratsenstein from Dortmund, Andrew Tu from Hong Kong, Dr 'Chummy' de Silva from Sri Lanka. Outside London, I had regular engagements such as small Samaritan conferences at the Hayes Conference Centre at Swanwick in Derbyshire, and the National Conference, at Loughborough that year; short trips, such as a week in Western Ireland, visiting Branches at Cork, Limerick, Galway and Waterford; a week in Scandinavia visiting Gothenburg, Lund and Copenhagen; a weekend with the Dublin Samaritans to give a lecture on sex; a weekend in Berlin.

Once the annual conference was over, I was free to go off on a proper trip, leaving on 21 September to visit our Branches in New Zealand. You will guess I didn't go there direct, but it's the journey back I want to tell you about. I don't think I've ever travelled so far in one day as I did on Saturday 16 October 1976. I got up early in Wellington, and was taken to the airport to catch an 8 a.m. plane to Auckland, where I changed to an Air New Zealand flight non-stop to Singapore. People thought I was brave, or perhaps foolhardy, to take this DC10 the day after a Turkish DC10 had crashed because the cargo door wasn't secured and blew off. I reasoned that the pilot would personally have supervised the closing of the cargo door, and I didn't worry at all.

That flight was a wonderful way to realize how big Australia is. You pass the Australian coast, you have a meal and a sleep and watch a film, and it's *still* Australia, on and on and on. I arrived in Singapore just in time to catch a plane to Colombo, Sri Lanka, where I was met at the airport by Sam Salviah and Nalini Ellawala, hustled through Customs and rushed to the bedside of my old friend Lakdasa, whose last illness was the reason for my sudden return. 'He won't know you,' they told me, 'but he was asking for you a few days ago.'

At the hospital, I greeted his wife Joan, who said, 'Bless you for coming, Chad. It's a comfort to me, even though Lak is slipping away.'

At this moment, Lakdasa sat up in bed and said, 'Chad, I knew you'd come.' I embraced him, and he told his wife to bring me the paper that he had prepared, and call the lawyer in. The paper was a legal document deeding part of the garden of Elsmere, his family house in Horton Place, to The Samaritans so that a custom-built Centre might be built on it. He signed it, and I thanked him, and he sank back and slept. It was just midnight on the day I had left Wellington at 8 a.m.

The following morning I was invited to lay the foundation stone, and all my familiar friends of 'Sumithrayo' (the Singhalese name for The Samaritans) gathered round. There were king coconut trees growing on the site, and I said what a pity it was that we couldn't drink to the new Centre in the milk of our own coconuts. Nalini said the only way to get them was to employ one of the men from the villages around who specialized in cutting them down. 'Like that man there?' I asked, pointing to a nearly naked man with a long rope wrapped round his body and a fearsome knife in his hand. They all gaped in amazement, and called the man over. He shinned up the tree, and threw down as many coconuts as we had ordered, and then slid down on the rope and expertly cut off the tops so that we could conveniently drink.

Just as they were preparing to drink a toast, I asked them to wait a moment, and told Nalini to tell the man in Singhala to prepare one for himself and join us. It was a wonderfully refreshing drink. Nalini paid the man well, and he said something to her and pointed to me. She translated: 'I have been cutting down coconuts for people ever since I was a boy, and this is the first time I have been invited to drink one.' I told them that although the upper classes like themselves were no more immune to suicidal depression than the poor, that peasant earning his living by the sweat of his brow fitly symbolized the dedication of our movement to suffering humanity.

Next I flew to Bombay, where I stayed in luxury with Leybourne Callaghan, head of Hoffman La Roche, who was also Irish Consul in Bombay. I was able to see dear Sarah Dastoor and her three Parsee social workers at Seva Niketan, Byculla, and also my friend Farida. Leybourne gave wonderful dinner parties with distinguished Indian guests, so that it was almost like a 'salon'. Not the best preparation for going to the airport at 4 a.m. – Leybourne always insisted on driving his guests in his car with the Irish pennant. On 19 October, my triplets' birthday, I flew to Bahrain, where I had an appointment to meet a Minister in the government and then fly home the next day in a beautiful VC10. On my arrival, there was no one to meet me and when I rang his office his secretary said that he had gone hunting – would I stay the night at the Gulf Hotel and meet him the following day?

I didn't want to stay in the Gulf Hotel, because the last time I had done that, I had wandered into what I thought was my bathroom, and it had turned out to be another bedroom with a sheik in bed between two wives, one of whom fixed me with a beady eye. I beat a hasty retreat, not knowing what outraged sheiks might do to nearly naked sleepwalkers – the act I put on as I backed away.

Arriving at Bahrain Airport, I saw an even more beautiful plane than the VC10 sitting on the tarmac. It was Concorde. I made a decision I've never regretted: I asked the air hostess when Concorde was leaving, and she said, 'Now.' I asked whether that meant in ten minutes, half an hour, or what, and she said, 'It means *now*.' If I wanted to fly I would have to decide at once and she would just have time to have my baggage security-checked and taped.

'How much extra will it be on a third-class ticket?' I asked her, and she replied, '192.'

'Dollars or pounds?' I asked.

'Dirhan, of course,' she snapped. I later discovered this is a lot more, and anyway I didn't have any. 'American Express?' I suggested, and she gave the standard reply, 'That'll do nicely, sir.'

Take off was rather sporty: after trundling across the uneven runway we suddenly pointed upwards at what appeared to be an angle of about 80° – the steward was hauling himself up the gangway like a gymnast to serve our drinks. In nine and a half minutes we were at 60,000 feet and by the end of the fourteenth minute we were doing Mach 2. I looked out of the tiny window and could hardly distinguish between the horizon and the empyrean. There was no vibration, no turbulence, and most of all, no noise – travelling at twice the speed of sound it could never catch up with us. Like the pre-war Rolls-Royce in which the loudest sound was the ticking of the dashboard clock, the only row to disturb the silence was produced by an American a few seats ahead who, instead of drinking his Dom Perignon like the rest of us, had ordered something in a glass with ice, which he kept banging against the side of the tumbler.

Except when eating the delicious food, I gazed out of the window: fortunately it was clear, and the world lay stretched below like a map. You could tell where you were by the shape of the land masses. Once we had crossed the Lebanese coast I could recognize the island of Cyprus by its shape, and thought how simple it must be to navigate: in a few minutes, I said to myself, we shall turn right and go up the middle of the Adriatic, sparing the folk on either side the sonic boom, and then as we approach Trieste we shall drop down below the speed of sound. This is exactly what we did: the Mach meter showed .982. Flying over the top of Mont Blanc was a beautiful experience: I managed to get a photo of it, which surprisingly came out very well.

We landed at Heathrow at 11.35, less than three and a half hours after leaving Bahrain – half the usual time by ordinary jets. I knew my house was still there because I had seen it from the plane, as I often do from a window seat on the starboard side, so I went straight to the City to have lunch and pick up my mail, wondering if anyone else having lunch had had breakfast in Bombay at 4 a.m. that day.

Lakdasa died four days later, and Charles had his party that Saturday, two days before his twenty-first. I was immediately in the thick of things: the annual service of the Worshipful Company of Carmen, and a luncheon; christening of my granddaughter Kate; lunch with Anthony Grey of the Albany Trust, and with Greta Meyersberg from Gothenburg; meeting with Win, Secretary of the PCC; meeting of the Deanery Synod; lunch with Rudolph Palumbo at Stone's

Chophouse; lunch with Monica from Boston; lunch with Jacques Conchon from Brazil; dinner with Margie; coffee with Nadir, breakfast (i.e. wedding breakfast) at the Berkeley with Ron and Sue Ferguson after blessing their marriage at St Paul's Knightsbridge; supper with my friend Cathy Jones; lunch with Peter Palumbo; and then, before the end of the year, nipping up to Glasgow, and to Rhyl, and over to Berlin to give four talks to Telefonseelsorge about Brenda.

Lest you forget, whenever I was in this country I had my clerical duties, not merely baptizing or marrying or burying relatives or friends, but doing the Sung Eucharist with the sixteenth- and seventeenth-century Masses sung unaccompanied in English, which was my chief delight and one of the things I most missed when I was abroad. I was shortly to miss it for nine years.

I don't want you to think that throughout 1977 I was staying put and behaving myself: I spent the whole of May and June doing a tour of twenty-five countries on behalf of The Samaritans, but I won't go into detail about that trip. Let us skip ahead.

What was important about 1978 was that we discovered that St Stephen Walbrook church was in danger of falling down. The damage it had suffered in the Blitz was reparable and had been repaired by the time I became Rector, but the building of skyscrapers all round, or rather the digging of enormous holes to put them in, had drained away the underground water, had lowered the water table, reduced the Walbrook to a trickle, and dried out our foundations, which, being of chalk, were strong when wet and as friable as blackboard chalk when dry. The walls were threatening to fall outwards, dropping the dome down in the middle. Evidently, drastic measures must be taken.

It was extremely fortunate for the church that I had my closest friend Peter Palumbo as my principal churchwarden (each year's Lord Mayor also held the post, but in an honorary capacity). I put the problem to him and asked him whether he would take complete charge of the restoration, appointing any committee he thought fit and having *carte blanche* to make any decisions without consulting me or anyone. This was a very wise thing to do. Peter engaged the distinguished architect Robert Potter, well known for having stopped the central tower of York Minster from falling down, and he set up monitoring equipment which he had invented himself and

331

which allowed him to see where there was movement and how much, to a fraction of a millimetre.

Peter engaged the late Lord De L'Isle to chair the Restoration Fund Committee, which met at Grocers' Hall – Nick MacAndrew, who was Master of the Grocers' Company that year, was on the committee throughout its existence. Messrs J.W. Falkner & Sons were engaged as the main contractors, and Ove Arup & Partners as engineers. The reason why the church had to be closed for nine years, until 1987, was that the work could not go on continuously. Bills had to be paid within two weeks of certification by the architect – we had to keep stopping to raise more money, which meant that the work had to be very carefully planned out in stages. Everybody concerned did what I think was a brilliant job, and although the cost was immense – it eventually reached £1.3 million – it was surely worth it to preserve for posterity Sir Christopher Wren's smaller masterpiece, with foundations designed to last for centuries.

By concealing his munificence behind the activities of the Restoration Fund Committee, my friend Peter (now Lord Palumbo) was able to keep everyone, including myself, in the dark as to the amount raised by them from various sources, and the amount contributed by himself, but I have no doubt that at this and at other times during my incumbency he has been the greatest benefactor that any church has had in this century.

It wasn't only money that he contributed and is still contributing. He took a close interest in the work throughout; no detail escaped his attention, and he insisted on everything being done in accordance with his own impeccable taste. Those who enter the church in the '90s find it immaculate, and can appreciate the wonderfully uncluttered space which Wren, who began the church in 1672, handed over to the parishioners in 1679.

Peter realized long before I did that the restoration of the church from foundations to dome gave the opportunity to bring it into line with current liturgical practice. At the time the church was built, even devout worshippers received the Sacraments only three or four times a year, but attended regularly and frequently to hear sermons. Wren provided them therefore with a beautiful little altar and a magnificent wine-glass pulpit with canopy, from which many famous preachers spoke for an hour or more to attentive listeners. Nowadays, battered by words from all directions, including radio and television, worshippers do not want sermons: I preach for three minutes or less at my Friday lunch-time organ recitals, and not at all at my Thursday lunch-time Sung Eucharists. What worshippers want nowadays is to gather round the altar as a family for the Sacrament.

At St Stephen Walbrook we are able to do this because Peter Palumbo, with my enthusiastic approval, invited his friend Henry Moore to sculpt an altar to go underneath the dome, with the seating round it in concentric sections of circles. We applied to the Chancellor of the Diocese for a faculty – you can't put anything important into, or take anything important out of, a church without legal permission from the Chancellor of the Diocese, which is called a 'faculty'. The hearing of the Consistory Court was of course in the crypt of St Mary le Bow, and we had Peter Boydell QC to represent us – he himself is Chancellor of two or three dioceses. But to no avail – the Chancellor refused a faculty on the ground that the proposed altar was not a table within the meaning of the act because it didn't have legs, and was in any case incongruous with Wren's architecture. In vain did I point out that no sect of Christendom, however weird, had worshippers gathering around the Holy Table with their legs underneath it: the faculty was refused. As you may imagine, the cartoonists had a wonderful time, showing it, for example, standing on four bricks and ecclesiastics stroking their chins as they regarded it to see whether it now had legs.

Peter decided that we should appeal to the Court of Ecclesiastical Causes Reserved. This ancient court had sat only once before in its history. It consisted of two High Court judges and three bishops. The judges were Lords Justices Lloyd and Gibson, and the bishops were Rochester, Chichester and Kenneth Woolcombe, Canon of St Paul's and former Bishop of Oxford. The hearings were in the Privy Council chambers in Downing Street, and Peter Boydell was again our advocate. It was an exciting day when I went along to Downing Street to receive the verdict. There was a demonstration in favour of Nimrod going on, and several TV cameras which I thought were covering the demo. The Clerk of the Court showed me a pile of paper weighing about a stone but said that I would perhaps be content for the time being with this – and here he handed me a slip of paper about half the size of a postcard - because the television gentlemen were waiting to interview me. On the slip of paper I read the beautiful words, 'In the matter of the appeal of the Rector and Churchwardens of St Stephen Walbrook, the appeal is allowed.' I was happy to share with the television reporters my joy that the Rector and churchwardens and Parochial Church Council and congregation of St Stephen Walbrook were *not* going to be prevented from worshipping at the altar they unanimously favoured.

Henry Moore had asked that the seating around his altar should be of a light timber such as beech, to contrast with the dark wainscoting, and Peter asked my son Andrew to design and make the pews and the four thrones for the Lord Mayor, the Patron, the Bishop and myself.

For a priest not to have an altar, not to mention a wonderful choir and organ, is a great deprivation. During the years 1978–87, when for most of the time the church could not be entered without a hard hat and annoyance to the workmen, I went nearly every Sunday to St Paul's Cathedral for the 11.30 Sung Eucharist, sitting in my stall 'Newington', the eighth from the altar on the left-hand side of the choir. The chief advantage of being a Prebendary (it means 'stipendiary', which is delightfully anomalous since there is no stipend), is that you have your own stall which you give up only at the United Guilds Service, when the Lord Mayor is accompanied by all his aldermen sitting in the choir.

During the nine years when my purely *ecclesiastical* duties were to administer a chalice most Sundays at St Paul's, and preach there once a year, I was still inhabiting my study, walled off from the rest of the building and accessible only through a little door in the porch. The Samaritans were still in the crypt, but had their own separate entrance; I was no longer their Director, but often dropped in for a coffee or a chat. They were more cramped than ever without 'Gulbenkian' (their name for the outer vestry) and had to divide the beautiful common room into small rooms for face-to-face befriending. These were named George, Godfrey and Diana. They had no room for the mass of papers, for which a place had to be found when the outbuildings in the church garden were pulled down and the church and the outer vestry cleared completely, so my small study was made even smaller by being piled high with cartons and several filing cabinets had to be transported to my garage at home. Until 17 September 1990 my biggest incentive to stay alive was that I couldn't bear to leave to someone else the masses of paper that have accumulated in the past thirty-eight years, and which no one but myself can sort into the one-tenth that should be kept and the nine-tenths which can be thrown away or, preferably, recycled.

During those nine years I still had all the administrative work which is inseparable from running a parish even if its church is closed for worship, and I still had, until 2 November 1986, when I retired from day-to-day work with The Samaritans after a third of a century, my work first as Chairman and later as President of Befrienders International, which involved much travelling both at home and overseas.

In 1978, for instance, I had to go to Newcastle to appear on Tyne/Tees TV's *Tell Me Why*, when Ludovic Kennedy seemed to be trying to make me feel guilty about my liberal attitudes towards sex, though perhaps as he didn't succeed in this he was merely drawing me out. Then I had to go to Blackpool to reopen the Branch there, which had been closed down years before for failing to give the service as advertised (the only such case, but it had a very salutary effect on the whole movement). Immediately after a conference at Swanwick I had to go to Nice to meet Dr M. Marois, Professor of Medicine in the University of Paris, about the proposed award to me and others of the Prix de l'Institut de la Vie. This was presented in Paris three weeks later. I took Susan with me because I thought she would enjoy the luncheon at La Tour d'Argent, but there was fog at London Airport and instead of arriving at 11 we arrived after the lunch was over. I sent her back alone the next day and went by train myself to Bienne to speak to the most Samaritan of the Swiss *postes*, going by way of Pontallier and Neuchâtel and coming back by way of Delle and Belfort – altogether, I've found six different routes to Switzerland by rail from Paris. I flew back to London the next day because I had to be at the Cathedral, robed, by 2.10 for the installation of the new Dean at 2.30. All my UK engagements were completed before 8 May, on which date I departed on another of my foreign tours until 21 August.

During that year there were of course clients to see, and delightful times with Peter Palumbo at Buckhurst Park, at Nadir's Jersey home, with André Tchaikovsky at Oxford and with other friends.

In spring of 1979 I took time off to campaign for election to the European Parliament, being driven in a loudspeaker van by Rosemary 993 all round the constituency of London South West. I had to cast my vote on 7 June and attend the counting on the 10th. The announcement on the 11th proved that an Independent has no chance against the domestic party machines, though I did get twice as many votes as any other Independent in the country. As things turned out, I am now glad I was not elected. The next day I was off to branches in the USA and Canada, going out via Halifax in order to see my niece Susan Gibson, who had changed from a little square toughie holding her own with my triplet boys to an elegant lady married to a psychiatrist and already known as an artist; and returning by way of Reykjavik, simply because I'd never done so before.

An advantage of being a churchless Rector is that one can travel abroad without having to find stand-ins. As usual, most of my travels were on Samaritan business, but any holiday I needed could be taken *en route*, in places it would have been uneconomical to travel to from home. It is impossible to have time off in a place where the local Samaritans have arranged a full programme, though in Bangkok in February 1981 I was able not only to fulfil every Samaritan duty, but also to visit some Cambodian refugee camps on the Thai side of the border. It was easy to distinguish the Khmer Rouge camps, with only surly or hostile young men in evidence, from the camps of their victims, where men and women of all ages, with their children, were pleading to be 'settled in a third country'. How could I or they have known that ten years later they would still be pleading, in vain?

Only friends living in Bangkok could have arranged that experience for me. It required a tourist to arrange a totally different experience. Before leaving England I had attended the wedding in Chelsea of a charming girl who told me she'd be on honeymoon in Bangkok whilst I was there, and said she and her husband would like to meet me for dinner. I thought this unlikely, but in fact they did take me to dinner and begged me to join them afterwards for a 'show' which had been highly recommended. After a long taxi-ride the girl wondered where we were.

'Patpong,' I told her; 'we've just passed the VD clinic run by a doctor friend of mine.'

We arrived at a dingy place unlike the many neon-lit topless bars and were shown to an upper room with tables and chairs round the floor space, on which a naked girl of maybe twelve was standing on a clean white towel doing surprising things with ping-pong balls and other small objects. There was a succession of these turns by different girls who didn't seem to me to have reached puberty but had no talent except the ability to smoke cigarettes in a way that exposed them to no risk of lung cancer. I'd finished my beer, so I suggested we might leave. But then there was the announcement of the Star of

336

the Show. Now, my seat was next to the undressing-room and loo, from which had emerged the little girl who was sitting next to me. Like the other girls seated next to customers, she had tried to fondle me and asked for a Coke. I made it clear I didn't want her to do that, and bought her *two* Cokes. She snuggled up to me as if she was my grandchild, and sucked at her straw. She spoke no English, but I knew how she would have got there. Her impoverished parents in the north would have sold her, or alternatively sent her to Bangkok to get whatever job she could and send money home. The tougher ones worked on building sites, the prettier ones worked in massage parlours or became bar girls, and the youngest worked in sweat shops or in places like the one we were in.

The Star of the Show turned out to be my little temporarily adopted granddaughter. She stood, walked with great dignity to the centre of the floor, spread her white towel, and carefully placed an empty beer bottle in the centre of it. Then, for perhaps ten minutes, she made love to that bottle. No, I'm not using a euphemism – you must have noticed that I don't go in for them much.

Everyone stopped chattering. It was no more (but no less) erotic than some ballet. Where, how, had she learnt to behave like a mature, sophisticated, passionate woman? Her act ended when she collapsed face down, orgasmically writhing, and then lay still while the applause went on and on. Then she fled to the undressing-room.

She emerged when the next act had begun, clasping a large rag doll, and snuggled up to me as before. I had a Coke waiting for her, and she sucked alternately at the straw and her thumb, a child again.

My hosts got up to go, and I got up with them, waving goodbye to the girl. At the door, she caught up with me and proffered a slip of paper on which the barmaid had written for her, 'I fuck you 100 baht.' I took the paper, inserted NOT after I, changed 100 to 200, and handed it back to her with the money. She ran to the bar to learn what it meant, and caught up with us again half-way down the stairs. She said something I didn't understand, and pressed her bottle into my hands, and flitted back. I still have the bottle, which reminds me to pray for her sometimes, and for all Thai girls sold into slavery.

You may be sure I sat in my stall on 29 July 1981 for the wedding of the Prince and Princess of Wales, when I had the King and Queen of

337

Sweden just in front of me, and the Queen of the Netherlands, whom I knew, diagonally opposite. Even more unforgettable than that moving and beautiful ceremony was the experience of sleeping at my church, getting up betimes to put on a morning coat, and then walking from my church to St Paul's along the middle of the road, the pavements being crowded with loyal citizens who had slept there all night and were disposed to cheer anything that moved – and specially loudly whenever the frequent police checks grudgingly allowed this eccentric pedestrian, waving his invitation, to pass.

I knew I wouldn't see myself on television, because the TV cameras were directly above my head, but it never occurred to me that there were also film cameras at work. Some months later I happened to be in Tonga; I was met by the Bishop and taken to a service of welcome, after which the congregation were shown films, one of which was about The Samaritans and the other was of the Royal Wedding; and there for the first time I saw myself large as life – or rather, small, at that distance.

That October, after one of my many visits to our Oporto Branch, I went to Lisbon to photograph Henry Moore's exhibition there, then set off for South America, New Zealand, Australia and India until Christmas. I usually go round the world westwards – it's less tiring, because the day you 'lose' is added bit by bit to your sleeping time.

I shall never forget the end of February 1982. I'd been invited by the French psychiatrist who ran it to attend a one-day SAR – 'Sexual Attitudes Restructuring' – as his guest. I think he regretted asking me, because at one point he was urging the participants to take every opportunity of having sexual intercourse as a valid pleasure in itself, without being too choosy; perhaps with the laudable intention of reducing guilt and inhibition in those who had come because their SAs needed R-ing. I didn't want to spoil this, but felt I must suggest mildly that fucking someone you're fond of is not only more moral but likely to be more enjoyable; which drew much applause. But my reason for remembering the day is that when we had to pair off, for uninhibited dialogue, the two guests were put together, so I drew the beautiful, brilliant, famous Nancy Friday, whose book *Men in Love* I often commend to Samaritans as the most useful book on sex they can read.

A month later, I was invited to Hamburg to the eightieth birthday celebrations of the philanthropist Dr Alfred Teopfer, who had set up the FVS Foundation and also the Johann Wolfgang von Goethe

338

Foundation of Basel. It was this latter which ten years before had awarded me the Albert Schweitzer Gold Medal 'for inspiring youth in the service of humanity' (most Samaritans were, and are, young). From this splendid occasion I flew to my pet Branch, Oporto, and thence, on All Fools' Day, to Belém, at the mouth of the Amazon, with its excellent Branch of CVV-Samaritanos. It was a privilege to stay at the house of the Director: nothing separates the traveller from the tourist more than this. Of course, they let one see the Amazon, which I'd previously seen only a thousand miles further up, near Manaus, and for the first time I understood why it was so difficult for early travellers to go ashore. In most places you just can't – on the river you are separated from the land by perhaps a hundred palisades, one after the other, each comprising trunks three to four inches in diameter growing out of the water something like a foot apart – more impenetrable than the tangled mass of rhododendron on the hills in the west of Ireland.

I'm not going to weary you with another itinerary. I'll just say that I was once again overwhelmed by the magnificence of Brasilia; moved to tears by the work done on babies and children with hare-lips and cleft palates at the specialist hospital in Bauru; and humbled by the dedication of Jacques Conchon and his colleagues and Samaritans from all over Brazil gathered for their annual conference at San Bernardo. On Easter Day I was able to celebrate the Holy Communion in English there for those who wanted it.

After another unsuccessful go at starting a Branch in Santiago de Chile, I flew across the South Atlantic from Rio de Janeiro to Cape Town, where I was met and put up by dear Cynthia Howard, who had heard nothing from me since I'd sent my flight number months before. I found the Cape Town Life Line just as unrepentantly preachy as the original one in Sydney. By the time I'd 'done' our African Branches and got home via Greece, Italy and France after eleven weeks, I felt I'd discovered a better itinerary than going round the world, because I'd cut out the Pacific.

A fortnight after my return, my dear friend André Tchaikovsky died of cancer in hospital in Oxford, where he lived. He was the most talented of my friends: a renowned pianist beginning to make his name also as a composer, and (what few except myself knew) a brilliant writer in his adopted language, English. I was privileged to read his autobiography a few pages at a time as he wrote it, and then, when to my great distress he told me he had destroyed it, many pages of the new version, which he may or may not have destroyed. Like many Polish Jews of the period, almost all his family had been murdered ('they made my mother into soap'), and he himself had had such a terrible life that I could not help feeling that his writing about it was a therapeutic exercise and that he had destroyed this because he found it too subjective to be just to others. When I read it I despaired of being able to write my own story in my native tongue as well as he wrote his in a foreign one.

I was asked by André's friend and agent Eve Harrison to conduct the cremation at Oxford, but not as a religious service because he was an unbeliever: would I please make it cheerful, even amusing? The chosen music was available on tape, and included his own 'Trio Notturno', which was to have had its première at Cheltenham three days later. As I entered the chapel, not robed, I noticed a piano at the back, and was greatly moved when a man sat at it, followed by a fiddler and a 'cellist: before playing the 'Trio' at Cheltenham, these good men would play it live at the composer's cremation.

After the ceremony his friend Kyung Wha Chung was very distressed, and I took her into the Botanical Gardens so that we could weep together.

That September I attended my first lunch of the Outsiders Club, founded by my friend Tuppy Owens for handicapped and disabled people to get to know one another and also if they wished to 'date' one another. Most would have preferred a lover who wasn't handicapped, but one who was was better than none. I did not share the popular belief that someone who does not appear sexually desirable could not possibly be desirous, or ought to be ashamed of it if they were. (The opposite fallacy, that one who appears desirable to you must be desirous of you is even more disastrous, leading to much sexual abuse and harassment.) I was honoured to accept Tuppy's invitation to become a Patron.

It had given me great pleasure when I was made an Honorary Liveryman of the Worshipful Company of Carmen in 1977. This entitled me to ply carts for hire in the City, if I'd had any carts, and heavy horses to pull them, though my brethren nowadays were more likely to ply intercontinental cargo aircraft. In October 1982 I was joined as an Honorary Liveryman by the Princess Royal, but unlike me HRH was to go on to become our Master. We all discovered her quality, and our admiration for her knew no bounds.

The other memorable event of 1982 was in November, when

Nadir Dinshaw, a friend of the Archbishop, preached in Canterbury Cathedral. I went, of course, and was proud to hear him deliver what must have been one of the best sermons of the year. I myself still had no pulpit, except once a year at St Paul's.

In January 1984 I was invited to visit our Branch in Bahrain and was delighted to discover there was a cheap ticket to nearby Dhahran by Austrian Airlines, which not many people grabbed because there was an eight-hour stop in Vienna. This suited me admirably: I was able to spend six hours there with The Befrienders, all of whom assembled at their centre in Seidlgasse, where we had the best seminar on sexual problems I had ever taken. Because the German-speaking 'hotline' was religious, our Samaritans had to take calls from many desperate Austrians.

A vivid memory from Bahrain was of a meeting for Leaders only when I was asked to give advice on the handling of a dozen difficult callers. I was happy in most cases to be able to say the Branch was doing fine and should in my opinion just persevere, but they'd saved until last a thick folder they wanted me to take away and advise on the following day. I said I didn't need to take it away as I could give my advice at once. 'Tell this character,' I said, 'though not necessarily in these words, to piss off. That if you never hear from him again, that will be too soon.'

'But, Chad,' they protested, 'you haven't read it!'

'I don't need to read it,' I told them. I hefted it in my hands and added, 'I've weighed it.'

When they got over the shock, they rejoiced: only two members of the Branch hadn't been victimized by this person, who had a talent for making people feel guilty if they wouldn't become his slaves.

On another cheap ticket in March, by enduring a very long flight by Air Canada to San Francisco via Toronto instead of a shorter one via the Arctic, I was able to return via Portland, Vancouver (cousins and a nephew), Lethbridge Alberta (where we have an excellent Branch), and the interesting change from Edmonton Municipal to ditto International airport. The reason for the stop at Portland was to be able to take a DC3 of Air Rajneesh to Rajneeshpuram, the large village built near Antelope Oregon by the disciples of this guru. My former secretary, Suzan Cameron, was a Sanyassin and was in charge of their airport. On my plane was a lady I thought sinister to whom everyone toadied, and when we arrived I wasn't allowed to deplane and embrace Suzan (or rather, Ma Alima) until a

341

huge welcoming party had borne this character tenderly away. I later learnt that Sheila was 'Bhagwan''s go-between, and later still that it was she who was responsible for the conflict with the State which led to Rajneesh's arrest and expulsion from the USA. He subsequently died in India.

I was most impressed by the building work, town-planning and horticulture achieved in so short a time, but the community did not seem to me at that time to be joyous and purposeful in the way Clent (for instance) had been. There was indeed a shadow over it which I didn't know about until after the bust-up. Suzan seemed to be interested only in 'the Ranch', as they called it, so our dinner in one of the restaurants was a bit strained, and I was soon in my huge, well-appointed bedroom in The Hotel, which at $90 a night from relatives and friends contributed to the coffers. In his early days in Poona, Rajneesh had attracted young middle-class Europeans by his discourses and the sexual freedom of his ashram, but in my bedroom at the Ranch there were notices admonishing me not even to engage in genital caresses without wearing the surgical gloves provided – if I had had anyone to share a bed big enough for four.

I decided to cancel my second night, and get the 8 a.m. plane back to Portland the next morning. The girls in charge of these arrangements were most helpful, but totally uncomprehending of a person who had come so far and was going away without experiencing the big event of each day, namely greeting (at a distance) Bhagwan as one of his large fleet of white Rolls-Royces conveyed him slowly through the adoring, flower-strewing crowds at 2 p.m. I was content to miss this.

I had to cut my fifth visit to Brazil down to a fortnight because, when I was staying with Michelle Maries at Sotogrande (she had made me her honorary grandfather) I had promised that if our friend Richard Denman, who had charge of the magnificent golf-course Las Aves, married our favourite golf pro, Jane Chapman, I would come and take the wedding. I never thought I'd have to fly back from Rio. The wedding in the little whitewashed church was a joyful occasion, worth the journey for me, and Michelle's birthday party two days later was a bonus.

I decided to accept Michelle's invitation to stay for another week because I had had an idea for a play, inspired by the way Nabil Shaban introduced a TV programme about the Outsiders' Club called *The Skin Horse* (a toy cuddled so much it had lost its hair). I knew I'd never be able to write it in London, hunted by people who hadn't been able to get at me when I was in North and South America. I called the play *Some Day I'll Find You,* and set it in the '50 before 'the permissive society' got going. The central character was Matthew, a quadriplegic who (as occasionally happens) wasn't impotent. He had been taken out of an institution by his good-hearted auntie who ran a boarding-house for business girls. The play explored the relationship between Matthew and these girls — and the resident maid, who was meant to be a minor character but bullied me until she had an important role. I had a lot of encouragement from Michelle, who had me read it to her at meals or whilst watching polo (she was secretary of the polo club as well as a keen golfer).

I sent it to several smaller theatres; after the Almeida complained about the violent and melodramatic ending, I rewrote the ending, but still had no luck with it. Theatres were not impressed by the fact that my TV play *Nobody Understands Miranda* had attracted $8\frac{1}{2}$ million viewers on BBC1 in 1972. Even after Max Stafford-Clark praised it highly in 1991 though not for the Royal Court, no Branch offered to put it on for my eightieth birthday.

May 1984 was dominated by the Enquiry into my friend Peter Palumbo's breathtaking plan to create a great square in front of the Mansion House, formed by demolishing property he and his father had patiently acquired over the years. Mansion House Square was to be dominated by a beautiful bronze building designed for the site by the famous Mies van der Rohe, facing Dance's Mansion House, and having Lutyens' fine Midland Bank and the adjoining bank on the north side, Bucklersbury House on the south, and St Stephen Walbrook, cleaned up, in the corner. I was enthusiastic about this imaginative scheme and submitted evidence in favour of it. You will know, of course, that after a favourable report by the Inspector, the project was turned down. I have never admired Peter more than when I saw the courage with which he bore the destruction of the longed-for fruit of endeavours which had occupied the whole of his adult life.

You must be thinking that my life consisted of nothing but interesting or exciting events, with undisguised holidays alternating with ostensible travels on business which were holidays in all but name. In fact, if you use a little imagination you will realize that when the Founder arrives for a few days at some far-flung outpost of the movement, the local Samaritans show great ingenuity in cramming in the maximum possible number of lectures, workshops, seminars, press conferences, radio and television interviews, and lavish solid and liquid hospitality from as many as possible of those who had offered it – and who can blame them? That was what I had come for, and of course I was happy to do what was expected of me. I'm usually happy doing my routine work at my church, but I don't call it a holiday. The reason why I don't tell you about all the boring things I have to do is that the last thing a writer wants to do is to bore his readers. So, just as a novelist does, I pick out the more memorable experiences.

One of these was a flying visit to the Army in Northern Ireland in June 1984. I had been several times to visit the Samaritans – in fact, I have visited all the Branches except Coleraine and Newry, and all in the Republic except the three newest – and felt reasonably safe because the IRA used The Samaritans to give bomb warnings, knowing that our rule of confidentiality would not allow us to pass on more than the message; but visiting the Army might have seemed different, even though we would not exclude anyone from our ministrations. I spoke on the history and ethos of The Samaritans with special reference to Northern Ireland, and I also spoke about bereavement and about anxiety. My host at dinner, Brigadier Colin Mattingley, later became Clerk to the Grocers' Company, and thus a neighbour in the City.

On my return I completed the revision of my book *The Samaritans in the '80s*, updated from the first version of 1965 and the two in the '70s.

On 4 July I had the fascinating experience of being photographed by Lord Snowdon at his Kensington studio. He was pleased with two prints, one of which I gave to my daughter Felicity. The other hangs in my library, looking across at my own best (amateur) photograph of great stone heads on Easter Island.

Whilst my church was closed the happiest month was July, when St Paul's put on great Masses with choir and orchestra doing at the Eucharist the big works of Schubert, Mozart, Haydn and Stravinsky. So far as we knew, in no other cathedral in Europe could you *worship* at these Masses, which were usually confined to the concert hall.

The other big event each July is Barnes Village Fair, when the lower Common is covered with stalls, several of which, like that of The Samaritans of Putney, include a few books, while one huge stall is devoted to nothing but books. Each year Susan would warn me, 'We don't need any more books'! I guess this 'we' was a wifely 'we' comparable to a royal 'we', and I had to agree that every shelf in the house was full. I seldom bought more than 200 books at the Fair, and always bought Susan a beautiful china cup, mug or teapot for her collection (she never said, 'We have enough mugs'). While she was absorbed in this, Girl Guides hired by me would creep up the stairs with my loot and hide it under my bed. I guess I'll have to think of something else if Susan reads this.

2 May, 1985 was a blissful day. Richard and Ruthie Rogers had invited me to baptize their latest, Bo, and Peter Palumbo had generously arranged for this to be done at Farnsworth House, the lovely and now famous house built for Mrs Farnsworth by Mies van der Rohe on the banks of the Fox River at Plano, Illinois. I had several times stayed there with him, and now the whole party was accommodated in Plano. Naturally, I took the opportunity to visit The Samaritans of Chicago: that dear, brave Branch had not then folded. I paid them another visit the next month.

This was the year my tiresome affliction called blepharospasm, convulsive involuntary screwing-up of the eyes, became so bad that I had to do something about it. Reading and writing took longer because of it, and crossing roads could be dangerous. My doctor at that time, Sandra Cotterell, even tried acupuncture. When that didn't work I went to Professor McDonald, who put me on pimozide. After a while I decided I preferred the blepharospasm to impotence, ditched the pimozide, and flew to Vienna for the IASP's twenty-fifth anniversary. I was one of the few who had been there with Professor Dr Erwin Ringel in 1960. As oldest and newest, my friend Onja Tekavčič of Slovenia and I jointly chaired a session.

At this time I was still President of BI for another year, and after our annual conference at York, where I twice presented a moving American film of families bereaved by suicide, I received an invitation from the Union of Socialist Youth in Poland to spend a week touring Poland as their guest. I had often visited our suicide-prevention colleagues in this and other Communist countries, but never before as an official guest. I was able to arrange to begin and end the week at our Embassy in Warsaw, taking an English service there on the Sunday, and being collected from there by the Poles.

At 9 on 21 October I was taken with my charming interpreter Ewa Turska to meet Mr Ungar at the Warsaw HQ, who was, I supposed, my host. From then until I was delivered back to the

Embassy at four on the 28th, my programme was arranged down to the smallest detail. It included paying my respects to officials in each of the four places on my itinerary: Warsaw, Piotrkow Trybunalski, Szczecin and Wrocław (the last two were formerly known as Stettin and Breslau), and in Warsaw I spent an hour or more at each of the Ministries of Justice, Foreign Affairs and Education. The logistics were exemplary, and my creature comforts were supplied as well as possible, not forgetting sightseeing and fine concerts in Szczecin and Warsaw. You may be wondering when there was time for what I'd presumably come for. I'm happy to say there was enough meeting with volunteers of Telefon Zaufania and promotion of Samaritan ideas at press conferences and on radio and TV to make the week most fruitful from my point of view, and the extensive press cuttings, with translations, which I received afterwards confirmed this. The saddest thing? Of three Branches represented at my meeting in Szczecin, one, Gdańsk, had severed its connection with us and joined IFOTES, on the retirement of dear old Professor Tadeusz Kielanowski. The most heartwarming? Two volunteers called Andrzej, one of them blind, travelled all night from Olsztyn to Piotrkow to join with the local volunteers plus some from Łodz (pronounced 'woodge') and Czestochowa, and then travelled back all night to be at work the next day. Olsztyn and Piotrkow are now members of BI. The most interesting sight? The great Panorama in Wrocław. The most depressing sight? Crowds of men waiting for buses to work, without caps, scarves, overcoats, jumpers or gloves, shivering, probably breakfastless. An official with whom I had had breakfast said, drawing on his fur-lined gloves, 'They do have overcoats, but don't bother to wear them until it gets cold.'

I had a fortnight before setting off round the world again. Apart from arrears of mail, I fitted in a Visitation by the Bishop; lunch with Peter; a meeting with another churchwarden, Lady Morse; a consultation with our architect Robert Potter; a Parochial Church Council meeting; the Council of Management of The Samaritans; a Clergy Chapter meeting; a visit to Milton Keynes Branch; three dinner parties; Sunday lunch with my son David and his wife and children; an evening talk to one of the London Branch's tutorial groups on the difference between befriending and counselling; a visit to Christie's depot to be photographed with my roll-top desk which I'd given for their sale in aid of The Samaritans; and most important of all, a meeting with Mr Stephen Halsey of the American Express Foundation. This had been arranged by another churchwarden (I have ten), Alderman Paul Newall, Alderman of the Ward of Wal-brook, and the magnificent result was that the Foundation granted us £100,000 to pay for the restoration and improvement of our famous Hill organ in the church, by Mr Frank Fowler, Organ Builder to HM The Queen. This was the third and definitive restoration made during my time as Rector.

From 13 November to 11 December I went round the world again, changing planes in Seattle for Honolulu, where I stayed with Fred Dailey and his wife Murph at the Hilton Lagoon and at Mokulea Polo Farm; the latter being the most peaceful place I know. Fred was the founder of polo in Hawaii, and had entertained the Prince of Wales at Mokulea. But I soon had to tear myself away to visit our Branches in Osaka, Japan; Seoul, Korea (where it's charmingly named Love-Line); our preparatory group in Manila, Philippines; and Hong Kong; and home by what was then British Caledonian. I didn't break my journey at Muscat because the authorities wouldn't allow the proposed Branch to advertise.

A week after my return I had the sad task of taking the cremation at Welwyn of 'Old Nell', Mrs Fletcher-O'Borne, aged ninety-seven. The next day Christie's held our auction, and my desk fetched £800 – not as much, of course, as Hard Rock memorabilia such as the pieces of a smashed guitar.

1987 was to be the year I would have my church back, though in January '86 this didn't look possible. A huge hole in the west end of the north wall allowed the spoil to be driven up a ramp to be carted away – one of the elegant pillars bore a sign BEWARE OF THE TRACTORS – and Henry Moore's altar was brought in this way. It's a skilled and expensive job moving objects weighing 8½ tons which mustn't be chipped.

In mid-April I went to Lincoln to preach at the fiftieth anniversary of the consecration of St Giles' Church, in which I had been ordained to the priesthood on St John's-Day-in-Christmas that same year. It made me feel old, especially as I still wasn't well and was foolishly still managing without a secretary, even though I knew Suzan would never come back.

I did some television again: TV AM; *Choices* (Am I my brother's keeper?) from the Greenwood; half a dozen Night Thoughts on *Hope* for Thames; a Central TV interview from Nottingham; and others. In the old days, Suzan had stopped counting at 500 appearances, here and abroad.

From 7 October to Christmas came the greatest joys of all. My dearest friend Peter had fallen in love and become engaged to a beautiful, witty and charming Lebanese girl, Hayat Mrouwa, and I thanked God, because I had prayed fervently that happiness might come to him. To know her is to love her. I was given the immense privilege of instructing her in the Christian faith, baptizing her, preparing her for confirmation and presenting her (to Bishop Kenneth Woollcombe, formerly of Oxford), giving her her first Communion, and eventually solemnizing the marriage. My only regret was that the lovely church which was by now as much Peter's as mine was unusable, so the Sacraments, up to and including Holy Matrimony, had to be at St James Garlickhythe.

On 2 November 1986 I retired officially from all Samaritan offices and responsibilities except the historical one of Founder. The movement had come of age, and I wanted it to go from strength to strength without me while I was still alive to see it. I was also conscious that most of the members hadn't been born when I started: they would have a better understanding of many current callers than I could possibly have.

The chief celebration was a birthday party for me at Grocers' Hall. I knew about half the Samaritans present, and told them not to hanker after the 'good old days' because we were now doing the job better, for more people, in more places. I said I'd sometimes felt like Frankenstein, having created something that took over my life, but I'd now proved I could get free without having to die.

BI announced that what I should like most as a retirement present – I pricked up my ears at this, wondering if Arabian Nights had been arranged, and if so, how many? – would be people giving money to BI to set up a bursary fund in my name, to help Samaritans from distant lands to come to conferences. This fund was set up, and serves a good purpose.

348

13

A T the Carmen's luncheon in January 1987, HRH The Princess Anne, by then our Master, gave me £1,000 from the Benevolent Fund for the Central London Samaritans, who before the year was out would leave the crypt and move to bigger premises at 46 Marshall Street, Soho. About this also I felt no sentimental qualms: the callers would benefit, and nothing else mattered.

In March 1987 I was to go on the best holiday I'd ever had in my life. I no longer had to include Samaritan visits, so I was able to pick on a huge country which had only one Samaritan Branch, and that was in its capital – Indonesia. I had long been intrigued by two of its thousands of islands, the starfish-shaped one called Sulawesi (formerly Celebes) and an enormous one you may not have heard of. Do you know where Kalimantan is? No? But everyone's heard of Borneo. The southern two-thirds belongs to Indonesia and it is called Kalimantan. In my boyhood I had dreamt of visiting the Dyaks and their longhouses in which a whole tribe lived a communal life, and Borneo was where they are. Kalimantan has some huge rivers, the biggest, as broad as the Danube, being the Mahakam. I told Peter I couldn't decide whether to explore the Mahakam River deep into the jungle, or to visit a sort of Shangri-la before the tourists find it, Torajaland in the highlands of Sulawesi. 'Why not do both?' asked Peter simply. I don't know when I've felt so elated.

I got some information from an obscure one-woman office set up by the Indonesian government, procured my air tickets and travellers' cheques, made my will, and flew to Jakarta, where I hadn't been since Bill Coombes had had to put me in an hotel because his Embassy was being repainted for the Queen's visit. Having a couple of days to wait for my flight, I broke my vow and telephoned our

Branch, Hotline Bersama. 'Do you speak English?' I asked. 'This is Chad Varah.'

'I don't believe it,' was the reply, with very little accent. 'It would be too much of a coincidence. Today an article about you covers the front page of one of our papers; I'll tell you how to get to us, and show it to you.'

I spent that day and the next very happily with them. I think the reason we seldom heard from them was that they were started by a lady from Singapore. They were gloomy about Kalimantan. Dysentery, they muttered darkly. 'We explorers', I said, (forgive me, Robin and Louella Hanbury-Tenison, who really are) 'take that in our stride' – though I suppose 'squatting' would be more accurate.

I flew to Balikpapan, found an hotel, and decided to check my cameras: Asahi-Pentax F 1.4 and Sankyo Cine-Camera, each with ten films. The shutter had jammed on the first, and the second, which I rarely used, wouldn't go because the batteries had corroded inside the handle. I walked along the main street, which has an open sewer in the middle, and saw a shop that advertised FILMS. I was happy to see that the proprietor was an old man because he was likely to speak Dutch. He was glad to do so. I asked him to show me his whole range of cameras. He put a neat little fixed-aperture, fixed-shutter-speed, fixed-focus job on the counter: it differed from a primitive Brownie only in having flash. That was his whole range. In the bright sun, I was to get wonderful photos with it, one of which is on the back of the dust-jacket.

The next day I took a taxi north to Samarinda, on the river, and found my guide-interpreter. He had a cook/laundryman and a 25-metre boat, four metres wide, with a 160-horsepower Mitsubishi engine and a crew of three, so that we could go very far by doing eighteen kph day and night – twenty-three or more coming back with the current. It was available for four to ten passengers, so I'd have to pay for four places. I was glad Samarinda was free of tourists: I wanted to be alone, in sole charge.

Conditions were fairly spartan. I slept on the deck on a mattress only an inch thick (why hadn't I demanded four, as I was four people?). Meals were bread, rice, fruit, coffee, beer and mineral water, with fish and prawns from the river. Every house on the bank had its privy by the water's edge, so the prognostication of 'dysentery' was soon fulfilled. My guide had stocked up with a dozen beers a day and was surprised I used only two; I think it was because he was making such a large profit out of me that he threw in a couple of shore excursions which I wouldn't have missed, and paid for me to be admitted as a member of the Banauq Dyaks at Tanjung Ysui, almost the remotest part of the jungle we reached before turning back.

I left my entourage to their own devices: they chatted, dozed and took turns at the wheel day and night. I sat and watched the nearer shore and the river craft, and the wildlife as the river narrowed; and, waking at 3 a.m. to make water, would see the Southern Cross blazing down on me from a cloudless sky. As the river narrowed beyond the great lake, the many mosques gave way to the occasional church: the Dyaks preferred Christianity because they loved palm wine and pork. One of my short trips was in an air-conditioned vehicle – a ramshackle lorry with no windscreen, that took us nine miles to a fair, with attractions from far and wide, including trussed pigs waiting to be slaughtered, and cocks fighting, and a bull in a wooden cage which would die by being speared by all the men who wished to appear brave (I did not stay for this). There were two taboo tents with fearsome men in one and female witches in the other. I naturally crept into the latter and got several photographs while they tried to decide what I was, with a huge straw hat, a pink bespectacled face, and a Sri Lankan guru shirt. I had some impressive curses put on me, free of charge.

The other excursion was one I shall never forget, for the Dance of Death is much more forbidden than the witches' tabernacle. It was an amazing piece of luck that at one riverside village where we stopped to buy fruit, my guide heard that this ceremony was taking place in a large hut several miles away in the jungle. Five corpses had been saved up, and the obsequies took twenty-eight days, on the fourteenth of which the Dance of Death was danced to a kind of gamelan orchestra, chiefly gongs of different pitch.

My guide (I don't mention his name, because he was guilty of logging in Sabah, to the north) hired a motor-bike and took me on the pillion along endless narrow tracks in the dark (its lights didn't work). After an interminable bumpy ride and getting lost several times, we got off and groped our way to a dimly lit building from which no sound came. We crept in, and sat on the floor. It was crowded. When my eyes became accustomed to the dimness, I could see the rows of solemn faces, the silent orchestra, a platform in a corner with shapes covered in rich cloth, and a cloth-covered box the size of a tea-chest hanging from the roof.

When the strange thrumming and throbbing began, nine young

351

men came in in single file, dancing to the music. They spun the hanging box, then the first five took something from it which they hung between their shoulder-blades. 'Coconuts,' whispered my guide. 'You can't fool me,' I whispered back. 'Skulls from the five corpses in the corner.' The young men had hair made of tow hanging down their backs, but their smocks didn't hide western trousers.

Next came nine young girls, much more elaborately dressed, and doing a prettier dance. They carried no skulls. I got a flash photograph of the leading girl, whose lovely face with frozen grief will always haunt me; and then we escaped. The dancers were teenagers who when children had been cherished by one or more of the dead.

At Tanjung Ysui my guide told me to explore the village and the jungle for two hours whilst preparations were made, then report to the longhouse. I was surrounded by charming children, and an old man who translated their Dyak into Dutch for me. I watched a blacksmith at his forge, with his seven-year-old son working the bellows. I watched a girl weaving, and bought some of her cloth. Then I wandered into the jungle, and came across a typical container of human bones, richly carved, on poles head-high.

When I reported to the longhouse, my guide told me to wait till the strangely attired chief finished a long question, which would be about my health, and then to reply, 'Beik' (I am well). I would then be purified by being asperged, sprinkled with powder, have smoke wafted at me, and then enter the longhouse. There we had to exchange gifts: mine to them was a carton of cigarettes (too weak for the men, but the girls liked them), and theirs to me was a plate which represented my life and must never be broken (baggage-handlers managed to break it, wrapped in clothes in my case). I had to sing 'a song from my own tribe', so I sang a couple of verses of 'Early one morning', and then the maidens danced for me – all were wearing the *infula*, the red and white twisted headband which I was now wearing, and still have.

Before I left, I had to – you'd never guess – sign the visitors' book. It was a tattered Victorian exercise-book given to the Banauq by an explorer in 1856; I was the seventh visitor since that one, the only Englishman and by far the oldest to reach them.

From Balikpapan I flew south-east to Ujung Pandang, formerly Macassar (don't get their hair-oil on the back of your chair). I'd arranged to be met by a guide, who turned out to be a member of the Toraja royal family: a small, mild fellow whom everyone jumped to obey, and who was the only Spanish-speaking Toraja.

352

His English wasn't bad, so we alternated. We set off northwards without delay, so as to reach Rantepao before dark, but stopped to see the Boogee people on the way to Parepare, which had a restaurant foreigners were allowed to eat at. The Boogee were feared pirates in the past, but now I suppose are smugglers. They were intrepid seamen, and their elegant boats, made without nails, could cross oceans – one went to Expo in Vancouver. I saw some Boogee girls weaving silk, told the driver to stop, and went and bought a piece of silk for Felicity.

On the way back to my car a pretty Boogee girl ran after me, prodded me below the belt, and said, 'Geev me your penis!' I decided to ignore this, and grinned feebly. 'Eef you liking me, geev me your PEEENS!' she persisted.

'What, in front of all these people?' I asked, with inappropriate jocularity, detaching myself from her clutches. I got into the car, where my guide was waiting for me, and took her photograph.

'Don't give money, ever,' he said in Spanish. 'Give a cigarette, a sweet, or a biro.' I handed her a spare ballpoint, and she was ecstatic. 'Your peens!' she exulted. I felt a fool.

I don't think I'll tell you about Torajaland. I don't want it spoilt before I retire there in the year 2010.

Back in London, the Hospital for Tropical Diseases cured my dysentery in a few weeks.

On 22 March I attended the ordination of some women deacons at St Paul's. I had always been in favour of the diaconate as a holy order in its own right and not merely as a probationary ministry before being priested, so even though only women were being made deacons, I was happy to see it. I had preached at St Paul's in favour of the ordination of women to the priesthood, but not to the episcopate. I had never in all my years as a priest had any need of my male equipment in performing my priestly duties, and the idea that only a male could represent Christ seemed to me to ignore the fact that it was humanity, not masculinity, that was taken into the Godhead at the Incarnation.

Some fervent supporters of the ordination of women were outraged by my pleading that they should not at present aspire to the episcopate. A woman may claim to have a vocation to the priesthood: any man or woman who claims to be called by God to sit in the House of Lords and receive a large income does not impress *me*. Those who say it is illogical to want women priests but not, for the time being, women bishops are thinking legalistically, not pastorally. I always want to consider the feelings of the laity whose servants we clergy are. Many of them cannot conscientiously believe that a woman can be a priest or that the Sacrament she would purport to consecrate would be valid. We ought not simply to ignore and unchurch such worshippers, even if we disagree with them. But neither can we permit them to impede what we believe to be God's will. They may absent themselves when a woman priest is officiating and go at another time or to another church, but it is not reasonable that they should have to go to another *diocese*, and perhaps find there a male priest who had been purportedly ordained by a woman bishop. I saw the consecration of a woman in Massachusetts as unChristlike, not because she was divorced or black, but because it seemed to me callously political.

On 25 April, Mother's youngest sister Aunt Lilian died in Peterborough at ninety-something and I wasn't able to go to the cremation because I'd already agreed to be on *Wogan* that day, with Derek Jameson substituting for Terry Wogan himself. He said he enjoyed having someone who wasn't a showbiz personality, but I guess he enjoyed the droll Kenny Everett too.

St Stephen Walbrook began to look as though it might be finished in six months. Part of me could hardly wait, and part was worried about what I'd *do* with it when I got it back. Nearly all our former regulars had attached themselves elsewhere, inevitably, and the competition between City churches had become more intense as the number of people wanting anything from us declined. I wasn't going to compete with those churches that had a handful on a Sunday morning – what good would it do the Kingdom of God if I poached one or two from each? I should of course recommence our splendid organ recitals on a Friday, and decided that Thursday would be a good day for my Sung Eucharist with the finest old Masses sung in English; but what else? My philosophy had always been not to beg for support for what was not much wanted, but to identify a crying need and fill it – hence The Samaritans. Time alone would tell what people wanted that wasn't being supplied.

Tuppy introduced me to Vieta, a Nichiren Buddhist to whom I taught counselling and who keeps me from getting into an ecclesiastical rut.

There were two sad things: the arrival in the garden in May of Henry Moore's beautiful sundial, with a gold bowstring as the gnomon, in memory of Denia Palumbo; and the funeral in the church, in July, which we hastily made just usable, of Rudolph Palumbo, Peter's father. I had been a friend of Rudolph, my nearest neighbour (in fact, at first I'd thought his charming Georgian office at 37a Walbrook was the Rectory) since a few days after my arrival in 1953, and we had taken to one another straight away. Peter, his only son, was at Eton, and he was very proud of him, but as so often happens, was more likely to say this to me than to the boy. When I got to know Peter he was at Oxford reading law at Worcester and playing polo for the University. My growing friendship with him was welcomed by Rudolph, who continued to treat me and Susan as 'family'. We were both very fond of him and kept in frequent touch by telephone. The day of his death was, cruelly, the day Peter received an adverse verdict on his proposed building by James Sterling in place of the one by Mies, and he knew that he had yet another fight on his hands.

At long last it was September, the month for which the Bishop had been booked a whole year. We had a PCC meeting and rehearsals and an open day for the Church Rate-payers. So all was set for the three re-dedication services: for the Lord Mayor, attending in State, on the 24th; the City clergy and the Ward on the 25th; and The Samaritans on the 26th. Then disaster struck.

On the eve of the Big Day I was crossing Butterwick at Hammersmith in front of a stationary bus. I heard a woman scream, and saw the bus a yard from me, out of the corner of my left eye – it had suddenly started and swooped at me. I knew this was death, and that I couldn't leap clear. But my guardian angel hurled me forward: I fell with my whole weight on my left wrist, and instinctively drew up my knees so that the bus wouldn't go over my legs. Astonished to be alive, I was helped up by an Inspector who had seen the whole thing, and was relieved that I wasn't going to sue the inattentive driver.

Nigel Dempster's headline was: *Egad, Chad! That was close*!

In great pain, and somewhat shocked, I was able to attend the re-dedication, and the consecration of the Henry Moore altar, but of course wasn't able to administer a chalice.

In his sermon, the Bishop did not mention Peter's generosity, nor the work of the Restoration Fund Committee, nor the Lord Mayor's encouragement to his parish church, nor our Patrons, the Grocers'

Company, nor Christopher Wren, nor Henry Moore, nor our architect Robert Potter, nor the contractors and craftsmen, nor the American Express Foundation, nor the organ and choir, nor the mission of a City church, nor The Samaritans, nor their Founder. He did, however, seem pleased that we used the Prayer Book.

The following day I had the great joy of celebrating the Eucharist at the Henry Moore altar and had the opportunity to thank all those I thought ought to be thanked.

The final event, on the Saturday afternoon, was a very informal one for any Samaritans who were able to attend, and for whom, whether they were Christians or not, St Stephen Walbrook was always to be loved as their birthplace.

The following day I did what I'd said on *Wogan* I would do on a Sunday, and preached for eight minutes at 1.05 and 1.35. Alas, the interval had been too great: people had forgotten, and few came. 'Monday School' the next day, which I'd defined as Sunday-School-on-a-Monday for intelligent adults, at 1.05 and 5.05, was also sparsely attended, and after a few weeks I had to abandon it.

My wrist was swollen and painful, so Peter sent me to Jean Clayton for physiotherapy ('H'm, why the delay?'), and it is thanks to him and to her that I now have full use of it.

On 9 October The Samaritans had a farewell-to-the-crypt party, and the following day moved to their commodious new centre in Soho. Their many lines were changed in 1991 to 071–734 2800.

The week after the Lord Mayor's Show was hospital week for us: Susan to Charing Cross with glaucoma, Charles to Princess Grace for a spine operation, and me to the National, Queen Square, where Dr Schott told me that, as I'd have to have botulin toxin injections round my eyes every few months for the rest of my life, I'd better be slotted into Dr Lees' clinic on the National Health. I'm still benefiting from that wise advice. The injections are painful, but worth it.

That week was also the one in which John Donat, son of Robert Donat the film actor, spent a whole day taking the beautiful photographs of the church which were used for our picture postcards. One of them in this book between pages 224 and 225.

On 2 November, The Samaritans' anniversary, I joined HRH The Duchess of Kent in front of the Mansion House to see off a Dennis Fire Engine crewed by half a dozen young men and two beautiful girls, who were going to drive it from North Cape to Cape Town to raise money for The Samaritans, calling at Branches of BI on the way. Unfortunately they missed Oporto, Coimbra, Bloemfontein and Kimberley, but what really mattered was that Chelsea Renton was badly burned in an accident in the Sahara and had to be flown home. She was amazingly brave, and is now back at work.

By December I'd reduced the Sunday sermonettes to one and given up the Monday School, but I made a point of giving a talk to all the groups who visited the church. Our Friday organ recitals were immensely popular, but we hadn't yet found how this lovely church could once again be used *as* a church, once a week at least. There were baptisms, weddings, memorial services and Livery services, but nothing regular – unless you count the Ward Service, held once a year. Correspondence, and visits from Samaritans from near and far, kept me busy, but I still longed for the Sung Eucharists we used to have, with the unaccompanied early Masses in English.

I've mentioned before what a burden correspondence is, but it became impossible when I had to be constantly away from my desk showing and guarding the church. As usual, the person who came to the rescue was Peter. When the National Safe Deposit which he owned was compulsorily purchased (in the Mansion House refurbishment its Court is to be transferred to the triangular building opposite), the employees were faced with redundancy. Peter, the most considerate employer imaginable, made arrangements for all who wanted to stay. One, Mr John Salter, he gave me as Security Guard. I can't imagine the job being better done than he does it, and because of him I'm now able to spend much more time at my desk.

On 1 May 1988 I was invited to preach at Magdalene College, Cambridge, which since 1954 had shared the patronage of my benefice with the Grocers' Company, and which by chance was creeping towards a majority amongst our churchwardens: Gerard Dent, former Master Grocer; Alderman Paul Newall, of our Ward; Sir Derman Christopherson, former Master (now retired); and the late Lord De L'Isle; to whom must be added our Treasurer, Charles Empson. I've had warm feelings for Magdalene ever since they gave C.S. Lewis a status which Magdalen College, Oxford hadn't given him.

On the Ascension Day Eric Evans was installed as Dean of St Paul's. He had long ago helped to start our Branch No. 9, in Bournemouth.

I took a Whitsun holiday at La Gazelle d'Or at Taroudannt, Morocco, and spent most of my time revising my book *The Samari-*

357

tans: Befriending the Suicidal. Soon after my return, fit as a violin, my son Andrew, who had become secretary of the Bespoke Furniture-makers' Association, borrowed the church for a 'Percipio' exhibition of craftsmanship called 'In Search of Magic'. It was an eye-opener to me and to those who came in off the street.

I'd tried preceding the 1 o'clock sermon on Sunday with Holy Communion at 12.30 for late risers, but that didn't attract a congregation either, so I abandoned Sundays, and faced the fact that the City dies at weekends and the best day to build up a service would be Thursday.

On 5 July I had the honour of being invited to preach at the annual Election Service of the Worshipful Company of Grocers, for the first time. Then the day after I preached at St Paul's the Cathedral was full of Bishops for the Lambeth Conference service, and as senior Prebendary present I said the vestry prayer. Now that I had practically given up counselling, I was becoming more and more a parson, and less and less a Samaritan – though we *had* had a Samaritans' Reception at Mansion House the previous week, and the following week I was on Radio 2 with my friend Claire Rayner. And I did of course attend the York Conference in September. After it, I went up to Blackburn to preach at Holy Trinity, not in the church but in the red-brick worship centre which was my successor's vicarage. I stayed with Ruth, widow of my loyal churchwarden Reg Rozee, and was chauffeured by their daughter Jean. The change in church life in forty years was poignantly demonstrated by the change from a congregation nearly filling a large church to one a room in a house could hold on a special occasion.

At St Stephen Walbrook our musical tradition was now to be revived: on Thursdays we were to have a Sung Eucharist with singers from Polyphony of London conducted by Stephen Layton, former Organ Scholar of King's, Cambridge. This was a most magnanimous seventy-seventh birthday present from Peter, which continues to give me greater spiritual satisfaction than anything else.

Something exciting was to happen before January 1989 was out. Glasnost had allowed a concerned young journalist, Natasha Boyarkina, to write openly at last in *Komsomolskaya Pravda* of the dreadful waste of young lives by suicide. Mrs Eugenia Donde of the BBC Russian Service, and I, prepared a response, commending the methods of The Samaritans in reducing suicide. We broadcast it on

6 February, and I did the most personal paragraph myself in my by-now rusty Russian. The response was a warm invitation from the Foundation for Social Inventions to me and another Samaritan to visit Moscow, all expenses paid. We then found it impossible to fix a date, and by the time we had fixed one, my intended companion, Anne Aston of Singapore, had had to go home as her ticket had expired. Eventually, by phoning Natasha, I discovered that shortage of hard currency had embarrassed Mr Alferov of FFSI, so I got her to inform him that I would pay my air fare and pay for a modest hostelry if they would be responsible for meals, transportation, hire of halls and such-like. This was agreed to with alacrity, and we had only to fix a date for me to go on my own.

On 9 March I had an honour I thought I hardly deserved: I was invited to deliver the annual Springfield Lecture at Graylingwell Post-Graduate Medical Centre attached to St Richard's Hospital, Chichester. I asked one of the leading psychiatrists to improve my text afterwards, and he added eight words.

Life goes on and so does death. On Wednesday in Holy Week I took the funeral service in my church of my dear friend and colleague Marcus Morris, and the cremation at Mortlake. As he was a priest, I had them place the coffin with head towards the altar, as the old custom was.

On 22 April I went to Lincoln to speak at the British Legal Association meeting, and took the opportunity of being in Eastgate to visit the nearby cemetery to look for the grave of the little girl whose body I'd buried there fifty-three and a half years before, but there was no trace of it.

Marcus's Memorial Service crowded St Bride's Fleet Street on the Ascension Day and there were many old colleagues to greet. ('Chad, do you remember the only time you were on the top of a *'bus* with Marcus and you were both for once wearing *dog*-collars' – Dewi Morgan must have had something at St Bride's, where we were both Chaplains of the Guild – 'and Marcus was planning your next story for the back page of *Girl*? He said he'd like you to *do* Ruth, and you said she was a lovely girl but you didn't find her strippable, and Marcus said if anyone could strip her in a really exciting way, you could, and two *prim* ladies turned round and saw two parsons and were outraged?' I was glad to be reminded – 'strippable' in the trade means 'patient of having his or her story told in strip-cartoon form'.)

I flew to Moscow on 12 May by BA 872 and was met by the

founder and other members of the Moscow 'Hotline' and Natasha Boyarkina. They had come in two cars, and drove me at once to my 'modest hostelry', which turned out to be Gostinitsa Sovyetskaya, the same VIP hotel where the Patriarch had lodged me in 1955 – in fact, I think I still had the same room, but now *I'd* be paying the £70 a night. They all gathered in my room to take refreshment and two of the three suitcases I'd brought with me, and to tell me of my programme. I was to visit the hotline founded eight years before and speak to them for six hours (of which half would be interpretation by Eugene).

On the Sunday I said I wanted to go to church and was taken to the Troitsa Church up in the Moscow hills, where after the service I found the choirmistress in the garden and presented her with the second volume of the Russian Church Music published by me (I had a copy of the first volume with me to present to the Patriarch). She was delighted with it, and fetched from the vestry a photocopy of my first volume – I'd sent it by my friend Michael Ramsey when he was Archbishop of Canterbury and invited the Russian Church to 'pirate' it. 'We use this every Sunday!' she said. 'We owe so much to Otets Chad Varah – I should so like to be able to thank him personally.' You may guess that I then embraced her. Later I was taken to visit the Novodevichi Monastery, and took part in a service; the Patriarch was away, but one of his staff took my book for him.

I was taken to the Crisis Clinic, where young people who had attempted suicide were helped as in-patients under a truly Samaritan type of woman, Galina. I was allowed to speak to about half the patients, with Alexander Poleev interpreting for me: afterwards they came up to me one by one and embraced me. I found it very moving.

I then had a wonderful consultation with the staff over a very long lunch, after which they asked me to interview one male and one female patient (who had volunteered for this) in the hearing of them all. Galina said afterwards that the woman had benefited greatly from an interview with someone who didn't know her history and whose style was so personal.

The next day was the big event, namely a lecture by me to psychiatrists and psychiatric nurses in the suicidology department of the Psychiatric Institute. I could not repress a shudder as I entered this infamous building where dissidents were punished with psycho-delotic drugs, but up on the sixth floor screams from the cellars wouldn't have been heard if this still continued. About 150 men and women made up the white-coated audience, with my friends in the front row, one of them armed with my rarely used cine-camera. A 'deputy director' was in the Chair: I suspected him of being the party stooge, if not KGB. A professional interpreter did a good job. I'd been given an hour and a half, of which half was for translation, so at the end of forty-five minutes I said: 'My time is up. I'm only about half-way through, but I think I'd better stop and invite questions.'

Five hands shot up. All five questions were the same: 'Why don't you complete your lecture, and then have questions?' I happily did so. After a couple of innocuous questions, a man in the back row asked what was my attitude to homosexuality and to sexual deviations? As you may imagine, I greatly welcomed this question, as I knew that homosexuality was severely punished in the USSR, or rather, didn't exist, but would have been very illegal if it *had* existed. Soon after I began my answer, my interpreter said she didn't know the technical words I was using, but Alexander came up and took her place for that question. You know already what my line on this subject was, and I didn't tone it down, nor did I try to shorten my reply.

As soon as I *did* sit down, the chairman said firmly, 'Since only one person was interested in that subject, we will now have questions on other subjects.' With difficulty I restrained myself from saying, 'You witless apparatchik, how do you suppose you can pass yourself off as any kind of a scientist if you deny the evidence of your senses? Seven-eighths of the audience were leaning forward, anxious not to miss a word!' Instead, I thanked Alexander and used the official interpreter for the remainder of the session.

Dr Ambrumova promised to send two young English-speaking hotline workers to our annual conference in September, but I suspected she wouldn't – and she didn't, that year or the next. Mind you, she must have needed determination and perseverance to start a suicide hotline in the conditions of 1981, and of the people she employed, those I met had been excellent. Back in London, I reported to Vanda, and we began the lengthy procedures involved in inviting Soviet citizens.

On 8 June we had a service at St Paul's to celebrate 800 years of the Mayoralty of London and the next day I set off for the IASP Congress in Brussels. Soon after my return, I met Dr 'Tiki' Tamura and his wife Yuko to discuss the setting up in the Central London

Branch of a Japanese-speaking line. This was established and still continues, though Tiki and Yuko returned to Japan in August 1991.

The time had come for my Alderman, Mr Paul Newall, to serve (if elected) as Sheriff of the City of London, a much older office than the Mayoralty. He was gracious enough to invite me to be his chaplain. I hadn't had this honour since 1960–61. My Alderman was duly elected. I would attend him on all important City occasions, wearing silver-buckled shoes, silk socks, cassock, gown, scarf, bands, tricorn hat and white gloves.

On 6 October I opened the Deaf Line at the Putney Branch. It, and Bolton to serve the north, had been provided with a machine which allowed deaf people wanting to ring The Samaritans to type their messages. These were displayed to the volunteer who could type the reply. The official ceremony was at Telecom Tower, but I wanted to be with Samaritans who would actually do the work.

On 8 November there were rehearsals of the Silent Ceremony and the ceremony at the Law Courts, followed by the Lighting-up Dinner at Guildhall; then two days later luncheon at the Mansion House before going to Guildhall to admit the Lord Mayor (the 'Silent Ceremony', most impressive; none of us made any mistakes).

Then on Saturday the 11th it was the Lord Mayor's Show, at which I rode with my Sheriff in his carriage, and Susan sat and watched from the balcony at the Mansion House, and also accompanied me the following evening to the Banquet at Guildhall.

On 13 December our Lodovico Cardi *Adoration of the Magi*, which had been beautifully restored and put in a contemporary frame, was re-hung in the church, and two days later we put in position on either side of the Henry Moore altar the beautiful brown earthenware candleholders by the famous Hans Coper, which Peter had bought to go there because he knew Henry Moore had admired them in his life-time. We bring them out only on great occasions, one of which was the day of the baptism of Petra Louise Palumbo, a glorious occasion with marvellous music. HRH The Duchess of York was one of the godmothers.

On 11 January 1990 was my Big Chance. As Aldermanic Sheriff's Chaplain, it was my duty to preach at St Lawrence Jewry to the Lord Mayor and Corporation. I assumed God wanted me to be a prophet for the occasion. As to whether I was, you must ask someone else. Catherine Ennis played the organ.

I wanted our hotline colleagues in Moscow to meet some typical volunteers, so I found a convenient package tour and chose eleven English Samaritans to come with me on it. We were booked to go on 27 January. When I mentioned this at home, the daughters-in-law and sisters-in-law present began to chorus, 'Chad, you are not, repeat NOT, going to Moscow on 27 January.'

'Oh yes, I am,' I told them.

'Oh no, you aren't,' they persisted.

After a bit of this, I said, 'Let's stop imitating prep school boys – *why* do you think I'll be persuaded to let eleven Samaritans go without me?'

'Because', they said, 'it's your wedding anniversary, and we're having a party at Michael's house.'

'You must have it without me,' I said. 'I've had lots of wedding anniversaries, and I've often remembered them.'

'Yes,' burst in Susan triumphantly, 'you've had *lots*. Forty-nine in fact.' Slowly it dawned on me. 'Yes,' chanted the chorus, 'it's your Golden Wedding and you are NOT going to Moscow that day.'

Those who did go to Moscow were led by my young churchwarden Anita Harding. They all enjoyed the visit and were glad to see the Crisis Clinic, but were disappointed that they weren't allowed to visit the hotline Centre (for fear invitations might be exchanged?).

There was a happy ending. Among the eighty Samaritans from overseas who joined 1,200 from the British Isles at York in September '91 were two from Moscow, Alekper and Sergei, who had come independently.

We had a splendid anniversary party in a marquee on Michael's lawn at Woking, with seventy of our extended family, nearly all except the North American ones. Tables were arranged so that no one was with spouse or sibling, and half-way through wives swapped with husbands and sisters with brothers, so we all renewed acquaintances well. Or made them: Lucy had never met Melissa, for instance, and they loved one another in a trice. Those of us who had the sense drank magnums of Haut-Brion.

Love-Line, our Branch in Seoul, was celebrating its tenth anniversary and invited Samaritans from all over the world. I said I would represent BI, as none of the others could get away, and booked a wonderful discount ticket via Frankfurt with Korean Airlines several weeks ahead.

Before setting out on 11 June, I checked the Frankfurt flight, but not, I'm ashamed to say, the continuation, with the result that I arrived in Frankfurt to find the Seoul flight had been changed at the beginning of June and had already gone. The next one my ticket would cover was the next day, arriving too late for the seminar, at which I was to speak no fewer than three times. The Lufthansa girl was splendid once she knew it didn't matter what it cost. She got my luggage rescued and rushed me to a JAL flight for Tokyo, where I could connect with a flight arriving Seoul at 9.20 p.m. the next day, if I wouldn't mind an extra £1,400. It was wonderful to wake over Siberia in the middle of the night and see some forest fires, and a little later to recognize Lake Baikal, before cloud obscured the view and I went back to sleep. The hostesses were so pleased I'd chosen Suntory (Japanese) whisky that they kept bringing it − it was surprisingly good.

After waiting all afternoon in vain, the welcome party from Love-Line had gone back to the hotel and hadn't received my cable because it wasn't Hotel Lotte this time, but New Naija. I found this out by becoming a caller in distress; then a taxi took me to where Shim Chul-ho, Han Sang-yup and other dear friends were waiting anxiously outside, cheering with relief that their chief speaker wouldn't be missing the next morning. What a fool I was not to remember that airline timetables change in June.

It was disappointing for Love-Line that no one came from the Americas except two girls from Brazil, no one from Asia except from Osaka, an hour away, and Jessamine Doe from Hong Kong; no one from Africa or Australasia; and no one from Europe except me. But those of us who *were* there had a wonderful four days, after which I had an even busier four days at our Branch in Osaka. My original discount ticket was available for my flight back on the 19th.

On the 25th my year as Sheriff's Chaplain terminated.

On the 30th at St Stephen Walbrook I had the great joy of blessing the marriage of my son Andrew to charming and talented Helen King.

On 16 July I was invited to preach at Aldershot, in the presence of HRH The Princess Alice, Duchess of Gloucester, for the Royal Corps of Transport, with which the Carmen's Company is closely connected.

*

There can be no doubt that the biggest and happiest event of 1990 was the Flower Festival in the church, arranged by the Lady Mayoress, Lady Bidwell, Lady Morse and her other helpers. No one had ever seen anything like it. Crowds came to see it, including passersby who couldn't resist the entrance arrangements. The entire building became a bower, and the scent was heavenly. At the end, surviving flowers were sold on the pavement. With this and sponsorships, a great deal was raised for the Lord Mayor's charities.

At York, Sheila Coggrave, the new Chairman, had me to chair the final Plenary and to speak. I compared The Samaritans to the TV programme *Casualty*, where those in most danger get first attention, and Sheila has developed this idea in a way which we hope will employ more usefully, from the point of view of suicide-prevention, the millions of hours given by our volunteers, some of which are wasted and some doing more harm than good. The ensuing debate has concentrated minds wonderfully.

Peter Palumbo had never been content simply (simply!) to restore the church. He had always intended to convert the crypt to vestries and remove the concrete entrance built for The Samaritans. This work began on 22 October. When it was completed, the church tower was covered with scaffolding and sand blasted. This revealed that much stone needed to be replaced.

It pleased me very much to be invited to go to the University of Bath the weekend of 15 December to take a seminar on sex for the National Night Line conference. Although Night Line is independent of The Samaritans and its function is different, we feel we have a lot in common with these students.

On 16 December there was a magical occasion at Westminster Cathedral, where the annual Carol Service had been dedicated to The Samaritans and HRH The Duchess of Kent and Chairman Sheila and I were special guests. Cardinal Hume was most gracious to us.

On 24 June 1991, those of us who were concerned with the christening next day of Peter and Hayat's second daughter Lana (it means 'ours') were invited to dinner by Richard and Ruthie Rogers in the house they had built. The christening was once again simple and dignified, with joyous music.

Two days later I set off for Beijing for ten days, with the aim of visiting the two hotlines we had been in correspondence with, to see if they were suitable to be linked with The Samaritans, and in any case to see if there was any way we could help them. I kept hoping we should have better luck than we'd had in Moscow, and this hope was fulfilled. Almost all the people I met were young: I was particularly impressed with the students running youth and teenage hotlines in Beijing and in Hangzhou, which I also visited.

On 15 July Robin and Louella's Pimlico Opera at the Royal Geographical Society in aid of Survival International was *Falstaff*, which I'd never seen before and much enjoyed. On 17 July I attended the AGM of CLB, with no intention of speaking, but when the counting of votes for the committee was prolonged, young Chairman Sarah asked me to fill the gap, and I told them about the KGB non-nun in this book, and about my heartening visit to China.

On 14 September I sat in my prebendal stall for the enthronement of David Hope as the 131st Bishop of London: the sixth to whom I have sworn canonical obedience. A banner outside proclaimed *Hope for the World*: I couldn't help thinking 'Hope for London' would have suited the occasion better. It would hardly have been practicable to refer to 'the eighteen boroughs which comprise the diocese of London'. I took Susan to the service, but of course *she* belongs to the diocese of Southwark, as we live south of the river.

On 17 September I went to York, as I do almost every year, for the Samaritans' conference, which now has extra days for those members of Befrienders International who come from outside the British Isles. I was given a difficult assignment: a seminar on the listening therapy I have named befriending, with an examination of the psychodynamics of it. I was very touched to be presented with an album containing hundreds of advance greetings for my eightieth birthday.

As I finish this book, which contains about two thirds of what I wrote and originally hoped to include, I have attained my eightieth birthday. The celebration on 12 November 1991 was arranged in my church by Befrienders International as a reception for the Patrons and other benefactors, headed by our Royal Patron, HRH The Duchess of Kent. They asked the internationally famous soprano Ann Mackay to give a recital, which she generously did without fee, accompanied by Julius Drake. She included some of my favourite songs, including three by Sibelius which I had translated for her from the Swedish. Rosemary 1662 did the catering and provided a rich cake which HRH helped me to cut. The following evening the Parochial Church Council attended a Sung Eucharist at the Henry Moore altar, when our choir, Polyphony, sang Monteverdi's Messa da Cappella and Messiaen's 'O Sacrum Convivium' and the choirmaster Stephen Layton played Bach's A minor prelude, after which we had a party in the Lord Palumbo room. The previous Saturday my wife Susan gave me a party in our home attended by all our children and grandchildren. 'CLB' gave me a party on 1 November at Grocers' Hall, where I was touched to find, in addition to current Samaritans, a good many from the early days, all of whom I remembered by name and number. Director Sian Greenbury presented me with a generous cheque (for the Chad Varah Bursary Fund of BI) and a bottle of vintage port to go with the ones sent by my dear Oporto Branch.

Several personal friends entertained me to lavish lunches and dinners. Letters, cards and telemessages flowed in from near and far, the nearest being the new Lord Mayor, Sir Brian Jenkins GBE, and the Master Grocer, Mr John Trotter, and the furthest being from as far as you can get, BINZ. It gave me particular pleasure to receive many large cards signed by all or nearly all the volunteers in a particular branch, and exotic cards with loving greetings in other languages or sometimes laborious English, of which the one that touched me most (from Brazil) read as follows: 'Congratulations for one more moment in your life. You have demonstrated me who the be human haven't limits when fetches to hear to yourself and everybody. Many thanks, for you exist.'

The Sunday before my birthday the Sunday Times concluded its eight-part '1000 makers of the 20th century', and I was included under V. This was a great honour, and I was well aware that my discovery of the listening therapy we call befriending, however valid, could not have proved the most effective means of suicide-prevention but for the unsung devoted practice of it by tens of thousands of Samaritans. If I have to any degree changed the world for good in this century, it has been through those who have done the work day and night and are still doing it.

The same day, Radio 4's 'Sunday' programme broadcast some of my thoughts, preceded by generous praise from Lord Palumbo and followed by the assurance from Simon Armson that there would always be a place for the Founder, whose advice was valued and who 'tells us when we aren't doing well.' I made an octogenarian resolution: in future I will confidently leave them to get on with it under Pieter De Bruijn of Harare, Zimbabwe, Chairman of BI, with

Vanda Scott as General Director, and in the British Isles Sheila Coggrave as Chairman of The Samaritans and Simon as Chief Executive. I can't tell them only when they *are* doing well as this is almost all the time.

In December the decision was made to repair the spire of the church.

The last event I want to record was one of the happiest. On December 14th I officiated at the wedding of Annabella Palumbo to Hugh Adams in St Stephen Walbrook, where I had baptised her in infancy. HRH The Duchess of York brought her two daughters: Princess Beatrice was one of the four small bridesmaids with the little page. It was a delightful reception at Grocers' Hall, where we have always felt at home.

At the time of writing, January 1992, I don't feel as though I'm ready to die (again) yet. I keep surprisingly well, thank God; I work a fifty-hour week on average, travelling eighteen miles a day by public transport; I still *care* very passionately about human suffering, and would like to continue to do something to alleviate it, on however modest a scale.

If you ask me what I most want to do in this regard, I think my answer may suprise you. I want to help to abolish the mutilation of the genitals of little girls, which happens to millions of them, mostly in Muslim countries and mostly in Africa, and is also happening in our own country, to our shame.

It is very difficult to get any public discussion of this question. People are afraid of offending those who shrilly and mindlessly denounce any interference with minority 'cultures', even though it has no place in Islam and is not enjoined by the Koran, but is a cruel and barbaric practice kept alive by malicious and avaricious old women. But in a country which has earls instead of counts, because the latter too closely resembles the most embarrassing of all four-lettered words, the subject is bound to be dismissed as 'not quayte nayce'. Well, I have spent my entire ministry dealing with what is 'not quayte nayce', and if I can't take this crusade up, who can? I should like to start an organization called MAGMOG. The acronym is for 'Men Against Genital Mutilation of Girls'.

Attempts to persuade women not to allow their daughters to be mutilated have largely failed, though brave souls are continuing the struggle in Ealing and elsewhere. In the Muslim world, men have, for better or worse, all the power, and my idea is to make use of this by persuading the men that they are being done out of their birthright if they have no choice but to marry a woman of their own community who instead of the beautiful genital organ which God so ingeniously contrived for her, has an ugly wound which the man's penis cannot penetrate without causing her agony. My researches show that Muslim men of the nationalities concerned *are* capable of being attracted to the idea of marrying a woman who can enjoy sexual intercourse and make it more exciting for them by being responsive. Indeed, some such men have had sexual experiences with Western women who have not been mutilated, and freely admit that they prefer it.

It may sound odd to say that Christians should keep safely any 'hard core' porno pictures they come across in order to pass them on to Muslim men whose womenfolk are likely to have been mutilated in infancy or early childhood. I have nothing but the bitterest contempt for the anti-porn campaigners who would rather baby girls should suffer the horrible torture which is done to them in, for instance, Somalia, than have pictures circulating which might excite men to masturbation (and why not?). As for those who say we should not interfere with the culture in which this barbaric practice has grown up, I would reply that it is not I but God who condemns it and that His curse must surely be upon all who practise or defend it. That curse might well take the form of being born the next time not only as an African woman, which is bad enough, but as an African Muslim woman in one of the countries where a little girl's mother and aunt hold her down with legs wide apart while an evil woman with a rusty knife or a sharp flint cuts away the inner labia and the clitoris and scrapes away all the tissue from the inside of the outer labia and then stitches these together leaving only a small hole for urination and menstruation. *This must end.*

It is a greater disgrace than suttee in India, which we abolished, and equal to child-bride murder-for-dowry, which we have no power to abolish. We do not govern the countries where this abomination of female genital mutilation persists, but it is shameful if we do not vociferously condemn it in the UN under Human Rights. What we can and must do is to stamp it out in this country, by prosecuting for child sexual abuse any who perform or consent to the operation and by enacting that any girl-children sent to a

369

country where it is practised to be thus mutilated shall not be allowed to return to this country (this will require genital inspection of returning children).

MAGMOG will urge men not to marry a mutilated girl but to insist on evidence of their bride's unmutilated state before marrying. This may seem hard on the mutilated girl unless you have enough imagination to see how much better her life would be without intrusion into her wound than in submitting to the torture of a man's conjugal rights. Men enabled by MAGMOG to have a happy sexual partner may be invited to contribute to the upkeep of unmarriageable girls or to offer them a home free of sexual obligations.

Of course, I may not live to see this through, or even begun. But before I die (again) I hope to save some little girls from a fate worse than death. As I am still getting on with the duties of this incarnation, I should like you, when the Inspector of Anatomy sends for my corpse, to finish this book, and my work, for me. So I will stop in the middle of this sentence and thank you for

NOT THE END

Index

MEMBERS OF BRANCH NO. I

2 Vivien, 193, 214, 279
3 Mary, 279
13 Barry, 280
44 Roger, 193, 234
61 Paul, 164
62 Rowena, 164
63 Ilse, 164
75 George, 193, 279
181 Mary, 216–9
200 Jennifer, 228
219 Jean, 81, 193, 209, 211–2, 238
235 Caroline, 228
250 John, 159, 190, 237
260 Mary, 190, 237–8
328 Jean, 238
332 Eric, 190
352 Nadir, 228, 236, 260, 311, 323, 327, 331, 335, 341
481 Leslie, 234, 237
505 Daphne, 234, 236
585 Godfrey, 279, 285–6
600 Diana, 279
606 Ann, 236
683 Mary, 285
700 Anna, 296
716 Dorothy, 283–5
874 Liz, 283–5, 327
990 Bill, 286
993 Rosemary, 335
1000 David, 286
1005 Norman, 286
1066 Corinne, 286
1100 Michael, 286
1134 Rex, 311, 314
1219 Margie, 327, 331
1345 Win, 330
1385 Amanda, 327
1493 Anita, 363
1500 'Miranda', 290
1662 Rosemary, 366
2772 Sarah, 366

ORGANISATIONS
Befrienders International, 189–90, 313–4, 316–7, 322, 335, 345, 348, 357, 363, 366–7
Council of Management, 313, 315, 346

IASP, 322, 345, 361
Love Line, 363–4
Sumithrayo, 328
The Befrienders, 322, 341
The Samaritans, 99, 156, 158–60, 165, 167–71, 176, 182, 184–6, 188, 190–1, 193, 206, 208, 211, 221, 224–5, 228, 232, 237–41, 252, 260, 267, 270, 276–7, 282–3, 286–92, 294, 296, 299, 303–4, 307–8, 311, 313–4, 316–7, 320–3, 324, 327–8, 331, 334–5, 338, 344–5, 348, 354–8, 362, 365, 367
The Samaritans Inc., 234–6, 238–9

PEOPLE
Abbott, Very Rev Eric, 42, 47
Abercrombie, Leslie, 156
Acland, Sir Richard, 73
Agu, Maureen, 322, 327
'Albert', 272–3
Alekper, 363
Alexander, 231
Alexii, Patriarch, 193, 196, 202, 205
Alferov, 359
Alice, HRH Princess, 364
Alima, Ma, 341
Allen, Godfrey, 152, 156
Ambrumova, Dr, 361
Andrews, Eamonn, 15, 50
Anne, HRH Princess, 349
Anseele, Eduard, 71
Appleton, Bp George, 303
Arkell, Marianne, 311
Arkell, Tom, 311
Armson, Simon, 367
Armstrong, Peter, 288
Arnott, Bp Felix, 242
Arthur, David, 232
Arup, Ove, 332
Ashcroft, Dame Peggy, 55
Ashdown, Bp Hugh, 77
Ashwell Wood, L., 141
Askwith, Bp Wilfred, 121
Asquith, Anthony, 101
Aston, Anne, 46, 359
Atkinson, Marie, 15
Aubert, Astrid, 51

Bach, J. S., 65
Baedeker, K, 72
Baker, 54
Baker, Bp John, 245–6
Bakker, Pastoor, 86
Balaszeskul, Ellen N., 316
Ballantyne, R. M., 22
Barton, Dr, 31
Bax, Arnold, 119
Baxter, Miss, 102
Beake, Mrs, 51, 92
Beatrice, HRH Princess, 368
Beattie, Jackie, 294
Beneš, Eduard, 94
Bernhardt, Sarah, 281
Bezruč, 50
Bhabha, Dr Amy, 260
Bhabha, Coovedji, 260
Bhabha, Kurshedji, 260
Bhabha, Naju, 260
Bidwell, Jenefer, 365
'Big', Mr, 277–8
Billig, Dr David, 323
Birtwhistle, Dr Percy, 34
Björnson, Björnstierne, 52
Blackie, ArchD, 75
Blackie, Prof James, 166, 228
Blackwell, Basil, 48, 58
Bloom, 'Farmer', 76
Bohlsen, Paul, 297
Boodell, Joe, 42
Bourne, Rev Christopher, 196, 201
Boyarkina, Natalia, 358–60
Boyd, 31
Boyd-Carpenter, John, 48
Boydell, Peter, QC, 333
'Bree Daniel', 302, 311, 320–2, 324–6
Březina, 50
Brierley, Betty, 113
Brierley, Cyril, 113, 117
Brittain, Doug, 30
Broatch, Liz, 253–6
Broomberg, Dave, 294
Browne, Anne, 296
Broza-Levin, Ruth, 323
Bruce, Mary, 190–1
Burger, Bruno, 303, 316
'Buz', 39
Byron, Lord, 22

Cabell, J. B., 41
Callaghan, Leybourne, 329
Callaghan, Rev Sidney, 234
Cameron, Duncan, 152
Cameron, Suzan, 320, 324, 327, 341–2, 347
Campbell, Miss, 139
Cantré, Jozef, 71
Cardi, Lodovico, 362

Carpenter, Bp Harry, 53
Carr-Gomm, Richard, 238
Carritt, David, 60
Carritt, E. F. 59–62
Carstairs, Prof Morris, 234
Casalis, Jean, 231
Casper, Sally, 312
Cauffield-Stoker, 57
Cézanne, 322
Chamberlain, Neville, 93
Chan, Mr 243
Chan Wah-Lok, 242–3, 269
Chapman, Jane, 340
Charlie, Uncle, 25, 49
'Charmian', 273
Chase, Rev Stephen, 76
Chaucer, 30
Chen Hua Loh, 242
Chipudhla, Joseph, 312
Christ, 353
Christie's, 346–7
Christison, Sandy, 33–4
Christopherson, Sir Derman, 357
Chung, Kyung Wha, 340
Churchill, Diana, 334
Churchill, Sir Winston, 162, 277
Clark, Norma, 148
Clark, Rev Roland, 148
Clarke, Arthur C., 134
'Claud', 226–7
Clayton, Jean, 356
Cobham, Alan, 19
Coggrave, Sheila, 365, 367
'Colibri', 173
Conchon, Jacques, 312–3, 322, 331, 339
Cooke, Erica, 297
Coombes, Bill, 258, 349
Coombes, Mrs, 258
Cooper, Fenimore, 22
Cooper, Joseph, 52
Cooper, Mrs, 21–2
Coper, Hans, 362
Cork, Fred, 156
Cork, Jim, 156
Cork, Mrs, 156
Cornelissens, Armand, 62, 70, 72, 74, 86
Cornelissens, Eva, 70
Cornelissens, Heliane, 70
Cornelissens, Tristan, 70
Cotterell, Dr Sandra, 345
Cross, Rev Aidan, 296
Culver, Michael, 288
'Cutie', 31–2, 37

Daddy, 17
Dailey, Fred, 347
Dailey, Murph, 347
Damascinos, ArchBp, 229
Dance, 343

Daniels, Rev R. N., 79, 85
'Dare, Dan', 130, 134–5, 137
Dastoor, Dr Sarah, 229, 260, 329
De Beer, David, 299
De Bono, Edward, 150
De Bruijn, Pieter, 367
De Clercq, René, 71
De Gennaro, Lino, 316
De Keijzer, Maria, 71
De Keijzer, Sidi, 71
Delbridge, Pat, 311, 321
De L'Isle, Viscount, VC, KG, 332, 357
Delius, 55, 93, 306
De Mel, Joan, 328
De Mel, ArchBp Lakdasa, 312, 314, 328, 330
De Mille, Cecil B., 30
Dempster, Nigel, 355
Dent, Gerard, 22, 357
Descartes, 51
De Silva, 'Chummy', 327
Devine, George, 55
Dickens, Charles, 22, 307
Dickens, Monica, 302, 307, 311, 331
Dinshaw, Hilla, 260
Dinshaw, Nadir, 260
Disraeli, 74
Dixon, 'Ginger', 30, 39
Doe, Jessamine, 318, 364
Dollinger, 87
Donaldson, Thelma, 294–5
Donat, John, 356
Donat, Robert, 356
Dondé, Eugenia, 358
Drake, 366
Drakeley, Dorothy, 144
Drakeley, Douglas, 144
Draminski, Andrzej, 346
Drinkwater, John, 47, 119
Dubash, Dinoo, 260
Dublin, Louis I., 306
Dugdale, Miss, 109–110
Dung, Hoo Flung, 243
Dunning, Jessica, 129

Eacott, 30
Eastoe, Harold, 27–8, 62–3, 66
Eccleston, Rev Alan, 109
Eckersley, John, 76
Edward III, 319
Eidem, ArchBp Erling, 97
Einstein, 46
Eldrid, Rev. John, 190–1, 314–6
Ellawalla, Nalini 328
Elliott, Elsie, 228, 243, 317
Emery, Jo, 294, 300
'Emmy-Nell', 120
Empson, Charles, 357
Ennis, Catherine, 362

Enthoven, Tom, 159
Evans, Rev David, 314
Evans, Very Rev Eric, 357
Evans, Rev Stanley, 196, 199, 201, 206
Everett, Kenny, 354

Falkner, J. W., 332
Farnsworth, Mrs, 345
Ferguson, Major Ronald, 331
Ferguson, Susan, 331
Finniston, Sir Edward, 320
Fisher, Miss, 116
Flecker, James Elroy, 55
Fletcher, Molly, 126–7
Fowler, Frank, 347
Fox, Dr R., 91, 234, 236, 238, 306
Frankenstein, 348
Fraser, Dr Joanna, 158
'Fred', 213
Freedman, Dr Al, 307
Freedman, Esther, 307
French, Mr Peter, 319
Friday, Nancy, 338

Gabriel, Archangel, 151
Gale, Dionne, 139
Galina, 340
Garbo, Greta, 200
Geijer, E. G., 53
Gérard, André, 305
Gérard, Francois-Bertrand, 305
Gérard, Marie-Thérèse, 305
Geuter, Frederick, 56, 65
Geuter, 'Mutter', 56
Gibbs-Smith, ArchD, 55
Gibson, Frederick, 145
Gibson, Mr Justice, 333
Gibson, Simon, 147
Gibson, Susan, 145, 147, 336
Gibson, Veronica, 145–7
Gillingham, Rev Frank, 154
Gladstone, 74
Gmeiner, Ilse, 64–5
Goethe, 338
Gooch, Godfrey, 334
Graham, Billy, 154
Green, Canon Bryan, 234
Greenbury, Sian, 367
Grey, Anthony, 330
Grieg, 52
Grimston, Edward, 76
Grove, Valerie, 311
Grut, Irina, 308
Guccione, Bob, 307
Gulbenkian, Calouste, 190, 279, 298, 334

Halliburton, Richard, 251
Halsey, Stephen, 346
Hampson, Frank, 130, 135, 137, 139, 141

373

Hanbury-Tenison, Louella, 327, 350, 366
Hanbury-Tenison, Robin, 350, 366
Han Sang-yup, 364
Harding, Anita, 363
Harding, Joel, 314
Haydn, 344
Heap, Sarah, 291
Heath Robinson, 271
Hemming, Dr James, 136
Hes, Dr, 322
Hicks, Bp Nugent, 78
Higgins, Terrence, 271
Higginson, Rev Basil, 228, 234
Hindle, Albert, 126
Hindle, Mrs, 111
Hine, Bp J. E., 24, 48, 75, 77–8, 291–2
Hine, Violet, 78
Hitler, 72, 93, 99, 106
Hodson, Phillip, 311
Hogarth, David, 22
Hollowday, Mark, 90
Hollowday, Stan, 90
Hollowday, Yana, 90, 92, 107, 308, 327
Holme, Stanford, 54–5
Holme, Thea, 54–5
Holmes, Sherlock, 306
Hood, Robin, 22
Hoodless, Arthur, 28
Hooper, Ann, 311
Hope, Bp David, 366
Hopkinson, Sir Alfred, 103
Hopkinson, Anne, 91, 96, 102–4, 108
Hopkinson, Jenny, 100
Hopkinson, Mary, 294
Hopkinson, Stephan, 76, 91, 94, 96, 99–100, 102–3, 106, 131, 294
Howard, Cynthia, 296
Howard, Euan, 296
Huddlestone, Bp Trevor, 299
Hugh-Jones, Maurice, 53
Hughes, Anne, 142, 299
Hulton, Edward, 132
Hume, Cardinal, 365
Humphreys, Nurse, 108–9, 119
Hurst, Very Rev Walter, 304

Ibsen, 22, 52
Ingeborg, 51, 97
Ingrid, 302
Isherwood, Jimmy, 113, 116–8
Isherwood, Kevin, 115–6, 118
Isherwood, Moira, 113, 115–6, 118

Jackson, Gordon, 288
Jacob, H. P., 33–5
Jameson, Derek, 354
Jammes, Francis, 90
Jenkins, Sir Brian, 367

Jenkins, Megs, 288
Joad, C. E. M., 175
Jolliffe, 54
Jones, Cathy, 331
Jones, Dr Maxwell, 223
Joseph, Sir Keith, 291
Joyce, 53
'June', 266
Junkin, Harry, 287–9

Kant, Immanuel, 50, 58–60
Karadjordjević, 48
Kastenbaum, Dr, 306
Kathleen, 24
Kaunda, Kenneth, 291
Kay, Very Rev William, 108
Keats, 22
Keble, John, 15
Kehr, Rev Otto, 232
Kennedy, Ludovic, 335
Kennedy-Bell, Canon, 131
Kent, HRH The Duchess of, 290, 356, 365–6
Keskanök, 254, 256
Khan, James Magi, 323
Kidd, Rev B. J., 58
Kielanowski, Prof Tadeusz, 191, 316, 346
King, Wearing, 53, 96–8, 100
Kinnock, Neil, 238
Kratsenstein, Beate, 327
Krebbers, Mrs, 70
Kuhn, Catherine, 327
Kurowski, Andrzej, 346

Lagerwij, Bp, 86
Lamartine, Alfonse de, 6
Langford-James, 54
Lasky, Lady, 322
Layton, Stephen, 358, 367
Leach, Donvé, 295
Lebedev, Tatiana, 206
Lee, Keskanök, 254, 256
Lees, Dr, 356
Len, 294
Lenin, 198
Leo XIII, 195
Lepidus, 157
Lermontov, 198
Lewis, C. S., 55, 129, 357
Liddon, 15
Lieven, Prince Leonid, 48, 199
Lillaz, Georges, 167, 231
Lily, 45
Lim, Janet, 290
Livingstone, Dr David, 270
Lloyd, John, 312
Lloyd, Mr Justice, 333
Lomax, Herbert, 119
Lord Mayor, The, 362, 365, 367

'Lorna', 266–7
Losanić, Princess Stanka, 48
Lund, 39
Lupait, 40
Lutyens, 343
Lytton, Lord, 22

McAlister Brew, Miss, 83
MacAndrew, Nick, 332
McClintock, Harris, 54
McDonald, Prof, 345
Machar, 50
Mackay, Ann, 366
McKechnie, Beth, 312, 324
McKechnie, John, 312–3, 324
McLean, Ruari, 135
Maincent, Yanine, 88–90, 114
Major, John, 238
Malcolm, Jacqueline, 297
Malcolm, Mr, 296
Malenkov, 197
Mao Ze Dung, 245, 247, 249
Mar Shimun, The 261
Maries, Michelle, 342–3
Marois, Prof, 335
Marryat, 22
Marsh, Jean, 288
Martonová, Dr Frantiska, 236
Maryam, 301
Mascall, Rev Dr Eric, 77
Matejić, Prince Michael, 42, 48
Meadon, Gilbert, 152, 156
Melissa, 363
Menninger, Karl, 306
Mens, Fr Rémi, 239
Merriman, Dr Basil, 191
Messiaen, 367
Meyersberg, Greta, 308, 312, 330
Milet De St Aubyn, Ap, 126
Millington, George, 334
Milne, Rev Ian, 304
Milner, 39
Moffatt, Rev Dr, 108
Molbs, Lavrinia, 28
Monteverdi, 366
Moore, Henry, 298, 333–4, 338, 347,
    355–6, 362, 366
Morgan, Rev Dewi, 359
Morris, Marcus, 129–33, 135–9, 141, 241,
    319, 359
Morse, Lady, 346, 365
Moses, 174
Mozart, 344
Musgrave, Rev James, 234

Naude, Anna, 295
Naude, Oubaas, 295
Netherlands, HM The Queen of, 338
Newall, Alderman Paul, 347, 357, 362

Newcastle, Duke of, 29, 36
'New South Wales', 222–4
Newton, Isaac, 63
Nikon, ArchBp, 201
Nimeiry, President, 300
Noble, Francis, 76
Noden, Peter, 237
Noffs, Rev Ted, 304
Nowell, Gilbert, 27, 65
Nowell, Harriet, 27, 65
Nowell, Hugh, 107
Nugent, Mr, 118

Oberon, Merle, 200
Obrenović, 48
O'Borne, Bob, 92
O'Borne, Nell, 92, 95–6, 100–1, 107, 347
O'Borne, Percy, 107
Odlum, Dr Doris, 191–3
Oecumenical Patriarch, 230
Oldfield, Miss, 79
Oldridge, Alec, 66–70
Oleg, 199
O'Meara, 39
Orme, Joyce, 84
Orme, Mrs, 84–5
Orme, Sid, 84
Orme, Sidney, 84
Orwell, George, 205
'Ovambo', Fr, 298
Owen, Bp Leslie, 77
Owens, Tuppy, 340, 354

Palmgren, 52
Palmstierna, Baron, 53
Palumbo, The Hon Annabella, 368
Palumbo, Denia, 355
Palumbo, The Lady, 5, 348, 365
Palumbo, The Hon Lana, 365
Palumbo, The Rt Hon Lord, 5, 302, 311,
    320, 327, 331–5, 343, 345–6, 348–9,
    355–7, 362, 365, 367
Palumbo, The Hon Petra, 362
Palumbo, Rudolph, 330, 355
Paree, Fr, 237
Pariiski, Prof, 198, 203
Park, John, 76
Parkes, Dr George, 42, 45, 50–1, 60, 63
Patriarch, The Ecumenical, 230
'Patricia', 267
'Patrick', 267
Pavamani, Premila, 312
Pavamani, Vijayan, 312
Pearn, 134
Pedder, Farida, 327, 329
Pendlebury, Dr, 119–20
Pepys, Bp Christopher, 228
Perry, Canon, 108
Peters, Mr, 132

Pilate, Pontius, 249
Pilkington, Dr Roger, 53, 302
Pitotti, Elena, 322
Plamenac, John, 48
Plimmer, Charlotte, 231
Plimmer, Dennis, 231
Ploeg, Cornelis, 104
Ploeg, Mevrouw, 104
Plzak, Dr Miroslav, 236
Poleyev, Dr Alexander, 360–1
Pollinger, 134
Portland, Duke of, 29
Potter, Robert, 331, 346, 356
Prager, Jack, 312
Price, Fr Hugh, 234
Pusey, 15
Pushkin, 199

Queen, HM The, 347, 349
Quibell, Mr, 93

Rachel, 109
Rachmaninov, 28–9, 52, 91
Radcliffe, 49
Rainsborough, Mr & Mrs, 253, 256–7
Rajneesh, 65, 327, 341–2
'Ramona', 271–2, 274
Ramsey, ArchBp Michael, 75, 360
Rasmussen, 257
Raymaekers, Pastoor, 126
Rayner, Claire, 358
Reade, Billy, 53
Reid, Rev Eric, 190
Rembrandt, 210
Renton, Chelsea, 357
Richter, 326
Ringel, Prof Erwin, 167, 322, 345
Ripley, 141
Roach, Rev Charles, 300
Robertson, Mrs, 303, 324
Rodrigues, Peggy, 323
Roe, Elizabeth, 300
Rogers, Bo, 345
Rogers, Lady, 345, 365
Rogers, Sir Richard, 345, 365
Rosen, Betsy, 302
Rosen, Martin, 302
Ross, Charlotte, 306
Rozée, Jean, 358
Rozée, Reg, 110, 358
Rozée, Ruth, 358
Royal, HRH The Princess, 340
Ruth, 359
Rutherford, 45

Sahlström, Ninnie, 308
St Aidan, 14
St Bride, 319
St Chad, 14, 21, 320

St Joan, 316
St John, 175
St Mark, 250
St Patrick, 139–40
St Paul, 44, 137, 174, 231
St Vladimir, 48, 199
St Willibrord, 86
Salter, John, 357
Salviah, Sam, 328
Sampson, Everard, 76
Sanders, George, 154
Sauter, Maryel, 188
Schubert, 344
Schwegler, 58
Schweitzer, Albert, 339
Schwyn, Pastor Ernst, 232
Scott, 22
Scott, Vanda, 313, 317, 367
Scott-Hansen, 51, 97
Scrimgeour, 159
Seaman, Rev Sir Keith, 303–4
Selver, Paul, 50
Sergei, 363
Shaban, Nabil, 342
Shafique, Dr, 323
Shakespeare, 22, 30–1, 61
Sharma, Kirun, 323
Shaw, 32, 61, 316
She, George, 42
Sheffield, Sir Berkeley, 93
Sheila, 342
Sheriff, 362
Sherwood, David, 53
Shim, Chul-ho, 364
Shucksmith, 17
Sibelius, 52, 346
Sibthorp, Ronald, 76
'Sidney', 207–8
Sidney, Philip, 72
Sihanouk, Prince Norodom, 250, 253
Sihvo, Jouko, 308
Sihvo, Marketta, 308
Simms, ArchBp George, 236
Slater, Dr Gordon, 79
Smalley, Maud, 111
Smith, Dr W., 18
Snowdon, Lord, 344
Soddy, Prof Frederick, 45–6, 125
Spinoza, 56
Stafford Clark, Max, 343
Stalin, 197–8
Staubo, Kari, 51, 97–8
Steiner, Dr Rudolf, 55
Stengel, Prof Erwin, 191–2, 235
Sterling, James, 355
Stockdale, Sir Edmund, 233
Stoneham, 156
Stratton, Commander Roy, USN, 307
Stravinsky, 344

Strettle, 'Tread', 159
Strindberg, 52
Stringer, Clem, 84
Stringer, Mrs, 84
Struve, Dr Pyotr, 206
Studholme, Sir Richard, 233
Sutton, Jean, 358
Sweden, HM King of, 337
Sweden, HM Queen of, 337
Synge, J. M., 119

Tamura, Dr 'Tiki', 361–2
Tamura, Yuko, 361–2
Tchaikovsky, André, 303, 311, 314, 322, 335, 339
Tekavčič, Onja, 345
Tennyson, Lord, 22
Thackeray, W. M., 22
Theron, Audrey, 296
Thompson (Aunt Lilian), 354
Thomson, Rev Bill, 234, 238–9
Thornton, Rev, 108
Tigris, 140
Toepfer, Alfred, 338
Tolstoy, 22
Trevellyan, Urith, 53
Trotter, John, 367
Tu, Andrew, 228, 241–3, 317, 327
Turska, Ewa, 345

Ulupinar, Nuran, 167, 224, 230–1, 261, 327
Ungar, Prälat, 322, 345
Uppleby, Mrs, 27

Van der Rohe, Mies, 343, 345, 355
Van de Woestijne, Karel, 71
Varah, Albery Veronica, 24
Varah, Alexa, 314
Varah, Andrew, 121, 291, 296, 358, 364
Varah, Audrey Mary, 24, 107
Varah, Charles, 330
Varah, David, 121, 308, 346
Varah, Dorothy Margaret, 24, 107, 109, 145, 147
Varah, Edmund, 320
Varah, Edward Chad, 24, 33
Varah, Elsie, 19
Varah, Felicity, 108–9, 120–2, 147, 160, 315, 344, 353
Varah, George, 16, 19
Varah, George Hugh, 24
Varah, Heidi Nicole, 302
Varah, Helen, 364
Varah, Hugh, 313
Varah, Ida, 19
Varah, Kate, 330
Varah, Liddon, 19, 29
Varah, Lucy, 363

Varah, Mary Elgiva, 24
Varah, Mary (mother), 354
Varah, Michael, 121, 363
Varah, Phyl, 147
Varah, Rosalind Mary, 24
Varah, Susan, 102, 105, 107–11, 117, 119–22, 126–7, 131–2, 139, 147–9, 153–4, 231, 294, 308, 311, 314, 335, 345, 355–6, 362–3, 366–7
Varah, Tamsen, 291
Varah, William Edward, Canon, 14
Varah, William Oswald, 16, 24, 147
Varah, Winfrid Edmund, 24
Vaughan, Cardinal, 195–6
Veljković, 48
Vera, 64
Vibeke, 51
Vieta, 354
Vincent, Isabel, 4, 317
Von Pataki, Koloman, 142
Vorontsov, Countess Tania, 48
Vrhlicky, 50

Wagner, Willou, 188
Wajid, Rev. Rafiq, 323
Wales, HRH Prince of, 319, 337, 347
Wales, HRH Princess of, 337
Walter, Dr, 64
Wand, Bp J. W. C., 156
Waterlow, 92
Waterlow, Lady, 96
Webb, Frank, 158
Wellow, Jane, 288
Welman, D. P., 124
Whanslaw, M., 95
Whanslaw, Susan, 95–6, 99–101
Wilde, John, 60
Wilde, Oscar, 43
Wilkinson, J. W. B., 32
Williams, Pam, 296
Wilson, Michael, 56, 65
Wogan, Terry, 354
Wolfenden, 200, 208
Woolcombe, Bp Kenneth, 333, 348
Woollaston, 78–9
Wrack, Mrs, 18
Wren, Alice, 100
Wren, Christopher, 154, 156, 332–3, 356
Wright, Frank, 76
Wrigley, Arthur, 55, 62–4
Wu, Mr, 245–50
Wynne, Greville, 72

Xenia, 109

York, HRH Duchess of, 362, 368
Yseult, 109

Zernov, Nicolai, 42
Zwart, Andries, 86, 126

PLACES

Aberdeen, 167, 228, 235
Aberystwyth, 314
Addis Ababa, 300
Adelaide, 303
Adriatic, 330
Afghanistan, 327
Africa, 228–9, 312, 364
Ailclyde, 140
Alberta, 322, 341
Aldershot, 204, 364
All Souls, 55
Amazon, 339
Amersfoort, 313
Amiandos, 90
Amsterdam, 126, 231
Angkor Thom, 251
Angkor Wat, 251–2
Antelope, 341
Antrim, 140
Antwerp, 239
Arctic, 341
Argyllshire, 311
Armagh, 236
Arrowe Park, 33
Ashmolean, 54
Ashqelon, 322
Asia, 229, 364
Aspet, 305
Athens, 167, 229, 231
Atlantic City, 322
Auckland, 304, 327
Australasia, 364
Australia, 316, 327, 338

Badajoz, 320
Bahrain, 329–30, 341
Bali, 303
Balikpapan, 349
Balliol, 192
Baltimore, 307
Bangkok, 252–3, 256–8, 303, 336–7
Barnes, 154, 344
Barrow Hall, 134
Barrow in Furness, 99–102, 104–5, 107–9,
    111
Barton on Humber, 13, 40, 62, 65–7, 91,
    108
Basel, 339
Bath, 365
Battambang, 252–3
Battersea, 131, 144, 147, 149, 159
Bauru, 339
Beaumont College, 61
Beck, The, 17
Beijing, 365–6
Belem, 339
Belfast, 167, 234–5
Belfort, 335

Belgium, 126, 237, 273
Belgrade, 229
Benidorm, 120, 316
Biel/Bienne, 232, 289, 335
Birchenough, 292
Birkenhead, 33
Birmingham, 125, 234
Blackburn, 108, 111–3, 117, 120, 125, 128,
    131, 136, 139, 147, 149, 358
Blackpool, 125, 335
Black Sea, 198–9, 202
Blantyre, 292
Bloemfontein, 295–6, 357
Bodleian, 43
Bolton, 362
Bombay, 229, 235, 260, 303, 327, 329–30
Bonn, 86
Borneo, 349
Borstal, 226
Boston, 79, 307, 322
Boston Spa, 16
Bournemouth, 167, 235, 357
Bradford, 313
Braithwell, 16
Brampton, 25, 49
Brasilia, 339
Brazil, 312–3, 339, 342, 364, 367
Brent, 185
Breslau, 346
Brigg, 93
Brighton, 235
Brisbane, 42, 324
British Isles, 312
Broome, 55
Brussels, 231, 361
Bucaramanga, 316
Budapest, 229
Bugada, 261
Bujumbura, 317
Bulawayo, 294
Bulgaria, 229
Burma, 257–8, 261, 312
Burundi, 317
Butterwick, 355

Cairns, 325
Cairo, 300–2, 316
Calcutta, 173, 257–9, 312, 316, 324
Cali, 316
California, 305
Cambodia, 251
Cambridge, 97, 148, 156, 235, 303, 322, 358
Cameron Highlands, 290
Canada, 166, 194–6, 321–2, 335, 341
Canberra, 304, 324
Canterbury, 75, 97, 195–6, 202, 205, 341, 360
Canton, 244–7
Cape Cod, 307
Cape Town, 296–7, 339, 356

Cardiff, 236
Carlisle, 99
Catholic Nursing Institute, 319
Celebes, 349
Central Africa, 24, 75, 317
Central America, 171
Central Europe, 90
Ceylon, 312
Chamonix, 128
Channel Islands, 289
Chelsea, 336
Cheltenham, 236, 340
Cherwell, 56
Chester, 101
Chieng Mai, 254–5
Chicago, 261, 316
Chichester, 333
Chile, 339
China, 244, 259
Chingola, 291
Chiswick, 173
Christ Church, 57
Christchurch, 304
Chum Tong, 254–5
City of London, 149, 166, 233, 252, 310,
    330, 340, 344, 354, 358, 362
Clapham Junction, 131, 139, 141, 149,
    151, 153–4, 323
Clarendon, 44–5
Clent, 55, 63–4, 66, 342
Cleves, 72
Clichy, 88
Cloak Lane, 214
Clumber, 29
Coimbra, 357
Colchester, 191
Colombo, 134, 303, 327
Constantinople, 194
Copenhagen, 166, 308, 327
Cork, 327
Costa del Sol, 321
Costa Rica, 306
Crowle, 67
Croydon, 236
Cuba, 166
Cumberland, 109
Cyprus, 90, 330
Czechoslovakia, 93–4, 191
Czestochowa, 346

Dallas, 317
Danube, 349
Darwin, 303, 316
Delhi, 312, 323
Delle, 335
Denmark, 97, 308
Denpasar, 363
Derby, 167
Deventer, 70, 74, 86

Dhahran, 341
Dili, 303
Djakarta, 303, 349
Dniepr, 199
Doetinchem, 72
Dona, 261
Dortmund, 327
Downing Street, 333
Dublin, 114, 116–7, 236, 327
Dukeries, 29
Dumbarton, 140
Dum Dum, 259
Dundee, 235–6
Durban, 295
Durham, 192, 235–6

Ealing, 367
East Australia, 325
Easter Island, 344
Eastern Europe, 46
East London, 316
Eastville, 16
Ecuador, 305
Edinburgh, 166, 210, 228, 235
Edmonton, 341
Egmond, 104
Egypt, 302
Eisenstaat, 322
Elgin, 296
Emmerich, 72
England, 104, 117, 121, 154, 171, 195,
    203, 235, 244, 249, 299, 308–9,
    319–20, 325–6, 336
Essex, 154
Europe, 167, 229, 239, 316, 344, 364
Everest, 260, 327
Evora, 316

Farnsworth, 345
Fiji, 304
Finland, 308
Fleet Street, 136
Fort Victoria, 316
France, 128, 173, 237, 339
Frankfurt, 308, 363–4
Freetown, 316
Frizington, 109
Frodingham, 19
Fuengirola, 316

Galway, 327
Gdansk, 191, 316, 346
Geneva, 167, 229, 231–2, 237, 239
Genoa, 316
Gent, 71
George, 296
George, The, 57
Geraldton, 316
Germany, 76, 104, 237

Gethsemane, 250
Ghana, 126
Glasgow, 167, 228, 235, 331
Gloucester, 364
Gold Coast, 126
Gomorrah, 82
Gostinitsa Sovyetskaya, 360
Gothenburg, 98, 308, 312, 327, 330
Goxhill, 66, 68
Grantham, 75
Great Zimbabwe, 292
Greece, 229, 339
Greymouth, 316
Grocers' Hall, 314, 332, 348, 367
Groningen, 71
Guildhall, 361
Gujarat, 260
Gweru, 316

Halifax, 335
Hamburg, 338
Hammersmith, 355
Hague, The, 71
Hampshire, 60
Han, 97
Hamilton, 303
Hampstead, 145, 147, 236
Handsworth, 125
Hangzhou, 365
Harare, 228, 312, 367
Harefield, 146
Harrow, 236
Havering, 236
Heathrow, 308, 330
Helsinki, 198, 308
Hertford, 86
Hiroshima, 46, 125
Hobart, 304
Holborn, 107
Holland, 71, 126, 313
Holland Park, 147
Hong Kong, 228, 235, 241, 243–5, 247,
    251, 317, 327
Honolulu, 347
Honiton Place, 286
Hotton, 126–7
House of Lords, 353
Hull, 17, 22–3, 235–6
Humber, 23, 66
Humber Bridge, 14, 66
Hungary, 67

Ijmuiden, 104
Illinois, 345
India, 231, 312, 323–4, 338, 369
Indonesia, 349
Iran, 261, 327
Ireland, 113, 118, 140, 167, 268, 339, 347,
    364

Isfahan, 261
Istanbul, 167, 229–30
Italy, 316, 339
Ivy, The, 136

Jacksonville, 306
Japan, 46, 347, 362
Jersey, 167, 229, 235, 323
Jerusalem, 303, 332
Johannesburg, 228, 299
Jougne, 128

Kabul, 323
Kalimantan, 349
Kalgoorlie, 316
Kampong Cham, 251
Kampong Thom, 251
Karachi, 228–9, 235, 316, 323
Keble, 42, 44, 48
Keele, 236
Kemi, 308
Kensington, 344
Kharkov, 90
Khartoum, 300
Khyber Pass, 323
Kiev, 48, 199
Kimberley, 357
Kitwe, 317
Kleve, 72–3
Knokke, 148–9, 151
Knysna, 296
Korea, 347
Kowloon, 235, 317
Krakow, 302
Kremlin, 204
Kroonstad, 295–6
Kruger Game Park, 295
Kuala Lumpur, 303
Kuching, 303
Kupang, 303

Lagos, 317
Lake Baikal, 364
Lake District, 103
Lake Nyasa, 292
Lambeth, 236, 358
Lancashire, 110, 122, 131, 195
Lancaster, 322
La Paz, 317
Law Courts, 362
Leatherhead, 236
Lee, 154
Leeuwarden, 71
Leningrad, 198–9
Lesotho, 295
Lethbridge, 322, 341
Liege, 126
Likoma, 292
Limpsfield, 144
Lima, 305

Limerick, 327
Lincoln, 14, 24, 67, 75, 77, 79, 90–2, 95,
    105, 112, 236, 308, 311, 347, 359
Lincoln Minster, 78, 96
Lincolnshire, 69, 92, 111
Lindisfarne, 14
Lisbon, 320–1, 338
Liverpool, 167, 195, 228, 235
Livingstone, 291
Lochearnhead, 236
Lodz, 346
Lok Fu, 241, 317
London, 16, 61, 67, 92, 107–8, 131–3,
    145–6, 149, 151, 153–5, 160, 177, 185,
    187, 203–4, 208, 228–9, 235–7, 259,
    286, 288–92, 302–3, 307–8, 310, 313–4,
    317, 320, 335, 346, 353, 358, 361–2
London Bridge, 276, 278
Lord Palumbo Room, 279
Lotte Hotel, 364
Loughborough, 327
Luanshya, 317
Lund, 97, 308, 327
Lusaka, 291, 317
Luxor, 302

Maastricht, 71
Macassar, 352
Mae Hpon, 254–6
Madrid, 320–1
Magdalen Bridge, 47
Magdalen College, 357
Majorca, 267
Mahakam River, 349
Malacca, 296
Malakoff, 88
Malaren, 97
Malawi, 292, 311
Malaysia, 257, 291
Malaga, 321
Malmö, 97–88, 308
Manaus, 339
Manchester, 167, 228, 234–6, 313
Manila, 317, 325, 347
Mansion House, 233, 343, 356, 362
Mars, 135
Martigny, 128
Massachusetts, 354
Maudsley Hospital, 164
Mbabane, 295
Mekong, 250–1
Melbourne, 304, 324
Mercia, 14
Mercury, 135
Milan, 322
Milton Keynes, 346
Mogadishu, 300
Mokulea, 347
Mont Blanc, 128, 330

Montevideo, 317
Montmartre, 87, 128
Montparnasse, 87
Montreal, 166
Montrouge, 88
Moody's Pass, 292
Moorea, 305
Morocco, 357
Mortlake, 359
Moscow, 193–4, 196–8, 200, 202, 205,
    359–60, 363, 365
Mount Nepean, 260
Moza Illit, 322
Mullingar, 113–5, 117
Munich, 93
Muscat, 347
Mutare, 292

Nadi, 304
Nagasaki, 46
Nairobi, 300, 317
Nanning 248, 250
Nashville, 304
Ndola, 291, 317
Netherlands, 71, 86, 104, 126, 128, 237
Neuchatel, 335
Newcastle, 77, 236, 335
New Holland, 23, 66
New Orleans, 306
New Theatre, 55
New York, 70, 307
New Zealand, 290, 304, 312, 327, 338
Nice, 322, 335
Nijmegen, 74
Nile, The, 302
Northallerton, 236
North America, 303, 316
North Cape, 356
Northern Ireland, 113, 116–7, 344
Northern Rhodesia, 291
Northfields, 322
Northamptonshire, 68
Northumbria, 14
North Vietnam, 250
Norway, 97
Nottingham, 28, 347
Novodevichi, 360
Nyon, 231

Odessa, 198–9, 201–2
Old Bailey, 233
Old Brumby, 19
Old St Peters, 21
Oliviershoek, 295
Oloztyn, 346
Olympia, 161
Omagh, 116
Oporto, 338–9, 357, 367
Orebro, 97

Oregon, 327, 341
Oriental Hotel, 245
Orpington, 236, 321
Oslo, 97
Ostend, 229–30
Osaka, 347, 364
Ottawa, 321
Oulu, 308
Oxford, 40, 42–3, 47–8, 51, 55–6, 59,
    61–2, 66, 68–71, 96–7, 101, 129, 138,
    235–6, 247, 333, 335, 339–40, 348,
    355, 357

Pacific Ocean, 339
Pakistan, 312, 323
Palmerston North, 312
Panama, 306
Papeete, 305
Papua New Guinea, 325
Parepare, 353
Paris, 87–9, 128, 150, 206, 229, 231, 305,
    322, 335
Patpong, 336
Pembrokeshire, 92
Peterborough, 354
Persia, 260
Perth, 303, 312, 324
Peru, 305
Peshawar, 317, 323
Philippines, 347
Piotrkow Trybunalski, 346
Plano, 345
Playhouse, The, 84
Phnom Penh, 249–50, 252–3
Poipet, 252–3
Poland, 86–7, 191, 345
Pontarlier, 335
Poona, 327, 342
Portland, 341–2
Port Elizabeth, 295
Port Hedland, 317
Port Louis, 317
Port Meadow, 49, 63
Port Moresby, 317, 325
Portsmouth, 196, 235
Port Talbot, 236
Port Vila, 317
Portugal, 327
Prague, 197, 229, 235, 302
Princess Islands, 262
Putney, 91, 100, 344, 362

Qatar, 261
Quito, 305, 317

Rajneeshpuram, 341
Rangoon, 257–8
Rantepao, 353
Rawalpindi, 323

Reading, 235, 289
Red Square, 204
Retford, 32
Reykjavik, 336
Rhine, 73
Rhodes House, 53
Rhodesia, 228, 235, 292
Rhyl, 331
Richmond, 295
Rio de Janeiro, 339, 342
Rochdale, 291
Rochester, 333
Romania, 194
Rome, 87, 167, 194–6, 229, 231, 300–1
Rosehill, 317
Rotterdam, 126
Rovanieni, 308

Sabah, 351
Sacubva, 292–4
Sahara, 357
St Bene't Sherehog, 155
St Bride, 359
St Chad's, 41–2, 66
St Clements, 43
St John's Hospital, 131, 147
St James' Garlickhythe, 348
St Lawrence Jewry, 362
St Lawrence Pountney, 155
St Martin-in-the-Fields, 236
St Mary's, 17, 21, 91
St Mary Abchurch, 155
St Mary Bothaw, 155
St Mary's Hospital, 236
St Mary le Bow, 333
St Paul's Cathedral, 233, 322–4, 338, 341,
    344, 353, 358, 361
St Pauls Cathedral, Calcutta, 259
St Peter's, 14, 17, 91
St Stephen Walbrook, 149, 152, 155, 165,
    191, 233, 312, 314, 331, 333–4, 343,
    354, 356, 358, 364
St Swithun London Stone, 155–6
Salisbury, 228, 235, 292
Salonica, 166
Saltsjobaden, 97
Samarinda, 349
Samlesbury, 120
San Bernardo, 339
San Francisco, 341
San Jose, 306
Santiago, 317, 339
Sarawak, 303
Saudia Arabia, 272
Scafell, 103
Scandinavia, 97, 308, 311, 327
Scholae Cancellarii, 75
Scotland, 121, 167, 191, 209, 232
Scunthorpe, 19, 313

Sea of Marmara, 262
Seattle, 305, 347
Seoul, 347, 363–4
Shangi-La, 255, 349
Sherwood Forest, 29
Shipston, 64
Shiraz, 261
Shwe Dagon, 257–8
Siberia, 205, 364
Siem Reap, 251
Singapore, 290, 303, 317, 327, 349, 359
Sisli, 230, 262
Sion, 313
Skiddaw, 103
Skyline, 292
Slovenia, 345
Sofia, 229
Sodom, 82
Soho, 191, 211
Somalia, 369
Somerset, 148
Sotogrande, 342
South Africa, 291, 295
South America, 305, 338
South Atlantic, 339
South Australia, 303
Southport, 129–30
South Vietnam, 250–1
Southwark, 140, 153, 366
Soviet Union, 193, 199, 200, 202–3, 206
Spain, 314
Sri Lanka, 327
Stanmore, 228
Stettin, 346
Stepney, 288–9
Stockholm, 97, 308
Stoke on Trent, 235
Stuttgart, 231–2, 240
Sulawesi, 349
Sunfield, 55
Surrey, 144, 216
Sussex, 208
Sutton, 216
Suva, 304
Swanwick, 308, 327, 335
Swaziland, 295
Sweden, 97, 312, 322
Switzerland, 128, 237, 289, 327, 335
Sydney, 297, 304, 324–5
Szczecin, 346

Tahiti, 305
Tampere, 308
Tanjung Ysui, 351–2
Taroudannt, 357
Tauranga, 304
Tehran, 261
Tel Aviv, 322
Telecom Tower, 362

Thailand, 253–4, 256
Thames, The, 92, 276, 278
Timor, 303
Tokyo, 241, 364
Tonga, 338
Tonle Sap, 251
Torajaland, 349
Toronto, 341
Torquay, 236
Townsville, 324
Trieste, 330
Trinity, 55
Troitsa Church, 360
Turin, 316
Turkey, 229, 327

Uddevalla, 98
Ujung Pandang, 352
Umeå, 322
Umtali, 292
Uppsala, 308
United Kingdom, 233–4, 335
United States, 312, 335, 342
Utrecht, 86

Vancouver, 305, 341, 353
Venus, 135
Victoria, 209
Vienna, 167, 229, 322, 327, 341, 345
Vincent Square, 281–2

Walbrook, 279, 347
Wales, 121
Wanchai, 235, 317
Wandsworth, 131
Ware, 167
Warsaw, 229, 345–6
Waterloo, 237
Waterloo Bridge, 276
Waterford, 327
Welbeck, 29
Welkom, 295
Wells, 148
Welwyn, 347
Wellington, 304, 327
West Berlin, 316, 327, 331
Western Australia, 303, 312
Western Ireland, 327
Westminster Abbey, 42, 77, 233
Westminster Bridge, 23
Westminster Cathedral, 365
Westmoreland, 99
Whalley Abbey, 129
Wickersley, 16
Wimbledon, 92, 236
Witzenhoek, 295
Woking, 363
Woolwich, 235
Wolverhampton, 236

Worcester, 53
Worcester College, 355
Worksop, 29, 32, 36, 40
Wroclaw, 346

Yarborough, 14
Yesilkoy, 261
York, University of, 291
York Minister, 331
York, 195, 345, 358, 365–6

Yorkshire, 111
Yugoslavia, 148

Zagorsk, 198
Zaire, 292
Zambia, 290–1
Zimbabwe, 228, 367
Zoo, The, 111
Zurich, 231
Zutphen, 72